Palgrave Macmillan's
Postcolonial Studies in Education

Studies utilizing the perspectives of postcolonial theory have become established and increasingly widespread in the last few decades. This series embraces and broadly employs the postcolonial approach. As a site of struggle, education has constituted a key vehicle for the "colonization of the mind." The "post" in postcolonialism is both temporal, in the sense of emphasizing the processes of decolonization, and analytical, in the sense of probing and contesting the aftermath of colonialism and the imperialism that succeeded it, utilizing materialist and discourse analysis. Postcolonial theory is particularly apt for exploring the implications of educational colonialism, decolonization, experimentation, revisioning, contradiction, and ambiguity not only for the former colonies, but also for the former colonial powers. This series views education as an important vehicle for both the inculcation and unlearning of colonial ideologies. It complements the diversity that exists in postcolonial studies of political economy, literature, sociology, and the interdisciplinary domain of cultural studies. Education is here being viewed in its broadest contexts, and is not confined to institutionalized learning. The aim of this series is to identify and help establish new areas of educational inquiry in postcolonial studies.

Series Editors:

Antonia Darder holds the Leavey Presidential Endowed Chair in Ethics and Moral Leadership at Loyola Marymount University, Los Angeles, and is professor emerita at the University of Illinois, Urbana-Champaign.

Anne Hickling-Hudson is associate professor of Education at Australia's Queensland University of Technology (QUT) where she specializes in cross-cultural and international education.

Peter Mayo is professor and head of the Department of Education Studies at the University of Malta where he teaches in the areas of Sociology of Education and Adult Continuing Education, as well as in Comparative and International Education and Sociology more generally.

Editorial Advisory Board

Carmel Borg (University of Malta)
John Baldacchino (Teachers College, Columbia University)
Jennifer Chan (University of British Columbia)
Christine Fox (University of Wollongong, Australia)
Zelia Gregoriou (University of Cyprus)
Leon Tikly (University of Bristol, UK)
Birgit Brock-Utne (Emeritus, University of Oslo, Norway)

Titles:

A New Social Contract in a Latin American Education Context
Danilo R. Streck; Foreword by Vítor Westhelle

Education and Gendered Citizenship in Pakistan
M. Ayaz Naseem

Critical Race, Feminism, and Education: A Social Justice Model
Menah A. E. Pratt-Clarke

Actionable Postcolonial Theory in Education
Vanessa Andreotti

The Capacity to Share: A Study of Cuba's International Cooperation in Educational Development
Anne Hickling-Hudson, Jorge Corona González, and Rosemary Preston

A Critical Pedagogy of Embodied Education
Tracey Ollis

Culture, Education and community. Expressions of the Postcolonial Imagination
Jennifer Lavia and Sechaba Mahlomaholo

The Capacity to Share

A Study of Cuba's International Cooperation in Educational Development

Edited by
Anne Hickling-Hudson,
Jorge Corona González, and
Rosemary Preston

THE CAPACITY TO SHARE
Copyright © Anne Hickling-Hudson, Jorge Corona González, and Rosemary Preston, 2012.
Softcover reprint of the hardcover 1st edition 2012 978-0-230-33880-7
All rights reserved.

First published in 2012 by
PALGRAVE MACMILLAN®
in the United States—a division of St. Martin's Press LLC,
175 Fifth Avenue, New York, NY 10010.

Where this book is distributed in the UK, Europe and the rest of the world, this is by Palgrave Macmillan, a division of Macmillan Publishers Limited, registered in England, company number 785998, of Houndmills, Basingstoke, Hampshire RG21 6XS.

Palgrave Macmillan is the global academic imprint of the above companies and has companies and representatives throughout the world.

Palgrave® and Macmillan® are registered trademarks in the United States, the United Kingdom, Europe and other countries.

ISBN 978-1-349-34192-4   ISBN 978-1-137-01463-4 (eBook)
DOI 10.1057/9781137014634
Library of Congress Cataloging-in-Publication Data

Hickling-Hudson, Anne.
    The capacity to share : a study of Cuba's international cooperation in educational development / edited by Anne Hickling-Hudson, Jorge Corona González, and Rosemary Preston
        p. cm.—(Postcolonial studies in education)
        1. Education—Cuba. 2. Education and state—Cuba. 3. Education—International cooperation. 4. Educational exchanges—Cuba. 5. University cooperation—Cuba. 6. Postcolonialism—Cuba. I. Hickling-Hudson, Anne. II. Corona González, Jorge III. Preston, Rosemary.

LA486.H54 2012
379.97291—dc23   2011025855

A catalogue record of the book is available from the British Library.

Design by Newgen Imaging Systems (P) Ltd., Chennai, India.

First edition: September 2012

Contents

List of Tables	ix
Series Editors' Preface	xi
Foreword and Acknowledgments	xv
Abbreviations	xix

Introduction: Cuba's Capacity to Share   1
Anne Hickling-Hudson, Jorge Corona González, and Rosemary Preston

Section 1   Cubans Sharing Education and Health Services: The Revolutionary and Material Basis

1. The Cuban Revolution and Internationalism: Structuring Education and Health   13
   Anne Hickling-Hudson, Jorge Corona González, Sabine Lehr, with Marina Majoli Viani

2. Challenging Educational Underdevelopment: The Cuban Solidarity Approach as a Mode of South-South Cooperation   35
   Jorge Corona González, Anne Hickling-Hudson, and Sabine Lehr

3. Cuba's Education System: A Foundation for "The Capacity to Share"   53
   Elvira Martín Sabina, Jorge Corona González, and Anne Hickling-Hudson

Section 2   Studying in Cuba: Returning Home to Work

4. Cuban Higher Education Scholarships for International Students: An Overview   73
   Francisco Martínez Pérez

5. The Children of the Isle of Youth: How Ghanaian Students Learned to Cope with "Anything in Life"   83
   Sabine Lehr

6 Studying in Cuba, Returning Home to Work: Experiences of Graduates from the English-Speaking Caribbean 107
   Anne Hickling-Hudson

7 Cuban Support for Namibian Education and Training 127
   Rosemary Preston

Section 3   Cuban Educators: Sharing Skills Internationally

8 Cuba's Educational Mission in Africa: The Example of Angola 141
   Christine Hatzky

9 Capacity Building in Latin American Universities: Cuba's Contribution 161
   Boris Tristá Pérez

10 "You Help Me Improve My English, I'll Teach You Physics!" Cuban Teachers Overseas 175
   Anne Hickling-Hudson

11 Cuba's Contribution to Adult Literacy, Popular Education, and Peace Building in Timor-Leste 197
   Bob Boughton

Section 4   The Global Reach of Cuban Education: Participant Narratives

12 Cubans Sharing Education: The Isle of Youth 217
   Oscar Elejalde Villalón interviewed by Anne Hickling-Hudson and Jorge Corona González

13 The Long Road to Neurosurgery: Reflections from Ghana on 18 Years of Studies in Cuba 225
   Samuel Kaba Akoriyea, with Sabine Lehr

14 The International Film and Television School in Cuba: For a Stronger Media Culture in the Global South 231
   Anne Hickling-Hudson and Melanie Springer

15 Air Raids, Bride Price, and Cuban Internationalism in Africa: A Cuban Teacher in the Angolan Civil War 241
   Marta Fernández Cabrera interviewed by Anne Hickling-Hudson

16 Teaching in Rural Jamaica: Experiences of a Cuban Teacher 249
   Emelina P. Pérez Herrera interviewed by Anne Hickling-Hudson

17 Cuban Cooperation in Literacy and Adult Education Programs Overseas 255
   Jaime Canfux Gutiérrez interviewed by Jorge Corona González and Anne Hickling-Hudson

18 The Role of the APC (Association of Cuban Educators)
    in Advancing Cuban Internationalism in Education   263
    *Lidia Turner Martí interviewed by Anne Hickling-Hudson
    and Alejandro Torres Saavedra*

Section 5   Endnote

19 Achievements, Celebrations, and Learning   273
    Rosemary Preston

Biographical Notes   277

Index   283

Tables

3.1	Factors contributing to the high performance of the Cuban educational system	56
3.2	Appendix 1: Network of institutions involved in higher education in Cuba, academic year 2009–2010	67
4.1	Overseas graduates from Cuban universities, by region of origin, 1961–2009	75
4.2	Number of foreign students studying in Cuba on Cuban scholarships, from different countries, 2005–2006	76
5.1	Geographic and socioeconomic background	91
7.1	SWAPO Manpower Survey (1988): Cuba's provision compared with the overall survey	133
10.1	Student numbers in the Namibian school system, 1999	184
18.1	Cuba-US seminarios, dates, participants, and provinces	269

Series Editors' Preface

Peter Mayo and Antonia Darder

The Capacity to Share: A Study of Cuba's
International Cooperation in Educational Development,
*Edited by Anne Hickling-Hudson, Jorge Corona
González, and Rosemary Preston*

This is a welcome volume on a postcolonial approach to education at the national and international level. It sheds light on the achievements of a country that captured the imagination of the world when on January 1, 1959, revolutionaries waged the first successful campaign against a Western-backed dictatorship in the region. The successful overthrow of the corrupt Fulgencio Batista regime and subsequent nationalization of assets, some of which were owned by the United States, meant a serious affront to the "Yankee imperialism" of Cuba's mighty next door neighbor. It also meant an end to Cuba as the financial and recreational playground of affluent US citizens and investors, as well as severing Cuba's role as another informal US colony influenced by the foreign economic policies of the Monroe Doctrine. With these momentous events, the possibility was that an alternative model could emerge from a region that had hitherto known only a colonizing model of governance, which had kept most of its inhabitants economically and politically disempowered.

It is not surprising, then, that the Cuban revolution served as a source of hope not only for the impoverished of Latin America but also for the rest of the Tricontinental World, to use a term adopted by the revolution's leading architect, the charismatic and tenacious Fidel Castro. He used the term during a visit to the UN and subsequently Harlem in New York City, where connections were made between the Cuban condition and that of one of the most impoverished US populations, namely, African Americans. This occasion and the use of the term, which connected with the name of the hotel where the Cuban delegation stayed, courtesy of the efforts of Malcolm X among others, captured a significant feature of the Cuban revolution, the subject of this volume—South-South international cooperation and solidarity. Castro's notion of "tricontinental" emphasized the idea of solidarity with those in the continents and regions of Latin America, Asia, and Africa, three areas in which colonialism had wreaked havoc and left deep structural problems.

But the notion of "tricontinental" was not merely determined by geographical boundaries. The link with African-Americans and their leaders suggests otherwise. Castro and his colleagues, including the formidable Ernesto Che Guevara, understood the implications of the existence of the "third world" in the "first world." Castro remained true to the commitment of solidarity with them when, even as recently as 2004, he offered Cuba's help to oppressed groups inside that very same country that has been a major cause of the Cuban people's hardships. These people included the impoverished of New Orleans, the home of jazz and blues—the music of the oppressed.

It is not surprising that the woes of impoverished North Americans were thrown into sharp relief for Cubans in the aftermath of Hurricane Katrina. True to form, Castro offered to provide help in the shape of Cuba's never-ending supply of highly trained doctors and health workers. Some took this as Castro's ultimate insult to his mighty neighbor; and indeed US leaders must have regarded it so, promptly and flatly refusing this offer of help. However, what this volume so clearly brings to light is the commitment with which Cuba sought to alleviate poverty and support the oppressed anywhere, irrespective of their home country and its relations with the Caribbean island state. It is primarily a commitment to the global South, defined widely. The poor and forsaken of New Orleans and other impoverished North American communities, themselves victims of a US war fought on two fronts (against the Iraqis and the United States' own people through social cutbacks to finance the Iraq war itself), are embraced as members of this global South.

There is no question that over the last five decades, Cuba has received much bad press in the Western media, which is hardly surprising given the revolution's disruption of the status quo, with respect to both material wealth and power at home and the larger geopolitics of the region. Indeed, the isolationist reaction of the Unites States and its blockade against Cuba led the revolutionary Cuban government to the only alternative path available within the Cold War scenario of the time. Cuba moved into the Soviet Union's orbit becoming a potential menace to the United States, given its geographical location—a situation that would come to a head with the Cuban missile crisis in 1962. The blockade and fomenting of counterrevolutionary attacks such as the *Bahía de los Cochinos* (Bay of Pigs) fiasco, as we would see later with the contra war in Nicaragua, served to make the revolutionary state more authoritarian in its efforts to weed out attempts at sabotage from within and without (not to mention the numerous attempts on Castro's own life). Yet, there has always been strong internal and external support for the social reforms and idealism of the revolution, even among North Americans, many of whom disagree with their government's policies toward Cuba.

The growing tensions in the region offered the Western media a field day, as if being in the USSR's orbit was not reason enough for portraying Cuba in a bad light. Yet, it is significant to note that there is no effort in this book to discuss the many controversial and contesting views of Cuba's politics. The volume, instead, simply seeks to do justice to a country that, much like Nicaragua after it, was forced to contend with all sorts of obstacles in its efforts to pursue a radical path, one that would serve as a revolutionary model to other countries within the US sphere of influence. Despite its problematic aspects, the Cuban revolution sought to evolve into an alternative political economic structure contesting the norms of that in the West, where capitalism has functioned to the benefit of the few at the expense of the many.

This volume courageously explores some of the notable international achievements of education in the Cuban model, linking these achievements to the revolution's educational and health systems that are the envy of many nations, including the much-heralded countries whose universities lead the world rankings. Though Cuban universities are not recognized in such rankings, their medical schools are widely considered to produce some of the best doctors in the world. Ask the many ambitious students from the formerly colonized countries of the Caribbean and Africa who strive to learn Spanish in order to gain admission to Cuba's medical schools. The same can be said of Cuba's science center lauded, in the late 1980s (Cuba now has many science centers), as a fine research institution in a program shown on *Rai* (Italian state) TV by that great connoisseur of Latin American affairs, Gianni Minà, editor of the Italian review *Latinoamerica*, who carried out a long televised and published interview with Castro himself. Or, ask former soccer superstars and other celebrities who went to Cuba to seek rehabilitation from life-threatening drug addiction.

Cuba places its educational and medical facilities at the service of not only its own people and such high-profile visitors, but also ordinary folk from countries in Africa, Asia, and many parts of the world. As part of its revolutionary commitment to international cooperation, with no strings attached, it provides thousands of scholarships and makes the products of these institutions (teachers, health workers, doctors) available for services overseas against token fees, depending on the receiving country's ability to pay. It is the bilateral, trilateral, or multilateral agreements in education generated by these forms of collaborations with other countries within the context of South-South cooperation that is the primary focus of this book.

This approach of horizontal South-South relations is contrasted with the more pervasive and dominant models of hierarchical North-South relations, which keep former colonies even today in a colonial bind. In addition, we now have the European Union joining the act with its Europe-aid programs, although it is to be said that the EU (like the US) is not monolithic. It contains spaces where people well aware of the problems of imperialistic models of "aid" use their influence in working groups and other EU epistemic communities to help develop less hierarchical forms of relations with "developing" countries. EU involvement requires studies of the kind carried out here with regard to the older and more well-known forms of North-South aid. We now also have the Union of the Mediterranean, which also involves North-South relations in a regional context. Of course, it remains to be seen what consequences the current "debtocracies" in southern European countries will have on such a project.

Whatever the case, the South-South model of mutual cooperation has been consistently promoted by Cuba, even in its most difficult economic restructuring days post-1990 and at the time of a US decision (still not revoked) to boycott any firm that engages in commercial relations with the Caribbean island. The book presents this model as an alternative for international exchange. It is based not on predominantly business interests or financial profit, but instead on the revolutionary humanist principle of communal sharing. The world's assets are viewed as the common birthright of humankind, rather than simply the individual rights of a few. In a "delinking" process, assets in the South can be exchanged in a complementary manner (e.g., Venezuelan oil at low prices and interest rates for Cuban teachers, doctors, and health workers). They can also be shared to enable traditionally subordinated people and countries to delink from the structural residue of their colonial past. The contributors to this volume not only analyze these cooperative patterns as aspects of policy that characterize this model, they also provide a human face to the model with contextualized narratives of the students and teachers who participate in it, both in Cuba and internationally.

Rightly so, however, Cuba is not romanticized here. Economic and socio-political difficulties and experiments are noted in relation to their implications for education. There is also what some view as an overproduction of qualified people without substantial enough economic investments to absorb them. Yet, this small country might be a real threat to the propagation of an unbridled and irresponsible globalized market economy, as this volume suggests. From the very early years of the revolution, to the present, Cuba's societal experiments in development and change have been the basis of its "capacity to share." In its approach to international cooperation, Cuba might serve as a credible and more viable alternative to US-led capitalism. This volume invites us to consider critically whether the country, tackling current difficulties and embracing current change, has the potential to develop—through its *capacity to share*—into a microcosm of another world that is possible.

Foreword and Acknowledgments

Anne Hickling-Hudson

This book emerges from 30 years of friendship and professional interaction with Cuba. I first visited Havana as a participant in the Caribbean arts festival, CARIFESTA, in 1979, and was overwhelmed by the Cuban organization of vibrant arts environments showcasing the region's artistic achievements, as well as by the fun, partying, music, and warm friendship of the people. I was born and raised in Jamaica, yet as a result of my British colonial education there, knew almost nothing about the culture of our nearest island neighbor.

As my postcolonial education proceeded, I continued to be surprised by Cuba. In Jamaica, Cuba's generosity was demonstrated when it funded the construction of a high school and a sports college, donated tertiary scholarships, and provided visiting experts in the 1970s and early 1980s. I was aware that at the same time, Cubans were helping Nicaragua, Guyana, and Grenada in health, engineering, and education. During my two years as an educational planner and teacher educator in Grenada, on leave from my teacher education post in Jamaica, I witnessed the difference it made to an impoverished country when Cubans supported the island's experiment in popular, revolutionary change led by Maurice Bishop. This ended with the tragic collapse of the Grenadian revolution and US invasion in 1983. Cuba contributed significantly to the building of an airport, the adult literacy program, the production of textbooks for students, and provided over 350 university and polytechnic scholarships for Grenadian young people who would otherwise have had no chance of post-school education. I visited Cuba several times as part of the team of educators sent by Grenada to negotiate the education agreements. This launched my fascination with the Cuban education system and its ability to support this kind of internationalism.

In the 1990s, I visited one of my nieces who spent two years as a student of economics on a Cuban-funded scholarship at a Cuban university. We traveled on local buses to visit her many friends from all over the Caribbean and the world, at several of the Cuban universities. Although she changed her field of study to languages and literature and finished her degree at the

University of the West Indies in Jamaica, her time in Cuba was a formative experience in internationalism for both of us. In the meantime, I had moved with my family from Jamaica to Australia, but several times during the 1990s traveled back to the Caribbean region. On these journeys, I visited Cuba to interview students and university professors there about the island's extensive international scholarship programs that continued even as Cubans struggled with the economic crises brought on by the US embargo and sharply intensified by the 1989 collapse of the Soviet bloc.

These experiences, together with those of like-minded colleagues, led to this book. When I presented a paper on my research on the Cuban scholarships at a US/Cuba conference in 2000, Jorge Corona González, in charge of international relations in Cuba's Ministry of Education, was a participant in the conference. He was deeply involved in the Cuban scholarship program and had never before heard it described and analyzed by an outsider. It was at this conference that Jorge and I envisioned, discussed, and planned this book. Rosemary Preston joined us in November 2004 on the occasion of Cuba's hosting of the 12th Congress of the World Council of Comparative Education Societies (WCCES) in Havana. I was then the president of the WCCES, with overall responsibility for working with teams of Cuban and international educators to organize the congress. Rosemary, fluent in Spanish and with a background of research in Latin American countries, led the WCCES committee that was helping the Cubans prepare and coordinate international links with global comparative educators coming to the congress. Among the leading Cuban organizers of the congress were professors who have contributed to this book—Elvira Martín Sabina, Lidia Turner Martí, and Alejandro Torres Saavedra.

I want to acknowledge the sustained international collaboration and commitment over a decade that has gone into the writing of *The Capacity to Share*. Co-editor Jorge Corona González organized part of the research in Cuba. I thank him for traveling with me to carry out many of the interviews set out in the book, and for helping to develop the introduction and first three chapters during my visits to Cuba in 2001, 2004, 2006, 2008, and 2010. His insider insights into Cuba's development, philosophy of solidarity, and organization of international programs were invaluable. Jorge's fluent bilingual skills enabled him to translate the complex ideas of his colleagues into excellent English for me when necessary. We were assisted by Elvira Martín Sabina, who as director of CEPES, the Centre for the Improvement of Higher Education at the University of Havana, provided us with office space, computer resources, and frequent cups of strong, intensely sweetened Cuban coffee. Elvira, a scholar specializing in the organization and management of the Cuban education system, guided and worked with us in the analysis in chapter 3 of how the development of Cuban education enabled it to become the foundation of the country's capacity to share. Sabine Lehr, inspired by her participation in the 12th Congress of the WCCES, decided to focus her PhD research on examining the experiences of people from Ghana who had studied in Cuba, and their career trajectories. She was awarded her doctorate in 2008 from the University of Victoria in Canada, and we were happy to invite her to contribute her knowledge to the contextual chapters. I am grateful to co-editor Rosemary Preston for applying her sharp editorial skills, particularly in the final phase of the project, to help improve the writing style and conceptual cohesiveness of the chapters.

The chapters in sections 2, 3, and 4 develop case studies around the themes of overseas students studying in Cuba and returning home to work, and Cuban educators sharing their skills with partner countries. Through Jorge Corona's and Elvira Martín's insider knowledge, I met several of the authors, who contributed their interesting insights on themes such as the experiences of Cubans teaching in Africa (Marta Fernández Cabrera) and Jamaica (Emelina Pérez Herrera), organizing adult literacy programs (Jaime Canfux Gutiérrez), and directing the organization of education on the Isle of Youth where thousands of young international students received the gift of schooling and post-school education (Oscar Elejalde Villalón). Lidia Turner Martí, a friend and colleague from the mid-1990s even before I had met Jorge and Elvira, provides insight into the practices of important voluntary associations that help tens of thousands of Cuban teachers and many of their Latin American colleagues to improve professional and research skills. I met Melanie Springer in the 1990s on one of my visits to Cuba interviewing international students. My interaction with her introduces us to the little-known International School of Film and Television in provincial Cuba and the grounding that it laid for Melanie's subsequent work as a media consultant in the Caribbean.

Several contributors focus on African case studies. Christine Hatzky, who researched her postdoctoral project on Cuban educators in Angola in the 1980s, shares with us her important work on this historical case study. Rosemary Preston's chapter adds to our understanding of the significance of Cuban internationalism in Africa, as it is grounded in research that she had done in the 1980s investigating the destinations of Namibians who had studied in Cuba and other countries during the traumatic years surrounding the birth of their nation. Sabine Lehr provides insight into another area of Africa, with her chapter on the significance of the program of Cuban scholarships for Ghana. Through Sabine, we meet Ghanaian neurosurgeon Samuel Kaba Akoriyea, who reflects on his 18 years of school, university, and postgraduate education in Cuba.

Other contributors provide case studies in Latin America and the Caribbean. Boris Tristá Pérez of CEPES shares with us his specialist knowledge and experience of university management and development in Cuba and in a partner Latin American country, while Francisco Martínez Pérez draws on his expert knowledge of the overall structure and organization of the Cuban scholarship program. In case study chapters, I discuss my research on the implications of the Cuban scholarships and Cuban teachers for the English-speaking Caribbean. My professional work in Australia brought me into contact with Bob Boughton, an expert in adult literacy education. His chapter discusses the Cuban contribution to a successful campaign and program of adult literacy in Timor Leste.

Alejandro Torres Saavedra helped by assigning two of his English language students at the Pedagogical University in Havana to work with me during my visits to Cuba on translating and writing up interview transcripts. He also helped to interview Lidia Turner Martí for her chapter, and assisted in translating it. He assisted Steven Smith of the Queensland University of Technology (QUT) while he was carrying out a research study in Havana, to visit many of the Cuban participants to help them complete tasks associated with the book. QUT has assisted me by giving me periods of study leave to pursue this research as well as some financial support for a few hours of research assistant time, and I thank Vinathe Sharma-Brymer for her work on the references.

Lastly, our book commemorates and celebrates the life of our colleague Marina Majoli Viani, who died in 2004. She was a professor of biotechnology at the University of Havana and researcher in the FLACSO-Cuba program of Cuban studies for overseas students (http://internationaldevelopmentstudies.artsandsocialsciences.dal.ca/Study%20Abroad/Cuba.php). Her research related to the impact of science and technology on Cuban society and development, and she contributed much of the material on Cuba's internationalism in health services that we present in chapter 1. Marina loved and deeply understood the ideals and global significance of the Cuban revolution and communicated this in an unforgettable way to visitors, including myself. This book is dedicated to her inspirational internationalist spirit. Together, editors, authors, and contributors from eight countries have demonstrated in this project what internationalism is able to achieve.

Abbreviations

ACS	Association for Caribbean Studies
AEC	Asociación de los Estados del Caribe
AELAC	Asociación de Educadores de Latinoamérica y el Caribe
AET	Africa Education Trust
AJOL	African Journals Online
ALADI	Asociación Latinoamericana de Integración
ALBA	Alianza Bolivariana para los Pueblos de Nuestra América
ALCA	Acuerdo de Libre Comercio para las Américas
ANC	African National Congress
ANZCIES	Australia and New Zealand International and Comparative Education Society
APC	Asociación de Pedagogos de Cuba
BAICE	British Association for International and Comparative Education
BBC	British Broadcasting Corporation
CA	California
CARICOM	Caribbean Community
CDR	Comité para la Defensa de la Revolución
CEA	Centro de Estudios de América
CECE	Comité Estatal de Colaboración Económica
CELAEE	Centro de Estudios Latinoamericanos de Educación Especial
CELEP	Centro de Referencia Latinoamericano para la Educación Preescolar
CEPES	Centro de Estudios para el Perfeccionamiento de la Educación Superior
CIA	Central Intelligence Agency
CIES	Comparative and International Education society
CITMA	Ministerio de Ciencia, Tecnología y Medio Ambiente
CMEA	Council for Mutual Economic Assistance
COMECOM	Council for Mutual Economic Assistance
CPE	Certificate of Primary Education
CSEC	Caribbean Secondary Education Certificate
CUJAE	Instituto Superior Politécnico José Antonio Echeverría

CXC	Caribbean Examinations Council
DAC	Development Assistance Committee
DR	Democratic Republic
DFID	Department for International Development
DVD	Digital Versatile Disc
ECLAC	Economic Commission for Latin America and the Caribbean
EFA	Education for All
ELAM	Escuela Latinoamericana de Medicina
ESBEC	Escuela Secundaria Básica en el Campo
FALANTIL	Forças Armadas de Libertação de Timor-Leste
FCE	Forum des Chefs d'Equipe
FCP	Fundamentos de los Conocimientos Políticos
FDTL	Forças de Defesa de Timor Leste
FEU	Federación de Estudiantes Universitarios
FNLA	Frente Nacional para a Libertação de Angola
FOCAC	Forum on China–Africa Cooperation
FNLA	Frente Nacional de Libertação de Angola
FRETILIN	Frente Revolucionária do Timor Leste Independente.
GCE	General Certificate of Education
GDP	Gross Domestic Product
GDR	German Democratic Republic
GEI	Grupo Especial de Instrucción
GELI	Griffith English Language Institute
GHASUC	Ghanaian Students Union in Cuba
GNI	Gross National Income
GNP	Gross National Product
GSAT	Grade Six Achievement Test
HDI	Human Development Index
HEART	Human Employment and Resource Training
HND	Higher National Diploma
HRD	Human Resource Development
HSRC	Human Sciences Research Council
I/NGO	International Non Government Organisation
IAU	Inter American University
IBON	IBON Foundation
ICAP	Instituto Cubano de Amistad con Los Pueblos
ICCP	Instituto Central de Ciencias Pedagógicas
IESALC	Instituto Internacional de la Unesco para la Educación Superior en América Latina y el Caribe.
IMF	International Monetary Fund
INCED	International Centre for Education in Development
INDER	Instituto nacional para Deporte y Recreación
INIDE	Instituto Nacional para Investigação e Desenvolvimento da Educação

INTRAC	International NGO Training and Research Centre
IPLAC	Instituto Pedagógico Latinoamericano y Caribeño
IPUEC	Instituto Pre-Universitario en el Campo
ISA	Institute of the Arts
ISCAH	Instituto Superior de Ciencias Agropecuarias Habana
ISCF	Instituto Superior de Cultura Física Manuel Fajardo
ISP	Instituto Superior Pedagógico
LA	Laos
LAC	Latin America and the Caribbean
MASTEP	Mathematics and Science Teacher Enhancement Programme
MDG	Millenium Development Goals
MED	Ministério da Educação
MEDICC	Medical Education Cooperation with Cuba
MEP	Ministerio de Economía y Planificación
MERCOSUR	Mercado Común del Sur
MES	Ministerio de Educación Superior
MIC	Ministerio de la Informática y las Comunicaciones
MINCULT	Ministerio de Cultura
MINED	Minsterio de Educación
MINFAR	Ministerio de las Fuerzas Armadas Revolucionarias
MININT	Ministerio del Interior
MINREX	Ministerio de Relaciones Exteriores
MINSAP	Ministerio de Salud Pública
MINVEC	Ministerio para la Inversión Extranjera y la Colaboración Económica
MPLA	Movimiento para a Libertacão de Angola
NDP	National Development Plan
NEPAD	New Partnership for Africa's Development
NGO	Non Government Organisation
NISER	Namibian Institute for Social and Economic Research
NJ	New Jersey
NORRAG	Network for Policy Review Research and Advice on Education and Training
NY	New York
OAS	Organization of American States
ODA	Official Development Assistance
OECD	Organisation for Economic Co-operation and Development
OREALC	Oficina Regional de Educación para América Latina y el Caribe
PCC	Partido Comunista de Cuba
PG	Post Graduate
PIS	Programa Integral de Salud
PLAN	People's Liberation Army of Namibia

PNDC	Provisional National Defence Council
RPA	República de Angola
RDTL	República Democrática de Timor-Leste
REDEES	Red de Estudios sobre la Educación Superior
S&T	Science and Technology
SACMEQ	Southern and Eastern Africa Consortium for Monitoring Educational Quality
SACU	Southern African Customs Union
SAF	South African Forces
SAP	Structural Adjustment Program
SE	South East
SIDA	Swedish International Development Agency
SSC	Student Solidarity Council
SWAPO	South West African People's Organisation
TV	Television
UAJMS	Universidad Autónoma Juan Misael Saracho
UCLV	Universidad Central de las Villas
UG	Under Graduate
UK	United Kingdom
UKFIET	UK Forum for International Education and Training
UN	United Nations
UNCTAD	United Nations Conference on Trade and Development
UNDP	United Nations Development Programme
UNESCO	United Nations Educational Scientific and Cultural Organization
UNE	University of New England
UNICEF	United Nations Children's Fund
UNIN	United Nations Institute for Namibia
UNITA	União Nacional para a Independência Total de Angola
UNSC	United Nations Security Council
UNTAET	United Nations Transitional Administration in East Timor
UNTL	Universidade Nacional de Timor-Leste
UNVTCN	United Nations Vocational Training Centre for Namibia
US	United States
USA	United States of America
USAID	United States Agency for International Development
UVic	University of Victoria
UWI	University of the West Indies
USSR	Union of Soviet Socialist Republics
WCCES	World Council of Comparative Education Societies
WI	Wisconsin
WP	Working Paper

Introduction: Cuba's Capacity to Share

*Anne Hickling-Hudson,
Jorge Corona González, and Rosemary Preston*

Why This Book?

Since 1959, international cooperation has been a key feature of Cuba's commitment to egalitarian social well-being. Aspects of this experience have been well documented, in general and with reference to specific initiatives across human development and occupational sectors. Others have been little examined, of which education is one. This book describes the internationalism of Cuban education policy as practised in Cuba and in other parts of the Global "South."[1]

The idea to document this experience originated at a conference in Havana. The meeting was organized by Cuban and North American scholars and sought to exchange information on educational development in the two countries. Research was presented on the work of young professionals in the English-speaking Caribbean, after they had studied at Cuban universities on Cuban government scholarships. The study attracted the interest of the Cuban educators who administered the scholarships. After some discussion, it was agreed to edit a collaborative book in which different contributors would report on their experience of international Cuban solidarity and sharing. It would focus on education, seek to increase knowledge of Cuban policy and practice, and more widely to deepen general understanding of international processes now often described as South-South cooperation.[2]

As structures of education are inseparable from the structures of society, a book such as this must introduce the economic and political contexts that frame Cuba's educational system and its international parameters.

Cuba, the Economy and Education

In 1959, Cuba was underdeveloped, and like other countries emerging from colonial or neocolonial regimes, it had inadequate public infrastructure and services. After the revolution, Cuba's political purpose was to build a socialist state. The hostility of the United States to this intention within an island state on its doorstep led Cuba to align with the then Soviet Union to resist US pressures. With many of the characteristics of less developed nations,[3] Cuba was for 30 years caught up in the Cold War, as a beneficiary of USSR support. Later, after the collapse of eastern European socialism, Cuba became isolated, as one of the few remaining socialist countries in the neoliberal global era. Hamilton (2002) provides this perspective on the significance of the Cuban path to development:

> Given the overwhelming global dominance of neoliberalism and capitalism today, Cuba is almost alone in providing an alternative socialist political, social and economic path to development. This path has undergone huge changes over the past four decades, and since the breakup of the Soviet bloc in the early 1990s Cuban socialism suffered greatly and has had to respond in unforeseen ways. Though changed fundamentally, the Cuban Revolution has not only managed to survive, surprising critics and supporters alike, but in the latter half of the 1990s developed further, despite the intensification of the US economic blockade of the country.[4]

From 1990, Cubans met the challenges and hardships of international economic pressures by imposing a "special period" of restructuring to overcome the devastation caused by the cessation of Soviet bloc trade and aid. The restructured economy improved and grew steadily. Between 1998 and 2002, growth in GDP was 3.4 percent a year.[5] According to Cuban government statistics for 2008, GDP peaked in 2006, at 12.1 percent. With the global financial crisis, it fell in 2008 to 4.1 percent,[6] but even this is healthy compared to other developing countries. Data published in 2011 rank Cuba at 51 on the UNDP Human Development Index (HDI), with a GNI pc of US$5.416, a higher HDI position based on lower income than Jamaica, Ecuador and other market economies of the Caribbean and Latin America.[7] The revolutionary government invested heavily in education, health, and the economy. By the twenty-first century, Cuba had a highly educated labor force and a high scientific and professional profile.

National income in Cuba derives from agriculture, tourism, genetic engineering, biotechnology, and other areas of science. Since the 1990s, joint partnerships with foreign enterprises, particularly in tourism, helped to expand and stabilize the economy. It rests on a number of solid pillars:

1. Well-educated human resources.
2. A highly developed biotechnology and genetic engineering sector—the seventh most important in the world. This supports human and animal health, and viable agricultural production. Cuba produces most of its own medicines and vaccines, and exports some of these internationally.
3. Partnerships in economic collaboration, mainly with Latin American members of ALBA (*Alianza Bolivariana para los Pueblos de Nuestra América*, known in English as "The Bolivarian Alternative for the Americas", see chapter 2), as well as with China, Russia, India, and Africa.
4. Expanding energy and water sectors that are becoming more efficient. Cuba's electricity system uses mainly Cuban oil, and there are joint enterprises with

several countries, including Venezuela, India, Brazil, and Spain, to explore for offshore oil. If successful, they will share with Cuba in the use of the oil. There has been an investment in building a network of small, medium, and large power plants throughout the country, which means power is no longer completely dependent on central plants. Water supply infrastructure is also being systematically expanded.

With globalization, Cuba is controlling its accommodation to the capitalist system through joint ventures and the opening up of opportunities for small businesses. It has incorporated foreign investment in tourism, but all schemes have to be approved by the central government to ensure their relevance to the interests of the country. Foreign investment is evaluated according to how it improves Cuba's financing facilities, achieves advanced technology, increases exports, and obeys the law relating to workers' conditions and the payment of taxes.

The global financial crisis of 2008 brought further difficulties for the Cuban economy. It displaced many thousands of workers from wage-earning jobs in state enterprises and government offices, pushing them into self-employment, family business, cooperative enterprise, or unemployment. All this has had enormous implications for education, as is demonstrated in the expansion of technical/vocational education for school leavers and a decrease in the number of university places (discussed in chapter 3). Structural adjustment has been introduced with a commitment to achieve "fundamental economic changes without abandoning Cuba's socialist essence."[8] For Haroldo Dilla, a Cuban scholar, "The government has been able to maintain political power in the midst of acute economic crisis, and it has done so with the support of the majority of the population.... Cuba's defense of its national sovereignty and social gains is the object of worldwide admiration and the sources of a solidarity movement of great moral and political value."[9] It is this solidarity movement that provides the framework for the South-South cooperation in education discussed in this book. We seek to understand how Cuban solidarity in education works, what principles and philosophy underpin it, how the Cubans organize and negotiate solidarity programs in the education sector with partner countries, and what enables them to carry out these programs on a large scale. We look at the experiences of a selection of the people involved in these programs, both in Cuba and in partner countries. We consider some of the challenges and benefits involved, for both sides.

Cuba's Promotion of International Solidarity

In spite of the attempt by US foreign policy to marginalize Cuba, Cuba has continued to play important roles in multi- and bilateral arenas. Its international collaboration has a long history. In the nineteenth century, Cubans joined with international liberation movements to fight colonialism, and they in turn allied with Cuban activists, eventually bringing an end to Spanish colonialism in the early years of the twentieth century. As soon as this happened, the United States exerted economic and political influence, controlling resources and local political alliances. This process was not defeated until the popular revolution of 1959.

Since 1959, international solidarity has been a key revolutionary concept. By the late 1960s, Cuba was active in the Non-Aligned Movement and shortly after became a leading instigator of South-South cooperation. In this role, it has been committed to policy development, knowledge, and exchange in and between low-income states.[10] In the last 50 years, Cuba has promoted solidarity as a national and international way of working and being. It is central to Cuba's revolutionary transformation and underpins education and training in its revolutionary principles. The ethos of solidarity was grounded in the USSR's support to Cuban education, enabling tens of thousands of Cubans (as well as Africans) to go to Eastern Europe for advanced study. In time, this enabled Cuba to help other countries of the less developed world by sharing the knowledge and expertise of qualified Cuban professionals.

With the collapse of the USSR in 1989, the loss of technical support, and the strengthening of the US embargo, education became essential for Cuba's survival. The maintenance of high-quality education and health services, together with a "vast framework of popular participation and mobilization,"[11] sustained morale internally, in the face of the crippling economic crisis. Today, Cuba has earned respect in many parts of the world for its levels of learning and sharing of knowledge, with its policy of internationalism integrating solidarity and South-South cooperation.

The Chapters of This Book

Against this background, the chapters of this book offer insights into the pioneering internationalization of Cuba's educational policy, at home and abroad. They highlight Cuba's innovative provision of schooling and post-school education to thousands of refugees from war-torn Africa, in the 1970s and 1980s; Cuba's funding of opportunities for international students to study in Cuban universities, colleges, and secondary schools; the work of Cuban teachers and professors in these educational institutions overseas, and the program of prestigious international conferences that exchange scholarship, keep Cuban scholars at the cutting edge of their fields, and publicize this knowledge globally. Case study chapters trace the destinations of former scholars once they leave Cuba, and describe Cuba's assistance to partner countries in fields ranging from adult literacy to professional development in university administration, medicine, and practical skills.

Drawing on dialogue between prominent educators in Cuba and the international community, the accounts show something of what can be achieved through political determination. They highlight the case of a less developed island territory, subject to protracted political and economic marginalization, yet morally supported by sympathetic states, many with similar experiences of exclusion engineered by the institutions controlling global resources and power.

Section 1 of the book provides an overview of Cuba's international education assistance, examining it in global and local contexts. In chapter 1, Anne Hickling-Hudson, Jorge Corona González, and Sabine Lehr provide an overview of the Cuban revolution, explaining how internationalism in education and health developed as the revolution unfolded. Chapter 2, by the same authors, starts by outlining the global educational crisis of huge educational gaps and deficits that continue to grow in spite of educational aid from North to South, and the attempts at South-South cooperation since the 1960s. The chapter then explores Cuba's solidarity policy as a unique approach to collaborating in development. The principles followed are those of negotiating agreements that respect sovereignty, refraining from conditionalities, and exchanging assistance based not on market norms (profits and competition), but on cooperation for mutual support. The authors analyze how Cuban solidarity works in the current agreements with Venezuela and other countries.

In chapter 3, Elvira Martín Sabina, Jorge Corona González, and Anne Hickling-Hudson show that without the revolution in Cuban education, it would have been impossible for Cuba to carry out the massive program of global educational assistance and collaboration described in the preceding chapters. In this chapter it is argued that Cuban internationalism rests on the excellent schooling and tertiary education that provides highly trained Cuban teachers, doctors, and engineers who go out in large numbers to assist and work in other countries. Cuba continues to pursue its ideals of achieving a combination of equity and high quality in education with the current reforms to the system. The three chapters of this section together, then, explain how the philosophy of solidarity, a hallmark of the revolution, together with the material strength of Cuban education, provide a foundation for Cuban internationalism. In the current global context, Cuba's unconventional policies help many countries to address entrenched educational problems.

The four chapters of section 2 discuss educational arrangements and programs for overseas students in Cuba, and present research on how the Cuban education of overseas students helped to shape their future careers in their home countries and elsewhere. Francisco Martínez Pérez in chapter 4 views Cuba's program of higher education scholarships to overseas students as one of the most significant ways by which the Cuban people express their solidarity with other developing countries and apply the principles of internationalism. This chapter discusses the main characteristics and achievements of the Cuban scholarship program. It also considers Cuban attempts to meet the main problems encountered in the program, and the impact of the program in an international context.

In chapter 5, Sabine Lehr explores the experiences of a number of former students and administrators involved in a South-South educational collaboration program between Ghana and Cuba. Through this program, Cuba provided full scholarships for secondary and post secondary studies and trained approximately 1,200 Ghanaians over the course of 20 years. The author discusses ways in which the program increased educational access for socioeconomically disadvantaged students in Ghana, in particular through the combination of secondary and post secondary studies. She explores the reintegration of graduates in their home country, with a focus on questions of work deployment. Finally, the relevance for developing countries of the Cuban model of combining academic and practical education is discussed.

Chapter 6, by Anne Hickling-Hudson, is a discussion of field research in which she interviewed undergraduates in Cuba and graduates who had returned home to work as professionals in the English-speaking Caribbean. The accounts of these graduates suggest that the Cuban university system has developed a curricular approach that is particularly suitable for preparing professionals to tackle the problems of material and social underdevelopment in the decolonizing conditions of the Global South. Students gain both the theoretical foundations of their field and an intensive practical and local experience of its implementation. This stands them in good stead as professionals in their own countries. The chapter discusses the policy implications of the experiences of higher education graduates in Cuba, regionally and globally.

In chapter 7, Rosemary Preston compares Cuba's educational provision for Namibians with that of other countries. She examines what is known of the post-return labor-market integration of Namibians who had studied in Cuba and of Cuban interventions in the new state following independence. As a framework, she draws on published histories to synthesize the experiences of Cuban internationalist contributions in Africa, from Algeria in 1960, to the end of the Angolan civil war in 1988 and Namibian independence two years later. The chapter presents Cuban support for Namibia as inseparable from Cuba's role in Angola and its frontier area with what was then South West Africa. It notes Cuban educational support for Namibian victims of South African attacks on refugees in Angola and for subsequent exiled groups.

Section 3 examines how Cuba shares its educational knowledge with other countries. It provides detailed examples of the Cuban civil mission in education overseas, describing political and administrative arrangements for Cubans to teach in other countries, as well as some of the actual education programs that they deliver. In chapter 8, Christine Hatzky explores Cuba's educational mission in Angola, the largest educational mission that it undertook overseas. About 10,000 Cubans educators carried out their internationalist duties in Angola as teachers and advisers between 1976 and 1991. Organized through regular requests from and negotiations with the Angolan government, the Cuban civil mission in Angola consisted of about 50,000 Cubans contributing their work in health, education, and civil engineering. The chapter explores the genesis, structures, and programs of this cooperation. It provides insight into the challenge and significance of the work of the Cuban educators in Angola, as well as its limits.

The chapter also discusses two outstanding educational initiatives that emerged in this unique example of South-South cooperation: the sending of brigades of Cuban higher education students to Angola and the establishment of Angolan schools on Cuba's Isle of Youth.

Boris Tristá Pérez in chapter 9 explains how Cuba, with its highly developed system of universities and postgraduate education, has been able to meet the requests from other countries for help in improving and expanding their postgraduate training systems. The strength of postgraduate education in Cuba is the foundation that enables Cubans to help other countries develop their postgraduate capacity. This assistance from Cuba involves not only the training of foreign postgraduate students in a wide variety of disciplines in Cuban universities, but also support given by Cuban academics to develop their administrative and curricular systems in Latin American universities elsewhere. The chapter presents a case study of how Cuba assisted the improvement of the university in Tarija, Bolivia, a project that illustrates the general approach of Cuban academics to university support.

In chapter 10, Anne Hickling-Hudson discusses her research on the work of Cuban teachers in schools and sports programs in Jamaica and Namibia. In a qualitative analysis based on in-country fieldwork, she shows how these programs operate in the two countries. Her framework comparing cross-cultural issues and national policies regarding the use of Cuban teachers facilitates the discussion of how decolonizing countries can benefit from Cuba's assistance in building teaching capacity, while Cuba in turn benefits from developing the expertise of its educators through this internationalist work. She also discusses the policy difficulties and future possibilities that arise from the program of lending educators.

Bob Boughton in chapter 11 discusses the case of Timor-Leste's national adult literacy campaign, launched in 2007 and supported by a small team of Cuban advisers. By 2010, over 26,000 people had completed a 13-week basic literacy course. Drawing on findings from in-country fieldwork, the author outlines the achievements of the campaign, and assesses the contribution that adult literacy makes to post-conflict peace building and the achievement of postcolonial independence. This innovative experiment in mass popular adult education, undertaken with high levels of local involvement, is contrasted with the more dominant neoliberal models of education and training for state building, favored by international agencies such as the World Bank.

Section 4 illustrates the global reach of Cuban education. Educators and former students, interviewed by authors in this book, describe in their own words, their involvement in Cuban internationalism in education. The first three narratives are about studying in Cuba. Oscar Elejalde Villalón was Rector at the Pedagogical College on the Isle of Youth and then became head of the educational division of the local government. In this post he directed education for young people from partner countries who had been provided with full scholarships to study at schools and colleges on the Isle. Elejalde describes how the program was organized and implemented, including the curriculum, extracurricular activities, and administration. Samuel Akoriyea, a Ghanaian neurosurgeon, provides an essay reflecting on his 18 years of studying in Cuba, from his schooling on the Isle of Youth to his professional training in Cuban universities in medicine and then neurosurgery. Melanie Springer of Barbados also narrates her experiences of education in Cuba. Interviewed by Anne Hickling-Hudson in 1996 and again in 2011, Springer describes her diploma program in media studies at the International School of Film and Television at San Antonio de los Baños, and comments on her career since then as a media professional in the Caribbean.

Two Cuban educators talk about their experiences while teaching overseas. Marta Fernández Cabrera describes the experience of going as a young professor of English studies to teach in Angola during the 1980s war between Angola and apartheid-dominated South Africa. The posting was full of wartime danger as well as opportunities to teach and learn. Emelina Pérez Herrera talks of the initial dissonance that she felt on leaving her professorial post in English studies at a Cuban university to teach Spanish for two years in the late 1990s at a high school in a remote mountain community in rural Jamaica. She soon threw herself into the challenges of teaching Spanish in an innovative way, through activities in drama, dancing, a Spanish language club, and a Spanish interschool camp. She was faced with the poverty of some of the families of school students, and the fact that some of them, though adolescents, were not literate. Both Pérez Herrera and Fernández Cabrera still work as professors of education in Cuba, and see their overseas postings as a highlight of their teaching careers.

The final two narratives are about structures and programs that facilitate Cuba's commitment in sharing its skills globally in adult literacy and other levels of education through professional associations, meetings, and conferences. Jaime Canfux Gutiérrez, a professor who has worked for 50 years in youth and adult literacy education and who was the director of the Literacy Studies Group at the Latin American Pedagogical Institute in Havana, describes the methods that Cuban literacy educators have used to carry out their mission of adult literacy education in partner countries that asked for this help. Lidia Turner Martí, one of Cuba's most famous educators and an emeritus professor of education, talks about three associations of Cuban educators that she helped to form and guide over several decades. The Association of Cuban Educators (APC), currently with 39,000 members, and the Association of Educators of Latin America and the Caribbean (AELAC), promote research and collaboration in the development of excellent teaching. They organize regular conferences and other events that bring together Cuban, international, and regional educators. Cuban educators have also regularly met with educators from the United States in an annual seminar that established professional links and friendships between these educators. This takes place in spite of the US government's long-standing blockade.

The interviews in Section 4 were conducted in different ways, determined by contributors' proficiency in English. The conversations with Oscar Elejalde and Jaime Canfux, were conducted in English and Spanish, with Jorge Corona González simultaneously translating Spanish responses into English. The same process was followed in the interviews with Lidia Turner Martí, with Alejandro Torres Saavedra providing the English translation. Marta Fernández Cabrera and Emelina Pérez Herrera, both professors of English at the pedagogical university in Havana, and Melanie Springer, were interviewed in English. All the English transcripts were later amended by interviewers and interviewees until a final version was agreed upon. Samuel Akoriyea wrote his own text. He co-edited it with Sabine Lehr by email.

In conclusion, Rosemary Preston reviews the achievements and promise of Cuba's educational internationalism. High levels of learning for Cubans at home and the renown of its international education and training, have constructed Cuba's international identity, encouraging partners to reciprocate and support the fragile Cuban economy. With neoliberalism and the collapse of Soviet aid, the revolutionary government retains solidarity as its rationale, at home and abroad, exporting expertise to some 50 countries, for mutual support and modest foreign exchange. Grounded in the teachings of Martí and Guevara, Cuba's educational internationalism has intellectual coherence, enabling its envoys abroad to show what can be achieved through motivation and commitment. Perhaps unplanned, Cuba's capacity to share, long a challenge to loan-based international technical assistance, can be seen to offer a way to mutually supportive international development.

Notes

1. In this book we use the terms "Global North" and "Global South" although acknowledging that they are problematic in many ways. They imply the division between the wealthy, economically developed countries in the northern hemisphere plus Australia and New Zealand, known collectively as "the North," and the poorer countries, "less" and "least" developed, located mostly in the Southern hemisphere, known as "the South." As nations become economically developed they may become part of the "North" regardless of geographical location, while many people living in the "North" are poorer than some living in the "South" (Reuveny and Thompson 2007). We recognize these limitations, and also recognize that the terms not only conceal the power relations that were more clearly understood in the superseded terms "First," "Second," and "Third" worlds, but also ignore the debate about what constitutes "development" (Sachs 2010).For this reason we also purposively use the term "underdeveloped" to reaffirm the notion so brilliantly conveyed by Walter Rodney in *How Europe Underdeveloped Africa*: (i) that colonialism deliberately underdeveloped the dependent countries with the consequence that most former colonies have not yet recovered from this process; and (2) that this process of deliberate underdevelopment continues to the present day. In fact, it is a component of economic globalization that, as discussed in

chapter 2 of our book, interferes with the contemporary development paradigm. We feel that postmodern expressions such as majority world (to signify that part of the world where the majority of the global population lives) conceal the very real power relations at play between rich and poor economies.
2. UNDP, 1978 and 2004.
3. Campling, L., 2006.
4. Hamilton, D., 2002:18.
5. ECLAC 1999 and 2003, quoted by E. Espinosa Martínez 2005:81.
6. Oficina Nacional de Estadísticas, 2009.
7. UNDP, 2007.
8. Carranza Valdés, quoted by D. Hamilton, 2002:32.
9. Dilla, H., 2000.
10. UNDP, 1978 (accessed February 17, 2010).
11. Dilla, H. 2000:34.

References

Campling, L. (2006) A Critical Political Economy of the Small Island Developing States Concept. South-South Cooperation for Island Citizens? *Journal of Developing Societies* 22: 235–285.
Dilla Alfonso, H. (2000) The Cuban Experiment. Economic Reform, Social Restructuring, and Politics. *Latin American Perspectives* 110, 27(1): 33–44.
ECLAC (Economic Development Division) (1999) *La economía cubana. Reformas estrucurales y desempeño en los noventa.* Mexico City: ECLAC and FCE.
ECLAC (Economic Development Division) August 2003. Current Conditions and Outlook. Economic Survey of Latin America and the Caribbean, 2002–2003.
Espinosa Martínez, E. (2005) Ethics, Economics and Social Policies: Values and Development Strategy, 1989–2004. In *Cuba in the 21st Century. Realities and Perspectives.* Edited by J. Bell Lara and R. A. Dello Buono. Havana: Editorial José Martí, 57–100.
Hamilton, D. (2002) Whither Cuban Socialism? The Changing Political Economy of the Cuban Revolution. *Latin American Perspectives* 124, 29(3): 18–39.
Oficina Nacional de Estadísticas (2009) *Anuario Estadístico de Cuba 2008*, La Habana. http://www.one.cu/aec2008/esp/05_tabla_cuadro.htm
Reuveny, R. X. and Thompson, W. R. (2007) The North-South Divide and International Studies: A Symposium. *International Studies Review*, 9(4): 556–564. Retrieved from http://www.wiley.com/bw/journal.asp?ref=1521-9488&site=1
Risquet Valdés, J. (2006) The Deep Roots of Cuba's Internationalism. http://www.tricontinental.cubaweb.cu/REVISTA/texto22ingl.html (accessed February 17, 2010).
Rodney, W. *How Europe Underdeveloped Africa.* Washington, DC: Howard University Press, 1982.
Sachs, W. (2010) *The Development Dictionary. A Guide to Knowledge as Power.* London: Zed Books.
UNDP (nd. from 1978) Special Unit for South-South Co-operation, http://tcdc.undp.org/summarypage.aspx (accessed February 17, 2010).
UNDP (2004) *Forging a Global South.* New York: UNDP.
UNDP (2011) Human Development Index (HDI) - 2011 Rankings.
United Nations Development Programme (2007) *Human Development Report 2007/2008.* New York, NY: Palgrave Macmillan. Retrieved from http://hdr.undp.org/en/media/HDR_20072008_EN_Complete.pdf

Section 1

Cubans Sharing Education and Health Services: The Revolutionary and Material Basis

1

The Cuban Revolution and Internationalism: Structuring Education and Health

Anne Hickling-Hudson, Jorge Corona González, Sabine Lehr, with Marina Majoli Viani

Introduction

Cuba is not a wealthy country. With a population of almost 12 million, it has an average annual GDP income of less than $8,000 per person, which is similar to that of Jamaica and many of the countries of the Caribbean region. It is a world away from the per capita income in rich countries, which varies from $30,000 to $48,000.[1] Yet, with limited resources, Cuba has the political will and organizational skills to have managed, since the 1960s, a massive, flexible, and targeted program of overseas assistance primarily to other low-income states, in education and other fields, such as health and engineering.

Sustained for half a century, Cuban assistance within the Global South is unique. Scores of countries are collaborating with Cuba, and research, though limited, suggests that Cuba's international solidarity has become a significant global resource.[2] Since the revolution, many thousands of full scholarships have been provided by Cuba to train large numbers of professionals in its universities and colleges, while teams of Cuban professors and other specialists have traveled to partner countries to deliver courses there. Tens of thousands of schoolchildren from sites of war, conflict, and poverty have been assisted in receiving schooling up to senior secondary and sometimes to tertiary level in Cuban institutions. Cuba has made a significant contribution to adult literacy and other adult education programs in many countries, including a number of richer states. It cooperates with several Spanish-speaking countries in curriculum and program development in fields such as disability, early childhood, and sports and physical education.

Cuban professors assist numerous South American universities with policy development and administrative and curricular improvement.

Cuba's educational internationalism, grounded in the philosophy of solidarity, is the central theme of this book. It describes how this international solidarity in education might provide insight into new ways in which aid administered by the multi- and bilateral systems might better resolve the serious problems of underdevelopment inherited from European and more recent North American colonial and imperial rule. This chapter sets the scene by providing an overview of Cuban collaboration, taking the case of health and education together as overlapping fields of learning and expertise produced by the same educational system. The Cuban revolution provides an essential framework for understanding this collaboration, its ideals and achievements, and its political and economic difficulties. This will be briefly outlined as the basis for the determination of Cubans to find new economic and social strategies for improving their own society, including its health and educational services, and to continue to expand their global solidarity programs. Cuba's internationalism is different in many respects from the interpretation of internationalism in wealthy countries.[3] A revolutionary and postcolonial ethos shapes the Cuban approach to internationalization, and that is the approach we explore.

The Cuban Revolution: Social Leveling and the Tackling of Challenges

The 1959 revolution can be seen as having its origins in the struggle against Spanish colonialism, which had shaped Cuba since the early sixteenth century, with a majority of very poor people controlled by a wealthy minority. Rebel forces had defeated the Spanish colonizers in the 1898 war of independence, only to see the US forces seize control of many of the country's economic and public institutions. For the next 60 years, the government of the United States in alliance with a series of Cuban regimes virtually controlled Cuba, directing a succession of Cuban governments. The island's economic and political institutions "were organized to develop the society within the US sphere of influence"[4] and US businesses had major shares in sugar, public utilities and communications, financial institutions, mining, and petroleum refining. In 1959, the 26th of July Movement, led by Fidel Castro, overthrew the dictatorial, US-backed regime of General Fulgencio Batista, which had illegally seized power in 1952. Within a year, it became clear that the new revolutionary government intended to make radical changes across Cuba, with nationalization of much private enterprise including US-owned businesses in retaliation to US threats, limitations on individual land ownership, social reform, and assistance to the very poor. When the United States broke off diplomatic ties with Cuba, Cuba established new links with the Soviet Union. The notorious 1961 invasion at the Bay of Pigs (*La Batalla de Girón*) was an unsuccessful attempt to overthrow the Cuban government by a US-trained group of Cuban exiles supported by the US military. Cuba's success in defeating this attack, in the words of historian Barry Higman (2011),

> helped elicit Castro's clear affirmation of the radical nature of Cuba's socialist revolution and his identification of himself as a Marxist-Leninist. Castro demonstrated his commitment to the defence of Cuba against US intervention by allowing the installation of Soviet ballistic missiles in October 1962. The United States demanded their withdrawal and the world waited in fear of atomic warfare, the great dread of the Cold War. Without first consulting the Cubans, the Soviet Union agreed to dismantle its weapons in return for an understanding that the United States would not invade Cuba or seek to overthrow Castro's government.[5]

In response, the United States imposed an enduring diplomatic and commercial embargo on Cuba, and intensified covert CIA operations against it. Nevertheless, by 1965, "Cuba was firmly established as the first socialist state in the Americas, a thorn in the underbelly of its capitalist northern neighbour."[6]

The revolution went through a series of phases analyzed by Martin Carnoy (1990) as initial transition (1959–1961); centrally planned development through agricultural diversification and rapid industrialization (1961–1963); fostering growth through export expansion; the development of socialist attitudes and values (1964–1970); and rationalization, economic growth, and material incentives (1970–1989).[7] Educational reforms were reflective of the larger societal changes, a point that we will further explore in chapter 3. Education was seen as a human right as well as a means of developing collective commitment and economic production capacity. Each sector of the education system was gradually developed, both quantitatively and qualitatively, with a focus on the adult literacy campaign, increased continuing education for newly literate adults, increased primary and secondary schooling, and the expansion of vocational and university education. In 1989, the collapse of the Soviet bloc and disappearance of its economic assistance to Cuba ushered in a period of crisis and economic restructuring, incorporating strictly controlled processes of capitalist-style business working in partnership and/or under the direction of the state. This model still underpins Cuba's political and economic strategy.

A deeply transformative process of social leveling took place as a result of the revolution. Haroldo Dilla (2000) comments on the disappearance of the old minority elites—the wealthy capitalists and a large portion of the middle classes—either through emigration or proletarianization. The remaining majorities of workers, small farmers, and peasants, those who had suffered most under the previous social order, were slowly reorganized around social and state ownership of the means of production. This reorganization was accomplished by massive state programs of employment, urbanization, health services, and the universalization and improvement of education to increasingly higher levels. The proportion of the population living in urban areas rose from 58 percent in 1953 to 73 percent in 1989.[8] The new society of workers now had opportunities to become skilled and educated because of the expansion of the education system, and to practice the forms of community political power, economic participation, and internationalism that were being developed through the revolution, while at the same time, state decision-making processes were highly centralized.[9]

Claudia Kaiser-Lenoir (2008) observes that the growing egalitarianism of the society was characterized by the fact that, from 1959 to 1990, "99 per cent of earnings came from salaries, with only a 1 to 5 differential between the highest and the lowest ones, something unheard of anywhere else, not just in Latin America, but the world."[10] She goes on to show that any scrutiny of indicators from international agencies such as the United Nations and the World Health Organization puts Cuba in the forefront of most poor countries in welfare measures benefiting the population. It is a model for health services and health outcomes, for pursuing the fight against urban and rural poverty, for achievement in sustainable development, and is placed by the UN Human Development Index Report (2007–2008) as "first in the world in the category measuring relationships between economic means and capacity for human development."[11] In 2007, Cuba ranked 51 among 177 countries in terms of its overall Human Development Index score ahead of countries such as Mexico, Panama, and Brazil. It led all 70 countries in the high human development category in terms of the percentage of GDP spent on education.[12]

These were fundamental achievements in the process of social transformation, but it was inevitable that many problems accompanied the revolutionary process. Some of the major issues that caused tension, debate, and different forms of resolution were (i) ideological struggles over conflicting models of socialism, (ii) the long evolution of the revolutionary state's political structures, (iii) trade-offs between the goals of developing collective, socialist consciousness and increasing production and consumption, and (iv) the conflict with the United States.[13]

Particularly severe were the problems of the crippling trade embargo imposed by the United States, which is estimated to have cost Cuba over $40 billion between 1959 and 1992,[14] and the collapse of the Soviet Union in 1989 accompanied by the sudden termination of Soviet financial assistance to Cuba. Recovery measures were put in place that gradually tackled the hardships of the transitional "Special Period" of 1989–1995 by a restructuring of the economy. The Cuban economy improved steadily. The GDP growth rate for 1995–2000 was estimated at 4.6 percent, and the rate for 2000–2007 was between 7.6 percent and 9.1 percent, depending on whether low or high estimates were applied. These remarkable growth figures have been attributed to Cuba's enormous human capital that has contributed to its growth performance through the export of services.[15]

Against this background, four phases of the development of Cuban internationalist cooperation can be identified.[16] The formative first phase spanned the period from 1959 to 1990. The political ideas and events that shaped this period were those of the postcolonial goals of the newly independent nations, Cuba's economic and political relations with the Soviet Union during the Cold War, the US embargo on trade with Cuba, Cuba's political participation in the Non-Aligned Movement, and Cuba's military assistance in southern African states in conflict with the apartheid regime in South Africa. In this period, Cuba was relatively isolated in Latin America and the Caribbean, with important exceptions. In the Caribbean, Cuban internationalism to some extent assisted Jamaica, Guyana, and Grenada, while in Nicaragua, 1979–1990, there was intense cooperation with Cuba during the Sandinista revolution.[17]

The second internationalist phase occurred after the collapse of the Soviet Union in 1989 and the withdrawal of Soviet assistance to Cuba. From 1989 to 1995, the resulting economic hardship of the "Special Period" was worsened by the impact of the increasingly harsh embargo imposed by the United States. In 1996, the United States passed the Helms-Burton Act penalizing foreign companies that do business with Cuba by preventing them from doing business in the United States. Yet, Cuba continued its international cooperation, although it had to be reduced.

The third phase from 1996 to 2004 saw the restructuring of Cuba's economy to allow limited market-based reforms to coexist with the socialist economy. The economy started to recover,[18] and new emphases in international cooperation developed in which relations with Latin America and the Caribbean became closer. The fourth phase of international cooperation is marked by the intense collaboration between Cuba and Venezuela that developed from 2004[19] and the continuation of economic restructuring.

In April 2011, at the first Communist Party congress for 14 years, Cubans recognized the steps that had been taken to move away from its classical socialist model toward more contemporary market socialism (Plummer 2011). Among the changes agreed on are job cuts in the public sector that employs 85 percent of the workforce, and the introduction of limited economic and market reforms that would allow Cubans to buy and sell property, and to start small businesses.[20] It is unclear what effect, if any, these changes will have on Cuba's international development programs in low-income states, not least since the new policies commit the treasury to repaying Cuba's external debt. Kaiser-Lenoir notes that economic restructuring in Cuba since the 1990s has been accompanied by broad and deep public consultation about measures to survive the crisis, including many self-generated initiatives undertaken by neighborhood groups to improve social conditions. All of this, she argues, helps to account for the fact that the Cuban government "has been able to survive, endure and even organize a leadership transition" in spite of the economic difficulties of the past two decades.[21]

The ability of the Cuban government to carry out its internationalist policies rests on the revolution's expansion of the system of education. This has enabled it to carry out research-based improvements in education and training sufficient to produce large numbers of medical and education specialists, and to strive for continuous development. The extensive network of universities and colleges in Cuba ensures that a relatively high proportion of its school leavers enter either five-year degree programs at universities or polytechnic vocational training at "middle-level" technical institutes. The Cuban economy is not yet developed enough to absorb as many graduates as the university system produces, leaving an excess compared to demand in most fields. It is this surplus expertise that enables Cuba to send large numbers of professionals, including teachers, doctors, and engineers, to work overseas, often for several years.

In the field of health, for example, Cuba expanded the number of doctors from 3,000 in the years immediately after the revolution, to 25,567 in 1986 (one per 399 inhabitants), and 60,248 in 1995 (one per 196 inhabitants). This rapid increase facilitated Cuba's solidarity policy of providing medical practitioners to other countries, including 2,000 sent to Central American countries hit by Hurricane Mitch in 1998. Since 2001, 2,173 doctors have worked abroad under Cuba's Comprehensive Health Program for Central America, the Caribbean, and Africa.[22] However, as discussed here, Cubans were carrying out internationalist policies in military assistance, health and educational services, and engineering, even while their education system was developing during the first 30 years of the revolution, with assistance from the East European bloc. So strong was the solidarity principle that, for example, hundreds of Cuban teachers suspended their own undergraduate studies to help teach for a few years in schools and colleges in Angola and other African countries, as is discussed in chapter 8.

Even at the height of their difficulties in the 1990s, Cubans maintained their commitment to their internationalism in health and education with the kinds of strategies outlined next.

Cuban Solidarity in Educational Development

While building a strong education system at home,[23] Cuba has also had over four decades of experience in international education, assisting other developing countries to improve their systems. Much less well known than Cuba's international health programs, its educational contributions are extensive. They continue to flourish despite the 1989 collapse of support from former East European trading partners, and the continuing devastating effects of the US blockade.

During the decades of partnership with Eastern bloc countries, prior to 1990, much of Cuba's educational assistance went to newly independent African countries that were still struggling to upgrade former colonial education systems while introducing socioeconomic and political changes to strive for the ideals of their new independent status. Not surprisingly, the stringencies of the early 1990s brought about a change in Cuban educational internationalism. The proportion of educational scholarship assistance directed toward African countries declined in relative terms while that to Latin America increased markedly.[24]

Financially, the largest educational contribution that Cuba has made to other countries has been through scholarships that cover the entire tuition and accommodation costs for foreign students to study at school, post-school, and university levels in Cuba. It is only since the 1990s that a small number of places, particularly in medicine, have been offered to overseas students willing and able to pay for at least part of the costs of their tuition. When Cuban educators are selected to work in overseas countries that have requested them, a cost-sharing arrangement is usually arranged in which the Cuban teachers and administrators receive local salaries in the destination country and pay a small portion of their earnings to their government, already paying their regular salaries to support families in Cuba. Educational assistance is provided without charge to the poorest countries, such as Haiti. Cuba's practice of charging partner states variable rates based on their ability to pay for human resources services rendered helps Cuba earn some much-needed foreign exchange.[25] It ought to be stressed, though, that Cuban educational assistance must not be narrowly assessed within either a political or economic context. Unlike much of the aid provided by the international financial institutions, Cuban assistance does not serve the larger goal of drawing participants into the market arrangements of economic globalization. It does not impose conditionalities on its partners, but enters into negotiated and agreed relationships with other countries based on specific economic and fiscal situations.

Cuba supports a range of international educational projects in other developing countries. Some of these are outlined here.

Contribution to School and University Teaching

Since the 1970s, Cuba has made an enormous contribution to teaching overseas students at every level of education, and Cuban professors have also regularly spent periods overseas to assist in university policy development and administration, as is discussed further by Boris Tristá Pérez in chapter 9 of this volume. It is estimated that by 2009, 50,000 international students had graduated from Cuban secondary and tertiary education institutions.[26] These students came from over 120 countries and studied on full scholarships in Cuba. Some 16,500 of them studied at university level and graduated with professional degrees.[27] From 1980 to the early 1990s, nearly a thousand teachers from Zimbabwe were trained in mathematics and science on Cuba's Isle of Youth, studying in a pedagogical institute affiliated with the University of Havana. In the mid-1990s, this institute was still providing scholarships not only to Zimbabweans, but also to Angolans and Namibians.[28] Thousands of tertiary-level scholarships are still being provided, especially in the health sciences and engineering. During the academic year 2007/2008 alone, a total of 2,481 international students graduated from Cuban institutions of higher education.[29] Cuba's Latin American School of Medicine (ELAM) takes in about 1,500 students every year and has overall 10,000 students mainly from Latin America and the Caribbean enrolled at any given time.[30] Another institution that provides opportunities for international students is the International School of Physical and Sports Education (*Escuela Internacional de Educación Física y Deportes*), which by 2010 had enrolled students from 78 countries.[31]

Between 1973 and 1985, 22,000 Cuban teachers were sent to work abroad.[32] Between 1978 and 1995, Cuba welcomed some 18,000 students from 38 nations for primary, secondary, and post secondary schooling, at the request of their governments.[33] Much of the education in Cuba took place on the Isle of Youth, where an innovative approach to internationalism was developed from about 1978 onward. The former Portuguese African colonies—Mozambique, Angola, Guinea-Bissau, Sao Tome and Principe—were highly represented among the countries whose young people received schooling and post-school education on the Isle of Youth. Other African countries that relied heavily on these schools were Ethiopia, Ghana, the Congo, and the Western Sahara. Hundreds of refugees from Namibia and apartheid-ruled South Africa were among the students.[34] Although most students now arriving in Cuba study at the university or technical college level, some international students needing assistance still receive schooling on the Isle of Youth, most notably refugees from Western Sahara who have previously lived in refugee camps.[35]

Today, Cubans continue to teach overseas in universities, colleges, and schools, including schools in several countries of the Caribbean where they are helping to fill gaps and to address serious weaknesses in mathematics and science, as is discussed in chapter 10. South Africa, for example, has benefited from such arrangements, based on a long-standing relationship in which Cuba assisted in its struggle against apartheid. In 2001, Cuba and South Africa signed an agreement for Cuban teachers to relieve shortages in South Africa, and two years later, the two countries embarked on a capacity-building program under which Cubans were to assist South African teachers in rural and disadvantaged areas in developing mathematics, sciences, and technology curricula.[36] Another major beneficiary of Cuban collaboration is the Bahamas: since 2003, some 80 Cuban educators have taught in 25 public schools there.[37]

Contribution to Adult Literacy and Continuing Education Campaigns

The solidarity principle in Cuban adult education overseas is expressed through the three pillars of the Cuban method: mass programs, high-quality programs, and low-cost programs. Cuban advisers in literacy and post-literacy use a variety of pedagogical methods, including radio and television. Cuban literacy education professors who lead the internationalist literacy campaigns are highly trained academics. The literacy system that they have designed has four components: preparation of materials, collaboration with and training of staff, video and classroom pedagogy, and evaluation.

Adult education collaboration with Cuban advisers has taken place in many countries including Colombia, Brazil, Mexico, Argentina, Guatemala, Haiti, Venezuela, Ethiopia, Nicaragua, Cape Verde, and Belize. Each program is negotiated with the respective country's government. The general principles of solidarity are followed: the teaching method (technology transfer) is freely given, and the rest of the cost is shared between Cuba and the partner country, depending on its possibilities. For example, in the case of Venezuela, Cuba provided the method, the TV sets, and the booklets required to teach the program, and Venezuela covered the transport costs, accommodation, and personal expense allowances for the Cuban advisers. However, in the case of Haiti (see Box 1.1), one of the poorest countries in the Americas, the whole literacy program is provided by Cuba. The number of beneficiaries in literacy programs is impressive: for example, in Panama, over 56,000 persons have benefited in the learning program based on the Cuban "Yes, I Can" method.[38] Cuba and Tanzania also hope to reach large numbers of Tanzanians through a mixed-method literacy program based on "Yes, I Can," involving the use of radio and television.[39] Bob Boughton discusses Cuba's adult literacy help to Timor-Leste in chapter 11 of this book.

Program Collaboration within the Education Sector

Cuban educators regularly cooperate with their colleagues in Spanish-speaking countries including Mexico, Colombia, and Venezuela in programs of curriculum development, infrastructure, special education, early childhood, and sports and physical education. Another aspect of collaboration is Cuba's provision of educational infrastructure. For example, the Cuban government donated three secondary school buildings during the 1970s in needy rural areas of Jamaica, and these schools are still being used. Secondary schools were also donated to the Dominican Republic.

Apart from more traditional sector collaboration programs, there are also a number of new areas in which Cuba offers expertise. Napier (2010) has pointed to community revitalization and small-scale organic agriculture projects as learning experiences based on social capital that could be applied in other countries.[40] Indeed, Cuba once again had proved its remarkable resilience after the collapse of the Eastern bloc when it transformed its capital-intensive agricultural system into more sustainable agricultural practices less dependent on oil.[41] The lessons learned in Cuba in this regard could assist other countries in preparing for a future without oil once global supplies start to decline.

Recently, Cuba has promoted literacy work involving people with disability in other countries. Cuban educators have taught basic literacy skills to over 270 mostly low-income Bolivians with different physical disabilities. This program was an outcome of the larger literacy program for more than

800,000 non-literate Bolivians who learned to read and write in indigenous languages between March 2006 and December 2008.[42] In 2010, Cuban professionals completed a contract in Ecuador where they had helped to carry out a bio-psychosocial and clinical-genetic study mapping the incidence of disability in the country. This aimed to enable the Ecuadorian government to devise policies related to work, recreation, sports, and health involving persons with disability.[43]

Cuban Solidarity in Health Development[44]

Medicine as practiced in Cuba is integral to the realization of global solidarity. When Cuban medical personnel share their knowledge, effort, and work overseas despite the dangers and difficult conditions they have to face, they are demonstrating the fundamental values of social commitment and self sacrifice in which they are trained. Medical solidarity, started in the 1960s, is implemented in the field of medical education, community medicine and emergency care, research, joint production of medicines, and technological development. The four principal modes of medical assistance are described below.

Cuban Medical Brigades Overseas: Community Medicine and Emergency Care

Solidarity medical brigades travel from Cuba at the invitation of overseas governments to provide medical care to very poor populations located in isolated areas, or to reinforce embryonic medical services, or to help after natural disasters have struck a community. The brigades offer healing and preventive medicine, including immunization, and assist local health workers to improve community health education. The first Cuban doctors went as a team to Algeria in 1963. Today, 24,950 Cuban health professionals serve in 67 countries,[45] making a significant contribution to staffing the health systems of the underdeveloped world.

Cuban medical collaboration overseas made considerable progress through the Integrated Health Program (PIS for *Programa Integral de Salud*), PIS for started in 1998.[46] This program provides a high quality of medical, social and human services to populations in isolated regions, extending medical coverage, social and health research, and community bonding. The integrated program consists of doctors of general medicine and specialists such as pediatricians, obstetricians, epidemiologists, surgeons, and anesthetists. This approach creates the capacity to provide primary, integrated health care with a specialist focus, for example, in mother-child immunization and medical assistance, the control of infectious and contagious diseases caused by parasites, and programs for improving the health of the elderly.

Emergency medical brigades responding to disasters comprise medical specialists, nurses, technicians, and assistants, supported by a range of materials. The brigades carry everything they need to do their job at a scene of disaster, including campaign hospitals, tents, medicines, food, and medical equipment such as X-ray machines. The brigades can carry out vaccination campaigns, and can take measures to protect the population from further environmental problems. Between 1960 and 1970, Cuba sent international medical brigades to help in 17 natural disasters, assisting the victims of eight earthquakes, six hurricanes, two floods, and a volcanic eruption. Some examples of the kinds of disasters in which Cuban medical brigades have been involved include the great earthquake in Managua, Nicaragua, in 1972, and hurricanes in the Caribbean and in Central America.[47]

Medical collaboration in response to catastrophes found a particular expression after the 1986 accident of the nuclear plant in Chernobyl, Ukraine. From 1990 on, Cuba started to welcome groups of children directly affected by the nuclear accident. The patients were assisted in La Ciudad de los Pioneros, east of Havana City. Specialists in general medicine, pediatrics, nursery, and psychology used their skills to help these children. The Immunology and Hematology Institute of the Pediatric Hospital of Havana was deeply involved. Within three years of the program starting, 11,700 children had been treated at La Ciudad de los Pioneros. Doctors treated 110 cases of leukemia and 15 cases of Hodgkins disease and other types of cancer. They performed 18 heart operations, as well as seven bone marrow transplants and two kidney transplants. Since 1990, Cuba has provided treatment free of charge to about 18,000 victims of the Chernobyl accident, and it continues doing so.[48] It is estimated that, by 2009, more than 38,000 Cuban health-care workers were active in more than 70 countries.[49]

Biomedical Collaboration in Research, and Countering Epidemics Overseas

Cuba shares with other countries its world-leading research and product development in health and medicine, as well as specialized services of the pharmaceutical industry and biotechnology. The latter includes the production of medicines including vaccines through chemical methods, and the development of genetic engineering. Cuba's innovative approach to international health collaboration includes:

1. Technological exchanges in the production and development of advanced drugs
2. Joint development of clinical tests, use of new medicines, and experimental vaccines
3. Therapeutic schemes applied to infectious diseases, such as resistant tuberculosis and hepatitis B and C among others
4. Antiretroviral therapy against HIV/AIDS, utilizing medicines produced in Cuba at affordable prices for poor countries.

Cuban doctors and researchers have also shown solidarity in helping to counter epidemics in other countries. They sent a million vaccines to

Uruguay, to prevent meningococcal meningitis. The vaccine had been created in Cuba when the disease appeared in 2002. Cuban doctors also helped in El Salvador with treatment and medicines to counter an epidemic of dengue fever.

Providing Specialized Health Care to Overseas Patients in Cuba

Medical assistance may be offered free of charge to thousands of people who come to Cuba seeking it. For many years, the International Center for Neurological Treatment has provided medical facilities for thousands of patients from different countries. Recently, the program was broadened to cover all types of pathologies. Patients coming from Venezuela have been provided with clinical treatments, rehabilitation programs, and complex surgical operations. This program began functioning in 2001, and by the middle of 2002, 1,000 patients had been assisted in more than 24 hospitals, with several hotels sheltering the patients and their relatives.

The Milagro ("Miracle") vision restoration program is one of the great success stories of Cuban medical internationalism. By 2008, doctors in Cuba had treated and performed surgery on over 1.14 million people from 33 countries. Cuba had established 51 full ophthalmological centers abroad in 12 countries, and had donated 87 overseas surgical stations.[50]

Cuban Education of Health Personnel: In Cuba and Overseas

Another form of collaboration is sending health specialists to teach overseas in order to help develop faculties of medicine for the training of local doctors, especially in Africa. In the period between 1966 and 1999, highly qualified Cuban doctors were sent overseas to share their knowledge. They facilitated the creation of seven faculties of medicine. Over the same period of time, 3,000 foreigners were trained in Cuban universities as specialists in medicine and dentistry.

Collaboration with Latin America began when Cuban brigades were sent to help in natural disasters. Later, other countries began to receive Cuban doctors supporting integral health programs. In this way, the collaboration expanded. The idea of creating the Latin American School of Medicine (ELAM) in Havana City, a school for training new doctors to serve in the poorer areas of Latin America, arose after the 1998 Hurricane Mitch disaster in Nicaragua. The objective of the school was to train doctors who came from very remote, isolated, and impoverished communities, so that these doctors would return home to work in their own communities, making it unnecessary to seek international medical assistance.

ELAM was established in February 1999 in refurbished buildings formerly used to train military personnel. At first, most students came from Central American countries including Nicaragua and Honduras. Then other countries in the region began asking for scholarships and the institution was officially inaugurated as a Latin American School of Medicine in

November 1999, the month during which the 11th Iberoamerican Summit took place. ELAM initially had a capacity to educate 2,000 students, but by 2005 it was enrolling 10,000 students from 29 countries and 101 ethnic groups, including 85 students from the United States.[51] There are also 1,000 students, mainly from Haiti and from Anglophone countries, studying at the Caribbean School of Medicine in Santiago de Cuba. ELAM, together with the Caribbean School of Medicine in Santiago de Cuba, is of great importance to Cuba's nearest neighbors.

The Cuban government provides the selected students with scholarships that finance all their needs. All Cuba requests is that they come from places with limited or no medical assistance, and that when they return, they offer services that favor the poor and the indigenous peoples. Cubans hope that these students create a new culture of medical practice and an image of doctors in society grounded in humanitarianism. This new culture does not prioritize the selling of medical services and merchandise, but is based on the principle of relieving pain and saving lives, because human lives and health cannot be objects of trade.

Cuban medical education requires that students see themselves as adults committed to going back to their communities, to relieve pain, and upgrade living conditions. It prepares them technically and culturally to face adverse social conditions. They learn to take heed of the social contexts in which they will practice, and the reaction of their more exclusive medical colleagues, which may not always be welcoming. The medical syllabus begins with a month of premedical subjects, to refresh and reinforce the knowledge previously acquired in secondary school. They then study two years of basic science at a senior school and at university level. From the third to the sixth year, the Latin American and Cuban students are trained together in the faculties of medicine at Cuban hospitals.

Cuban doctors teach medical students overseas by means of televised classes and hands-on instruction in local polyclinics, for example, in Venezuela, Cuba played an important role in the establishment of schools of medicine in Equatorial Guinea, Eritrea, and the Gambia. Similar schools are planned for other countries.[52] In October 2010, a Cuban program began in Zambia, which aims to map malaria-breeding places and apply biolarvicides to reduce its annual toll on the Zambian people.[53]

Cuba's Solidarity Assistance to Haiti

Haiti, a Caribbean country of some 6 million people, has for decades been renowned for the extreme poverty of the majority of its people. With the 2010 earthquake, the country was devastated. The death toll rose to 220,000, with another 1.5 million people homeless, most in precarious conditions, many facing cholera, 18 months later.[54] Assistance to Haiti is an example of the large-scale medical and educational help that Cuba offered, at no cost to a destitute neighbor. The point here is that help on a generous

Box 1.1 Haiti

The impoverished situation of Haiti stems from two centuries of what many scholars see as systematic oppression and abuse from wealthy countries, particularly France and the United States. This followed the first successful African slave revolution in history in which enslaved Africans in the French colony of Hispaniola organized an army that drove out their French slaveowners, defeating the well-armed troops of Napoleon. They renamed their country "Haiti," and established a state led by Haitian Africans. Noted Caribbean historian Sir Hilary Beckles, describing these events, makes this comment:

> (F)or too long there has been a popular perception that somehow the Haitian nation-building project, launched on January 1, 1804, has failed on account of mismanagement, ineptitude, corruption. Buried beneath the rubble of imperial propaganda, out of both Western Europe and the United States, is the evidence which shows that Haiti's independence was defeated by an aggressive North-Atlantic alliance that could not imagine their world inhabited by a free regime of Africans as representatives of the newly emerging democracy. (Beckles 2010, *Nation News*, 17 January)

The French, supported by the British and the newly independent Americans, refused to recognize Haiti and joined in a strategy of strangling its economy by denying access to world trade. By 1825, Haiti's economic straits led its rulers to agree to pay massive reparations to France in return for recognition of its sovereignty. This payment, amounting to 70 percent of Haiti's foreign exchange earnings, continued until 1922. It has been estimated that the modern value of these reparations to France is US $21 billion, and some Haitians are pressing the demand that France should pay back this sum, which "was illegally extracted from the Haitian people and should be repaid. This could rebuild Haiti and place it in a position to re-engage the modern world" (Beckles 2010).

"Assisting France to collect reparations" from Haiti provided a pretext on which the United States invaded Haiti in 1915. US exploitation of Haiti's resources, as well as its violent military interventions, escalated during the twentieth century. In 2004, Haitians "were celebrating their bicentennial when the U.S. kidnapped and exiled (for the second time) their popular President Jean-Bertrand Aristide who won two landslide victories in internationally monitored elections. The majority of Haitians have demanded his return ever since" (Kiilu Nyasha <kiilu2@sbcglobal.net> January 15, 2010).

scale is needed to make a difference in the worst situations in the poorest countries. The example of Haiti demonstrates how bilateral cooperation in health is enhanced and supplemented by educational initiatives.

Cuba's solidarity with Haiti pre-dated the earthquake. A disaster relief and reconstruction program had been in place since 1998, when the devastation of Hurricane George killed more than 30,000 people in Central America and the Caribbean, making 2.4 million homeless.[55] Such an extended program shows how an emergency relief initiative grew into a solidly structured program of bilateral assistance. After hospital care was reinforced during the emergency phase, Cubans started to send doctors and nurses into remote Haitian areas. The next phase strengthened frontline health services, developed an epidemiological surveillance system, instituted a school of medicine to train health workers through a variety of media, and dispatched recently graduated Cuban medical personnel to work alongside Haitian colleagues.[56]

When the earthquake shook Haiti in January 2010, around 400 Cuban internationalist professionals, primarily health workers and literacy teachers, were already working there.

Currently, there are 660 young Haitians studying in Cuba on scholarships from the Cuban government. Of these, 567 are training to become doctors. Up to 2009, 550 Haitian doctors had graduated from the Latin American School of Medicine. As a result of Cuba's contribution to education, 16,000 Haitians have learned to read and write. Since 1998, over 6,000 Cuban health professionals have done tours of duty in Haiti. They have performed more than 14 million medical consultations and over 231,000 surgical operations. They have assisted in the delivery of over 112,000 babies, and through Operation Miracle have performed eye operations on some 44,000 Haitians, to save or improve their sight.[57] Cuba cooperates with Haiti not only in health and education, but also in sectors such as agriculture, energy, fisheries, and communications.

Cuban doctors and other health professionals started to offer services immediately after the 2010 earthquake. For the first four days, while other countries and international agencies were getting organized, the Cuban health workers were offering the principal medical assistance received by the Haitian people. Under a medical cooperation agreement between Cuba and Haiti signed in 1998, there were already 344 Cuban health professionals in Haiti before the earthquake.[58] After the earthquake, more health workers arrived from Cuba to reinforce the medical brigade in Port-au-Prince. Among them were specialists from the Henry Reeve Medical Brigade for emergency situations, with experience in similar disasters. Cuban doctors organized medical facilities by revamping three field hospitals and building five new ones, five diagnostic centers, and an additional 22 care posts, aided by financial support from Venezuela. Cubans operated nine rehabilitation centers staffed by nearly 70 Cuban physical therapists and rehabilitation specialists.[59]

The Cuban medical brigade carried medicines, food provisions, serum, and plasma bags with them. By January 14, Cuban health workers had treated 1,987 patients who had suffered in the Haitian earthquake. They had performed 111 surgical interventions at assistance locations both in Port-au-Prince and on its outskirts. The reach of the Cuban health workers was considerably extended by the fact that some 400 young Haitians who had been recently trained as doctors in Cuban universities worked to save lives, side by side with the Cuban reinforcements.

The effectiveness of Cuba's internationalist work has been extended by the government's willingness to support the Haitian people in cooperation with a range of other countries. For example, at the request of the US government, Cuba immediately authorized US airplanes to use Cuban airspace in the eastern provinces nearest to Haiti to evacuate Haitians to hospitals in Florida.[60] Cuba also cooperated with Venezuela, Namibia, and Norway, China, the Dominican Republic, Mexico, and Russia to extend interventions after the earthquake.

Conclusion

The assistance provided by Cuba to other developing countries is an example of the radically new kinds of relations that are needed to tackle the crisis left by a flawed, neocolonial model of development in which countries weakened by colonialism have been offered, for the most part, only inadequate and conditional aid from the wealthy countries. Although in some areas, including education, the old model of aid from the "North" has recently been improved, as is discussed in the next chapter, the improvements are far from enough to tackle the enormous problems of impoverished underdevelopment left by colonialism.

The overview of Cuban educational and medical aid provided in this chapter demonstrates a model of assistance from highly qualified professionals on a very large scale. The assistance is made possible through the principles of mutual solidarity and collaboration, in which partner countries receiving help from Cuba, support Cuba, in turn, in a variety of ways. Cuba does not expect or ask for equivalent value to be a feature of this reciprocal support. Its provision of highly significant assistance to the most impoverished countries, such as Haiti, without expecting anything in return, is another feature of the solidarity principle. It is clear that wealthy countries could provide more effective assistance to the poorer countries if they were to consider implementing a model of internationalism on the much larger and more generous scale illustrated by Cuban internationalism in education and health. They could afford to implement this more easily than Cuba can.

Cuba's internationalist work faces numerous challenges. Among those identified by the Cuba-US group "Medical Education Cooperation with Cuba" (MEDICC), are the political and social instability in some developing countries, the sheer size of the effort and resources needed to make a difference in the health status of the poorest countries, and the fact that this can put a strain on domestic health facilities in Cuba. There are sometimes barriers to access and occasional problematic treatment found in the various health systems staffed by Cubans, initial concerns from in-country medical associations fearful of job displacement, the need to expand the skill set of Cuban physicians serving abroad, who confront circumstances and infectious diseases long absent from the Cuban health picture, and the negative effects of the US embargo that continue to generate barriers for Cuban health care at home and abroad.[61] These observations are important in suggesting some of the difficulties that may also face educational cooperation.

Cuban South-South cooperation is important in improving broader political, cultural, and ultimately economic relationships between developing countries. A criticism frequently made against Cuba is that it "overtrains" its citizens without providing sufficient employment opportunities in a depressed economy. This chapter has provided examples of how highly trained Cuban professionals are not restricted to the domestic job economy, but are finding a meaningful role beyond the country's borders. Cuba has successfully demonstrated that aid and trade can be based on principles of equality, social justice, and partnership, thus evading the problems of the development assistance approach prevalent in traditional North-South aid and trade relationships, discussed in the next chapter. South-South collaboration in education and other fields could increase development on political and cultural as well as economic fronts.[62] These are issues that invite deeper exploration as postcolonial educators consider the value of forging an approach to collaboration that would be independent of traditional direction and financing with strings from the wealthy countries of the "North."

Notes

1. Cuba's Gross Domestic Product (GDP) per capita (or purchasing power parity, PPP) averaged $6000 over the past five years, ranging from $3000 in 2005 to $11,000 in 2008. In 2008 Jamaica's GDP per capita was $7,500 while Australia's was $36,700, Canada's was $38,700, that of the UK $35,000 and the United States $46,300. Source: CIA Factbook. http://www.indexmundi.com/g/r.aspx?v=67&l=en Retrieved 9 June 2011.
2. See, for example, De Vos, De Ceukelaire, Bonet, and Van der Stuyft, 2007; Gorry, 2008.
3. Unterhalter and Carpentier, 2010; Luke, 2010. For example, Allan Luke argues that "...while the recruitment and training of international students served and serves the interests of ideological and cultural incorporation by nation states, and the production of specialized technical expertise for globalizing industry—its major function in many American and Commonwealth universities now is revenue generation in the face of declining state and endowment funding" (47–48).
4. Carnoy, 1990: 155.
5. Higman, 2011: 255.
6. Ibid.
7. Carnoy, 1990:159.
8. Dilla, 2000.
9. Carnoy, 1990:169–171, Lutjens, 2000.

10. Kaiser-Lenoir, 2008:299, see also Carnoy, 1990:167–168.
11. Kaiser-Lenoir, 2008:296–297.
12. United Nations Development Programme, 2007.
13. Carnoy, 1990:159.
14. Hammett, 2004.
15. Brundenius, 2009.
16. De Vos, De Ceukelaire, Bonet, and Van der Stuyft, 2007.
17. Azicri, 1988:220–221.
18. Brundenius, 2009.
19. Gott, 2005.
20. *BBC News*, 2011.
21. Kaiser-Lenoir, 2008:307.
22. Hammett, 2007.
23. Carnoy, Gove, and Marshall, 2007; Richmond, 1990; United Nations Educational, Scientific and Cultural Organization (UNESCO), 1998.
24. Ministerio de Relaciones Exteriores de Cuba, n.d.
25. Eckstein, as cited in Hammett, 2004.
26. Martín Sabina, 2009.
27. Fiddian-Qasmiyeh, 2010; Martín Sabina, 2002.
28. Zeigler, 1995:27.
29. Martín Sabina and Viña Brito, 2010. The United Nations Office of the Special Adviser to Africa (2004) concluded that 29,106 African students had graduated from Cuba's higher education institutions between 1961 and 2002. This figure appears inconsistent with data provided by Elvira Martín Sabina and Silvia Margarita Viña Brito (2010) who cite the figure of 29,039 students from 129 countries graduating from Cuban higher education institutions between 1961 and 2008. The discrepancy is likely to be the result of different ways of including graduates from post secondary vocational training institutions in the data.
30. *Escuela Latinoamericana de Medicina ELAM*; Harris, 2009.
31. Martín Sabina and Viña Brito, 2010; EcuRed, 2012.
32. Lutjens, 2000:328.
33. Elejalde Villalón, 2011.
34. Zeigler, 1995; Gonzales, 2000; Gleijeses, n.d.
35. Fidian-Qasmiyeh, 2010
36. Napier, 2010
37. http://www.cubaminrex.cu/English/Cooperation/2010/CUBAN.html
38. http://www.cubaminrex.cu/English/Cooperation/2010/14-06-10-3.html
39. http://www.cubaminrex.cu/English/Cooperation/2010/0218.html
40. Napier, 2010.
41. Wright, 2009
42. http://www.cubaminrex.cu/English/Cooperation/2010/Cubans%20Help.html
43. http://www.cubaminrex.cu/English/Cooperation/2010/ECUADOR.html
44. Most of the section on the health sector was prepared for us by our colleague Marina Majoli Viani just before her death in 2004. She was a professor of biotechnology at the University of Havana, and was dedicated to supporting Cuba's internationalist health policy for solidarity in global development. We have used her words, but have updated some of her information with later references and occasional additions to her text.
45. Frank and Reid, 2005.
46. De Vos, et al., 2007.
47. Huish and Kirk, 2007; Saney, 2006.
48. Huish and Kirk, 2009.
49. Gorry, 2008b.

50. Gorry, 2008a and 2008b.
51. Keck, 2007, see also Frank and Reed, 2005.
52. *Granma International*, as cited in Saney, 2006; United Nations Office of the Special Adviser on Africa, 2004.
53. http://www.cubaminrex.cu/English/Cooperation/2010/25-10-10.html
54. Disasters Emergency Committee, 2010.
55. Gorry, 2008b.
56. De Vos, et al., 2007.
57. Appelbaum, 2009.
58. Fawthrop, 2010.
59. Fawthrop, 2010.
60. "Cuba Aids Haiti," 2010; Fawthrop, 2010.
61. *MEDICC*, 2007.
62. Tikly, 2004:124.

Bibliography

Appelbaum, D. (2009) Fact Sheet: Cuban Medical Cooperation with Haiti. *Medical Education Cooperation with Cuba (MEDICC)*, January 15, 2009. http://www.medicc.org/ns/index.php?s=104, Accessed June 9, 2011.

Azicri, M. (1988) *Cuba. Politics, Economics and Society.* London: Pinter.

BBC News Cuban May Day Marchers "Back Economic Reform." May 1, 2011.

Beckles, H. (2010) 'The hate and the quake', *Nation News* (Barbados newspaper), 17 January.

Blue, S. A. (2010) Cuban Medical Internationalism: Domestic and International Impacts. *Journal of Latin American Geography* 9(1), 31–49. doi: 10.1353/lag.0.0071.

Brundenius, C. (2009) Revolutionary Cuba at 50. *Latin American Perspectives* 36(2), 31–48. doi: 10.1177/0094582X0933196.

Carnoy, M. (1990). Cuba. In *Education and Social Transition in the Third World.* Edited by M. Carnoy and J. Samoff. Princeton, NJ: Princeton University Press, pp. 153–208.

Carnoy, M., A. Gove, and J. Marshall (2007) *Cuba's Academic Advantage: Why Students in Cuba Do Better in School.* Stanford, CA: Stanford University Press.

Castro, F. (2000) Cuba and the Struggle against Global Poverty. *Socialism and Democracy* 14(2), 1–25. doi:10.1080/08854300008428261.

Cuba Aids Haiti Relief. (January 22, 2010) *VOANews.com*. Retrieved from http://www.voanews.com/policy/editorials/a-41-2010-01-21-voa1-84649797.html

De Vos, P., W. De Ceukelaire, M. Bonet, and P. Van der Stuyft (2007) Cuba's International Cooperation in Health: An Overview. *International Journal of Health Services* 37(4), 761–776. doi:10.2190/HS.37.4.k.

Dilla Alfonso, H. (2000) The Cuban Experiment. Economic Reform, Social Restructuring, and Politics. *Latin American Perspectives* 110, 27(1), January, 33–44.

Disasters Emergency Committee. (July 10, 2010) *Haiti Earthquake: Facts and Figures.* Retrieved from http://www.dec.org.uk/item/425.

Elejalde Villalón, O. (2011) 'Cubans sharing education: the Isle of Youth'. See Chapter 12 in this volume.

Escuela Latinoamericana de Medicina [Latin American School of Medicine]. EcuRed, http://www.ecured.cu/index.php/Escuela_Latinoamericana_de_Medicina, accessed 5 April 2012.

Fawthrop, T. (February 16, 2010) Cuba's Aid Ignored by the Media? *Al Jazeera*. Retrieved from http://www.aljazeera.com/focus/2010/01/201013195514870782.html.

Fiddian-Qasmiyeh, E. (2010) Education, Migration and Internationalism: Situating Muslim Middle Eastern and North African students in Cuba. *Journal of North African Studies* 15(2), 137–155. doi:10.1080/13629380802532234.

Frank, M., and G. Reed (2005) Doctors for the (Developing) World. *MEDICC Review* 7(8), Aug/Sept 2005, Retrieved June 13, 2011 at http://www.medicc.org/publications/medicc_review/0805/spotlight.html

Gleijeses, P. (n.d.) *The Massacre of Cassinga*. Retrieved January 3, 2008, from Cuban Embassy to South Africa Website: http://emba.cubaminrex.cu/Default.aspx?tabid=6027.

Gonzales, D. (2000) Cuban-African Relations: Nationalist Roots of an Internationalist Policy. *Review of African Political Economy* 27(84), 317–323.

Gorry C. (2008a) Sight for Sore Eyes: Cuba's Vision Restoration Program. *MEDICC Review* 10(2). Retrieved November 20, 2011, from http://www.medicc.org/mediccreview/index.php?issue=4&id=37&a=vahtml

Gorry, C. (2008b) Cuban Health Cooperation Turns 45. *MEDICC Review* 10(3), 44–47. Retrieved November 20, 2011 from http://www.medicc.org/mediccreview/articles/mr_22.pdf

Gott, R. (2005) *Hugo Chávez and the Bolivarian Revolution*. London and New York: Verso.

Hammett, D. P. (2004) From Havana with Love: A Case Study of South-South Development Cooperation Operating between Cuba and South Africa in the Health Care Sector. Edinburgh, United Kingdom: Centre of African Studies, University of Edinburgh.

Hammett, D. P. (2007) Cuban Intervention in South African Health Care Provision. *Journal of Southern African Studies* 33(1), March, 63–81.

Harris, R. (2009) Cuban Internationalism, Che Guevara, and the Survival of Cuba's Socialist Regime. *Latin American Perspectives* 166, 36(3), 27–42. doi: 10.1177/0094582X09334165

Hickling-Hudson, A. (2000) The Cuban University and Educational Outreach: Cuba's Contribution to Postcolonial Development. In *Local Knowledge and Wisdom in Higher Education*. Edited by G. R. Teasdale and Zane Ma Rhea. London: Pergamon, 187–208.

Hickling-Hudson, A. (2004). South-South Collaboration: Cuban Teachers in Jamaica and Namibia. *Comparative Education* 40(2), May, 289–311.

Hickling-Hudson, A., J. Corona González, R. Preston, and E. Martín Sabina (2004) The Internationalism of Cuban Education: Pioneering Cooperation between Postcolonial Countries. Panel of four papers presented at 12th Congress, World Council of Comparative Education Societies (WCCES), Havana, Cuba, October 25–29.

Higman, B. W. (2011) *A Concise History of the Caribbean*. Cambridge: Cambridge University Press.

Huish, R., and J. M. Kirk (2007) Cuban Medical Internationalism and the Development of the Latin American School of Medicine. *Latin American Perspectives* 34(6), 77–92. doi:10.1177/0094582X07308119

Huish, R., and J. M. Kirk (2009) Cuban Medical Internationalism in Africa: The Threat of a Dangerous Example. *Latin Americanist* 53(3), 125–139. doi:10.1111/j.1557-203X.2009.01045.x

Kaiser-Lenoir, C. (2008) A Contribution to the Assessment of a Changing Cuba. In *A Changing Cuba in a Changing World*. Edited by M. Font. New York: The Graduate Center, City University of New York, 296–297.

Keck, C. W. (2007) Cuba's Contribution to Global Health Diplomacy. In Global Health Diplomacy Workshop, March 12, 2007.

Lehr, S. (2008) *The Children of the Isle of Youth: Impact of a Cuban South-South Education Program on Ghanaian Graduates*. Doctoral thesis, University of

Victoria, Victoria, Canada. Retrieved from http://dspace.library.uvic.ca:8080/handle/1828/1243.

Luke. A. (2010) Educating the Other: Standpoint and Theory in Higher Education. In *Global Inequalities and Higher Education*. Edited by E. Unterhalter and V. Carpentier. Basingstoke and New York: Palgrave /Macmillan, 43–65.

Lutjens, S. (2000) Política educativa en Cuba socialista: lecciones de 40 años de reformas [The Politics of Education in Socialist Cuba: Lessons of 40 Years of Reforms]. In *Cuba: construyendo futuro* [Cuba: Building the Future]. Edited by M. M. Pérez, M. Riera, and J. Valdés Paz. Barcelona: Fundación de Investigaciones Marxistas/Viejo Topo, 287–330.

Martín Sabina, E. (2002) La educación superior de Cuba en la década del 90 [Higher Education in Cuba in the 1990s]. Havana, Cuba: Editorial Félix Varela.

Martín Sabina, E. (2009) Thoughts on Cuban Education. *Latin American Perspectives* 36(2), 135–137. doi:10.1177/0094582X09331817

Martín Sabina, E., and S. M. Viña Brito (2010) La educación superior en Cuba: Estabilidad y cambios [Higher Education in Cuba: Stability and Changes]. *Educación Superior y Sociedad*, 15(1), 69–89. Retrieved from http://ess.iesalc.unesco.org.ve/index.php/ess/article/view/369/309.

MEDICC 2007. Cuba and the Global Health Workforce: Health Professionals Abroad. http://www.saludthefilm.net/ns/cuba-and-global-health.html. Retrieved June 9, 2011.

Ministerio de Relaciones Exteriores de Cuba. (n.d.) *Scholarships program*. Retrieved February 1, 2008, from http://www.cubaminrex.cu/English/cooperation/scholarship%20program.htm

Napier, D. B. (2010). Education, Social Justice, and Development in South Africa and Cuba: Comparisons and Connections. *Globalization, Comparative Education and Policy Research* 10(1), 33–48. doi:10.1007/978-90-481-3221-8_3.

Nyasha, K. (2010) 'The Haitian Tragedy and Mainstream Media Response. In *Bay View*, 16 January.

Pérez López, J. F. (2008). Recent Cuban Foreign Trade Patterns. *Nueva Sociedad 216*. Retrieved from http://www.nuso.org/upload/articulos/3541_2.pdf.

Plummer, R. (2011) Cuba Inches towards Market Socialism. *BBC News*. March 27. http://www.bbc.co.uk/news/business-12565417

Richmond, M. (1990) The Cuban Educational Model and Its Influence in the Caribbean Region. In *Education in Central America and the Caribbean*. Edited by C. Brock and D. Clarkson. London, UK: Routledge, 63–99.

Saney, I. (2006). African Stalingrad: The Cuban Revolution, Internationalism, and the End of Apartheid. *Latin American Perspectives* 33(5), 81–117. doi:10.1177/0094582X05281111.

Tikly, L. (2004) Globalisation and Education in Sub-Saharan Africa. In *Disrupting Preconceptions: Postcolonialism and Education* Edited by A. Hickling-Hudson, J. Matthews, and A. Woods. Flaxton, Brisbane: Post Pressed, 109–126.

United Nations Development Programme (2007) *Human Development Report 2007/2008*. New York, NY: Palgrave Macmillan. Retrieved from http://hdr.undp.org/en/media/HDR_20072008_EN_Complete.pdf

United Nations Educational, Scientific and Cultural Organization. (1998) *World Conference on Higher Education. Higher Education in the Twenty-First Century: Vision and Action. Final Report* (Technical report). Paris: UNESCO. [Electronic version]

United Nations Office of the Special Adviser on Africa. (2004) South-South Cooperation in Support of the New Partnership for Africa's Development: Experiences of Africa-Latin America and the Caribbean. New York, NY: United Nations. Retrieved from http://www.un.org/esa/africa/South South.pdf

Unterhalter, E. and V. Carpentier (2010) Introduction: Whose interests Are We Serving? In *Global Inequalities and Higher Education*. Edited by E. Unterhalter and V. Carpentier. Basingstoke and New York: Palgrave /Macmillan.

Wagner, S. (2004, December 16) Venezuela and Cuba Sign New Cooperation Agreements. *Venezuelanalysis.com*. Retrieved August 27, 2009, from http://www.venezuelanalysis.com/news/840

Wright, J. (2009) *Sustainable Agriculture and Food Security in an Era of Oil Scarcity: Lessons from Cuba*. London, UK: Earthscan.

Zeigler, L. (1995) Cuba's African Connection: International Education on the Other Side of the Cold War. *International Educator* (Winter), 24–28.

2

Challenging Educational Underdevelopment: The Cuban Solidarity Approach as a Mode of South-South Cooperation

*Jorge Corona González,
Anne Hickling-Hudson, and Sabine Lehr*

Introduction

This chapter analyzes the role played by overseas aid in education. Taking a postcolonial perspective, it explores overseas aid for the human development of beneficiary countries, given the context of the educational legacies of colonialism, the challenges being raised to these legacies, and the difficulties and ambivalence involved in change.[1] A postcolonial study of Cuban educational aid illustrates the complexities of the manner in which the disengagement from colonial legacies in education is taking place, and facilitates the discussion of alternatives that might become possible if postcolonial societies were able to disentangle themselves from the constraints of their colonial histories.

Deep socioeconomic divisions and inequalities prevail in the education systems that remain after the formal ending of colonialism in many countries of the global "South."[2] The educational reforms of the decolonizing period, including expanded access, improved teacher education, and curriculum change, have often failed to alter fundamentally the flawed education models inherited from colonial times. Entrenched disparities of social class, gender, ethnicity, resourcing, and location have been hard to shift, and constitute a barrier to effective national development. Aid has been provided by the wealthy countries of the Global "North," including those of Western Europe, the United States, and Canada, but this has been too inadequate and poorly targeted to help the South systematically develop its education systems.

The OECD's 2005 Paris Declaration on Aid Effectiveness and the 2008 Accra Agenda for Action were the outcome of a process of discussion and negotiation between donor countries and impoverished countries receiving educational aid. These declarations agreed on an improved approach to aid in order to increase aid effectiveness. There is some progress toward this goal, but far from enough is being done to tackle the massive problems of education.[3] Moreover, the global socioeconomic divide is not narrowing. It is this situation that makes it imperative for all nations to consider different approaches to educational assistance and exchange.

In this chapter we introduce global modalities of educational aid in order to understand the unique approach that Cuba takes. We argue that

1. Traditional "North-South" approaches to educational aid (referred to in the literature as "aid architecture") have not had the desired effects in tackling the crisis of quantity and quality. Since the 1990s, aid architecture has been slowly improving, but remains inadequate.
2. South-South cooperation approaches, within the Non-Aligned Movement, have achieved some useful exchanges between countries, but on such a small scale that these approaches remain at the margins of aid processes.
3. Cuba's internationalism with its philosophy of solidarity, a South-South modality that fits within the framework of socialist internationalism, appears to be a promising strategy in the search for a justice-based approach to aid and exchange.

The Global Educational Crisis and the Role of Aid

Knowledge is a vital asset to economic growth and human development. The education crisis enmeshing most underdeveloped countries means that the knowledge base of their populations remains inadequate. Weak education systems are a component of the present unjust global order that condemns two-thirds or more of the world's people to live in poverty, ill-health, and hunger. The "Education for All" goals reiterated at the conference in Dakar in 2000 are so far from being achieved that at the present rate, they would not even be reached by the end of the twenty-first century. Although access to schooling has been expanded everywhere, it is still far from being equitable in terms of quality, and is not guaranteed for all, not even at the primary level. UNESCO's 2010 overview indicates the contours of the global education crisis. Poverty is accompanied by a high rate of nonliteracy, inadequate access to schooling and higher education, discrimination against women and the poor, and school ineffectiveness. Sixteen percent of the world's adult population, some 759 million adults, are nonliterate, of whom two-thirds are women. About 72 million children of primary school age are out of school. It is estimated that 44 percent of this number will never have access to schooling. Additionally, many children drop out of primary school before completion, a trend that affects 13 percent of children in Asia, and 9 percent in Sub-Saharan Africa. In 2007, approximately

71 million adolescents who should have been in secondary education were not attending school (20 percent of the age group). Schooling is so poorly resourced that millions of people finish school without basic competencies in reading, writing, and arithmetic. The higher education and vocational education sectors are both so underdeveloped that countries cannot train adequate numbers of professionals and skilled workers.[4]

Development as a process of equitable and sustainable economic growth aims to bring about social equity, autonomy, freedom of decision making, equal opportunities, equality between men and women, employment for all, and the conservation and protection of the environment and of nations.[5] The Millennium Development Goals (MDGs) constitute a small global step toward acknowledging not these broad ideals of development, but rather, a minimal consensus that something must be done to tackle global inequity. The MDGs aim to eradicate extreme poverty and hunger, improve health care, promote gender equality, and work toward environmental sustainability and a global partnership for development. The funds needed to accomplish these goals, at the minimal level outlined, are estimated at US $150 billion, a sum that could be found if the developed countries were sincere about their commitment to the MDGs. If wealthy countries were to increase their aid to just 0.7 percent of their respective GDP as they have promised at past international meetings, this would add $160 billion a year to development. However, the amount of development assistance given is miserly: Steven Klees estimates that it comes to about $10 US per capita a year, and asks: "What kind of development do we think we can buy for $10 per head per year? ....In 2008, ODA [official development assistance] to all of Africa was about $35 billion, less than the U.S. bailout of the auto industry."[6]

The emergence of the new development compact in education at the turn of the twentieth/twenty-first century constitutes another global step in acknowledging equity ideals. Between 1996 and 2006, education was accorded a more important position than previously in the agendas of donor countries and agencies. The new approach to aid architecture can be summarized as an emphasis on poverty reduction, support to national budgets, cooperation between bilateral and multilateral agencies, more harmonized methods of aid delivery across socioeconomic sectors, and a modified language that talks of partnerships instead of conditionalities.[7]

However, there has only been a limited implementation of sector-wide approaches to aid, a decade after their introduction.[8] This may be because some donors worry about corruption, governance ability, or lack of capacity in partner countries, or show skepticism toward pooled approaches. The new paradigm of North-South educational aid claims to focus on the poorest countries, yet there is often a pragmatic targeting of those nations that appear to be most capable of utilizing the aid effectively, rather than the poorest ones. The paradigm still focuses largely on primary schooling, with little attention to other educational sectors, particularly higher and vocational. The new aid paradigm has yet to show its potential. Ridell (2007) observes that while donors stress the importance of partnership between donors and recipients as being necessary "for aid to have a positive impact, in practice, the overall aid relationship remains extremely lopsided with donors remaining almost wholly in control."[9]

UNESCO's Global Monitoring Report 2010 concludes that the number of children out of primary school is decreasing, but a much stronger focus on marginalized children is required to get all children into school. The poorest countries are still struggling to reach universal enrolment, but richer countries also have significant out-of-school populations, indicative of the equality gap. The report concludes that the target of universal primary education set for 2015 will be missed, with an estimated 56 million children still out of school by then.[10] Apart from this problem, implementation of the "Education for All" goals has also been criticized for its excessive focus on primary schools and thus only on children.[11] Furthermore, the insistence that increasing numbers of children and young adults with basic literacy skills constitutes progress is ill-conceived. UNESCO has recognized a greatly expanded concept of literacy, and points out that most bilateral and multilateral agencies still define literacy primarily as a very narrow skill set that does not take into account cultural, national, regional, or community contexts.[12]

Aid from wealthy countries can play an important part in helping with educational change, but the question is whether current aid structures and strategies can realistically meet goals of transformation. Some scholars argue that they cannot. Klees (2010) points out that the financial and aid regime steered by the World Bank and the IMF has resulted in the biggest concentration of wealth that the world has ever seen, and adds that these two agencies have imposed a great deal of bad advice on the global education sector.[13] Samoff's view (2009) is that the aid system "is in fact working very well. Its essential role is not to achieve publicly stated objectives but rather to maintain a global political economy of inequality."[14] Similarly, Hammett (2004) argues that the aid policies of the former colonial powers are to a large extent a facade, promoting their continued access to natural resources and markets to favor their own economic progress and to further their strategic interests.[15] Wealthy countries often have a contradictory position with regard to educational aid. With one hand they offer limited amounts of aid, and with the other they counteract it by measures that deepen poverty and crisis. This includes encouraging the migration of highly skilled professionals who received expensive higher education in developing countries, and facilitating permanent residency for a high proportion of professionals who obtained their degrees in wealthy countries.[16] If aid conditionalities insist on a continuation or reintroduction of European colonial languages for instruction, suppressing the promotion of indigenous languages, the publishing industries of the former colonial powers will continue to profit directly from these language policies.[17] Wealthy countries may contribute aid to supporting the education of teachers in poorer countries, but such efforts could be neutralized if at the same time these countries carry out aggressive recruitment campaigns to attract hundreds of these teachers to fill gaps in the schools of London and New York, as has been occurring in the Caribbean and elsewhere over the past decade.[18]

Development assistance goals appear to run counter to the economic interests of industrialized countries to maximize profits by whatever means. In this context, can meaningful change be achieved? Recent analyses have been skeptical. Escobar observes, "Although the [development] discourse has gone through a series of structural changes, the architecture of the discursive formation laid down in the period 1945-55 has remained unchanged, allowing the discourse to adapt to new conditions. The result has been the succession of development strategies and substrategies up to the present, always within the confines of the same discursive space."[19]

It is against this background that we discuss the importance of considering alternative models of development assistance such as the model of "South-South collaboration," which is evident in Cuban internationalist policy in education, health, and other areas. We consider the movement for South-South cooperation in education, pointing out the limitations of scale but arguing that this approach could become a vital contributor to tackling the global educational crisis. This discussion provides the context for this book's focus on the role of the distinct Cuban model of development collaboration.

South-South Development Cooperation

Parallel to the traditional "North-South" or "vertical" development assistance model, an alternative model has emerged, which is frequently termed "South-South" or "horizontal" development cooperation. While Cuba began to support countries emerging from colonialism in the early 1960s, the language of South-South cooperation was only adopted in aid policy towards the end of the decade. Newly decolonizing countries tried to find ways to cooperate among themselves to gain more autonomy from the former colonial powers through finding solutions within their own regions to the critical problems they were facing.[20]

Any consideration of South-South linkages for development inevitably raises questions concerning what type of development is desirable, and toward what goals countries might aim to develop. It is no longer appropriate to think that development models widely espoused in today's industrialized countries are the only appropriate development paradigms. The widespread failure of structural adjustment policies as a means of alleviating poverty and of contributing to development in lower-income countries shows that policies rooted in Northern thinking patterns will often not achieve the desired results in environments characterized by very different socioeconomic realities. Specific and localized bilateral collaboration mechanisms such as the assistance program in the health-care sector between Cuba and South Africa, or the collaboration in the education sector between Cuba and its partners, appear to be a promising alternative approach. These initiatives are designed for the mutual benefit of the collaborating partners through addressing particular gaps in the respective countries' economic and/or social systems.

The main conduit that led to the emergence of the South-South concept was the Group of 77 (G-77). This intergovernmental alliance of 77 developing countries formed the Non-Aligned Movement on the occasion of the first session of the United Nations Conference on Trade and Development (UNCTAD) in Geneva in 1961.[21] The goal was to assert, improve, and defend "Third World" economic and political interests without being structurally aligned to either the capitalist or the communist power blocs. By the late 1980s, however, it had become clear that the development desired was not taking place in most of the 77 countries. In his 1987 book, *Up the Down Escalator,* Michael Manley analyzed the experience of the agricultural, finance, and bauxite sectors in Jamaica (of which he was prime minister during periods between the 1970s and 1990s), arguing that hard-won advances by Third World countries appearing to put them on the "up" escalator were likely to be eroded because of structural imbalances built into the larger escalator of the international system perpetually putting the poorer countries on the downward path. Manley advocated the argument that solidarity built up in the "South-South" process would give countries in the Global South a chance of achieving economic independence from the "North":

> Jamaica cannot start a shipping line of any significance by itself, but the eleven countries of the Caribbean Community (CARICOM) can. Jamaica can, simultaneously, join with Mexico, Panama, Costa Rica, Nicaragua, Venezuela and Cuba to develop a very large shipping line.[22]

The Non-Aligned Movement has continued into the twenty-first century. Cuba has chaired the movement on two occasions, and Egypt chaired the fifteenth summit of the movement in 2009. A G-77 declaration during a South summit in Havana in 2000 recognized regional cooperation through harmonization of economic and social policies as the most meaningful approach for South-South cooperation, describing it as "a crucially important tool for developing and strengthening the economic independence of developing countries and achieving development, and as one of the means of ensuring the equitable and effective participation of developing countries in the emerging global economic order."[23] The ethos of South-South cooperation informs the New Partnership for Africa's Development (NEPAD) that rests on the principle of finding African solutions to African problems. The founding principles of NEPAD, adopted as a strategic framework by the Organisation of African Unity in 2001, "provide an enabling environment within which African states can pursue bilateral and multilateral development projects, including South-South cooperation." This includes exploring links with China. The South African government is one that "views alignment with China as a priority to encourage development in the South and to challenge...North-South post Cold War hegemony."[24]

Examples of South-South collaboration include a number of regional free trade agreements, such as the Common Market of the Southern Cone (MERCOSUR) which includes Argentina, Brazil, Paraguay, Uruguay, with Bolivia, Chile, Colombia, Ecuador, and Peru as associate members; the Southern African Customs Union (SACU); the free trade agreement that links MERCOSUR and SACU[25]; the Caribbean Community (CARICOM), regional trading network for countries of the English-speaking Caribbean; and ALBA, an international cooperation organization that promotes collaboration and regional economic integration among Latin American and Caribbean countries. A certain level of South-South cooperation in the industrial and utility sectors exists outside the large-scale trade schemes. Notable examples include those between Latin American and African countries, which have worked together to enhance expertise in the energy and information sectors, and in the communication technologies sector, using intermediate technologies that are better adapted to African needs than the sophisticated products imported from industrialized countries. Other South-South collaborations focus on science and technology, higher education and research development, and knowledge networks.[26] African Journals Online, AJOL (http://ajol.info/index.php/), a nonprofit organization in South Africa, is a large collection of peer-reviewed African-published scholarly journals, established to facilitate access for African scholars to their African colleagues' work, and to make African scholarly work accessible to other parts of the world.

Educational cooperation between African and Latin American countries has been in existence for decades. This collaboration between educators strives to address the inadequacies of the education systems inherited from European colonialism, addressing the educational needs of learners in Southern communities with similar structural, economic, and demographic characteristics. The main Latin American countries involved in the provision of educational assistance to Africa have been Brazil, Cuba, and Mexico. Through scholarship programs, training of African students both in Latin America and in Africa, as well as capacity-building programs and the establishment of educational institutions in African countries, these three Latin American countries have made a sizeable effort to build up formal professional training on the African continent.[27]

South-South cooperation for development in education is also notable in Asia and in Africa. For example, a special relationship between Vietnam and Laos facilitated Vietnam acting as a donor/partner in the development of education policy in Laos (Faming 2009). An interesting case of South-South collaboration is China's newly expanded relationship with African countries, as confirmed at the Beijing Forum for China-Africa Co-operation (FOCAC) Summit in November 2006. King has pointed out that China sees this relationship as a South-South linkage rather than an aid relationship, and that it is demonstrating this distinctiveness by its lack of engagement with the dominant aid discourse and donor organizations.[28]

South-South cooperation can be observed to varying degrees in other sectors, most notably health,[29] in particular population and reproductive health[30]; food security; animal and plant pests and diseases; agriculture and environment; and entrepreneurship and development of small- and medium-size enterprises Successful South-South projects and networks include a number of bilateral agreements under which Latin American countries work with African partners to strengthen agricultural research institutes, to support subsistence farming as a development strategy, and to transfer locally appropriate technologies and technical knowledge in agriculture.[31]

Over the past 30 years, South-South cooperation has been promoted by the United Nations Development Program through its activities.[32] It is somewhat paradoxical that a movement that started as a counterforce to the systems put in place by the former colonial powers has been to some extent incorporated into dominant development discourse. There is a trend toward embedding South-South development cooperation into the global operations of organizations located in and controlled by the rich countries. The movement has remained small in scale and on the margins of traditional international aid.[33] Meaningful South-South cooperation is more likely to occur if developing countries act on the recognition that they have much endogenous knowledge to share.[34] It can be argued that a genuine South-South model of development assistance must be controlled by the Southern partners, as is the case with Cuban South-South assistance.

Cuba's Solidarity Approach: Mutual Assistance and Support

The Cuban model of internationalism is different from that of the North-South model of official development assistance. Its underlying principle is solidarity, and even though economic considerations also play a role, they have never been the driving force behind the Cuban approach. In this section we provide an overview of the principles of Cuban solidarity, exploring their implications for the special type of South-South collaboration that Cuba has developed.

What Cubans describe as "solidarity" principles characterize the internationalist cooperation agreements that Cuba shares with numerous countries. Some of these agreements and the principles on which they function are very different from principles underlying aid given by rich to poorer countries, as the following list might suggest:

1. Respect for the national sovereignty and self-determination of the countries involved;
2. No conditionalities;
3. Agreements take account of the different economic levels of each country, so that countries can help each other on the basis of solidarity rather

than following only the rules of the market. In education, this means that a cost-sharing principle that includes paying local salaries to Cuban educators is worked out with countries that can afford it, while the poorest countries are given Cuban assistance for little or no payment;
4. A variety of approaches to bilateral financing are identified;
5. The joining of a third party is admitted if this party agrees with the general solidarity principles (the third party could be, for example, UNESCO, UNICEF, the UNDP, or it could be another country);
6. Technologies and knowledge are transferred to poor countries in need of them without payment for "intellectual property," on the basis that knowledge is the patrimony of humanity, and not private property for profit. This means, for example, that the Cuban-designed adult literacy materials and approaches to medical training are shared, not sold.

Cuban internationalism has always been based on these principles of solidarity, stemming from the ideas of Simon Bolívar and José Martí. Cuba's ongoing internationalism, originally based on its foreign policy support for liberation movements, particularly on the African continent, reflects the country's commitment to support underdeveloped countries.[35] International solidarity is one of Cuba's success stories, along with health care and education. Cuban solidarity is mostly focused on, but not limited to, countries of the global "South." For example, Cuba also offered to send medical personnel and emergency supplies to New Orleans when the city was hit by Hurricane Katrina in 2005—an offer that the United States rejected.[36] Hammett makes the point that Cuba is able to empathize with the partners in negotiation procedures, as it will have experienced similar problems.[37] Harris has distinguished the socialist "version" of internationalism from the liberal or bourgeois version, arguing that Cuba's practice of socialist internationalism is based on a strong critique of exploitation, inequality, and social injustice, which is not necessarily the case with liberal internationalism.[38]

The principles of "solidarity" were formally articulated in an agreement signed on December 14, 2004, by the presidents of Venezuela and Cuba. The agreement was signed under the auspices of the new integration model, ALBA ("The Bolivarian Alternative for the Americas"), based on an initiative of the Venezuelan president, Hugo Chávez.[39] It aims for collaboration between Latin American and Caribbean countries based on solidarity, mutual benefits, and mutual respect. ALBA's four basic anticapitalist principles are: complementary action, cooperation, solidarity, and respect for the sovereignty of nations.[40] ALBA represents an alternative to the *Acuerdo de Libre Comercio para las Américas* (ALCA—the Free Trade Agreement for the Americas), designed by the US government and negotiated bilaterally with countries that agree with this direction.

Socialist ideas of development are opposed to the "market" principles articulated in ALCA-type agreements. The view of the Cuban government is that neoliberal agreements based on markets and free trade are disastrous for the region, and that ALCA would bring about the deepening of unequal dependence on the United States.

Although some may see the recently approved Cuban economic reform package as a step toward abandoning socialist economic principles and moving in the direction of free trade, the economic reforms stress Cuba's continued commitment to the socialist planning system. Specifically, the economic and social policy guidelines emphasize Cuba's ongoing prioritization of its participation in the ALBA and the economic integration with other regional commercial initiatives, such as the Latin American Association for Integration (ALADI), the Association of Caribbean States (AEC), CARICOM and PetroCaribe. International collaboration will continue to be based on international solidarity principles, but will place enhanced emphasis on compensation for at least the costs of solidarity collaboration, where possible. The economic reforms foresee the establishment of an international economic association that will evaluate and approve participation in any foreign investments and will exercise control over the fulfilment of regulations and commitments by the foreign partner.[41]

The continued application of solidarity principles in Cuba's foreign trade relations means that partner countries agree to exchange assistance based not on the "laws" of the market (profits, competition, protection of intellectual property rights), but on cooperation for mutual support. These agreements thus successfully combine "aid" and "trade" components. It is necessary for the collaborating countries to have identified common interests. Countries of the global "South" have been conditioned to look toward the global "North" for ideas, information, and innovation. The information gap thus created must be overcome: the countries of the global "South" have to learn to find out more from each other about their mutual needs, strengths, and weaknesses, in order to effectively collaborate. Once this baseline analysis has been carried out, the funding situation must be worked out; and the collaborating countries have to negotiate financial agreements in relation to their economic situation. An important strategy for the negotiation of common interests and support between Cuba and partner countries is that of collaboration agreements through joint commissions. Periodic negotiation meetings take place either in Cuba or in the partner country. During these meetings, cooperation agreements are drafted in different fields of socioeconomic development. A great number of such agreements already exist and are based on respect for the varied interests and approaches of other countries.

The ALBA mechanism utilizes many strategies that Cuba has employed over the past few decades in its international collaborations. Under their bilateral ALBA agreement, Cuba and Venezuela negotiated mutual support relating to their strengths and weaknesses. After decades of capitalist utilization of oil wealth, Venezuela (population approximately 28 million) remained underdeveloped, with the majority of the people living in poverty. The country experienced problematic health and education patterns, distorted industrial patterns (imports were completely financed with oil money), and a skewed agricultural sector (vast estates juxtaposed with a dependent and impoverished peasantry). Cuba, in spite of turning around its post-Soviet economic difficulties with the achievement of economic growth within a decade, continued to experience underlying economic weaknesses similar to those in many decolonizing countries. For example, it is obliged to invest almost all of its hard currency in buying oil, food, and manufactured goods. Domestic agriculture has improved, but not to the point where Cuba can do without considerable imports of milk powder, meats, beans, flour, cooking oil, and other staples. Cuba is also struggling to improve its housing and transport systems. After 1989, the Cuban government sought funding, markets, and advanced technology from capitalist investors and established strictly regulated joint ventures with capitalist enterprises in tourism, mining, light industry, and telecommunications.

Given the needs in each country, Cuba negotiated to provide Venezuela with the assistance of more than 15,000 medical professionals, as well as other professionals—teachers, sports instructors, education planners, and engineers. In addition, some 2,000 annual scholarships are granted to Venezuelan students for studies in Cuba. In turn, Venezuela undertook to provide Cuba with significant supplies of oil with credit facilities at a low rate of interest. It also transfers technology and finances development projects in the agricultural, service, energy, and infrastructural sectors, and offers scholarships to Cubans in the energy sector. Cuba and Venezuela further agreed to eliminate any protective tariffs on goods imported from the other country, and agreed upon additional concessions involving ship and air traffic.[42] A further notable solidarity agreement between Cuba and Venezuela is "Operation Miracle," designed to restore sight to Latin Americans who could not afford medical treatment. The program combines Cuban human capital with Venezuelan petroleum capital; as of 2007, Cuba had performed 750,000 eye surgeries on patients from over 20 countries in South America and the Caribbean.[43]

Cuba has spent and continues to spend billions of dollars on assistance shaped by its solidarity approach. Eckstein estimated that between 1963 and 1989, Cuba spent $1,537.2 million on international assistance[44], equivalent to 0.7 percent of Cuba's GDP for this period—an overseas development assistance figure promised, but not delivered, by many wealthy, developed countries. The Cuba/Venezuela interaction described above illustrates the "solidarity" approach of aid and trade within a framework of mutual support and cooperation. Cuba provides to partner countries the skilled work of its highly trained professionals, whose internationalism is applied both in overseas settings through a range of direct work projects in many fields, and in Cuba through scholarships and high-level medical assistance. The support to Cuba from those partner countries occurs in a variety of ways according to the possibilities of each country. This includes support through cooperative economic projects, support in international political forums, educational exchanges through conferences and other projects, and the opportunity for Cuban professionals to broaden their work experience and international networks, and at the same time earn some foreign exchange. They are usually paid local salaries in countries that can afford this. Cuban internationalists are asked to pay a portion of their earnings to their government to help with administrative costs, and are able to use the rest as personal and family income. Apart from the solidarity motivation, international missions thus have recently not only contributed positively to Cuba's macroeconomic position, but also hold incentives for Cuban professionals to improve their livelihoods. Roughly 185,000 Cubans participated in international missions during the ten-year period from 1998 to 2008, and they were active in 160 countries around the world.[45]

Conclusion

This chapter has outlined features of the global educational crisis that is being experienced by most developing nations, arguing that the severe weaknesses in their education systems hamper the expansion of their knowledge base to deal adequately with the challenges of the twenty-first century. Educational problems are so large that they need to be tackled with the assistance of international aid. Although the new architecture of North-South educational aid is promising, it is inadequate to tackle the problems of neocolonial models of education. There is much promise in the bilateral collaboration of South-South cooperation, but it is still on too small a scale to tackle the educational crisis. More effective models of aid and collaboration are needed globally.

This discussion of aid and cooperation models provides insights that help to frame the different chapters in this book. In the new aid paradigm, Western donors are now talking in terms of wanting "partnerships" to replace the outmoded past relationships of donors/recipients/conditionalities, but the partnership goal has not been achieved. The Cuban cooperation/solidarity model is not "official development assistance" along the lines of North-South aid. It operates as a philosophy of solidarity that can range from an equal partnership between countries able and willing to help each other, to a relationship whereby Cuba provides assistance expecting no return. This model of cooperation can suggest how partnerships could work, and what is needed in them. As Harris (2009) argues, the type of internationalism practised by the global "North" does not effectively critique and oppose the inequality of wealth and power that characterizes the international system. The socialist version of internationalism as practised by Cuba does provide such a critique.

Cuban educational cooperation is one element in a broad tapestry of global educational assistance. Other strands in the tapestry include quite separate endeavors, such as help from foundations, cultural diplomacy organizations, and faith-based organizations. Cuba provides socialist solidarity, with goals of strengthening the international position of the working class. A key achievement of this solidarity model is capacity building in other countries through contributing to the education of skilled workers and professionals, many of whom cannot afford to study in their own countries. Another achievement is the loan of Cuba's own professionals to lead or assist specific projects in the partner country. A further Cuban achievement has been the contribution to liberation politics in Africa. Cuban cooperation has had some welcome side effects as its partners tend to support Cuba in international forums. Cuba benefits from sending thousands of its professionals to work overseas, in the sense that hard currency is earned and skills are honed by being applied to difficult and demanding projects. Cuba establishes an independent global profile of solidarity, which brings it political support from the majority of countries in the world, thus providing a measure of protection from the implacable hostility of the United States government.

North-South aid and South-South cooperation are not mutually exclusive. It is essential that they coexist. We suggest that North-South aid could in many cases be improved if it were to be influenced by examples of the approach of South-South aid. Wealthy countries and agencies could make more effective use of the money that they spend. The Cuban approach to South-South collaboration discussed in this book is not a panacea that will solve global education and development problems. Many aspects of the approach, however, could point to effective ways of tackling the crisis in global education outlined in this chapter.

Notes

1. See Hickling-Hudson, Matthews and Woods 2004, Hickling-Hudson 2011, Tikly 2004.
2. For discussions of global poverty and underdevelopment see Rodney, 1982; Samoff, 1994; Chossudovsky 1998; Castro, 2000. For education, poverty and inequality see Kozol 1992; Welch, 2000; Samoff, 2003; Tomasevski, 2003; Farrell, 2007;Tarabindi, 2010, Brock, 2011.
3. Mundy, 2006; Benavot, 2010; Colclough, King, and McGrath 2010.
4. UNESCO 2010.
5. United Nations Development Program (UNDP), 2005.
6. Klees, 2010.
7. Mundy, 2006.
8. Colclough, C., K. King, and S. McGrath, 2010.
9. Riddell, 2007, as summarized by Klees, 2010.
10. UNESCO, 2010.
11. Duke and Hinsen, 2006.
12. UNESCO 2006, EFA Global Monitoring Report, "Literacy for Life."
13. Klees, 2010.
14. Samoff cited by Klees, 2010.
15. Hammett, 2004, p. 10.
16. Lehr, 2008a; Lehr, 2008b.
17. Brock-Utne, 1995.
18. See Jules, 2006.
19. Escobar, 2005, p. 89.
20. Abdenur, 2002.
21. Group of 77, n.d.
22. Manley, 1987, p. 226.

23. Group of 77, 2000. "Havana Programme of Action," available at http://www.dfa.gov.az/events/multilateral/action.htm
24. Hammett, p. 65, "Cuban Intervention in South African Health Care Provision," *Journal of Southern African Studies* 33, no. 1 (March 2007): 63–81; see also NEPAD 2006.
25. Ary-Plonski, 2000; White, 2004.
26. See Ekoko and Benn, 2002; Kahn, 2001.
27. United Nations Office of the Special Adviser, 2004.
28. King, 2009, King, 2010, see also Davies, 2008, and Nordveit, 2009.
29. See Hammett, 2004; UNDP, 2004; United Nations Special Adviser, 2004.
30. Ekoko and Benn, 2002.
31. Hammett, 2004; UNDP, 2004; United Nations Office of the Special Adviser, 2004; Ekoko and Benn, 2002.
32. UNDP, 2004.
33. Ekoko and Benn, 2002.
34. Wolhuter, Steyn, and Steyn, 2003.
35. Gonzales, 2000.
36. Brundenius, 2009.
37. Hammett, 2004, p. 11.
38. Harris, 2009.
39. Alianza Bolivariana para los Pueblos de Nuestra América (ALBA), 2004. See also introductory chapter of this book, page 2.
40. ALBA, 2009.
41. Cameron, M., 2010.
42. ALBA, 2004; Wagner, 2004.
43. Huish and Kirk, 2007; see also Huish and Kirk, 2009, and Pérez-López, 2008.
44. Eckstein, 1994.
45. Blue, 2010; Harris, 2009.

Bibliography

Abdenur, A. "Tilting the North-South Axis: The Legitimization of Southern Development Knowledge and Its Implications for Comparative Education Research." *Current Issues in Comparative Education* 4, no. 2 (2002): 57–69.

Alianza Bolivariana para los Pueblos de Nuestra América. "10 Points to Understand the Alba: Constructing the Alba from within the Peoples". Retrieved from: http://www.alianzabolivariana.org/modules.php?name=Content&pa=showpage&pid=1980." 2009.

———. "Acuerdo Entre El Presidente De La República Bolivariana De Venezuela Y El Presidente Del Consejo De Estado De Cuba, Para La Aplicación De La Alternative Bolivariana Para Las Américas [Agreement Between the President of the Bolivarian Republic of Venezuela and the President of the State Council of the Republic of Cuba Concerning the Application of the Bolivarian Alternative of the Americas]. Retrieved from: http://www.alianzabolivariana.org/modules.php?name=News&File=Article&Sid=81." 2004.

Ary-Plonski, G. "S&T Innovation and Cooperation in Latin America." *Cooperation South* 1 (2000): 99–107.

Benavot, A. "International Aid to Education. Moderated Discussion." *Comparative Education Review* 54, no. 1 (2010): 105–24.

Blue, S. A. "Cuban Medical Internationalism: Domestic and International Impacts." *Journal of Latin American Geography* 9, no. 1 (2010): 31–49.

Brock, Colin, *Education as a Global Concern*. London: Continuum Publishing Group (2011): 41–68.
Brock-Utne, B. "Cultural Conditionality and Aid to Education in Africa." *International Review of Education* 41, no. 3–4 (1995): 177–97.
Brundenius, C. "Revolutionary Cuba at 50." *Latin American Perspectives* 36, no. 2 (2009): 31–48.
Burbach, R. *Globalization and Postmodern Politics: From Zapatistas to High-Tech Robber Barons*. London: Pluto Press, 2001.
Cameron, M. (unofficial translation) (2011). Draft economic and social policy guidelines for the party and the revolution. Retrieved from http://www.walterlippmann.com/pcc-draft-economic-and-social-policy-guidelines-2010.pdf.
Castro, F. "Cuba and the Struggle against Global Poverty." *Socialism and Democracy* 14, no. 2 (2000): 1–25.
Chapman, D. and J. Quijada. "An Analysis of USAID Assistance to Basic Education in the Developing World." *International Journal of Educational Development* (2008).
Chossudovsky, M. *Global Poverty in the Late 20th Century*. Available online at http://www.transnational.org/SAJT/features/chossu_global_poverty.html.
———. *The Globalisation of Poverty. Impacts of IMF and World Bank Reforms*. London: Zed Books, 1998.
Colclough, C., K. King, and S. McGrath. "The New Politics of Aid to Education: Rhetoric and Reality." *International Journal of Educational Development* 30 (2010): 451–52.
Davies, M. "How China Delivers Development Assistance to Africa." In http://collection.europarchive.org/tna/20080305120132/http://dfid.gov.uk/pubs/files/china-dev-africa.pdf: Department for International Development [DFID], Beijing 2008.
De Vos, P., W. De Ceukelaire, M. Bonet, and P. Van der Stuyft. "Cuba's International Cooperation in Health : An Overview." *International Journal of Health Services* 37, no. 4 (2007): 761–76.
Duke, C. and H. Hinzen. "Basic and Continuing Adult Education Policies." *Adult Education and Development* 66 (2006): 131–66.
Eckstein, S. *Back From the Future. Cuba Under Castro*. NJ: Princeton University Press 1994, and Psychology Press, 2003.
EFA, and Global Monitoring Report Team. "Education for All. The Quality Imperative." In *UNESCO 2004. Summary*, 11–14. Paris: UNESCO, 2005.
Ekoko, F., and D. Benn. "South-South Cooperation and Capacity Development." *Development Policy Journal* 2 (2002): 119–30.
Ellerman, D. "Reflections on the Paris Declaration and Aid Effectiveness." *NORRAG News* (2009).
Escobar, A. "The Making and Unmaking of the Third World through Development." In *The Post-Development Reader*. Edited by M. Rahnema and V. Bawtree, 85–93. London: Zed Books, 2005.
Faming, M. "A New Role for an Old Tale: Vietnam as a Donor to Laos." *NORRAG News* (2009).
Farrell, J. " 'Equality of Education: A Half-Century of Comparative Evidence Seen from a New Millennium.' " In *Comparative Education: The Dialectic of the Global and the Local*. Edited by R. Arnove and C. A. Torres, 129–50. Lanham, MD: Rowman and Littlefield, 2007.
Fiddian-Qasmiyeh, E. "Education, Migration and Internationalism: Situating Muslim Middle Eastern and North African Students in Cuba." *Journal of North African Studies* 15, no. 2 (2010): 137–55.

Galeano, E. "To Be Like Them." In *The Post-Development Reader.* Edited by M. Rahnema and V. Bawtree, 214–22. London: Zed Books, 2005.

Gonzales, D. "Cuban-African Relations: Nationalist Roots of an Internationalist Policy." *Review of African Political Economy* 27, no. 84 (2000): 317–23.

Gorry, C. "Cuban Health Cooperation Turns 45." *MEDICC Review* 10, no. 3 (2008): 44–47.

Group of 77. "About the Group of 77. Retrieved July 7, 2009, from http://www.g77.org/doc/." n.d.

———. "Havana Programme of Action." Edited by http://www.dfa.gov.az/events/multilateral/action.htm., 2000. http://www.g77.org/summit/ProgrammeofAction_G77Summit.htm.

Hammett, D. P. "From Havana with Love: A Case Study of South-South Development Cooperation Operating between Cuba and South Africa in the Health Care Sector." Edinburgh: Centre of African Studies, University of Edinburgh, 2004.

Hammett, D. P. "Cuban Intervention in South African Health Care Provision." *Journal of Southern African Studies* 33, no. 1 (2007): 63–81.

Hickling-Hudson, A. Teaching to Disrupt Preconceptions: Education for Social Justice in the Imperial Aftermath. *Compare*, Vol. 41, No. 4, (2011): 453–465.

Hickling-Hudson, A., J. Matthews, and A. Woods. "Education, Postcolonialism and Disruptions." In *Disrupting Preconceptions: Postcolonialism and Education.* Edited by A. Hickling-Hudson, J. Matthews, and A. Woods, 1–18. Flaxton: Post Pressed, 2004.

Hoogvelt, A. *Globalisation and the Postcolonial World. The New Political Economy of Development.* Basingstoke: MacMillan, 1997.

Huish, R. and J. M. Kirk. "Cuban Medical Internationalism and the Development of the Latin American School of Medicine." *Latin American Perspectives* 34, no. 6 (2007): 77–92.

Huish, R. and J. M. Kirk. "Cuban Medical Internationalism in Africa: The Threat of a Dangerous Example." *Latin Americanist* 53, no. 3 (2009): 125–39.

Jules, D. "Power and Educational Development: Small States and the Labors of Sisyphus." In *Current Discourse on Education in Developing Nations: Essays in Honor of B. Robert Tanachnick and Robert Koehl.* Edited by M. O. Afolayan, D. Browne, and D. Jules, 17–29. New York: Nova Science Publishers, 2006.

Kahn, M. J. "Developing Mechanisms to Promote South-South Research in Science and Technology: The Case of the Southern African Development Community." *African Sociological Review/Revue Africaine De Sociologie* 5, no. 1 (2001).

King, K. "China's Cooperation in Education and Training with Kenya: A Different Model?" *International Journal of Educational Development,* 30 (2010): 488–96.

King, K. "Moyo on Aid Effectiveness and China in Africa." *NORRAG News* (2009).

Klees, S. "Aid, Development and Education." *Current Issues in Comparative Education* 13, no. 1 (Fall), 2010.

Kozol, J. *Savage Inequalities: Children in America's Schools.* New York: Harper Perennial, 1992.

Lehr, S. "Ethical Dilemmas in Individual and Collective Rights-Based Approaches to Tertiary Education Scholarships: The Cases of Canada and Cuba." *Comparative Education* 44, no. 4 (2008a): 425–44.

Lehr, S. "The Children of the Isle of Youth: Impact of a Cuban South-South Education Program on Ghanaian Graduates." Unpublished PhD dissertation, University of Victoria, Canada 2008b.

Martín Sabina, E. "Thoughts on Cuban Education." *Latin American Perspectives* 36, no. 2 (2009): 135–37.

Manley, M. *Up the Down Escalator. Development and the International Economy: A Jamaican Case Study*. London: Andre Deutsch, 1987.
Mundy, K. "Education for All and the New Development Compact." *International Review of Education* 52 (2006): 23–48.
NEPAD "New Partnership for Africa's Development. Nepad in Brief. Retrieved July 7, 2009, from Http://Www.Nepad.Org/2005/Files/Inbrief.Php." 2006.
Napier, D. B. "Education, Social Justice, and Development in South Africa and Cuba: Comparisons and Connections." *Globalization, Comparative Education and Policy Research* 10, no. 1 (2010): 33–48.
Noddings, N. *Educating Citizens for Global Awareness*. New York: Teachers College Press, 2005.
Nordtveit, B. H. "New Voices in the Aid and Development Discourse: China's Growing Partnership with Africa." *NORRAG News* (2009).
OECD. "Paris Declaration and Accra Agenda for Action."
Organisation for Economic Co-operation and Development. "DAC List of ODA Recipients: Effective for Reporting on 2009 and 2010 Flows. Retrieved from http://www.oecd.org/dataoecd/32/40/43540882.pdf." 2009.
———. "2008 Survey on Monitoring the Paris Declaration: Making Aid More Effective by 2010." Paris, 2008.
———. "Aid Effectiveness. 2006 Survey on Monitoring the Paris Declaration. Overview of the Results. Retrieved from http://www.oecd.org/dataoecd/58/28/39112140.pdf," 2007.
Pérez-López, J. F. "Recent Cuban Foreign Trade Patterns." In *Nueva Sociedad 216. Retrieved from* http://www.nuso.org/upload/articulos/3541_2.pdf, 2008.
Reuveny, R. X. and W. R. Thompson. "The North-South Divide and International Studies: A Symposium." *International Studies Review* 9, no. 4 (2007): 556–64.
Richmond, M. "The Cuban Educational Model and Its Influence in the Caribbean Region." In *Education in Central America and the Caribbean*. Edited by C. Brock and D. Clarkson, 63–99. London: Routledge, 1990.
Riddell, R. *Does Foreign Aid Really Work?* New York: Oxford University Press, 2007.
Rodney, W. *How Europe Underdeveloped Africa*. Washington, DC: Howard University Press, 1982.
Samoff, J. *Coping with Crisis: Austerity, Adjustment and Human Resources*. London: Cassell, 1994.
———. "No Teacher Guide, No Textbooks, No Chairs: Contending with Crisis in African Education." In *Comparative Education: The Dialectic of the Global and the Local*. Edited by R. Arnove and C. A. Torres, 409–45: Lanham, MD: Rowman and Littlefield, 2003.
———. "The Fast Track to Planned Dependence: Education Aid to Africa." In *International Political Science Association XXI World Congress*. Santiago, Chile, 2009.
Saney, I. "African Stalingrad: The Cuban Revolution, Internationalism, and the End of Apartheid." *Latin American Perspectives* 33, no. 5 (2006): 81–117.
Tarabini, A. "Education and Poverty in the Global Development Agenda: Emergence, Evolution and Consolidation." *International Journal of Educational Development* 30 (2010): 204–12.
Tikly, L. "Globalisation and Education in Sub-Saharan Africa." In *Disrupting Preconceptions: Postcolonialism and Education*. Edited by A. Hickling-Hudson, J. Matthews, and A. Woods. Flaxton: Post Pressed Publishers, 2004.
Tomasevski, K. *Education Denied: Costs and Remedies*. London: Zed Books, 2003.
UNDP. "Human Development Report," 2005. In *Full text available at* http://www.undp.org/hdro/index2.html

UNESCO. "Education for All Global Monitoring Report 2010: Reaching the Marginalized." *Retrieved from:* http://www.unesco.org/en/efareport/reports/2010-marginalization/. Oxford: Oxford University Press, 2010.

———. "Literacy for Life: EFA Global Monitoring Report." 2006.

———. "World Conference on Higher Education: Higher Education in the Twenty-First Century: Vision and Action." In *Final Report.* Paris: UNESCO, 1998.

United Nations Development Programme. "Human Development Report 2007/2008." New York, Palgrave Macmillan, 2007.

———. "Forging a Global South: United Nations Day for South-South Cooperation. Retrieved July 7, 2009, from http://ch.undp.org.cn/downloads/ssc/forgingaglobalsouth.pdf." 2004.

United Nations Office of the Special Adviser on Africa. "South-South Cooperation in Support of the New Partnership for Africa's Development: Experiences of Africa-Latin America and the Caribbean." New York, NY: United Nations, 2004.

Wagner, S. "Venezuela and Cuba Sign New Cooperation Agreements." 2004.

Welch, A. "Quality and Equality in Third World Education." In *Third World Education: Quality and Equality.* Edited by Anthony Welch, 3–28. New York: Garland, 2000.

White, L. "South Atlantic Relations: From Bilateral Trade Relations to Multilateral Coalition Building." *Cambridge Review of International Affairs* 17, no. 3 (2004): 523–37.

Wolhuter, C. C., S. C. Steyn, and H. J. Steyn. "Learning from South-South Comparison: The Education Systems of South Africa and Madagascar." *South African Journal of Education* 23, no. 1 (2003): 29–35.

Wright, J. *Sustainable Agriculture and Food Security in an Era of Oil Scarcity: Lessons from Cuba.* London: Earthscan, 2009.

Zeigler, L. "Cuba's African Connection: International Education on the Other Side of the Cold War." *International Educator* (Winter, 1995): 24–28.

3

Cuba's Education System: A Foundation for "The Capacity to Share"

*Elvira Martín Sabina, Jorge Corona González,
and Anne Hickling-Hudson*

Introduction

In this chapter we discuss Cuba's success in bringing about comprehensive national educational change that has gone some way toward achieving a combination of equity and high quality in education. This kind of change is different from the reform that in some countries does not substantially change social stratification, leaving in place a system of high-quality education for the minority and education of a much poorer quality for the majority of the society. Our outline of features of the Cuban revolution, including its internationalist "solidarity" policy, has provided a context for discussing in this chapter the model of educational development in Cuba, and the current reforms in the system. This is the foundation for understanding that without the revolution in Cuban education, and the continuing efforts to improve it, Cuba would not have been able to implement and continue the massive program of global educational assistance and collaboration described in this book.

Good general and technical schooling and good university education equip Cubans with internationally recognized levels of knowledge and professional skills, which are deployed by the highly trained Cuban teachers, doctors, engineers, and other professionals who go out in huge numbers to assist and work in other countries. This education also provides essential skill formation for the thousands of young people from other developing countries provided with scholarships or subsidized education by Cuba. Education of a high quality is part of the material basis of the capacity to share.

Fundamental Educational Changes in Cuba

The Cuban revolution has achieved fundamental changes in education. It has done so in spite of retaining an education system with the essential hallmarks of the modernist European model designed and developed in the nineteenth and twentieth centuries. The school and university buildings, the classroom organization, and the teaching and learning processes that are deployed in Cuba are similar to those that are used all over the world. What Cuba has changed is what happens within this framework between educators, students, their communities, and their government. The change process has, of course, experienced problems and errors, and Cuban authorities are still far from being satisfied with the system in terms of quality assurance, because their objective is to provide lifelong education of a high quality for all. However, Cuba's approach to educational development deserves the attention of the world because of its effectiveness. It is obviously not feasible in its entirety for many countries that lack a supportive political context, but aspects of the Cuban approach are worth considering in the struggle to find a more successful education system.

Cubans, rather than following a policy of decentralized, localized, and uncoordinated change, have structured education by agreeing on national goals of equity and quality, centralizing policy to achieve these goals, decentralizing management, finance, and local practice, and supporting the implementation of the entire system at the highest political level. The centralized policy and planning approach is based on a national consensus that is voiced through several levels of popular representation in professional and mass political organizations.[1]

As a result, Cuba is now one of the few countries of the Global South on the way to achieving an educational structure that facilitates lifelong education for all. Lifelong learning cannot be claimed if there are deep weaknesses in the structure of education, such as those that result in illiteracy and wide educational disparity between male and female, rich and poor. It is even unlikely that the goal can be achieved where high user fees prevent poorer people from utilizing educational services. Equal socio-educational opportunity is a necessary condition for lifelong education, and this precondition has been established in Cuba. Lifelong learning in Cuba has the goals of preparing citizens to be a productive part of the economy and to be socially and politically responsible as the society defines it. Putting in place a system that facilitates access to lifelong learning is the aim of the current Cuban transformation programs. These are currently being implemented at all levels of education throughout the society, with the active participation of teachers, parents, and other citizens.

The fundamental educational changes pursued throughout the Cuban revolution were, first, universalizing literacy and access to schooling, second, transforming the content of education to serve the goals of the revolution for equity and planned socioeconomic development, and third, qualifying teachers with a high level of education in five-year degree programs and further in-service training to carry out these aims. It has often been pointed out that Cuban education combines the three foundational principles of work, study, and research.[2] This is comprehensively described in chapter 12 by Oscar Elejalde Villalón. For ten years, he was director of education from primary to tertiary levels on Cuba's Isle of Youth, where thousands of overseas students as well as those born in Cuba were educated. As in all school systems, the foundation is laid by academic work in all the curriculum subjects. In the Cuban model, however, practical productive work is embedded in the curriculum to train students in a culture of combining study and work, theory and practice. The research engaged in by students when they are old enough gives them practice in experimenting with problem-solving approaches for practical needs.[3]

Part of the educational program is devoted to promoting social commitment, which includes values such as dedication to the national interest, internationalist solidarity, and discipline. Many of the research projects are linked to helping national economic enterprises, and social projects tackle their problems. Saloman Berman (2008) explains the vital importance of the "praxis" principle of socialist education, saying that Cuban leaders know well that a complete commitment to socialist values and ideals can neither be transmitted nor formed by spoken and written language alone. "Their insistence that theory must be complemented by praxis, that is by theoretically informed action, simply cannot be overstated."[4] This principle means that education at all levels incorporates practical work, which orients the learner into appreciating its value. Besides this, practical work is promoted in ways that go beyond the incentive of material rewards, providing moral incentives too "such as the public recognition for a worker or a group of workers as outstanding. Work that involves no rewards at all, or voluntary labor, is often done in the framework of the mass organizations", and its goal, and often the outcome, is to promote the "joy" of work, an internal system of human motivation.[5]

So effective has been the achievement of high quality in formal schooling that Cuban primary school students ranked first by a very wide margin in a UNESCO assessment of language and mathematics carried out across 13 Latin American nations: Argentina, Bolivia, Brazil, Chile, Colombia, Costa Rica, Cuba, Dominican Republic, Honduras, Mexico, Paraguay, Peru, and Venezuela.[6] According to the Caribbean Education Task Force (2000) comprising academics and government officials, the following are among the factors that have contributed to the high performance of the students in the Cuban educational system, and that represent important lessons to be learned by other countries in the region.

Arriving at similar conclusions to these general points is a detailed study by Carnoy, Gove, and Marshall (2007), *Cuba's Academic Advantage*, in which the authors seek to explore the reasons for the remarkable academic success of Cuba's school students compared to students in Brazil and Chile. This comparative study of factors at the levels of individual, classroom, school, and country led to the conclusion that "social context" variables

Table 3.1 Factors contributing to the high performance of the Cuban educational system

1. sustained high levels of investment in education
2. high levels of non-salary expenditures (approximately 40 percent of the education budget)
3. provision throughout the country of low-cost, high-quality instructional materials, adapted to local realities
4. a consistent policy environment supportive of high-quality education
5. high professional status of teachers; regular in-service professional development through formal and informal methods
6. involvement of teachers in applied research aimed at improving learning outcomes
7. emphasis on evaluation and accountability throughout the system and aimed at school improvement through identification of problems and formulating and implementing plans of action
8. a system of "emulation" rather than competition in which collaboration among peers is emphasized, high-performing schools serving as a model to others
9. wide stakeholder participation in school management
10. strong commitment and support to rural children and those with special needs, ensuring access and provision of incentives to teachers who work in remote areas
11. linking school and work through "labor education" emphasis on technical vocational education (50 percent of students who complete grade 9 pursue these subjects)
12. provision of "values education" as a core subject in the curriculum.[7]

are essential in explaining Cuba's academic effectiveness. Education systems are more likely to achieve high levels of student learning if students live in a sociopolitical context outside school that provides for "the safety, health and moral support needed to function well in a classroom environment."[8] These essential conditions are provided in Cuba. Additional conditions of a productive social context include a balance between national control and community participation. The Cuban state sets high standards for schools and teachers, and enforces them by balancing a high level of teacher preparation, central monitoring, and drawing on the commitment of families, communities, and school administrators.[9]

Cuba has already fulfilled UNESCO's Education for All (EFA) objectives. The EFA Global Monitoring Report of 2005 reported on case study research into 11 countries that have demonstrated strong commitment to EFA—Bangladesh, Brazil, Canada, Chile, Cuba, Egypt, Finland, Republic of Korea, Senegal, South Africa, and Sri Lanka. The research found that four of the countries have achieved high standards of educational quality: Canada, Cuba, Finland, and the Republic of Korea.[10] Cuba was then the only one categorized as a lower-middle-income country, while the other three were high-income nations. UNICEF observers note that Cuba is among the countries making the greatest progress toward the goals of the UN Convention on the Rights of the Child.[11]

A profile of major features of Cuban achievements in education demonstrates the strength of the system. A foundational indicator of its effectiveness is that there is full literacy. Due to the National Literacy Campaign of 1961, and the developments in adult education that followed, adults who had previously been deprived of formal education were able to move from basic literacy, to post literacy, to equivalent primary and secondary schooling.[12] Another indicator of effectiveness is the equitable distribution of education throughout the country. This is shown by the 99 percent rate of school enrolment for students aged between 6 and 14 years, and the widespread network of universities and other post-school institutions in each province. The proportion of the population completing university-level education is much higher than in most other developing countries, and is similar to that in some of the wealthy, developed countries. Statistical data indicate that in 2009–2010 there was 52.9 percent university enrolment of the 18–24 cohort, of which 61.3 percent were women, and that university graduates comprise 8.81 percent of the whole population, and 14.64 percent of the workforce.[13]

Teaching is internationally recognized as being of extraordinarily high quality, as was demonstrated by the UNESO-OREALC evaluations of 1997 mentioned earlier. University quality is also highly regarded internationally, as is discussed in chapters 4 and 9. Among the strategies that contribute to this educational effectiveness are the systematic professional development of educators, the facilitation of learning through audiovisual aids, two educational television channels, and the state-funded production and provision of textbooks and other publications to support the general cultural level of the population.

The strength of Cuba's education system is all the more remarkable when it is compared to the weakness of the system that preceded it. In the 1950s, Cuba had very little technological development, and it had an economic structure characterized by underdevelopment and inequality. Education showed the typical deformities left behind by colonialism. High-quality, prestigious education was reserved for the privileged minority with high incomes. Higher education, also for the minority, did not match the needs of socioeconomic development for the majority of the population Just over half (56 percent) of the children went to primary school, and only 28 percent of those continued their studies at the secondary level. According to the 1953 census carried out by the Batista government six years before the revolution, 1 million people could not read and write, amounting to 23.6 percent of the population over 10 years of age. In the rural areas, the percentage rose to 41.7 percent, with a higher incidence among women. Educational services were inadequate, yet there were thousands of teachers without a job.[14]

Cuban educational transformation has gone through three major phases of change since the 1960s.[15] The first phase was initiated by the 1961 National Literacy Campaign, accompanied by the 1962 University Reform process, which pursued the goals and strategies for establishing a cultural and practical link between university and society. The second phase, from the 1970s onward, achieved mass secondary education, the restructuring of higher education, and the expansion of a network of universities and polytechnic schools throughout the country. The third phase, starting from the late 1990s and continuing today, implements changes in primary, secondary, and university education that will expand the extent to which Cuba's cultural resources become available to the whole population. In all three phases, Cubans extended their achievement of organizing education to guarantee free access for all, while at the same time recognizing that free access does not guarantee the provision of education of a high quality for all. The Cuban interpretation of quality in education is demonstrated in the integration of study, work, and research and the application of these three dimensions to improving the society. These goals can be implemented through pedagogy because of the high level of training and motivation and the regular professional development of Cuba's teachers. However, educational reforms and social change can sometimes become problematic and lead to a decline in quality, so efforts for improvement must continue to be made.

During the four decades of sustained social and political endeavor that led to the current high level of educational development, five key factors ensured success:

1. the absolute commitment of the state to the educational project,
2. the philosophy of valuing education, and the moral impulse in politics,
3. extensive popular participation in educational initiatives,
4. the capacity to change the system in response to the social and economic development of the country and the personal needs of the people, and
5. the assistance of the Socialist bloc in upgrading higher and vocational education.

In the 1960s and 1970s, Cuba received thousands of scholarships to send students to study in the Soviet Union and East Germany as well as other East European countries. This was pivotal in leading to a rapid development of education and skill levels in Cuba. Cuba's appreciation of this assistance strengthened its deep commitment to the principles and values of a "solidarity" approach, and led it to provide, in turn, extraordinary levels of assistance in health, education, and construction to other developing countries. However, internationalism might not have developed to such an extent without a particular ethos that grew out of Cuba's history. In his article "Education, Revolution and Revolutionary Morality in Cuba," Antoni Kapcia analyzes the roots of the revolution's educational ethos. He observes that a foundation of this ethos is Cuba's long-established, profound, and consistent belief "in the liberating power of education and culture and...in 'moralism,' in the moral impulse in politics."[16] This is related to the attachment of Cubans to the ideas and example of national heroes such as José Martí and Che Guevara, as well as their "deep sense of communal solidarity and struggle" that was reinforced by Cuba's position "as an embattled enclave."[17]

Among the major drivers of educational change in the Cuban revolution were the literacy and post literacy campaigns, the expansion of schools and adult education throughout the country, and the expansion of a teacher-training approach that shaped teachers capable of working in the most remote and economically depressed areas. At the same time, the development of its higher education sector was the cornerstone of the country's ability to utilize highly skilled professionals in the improvement of its economy and social services (see Appendix 1, page 67). Schoolteachers and university lecturers alike implemented a model of education that sought to inculcate habits of integrating theory and practice as well as to promote socialist values.

Educational Research

Systematic research has been central to the improvement of education in Cuba. Educational research is carried out in a number of institutions including pedagogical universities and dedicated research agencies. Research results are communicated to and discussed by teachers, people's mass organizations, and the government. This process becomes the foundation of the efforts to advance specific components of Cuban education. The content as well as the skills developed in the process are shared with educators in other countries through institutions, courses, meetings, conferences, and professional associations.

A brief outline of the education research structure is provided here, based on the practitioner knowledge of two of the authors of this chapter. Educational research on the school system is organized and carried out by the Ministry of Education (*Ministerio de Educación,* or MINED) and many organizations for which it has responsibility. The Division of Science and Technology in MINED articulates policy issues in education, guided by CITMA (the Ministry of Science, Technology and the Environment), Cuba's central research and policymaking institute. Out of these issues, the MINED identifies the research necessary to improve the education sector. They ask the following institutions to carry out the research:

1. ICCP—*Instituto Central de Ciencias Pedagógicas* (Central Institute of Pedagogical Sciences)
2. The 16 pedagogical universities
3. IPLAC—*Instituto Pedagógico Latino Americano y Caribeño* (Pedagogical Institute of Latin America and the Caribbean)
4. CELAEE—*Centro de Estudios Latinoamericano de Educación Especial* (Center for Latin American Studies in Special Education)
5. CELEP—*Centro de Estudios Latinoamericano de Educación Prescolar* (Center for Latin American Studies in Pre-School Education)

Research in higher education takes place through a structure relating to the Ministry of Higher Education (*Ministerio de Educación Superior,* MES) that manages 14 universities specializing in engineering, agriculture, natural sciences and mathematics, humanities, law, economics, and others. Research in higher education is carried out through the Network of Research Centres on Higher Education (REDEES—*Red de Estudios sobre la Educación Superior*). The mission of these 17 centers is to contribute to the continuous improvement of the Cuban system of higher education. CEPES (the Centre for Improvement in Higher Education) is the major research arm of the Ministry of Higher Education. Located at the University of Havana, CEPES carries out national and international research into higher education, and it collaborates in this research with universities overseas. The research at CEPES focuses on pedagogy, psychology, management, administration, and information technology as these relate to higher education.

Some universities are managed and administered by their specific ministries—for example, health, culture, and sports. However, the Ministry of Higher Education is responsible for defining national policy issues, for carrying out accreditation processes, and for advising other ministries on the general principles, changes, and reforms in higher education.

The next section outlines the important structural developments in the current phase of education policy. It is based on the involvement and knowledge of two of the authors of this article in policy, planning, and implementation of educational reform in Cuba. We outline these reforms and explain the changes that are being made as a result of constant monitoring and evaluation. The goal is to bring about improvement of the system by expanding the access of the population to learning and culture while at the same time remaining within the country's economic means. As was explained in the introduction to this book, Cuba, like other developing countries, was hard hit by the global financial crisis of 2008 and suffered a contraction of its economy, which has influenced the social context.

Developments in Current Educational Policy and Practice in Cuba

Early Childhood Education: "Teach Your Child"

This is a massive program of parental involvement in preschool education, which, together with education in kindergartens, encompasses over 99 percent of children between 0 and 5 years of age. "Teach your Child" is a non-institutional program, launched in 1992 as the result of ten years of research on preschool education. It is based on active participation of the parents, the family doctor, and other community members. Parents receive advice on the activities they can carry out with their children, at the different stages of their development, to stimulate them to learn. One of the parents or another family member can act as a teacher, with the help of professional teachers living in the community and of a series of guiding booklets developed by experts. The family doctor checks regularly on the healthy growth of the child. So the teacher, doctor, and parents understand the child as a whole, and learning becomes more effective in this context. Research is being carried out on the impact of this program, which is backed by UNICEF. Similar programs are being applied in Guatemala, Colombia, Venezuela, and some Mexican states.

Primary and Secondary Education: Small Classes, Individual Attention, and the Comprehensive Teacher

In primary school education, class sizes are being reduced as Cuba's means allow, with the goal of helping the teacher to give increased individual attention to each child. The initial target was to have 20 or fewer children per class, but this is applied with flexibility according to organizational needs and economics. A teacher has the option either of staying with the same class of students from the first grade until the sixth grade, or of staying with the class from first to fourth grade, with another teacher at the fifth and sixth grades. The teacher gets to know the students and their families, and he or she can maintain the close and affectionate relationship that is so important in the early years. This ensures that the diverse needs of all students are addressed. The availability of TV sets, videos, and computers in all classrooms helps both teachers and students.

Basic secondary education has undergone profound innovations and remodeling. Traditionally, secondary teachers have been trained as curriculum specialists teaching one or two particular subjects. The present trend is increasingly to train teachers in the way that primary teachers are trained, that is, as "comprehensive teachers" who are capable of teaching a range of subjects. They will take comprehensive responsibility for the education of no more than 15 students through grades 7, 8 and 9, and will be in close contact with the students' parents, offering attention to the developmental needs of each adolescent as well as of the group.

There were debates among educators in regard to this reform. Some argued that the comprehensive teacher would not be able to ensure a high quality of subject learning at the secondary level. Others disagreed, arguing that the proliferation of curriculum subjects (teaching subjects rather than children) was not the best approach in the formation of young adolescents. In the first phase of the reform, the latter view was accepted. Educators carried through their goal of achieving an integrated curriculum through training a comprehensive teacher. This meant big changes in the teacher education curriculum. Experience in the first few years of the reform showed that modifications were needed. The goal of the integrated curriculum is still dominant, but the strategies of teacher preparation have been modified. The secondary teacher is being prepared to teach several subjects, but the emphasis is now on preparation across one group of subjects rather than the full range. The groups of subjects among which secondary student teachers can choose to specialize include mathematics and the sciences, or the humanities, the expressive arts, foreign languages, or physical education. The choices for study are therefore integrated around related subjects rather than across the entire curriculum.

To improve methods and content knowledge, schoolteachers are encouraged to watch video classes taught by top-level teachers in any subject. Teachers utilize educative games and computers to improve the quality of students' learning in mathematics, the natural sciences, geography and history. The aim is for the middle secondary teacher to become a holistic educator rather than just a teacher of subjects. Teachers supervise the behavioral and intellectual development of each child, as well as guide their academic development with the assistance of educational software developed by experts. Changes in the approach to secondary teaching are being evaluated for quality assurance each year.

The reduction of class sizes at both primary and secondary levels is an educational reform of immense significance. Teachers with 15 to 20 students to a class are much more likely to be able to provide training in social activities that link theory to practice than teachers in larger classes. They are more likely to be able to teach in a way that combines the development of knowledge with an understanding of values and norms, and to promote reflective and flexible ways of thinking to foster stable self-esteem. Teachers can thus develop a closer relationship with their students, which enables them to take into consideration the students' individual differences and family backgrounds in relation to their learning process.

Cuba achieved the training of thousands of new young teachers, the reduction of class size, and the professional evaluation of the new reforms, by increasing the education budget by several million dollars annually between 2003 and 2008. While education comprised 14–16 percent of the national budget between 1990 and 2001, by 2003 it rose to 19 percent.[18] However, with the global financial crisis of 2008, the education budget had to be reduced. This contraction has brought about some changes. Most of the boarding schools in the countryside have been phased out, with their land being leased to people who want to farm it. Most students now attend day schools near their homes. Boarding at school is only for children of the poorest families.

Special Education: A Combination of "Mainstreaming" and Special Schooling

Special education services have been "mainstreamed"—that is, provided to children with disabilities/special educational needs, in an integrated way in regular schools. However, some acute problems require more specialized attention than teachers can provide. For children with such problems, there are diagnostic centers, and a visiting teacher program in hospital classrooms, in pupils' homes, and in diagnostic centers. There are still about 500 special schools in the country, supplied with computers, videos, and television sets, for children with special needs. Parents and teachers decide together when these children are ready to attend a regular school.

Increased Practical Experience in Teacher Education

The education reforms put in place a new teacher education program that requires more teacher education to take place in communities than was the case before. For many decades, the five-year degree in education took place mainly in the pedagogical universities. In the new program, the students completed one year of preparation in accelerated undergraduate study at the university, and then carried out practical teaching combined with university study for the rest of their degree program. From their second year onward, each student began teaching in a school in her or his own municipality and attended a local university outreach center for lectures. All students were guided by an experienced teacher-mentor who acted as their personal tutor. As well, their lecturers from the pedagogic universities visited them at the school, and the students visited the outreach center to attend classes taught by these lecturers.

The evaluation of the initial phase of the new program led to the conclusion that students needed more than one year of full-time university study. The foundation course at universities was extended to two years, and student teachers now spend three years in combined work placements and university studies. Another important change that was begun in September 2010 was the introduction of post ninth-grade middle-level technical institutions to train some primary and early childhood teachers as well as teachers of children with disabilities.

Extending Training Programs for Workers and Middle-level Technicians

A very successful program implemented in the first decade of the twenty-first century treated study as a full-time job. This program was established to deal with the problem of young people who left school after the ninth grade and were not employed. Some left because of early pregnancy, others to provide extra support for their families. The problem was analyzed by the government, student councils, and the Communist Youth organization, and it was decided that this group of young people should be offered the chance to go back to school and be given a monthly payment. About 110,000 students between 17 and 29 years of age went into this program. It provided them with school upgrading, the possibility of access to professional studies, and job opportunities. Students receive economic support and are officially regarded as being employed, in an effort to improve their self-esteem. The program is taught by retired teachers and current teachers in their respective municipalities. By 2010, this program had nearly accomplished its task, and will be phased out when the last graduates have completed their studies.

Another program that has to a large extent fulfilled its goals is that of a ten-month course to train social workers. Delivered by university professors, this course was for young people who have completed grade 11 or 12 at senior high school. Graduates from the program can enrol in part-time university courses at their municipal university branch. Technical schools that train middle-level technicians in agronomy, industry, and information technology are once again being extended. These polytechnics are already showing their potential in producing mid-level technicians for the economy.

Before 2010, 40 percent of the graduates from grade 9 went to technical schools (polytechnics) and 60 percent to senior high schools. Now, the proportions are reversed—60 percent to technical schools and 40 percent to senior schools. The change is a response to the demands of Cuba's new economic situation. With expanded opportunities for joint ventures, more employment in family and cooperative enterprises, as well as a more highly developed and efficient state sector, the education system must produce more people trained in vocational and technological skills that are intended to increase productivity and efficiency. The technical schools offer three sets of subjects: general, technical, and mid-level professional. The respective curricula provide three years of training after grade 9 for young graduates to leave with mid-level skills for industry, agriculture, and service industries. On graduation after grade 12, the 40 percent of students who go into senior high schools for a general academic education can apply either to go to university for a five-year degree, or into the technical stream for a two-year program that qualifies them to become mid-level technicians.

The Extension of Higher Education

In 1959, Cuba's university system consisted of three comprehensive public universities and a few private ones. Since the revolution, Cuba has created a network of 64 comprehensive, medical, technical, pedagogical, sports, and arts universities. In the first decade of the twenty-first century, there was another large expansion of the university system that enabled up to 50 percent of the 18–24-year-old cohort to enroll in university studies.[19] However, with the current economic restructuring requiring more people with mid-level technical and vocational training, the proportion of university entrants will be somewhat reduced, although the numbers in university studies remain larger than was the case in 2000.

This expansion of the university took place because of the introduction of the Municipal University Centres (SUMs), an innovation of the University Municipality Branch Program developed since 2000. In the country's political-administrative division, the municipalities are the basic management level. The SUM forms part of the structure of a nearby university. These branches of the existing network of universities aim to provide additional opportunities within communities for people to undertake university studies. SUMs are distributed in 169 municipalities. School buildings are used in the evenings for university classes,[20] and the SUMs provide flexible learning to suit students' needs. Some are part-time students who continue to work at other jobs, while others are full-time students. In the first phase of the SUM program, students could study without limits of time or age, until graduation. Now, based on evaluations, some time limits are being set.

This model of municipal university branches facilitated a large increase in undergraduate education, and some postgraduate study was also facilitated by it. For example, SUMs are attended by many teachers who wish to upgrade their qualifications. Twenty-five percent of the existing teaching force is currently enrolled in masters degree programs offered by the pedagogical universities utilizing an "open learning" approach that mixes distance and on-site classes through the SUMs. In the 2009–10 academic year, the university system had over 62,000 full-time academic staff plus over 90,000 part-time lecturers.[21]

To achieve a mass expansion of higher education, the old concept of the ivory tower has to be left behind. The municipal university campuses help Cuba to progress beyond the goal of taking the university *to* the community, and facilitate the goal of the university *in* the community. Municipal university centers have a small number of full-time staff seconded from the central university campus. They work with local professionals who serve as part-time teachers, with advice from full-time academics at the central campus. Those who teach in the centers have undergone a rigorous process of selection and training. The SUMs offer studies in several tutor-assisted undergraduate distance-learning programs. Graduates from the SUMs are intended to attain the same standards as those graduating from full-time programs. The continuing implementation of this innovation is contributing to the transformation of the entire higher education subsystem. Universities have to learn to plan and work flexibly under conditions of change, and to make efficient use of teamwork within the academy, both at the central university campus and in the municipality.

Although this university expansion is currently being reduced in scale compared to the situation in 2004 and 2005, it is still a major aspect of the improvement of education in the Cuban revolution. The first component of change was the universalization of literacy and primary education. The second was the universalization of secondary education. Expanded university education is the third component of improvement in the educational system. It included a large increase in specialist education at the vocational universities that trained health professionals, engineers, agriculturalists, teachers, and others. By the 1990s, enough teachers were trained to allow a proportion of teachers to upgrade their qualifications and participate in solidarity programs of teaching in other countries. More university opportunities in the twenty-first century will provide many more people with the possibility of attaining high levels of culture in a system of lifelong learning. It will also enable the benefits of university research to be percolated more effectively throughout local communities and workplaces.[22] What is envisaged is a circular flow of ideas and knowledge in which the movement for science and technological innovation, through organizations such as the Forum of Science and Technology, supports the municipal university campuses, which in turn contribute to boost existing opportunities.[23]

The number of university students is likely to diminish in the short term because of the steps being taken to improve the quality of the students having access to university entry, and also to improve the university accreditation process nationally. Another reason is that high school graduates have increased opportunities for studying to become mid-level technicians in technical schools and colleges. Earlier, senior high school graduates who had completed grade 12 had only one option for higher education—that of going to university. Now they have the option of doing a two-year technicians' course rather than a five-year university degree. There is a demand for more qualified technicians to match the changing conditions of the economy, and their qualifications will be accredited if they want to continue into a university degree program.

Conclusion

The millennium goals of sustainable development, agreed upon at the United Nations, have outlined a vision of modest progress for poorer countries. Over the past half century, the wealthy countries of the global "North" have financed some programs of educational aid that have been working well in such countries. But it is clear that these programs of aid are insufficient compared to the great need for the type of aid and solidarity that would promote systematic and sustainable progress in education. It is also clear that if globalization continues to be shaped by the doctrines of neoliberalism, the goals of achieving a more equitable global society are unlikely to be met. Instead, current trends for increasing poverty and wider disparities between rich and poor will continue.

Given this political situation, the Cuban model of education and its current reforms constitute an alternative way of conceptualizing education and its role in development. Despite the world financial crisis, the continued economic barriers sustained by the US blockade, and its economic status as an underdeveloped country, Cuba has been able to accomplish and sustain significant achievements in educational development as has been acknowledged by numerous experts, national governments, and international agencies such as UNESCO and UNICEF.

Cuba developed its education system with massive help from the former Socialist bloc, and as a result was able to excel in producing large numbers of educated people, including young professionals and skilled technicians, who were charged to apply their knowledge to socioeconomic development. In spite of the severe blow of the collapse of Soviet assistance, Cubans surmounted the crisis by instituting a transitional "special period" of intense restructuring of their economy and society. During the hardships of restructuring, great efforts were made to maintain the essentials of the educational system, and when the economy started to recover and grow as a result of new strategies and alliances, significant changes were launched in an effort to improve every sector of education. While in primary and secondary education the general global trend is to try to change education by changing the content of study plans, programs, and textbooks, Cuba is taking a different approach with the significant change of transforming most teachers into comprehensive educators responsible for the continuous overall education and caring support of small class groupings of students, with the help of the new technologies of information and communication. While the global trend is to try and expand higher education through a "user pays" approach, in Cuba the state provides higher education, and the innovative University Municipality Branch Program is massively expanding access to university studies for thousands of citizens, especially youngsters, using alternative scheduling, as described earlier, in existing schools and other community facilities.

Cuba's intense focus on maintaining and improving the breadth and quality of the education system was accompanied by a philosophical commitment to international solidarity, and Cubans showed the will to collaborate in assisting and cooperating in social development projects on a global scale. It is this combination of preparedness, values, and vision that has enabled Cuba to pioneer a unique program of collaboration in education with many impoverished countries in Africa, Asia, and the Caribbean. The Cuban approach to education demonstrates that equitable and high-quality education can be pursued and achieved by countries in the Global South if there is political will and commitment based on solidarity and cooperation, regardless of an economically underdeveloped status and an adverse international context. Moreover, Cuban solidarity can assist these countries to move faster toward that vision in a global period when their future sustainability depends on massive educational improvements. It is this optimistic belief in the capacity for collective transformation on which Cuba's sharing of its educational capacity is based.

Appendix I

Table 3.2 Network of institutions involved in higher education in Cuba, academic year 2009–2010

Government ministries and organizations	Total number of institutions organized by ministries and organizations	Universities	Higher education institutes	University centers	Schools and academies
MES Ministry of Higher Education	17	11	2	4	
MINED Ministry of Education	16	16			
MINSAP Ministry of Public Health	14	13			1 (ELAM)
INDER National Institute for Sports and Recreation	2	1			1 (International School of Sports)
MEP Ministry of Economics and Planning	1		1		

Continued

Table 3.2 Continued

Government ministries and organizations	Total number of institutions organized by ministries and organizations	Universities	Higher education institutes	University centers	Schools and academies
MINCULT Ministry of Culture	1		1		
CITMA Ministry of Science, Technology and the Environment	1		1		
MINREX Ministry Of Foreign Affairs	1		1		
MIC Ministry of Information and Communication	1	1			
PCC Cuba Communist Party	1				1
MINFAR Ministry of Revolutionary Armed Forces	9	1	2		6
MININT Ministry of the Interior	1		1		
TOTAL	65	43	9	4	9

Source: Prontuario 2009–2010 pp. 23–24.
Note: In Cuba, higher education institutes provide courses and postgraduate qualifications in one specialist area of knowledge, such as medical sciences, pedagogical sciences, and technical sciences. A university center is the first stage of a university that is growing. When the institution reaches the required academic maturity, it can become a university. Universities offer a wide range of degrees across many disciplines

Notes

1. López García, 2005.
2. See Carnoy and Samoff, 1990.
3. Elejalde Villalón, 2006.
4. Berman, 2008, p. 166.
5. Berman, 2008, p. 168.
6. UNESCO-OREALC, 1997.
7. Caribbean Education Task Force, 2000.
8. Carnoy et al., 2007, p. 154.
9. Carnoy et al., 2007, see especially chapter 7.
10. EFA Global Monitoring Report Team (2005) *Education for All: The Quality Imperative.* UNESCO, Paris 2004.
11. Convention on the Rights of the Child, 1989; www.ohchr.org
12. Carnoy and Samoff, 1990, pp. 176–178.
13. Ministerio de Educación Superior, *Prontuario*, 2010.
14. Ministry of Education, 1981, pp. 17–18.
15. Martín Sabina and Corona González, 2005, Gómez, 2003, Gómez, 2004.
16. Kapcia 2005, pp. 403–404.

17. Kapcia, p. 404.
18. See Appendix 1.
19. Ministry of Higher Education, Statistics Department, 2010.
20. See Martín Sabina, 2003.
21. Ministerio de Educación Superior, *Prontuario* 2010, p. 34.
22. Martín Sabina, 2003.
23. Vecino Alegret, 2006, p. 13.

References

Berman, S. "Bound to Outlast? Education for Socialism." In *A Changing Cuba in a Changing World*. Edited by Maurice A. Font, 138–73. New York: The Graduate Center, City University of New York, 2008.
Caribbean Education Task Force. "A Caribbean Education Strategy. Discussion Draft." In *Report No. 20452-LAC*, 2000.
Carnoy, M., A. Gove, and J. Marshall. *Cuba's Academic Advantage: Why Students in Cuba Do Better in School*. Stanford, CA: Stanford University Press, 2007.
Carnoy, M. and J. Samoff. *Education and Social Transition in the Third World*. Princeton, NJ: Princeton University Press, 1990.
Castro, Fidel. "Keynote Address; Official Inauguration of the School Year 2002–2003." http://www.cuba.cu/gobierno/discursos 8/26/05, 2002.
ECLAC. "Current Conditions and Outlook." In *Economic Survey of Latin America and the Caribbean, 2000-2003*, Economic Development Division, 2003.
———. "Preliminary Overview of the Economies of Latin America and the Caribbean, 2003." Economic Development Division, 2003.
Education, Ministry of. "Report to the National Assembly of Popular Power, Republic of Cuba," 1981.
EFA, and Global Monitoring Report Team. "Education for All. The Quality Imperative." In *UNESCO 2004. Summary*, 11–14. Paris: UNESCO, 2005.
Elejalde Villalón, O. "Cubans Sharing Education: The Isle of Youth". Interview conducted by Anne Hickling-Hudson and Jorge Corona González, Havana, 2006. See chapter 12 herein.
Espinosa Martínez, E. "Ethics, Economics and Social Policies: Cuban Values and Development Strategy." In *Cuba in the 21st Century: Realities and Perspectives*. Edited by J. Bell Lara and R. Dello Buono, 59–99. Havana: Instituto Cubana del Libro, 2005.
Gómez Gutiérrez, L. "Cuba: The Profound Educational Revolution." In *Keynote Address:12th World Congress of Comparative Education*, 3–4. Havana: World Congress of Comparative Education, 2004.
Gómez Gutiérrez, L. "The Development of Education in Cuba." In *Keynote Address*. Havana: International Pedagogical Congress, 2003.
Hickling-Hudson, A. "The Cuban University and Educational Outreach: Cuba's Contribution to Post-Colonial Development." In *Local Knowledge and Wisdom in Higher Education*. Edited by G. R. Teasdale and Z. Ma Rhea, 187–207. New York: Pergamon, 2000.
Kapcia, A. "Educational Revolution and Revolutionary Morality in Cuba: The 'New Man', Youth and the New 'Battle of Ideas.'" *Journal of Moral Education* 34, no. 4 (2005): 399–412.
López García, D. L. "A Guide for Understanding the Cuban Political System." In *Cuba in the 21st Century: Realities and Perspectives*. Edited by J. Bell Lara and R. Dello Buono, 101–14. Havana: Insituto Cubana del Libro, 2005.

Martín Sabina, E. "Higher Education in Cuba in the 2000s: Past and Future." In *47th annual Conference of The Comparative and International Education Society.* New Orleans, LA, 2003.

Martín Sabina, E., and J. González Corona. "Learning and Livelihood Education: Reflections on the Cuban Experience." In *8th UKFIET International Conference on Education and Development.* University of Oxford, UK, 2005.

Ministerio de Educación Superior. "Prontuario 2009-2010." (Higher Education Compendium). 23, 2010.

UNESCO-OREALC. "First International Comparative Study of Language, Mathematics, and Associated Factors for Students in the Third and Fourth Grade of Primary School. 2nd Report." Santiago de Chile, 1997.

Vecino Alegret, F. "The Universalization of the University for a Better World.' Keynote Address of the Minister of Higher Education." Paper presented at the Universidad 2006: 5th International Congress on Higher Education, Havana, February 13–17, 2006.

Section 2

Studying in Cuba: Returning Home to Work

4

Cuban Higher Education Scholarships for International Students: An Overview

Francisco Martínez Pérez

Introduction

Cuba's program of higher education scholarships to overseas students is one of the most significant ways by which the Cuban people express their solidarity with other developing countries. Many of these countries have not had the opportunity to develop their higher education sector extensively, and Cuba's provision of fully funded scholarships to the young people of these countries demonstrates how the Cuban government applies the principles of internationalism. In this chapter, the author discusses the main characteristics and achievements of the Cuban scholarship program in a manner that illustrates the principles discussed in chapters 1 and 2. The chapter also considers how Cuba is attempting to meet the main problems encountered in the program, and discusses the impact of the program in an international context.

An Overview of the Development of the Overseas Scholarship Program

The program of overseas scholarships is directed toward countries of the Third World and toward young people coming from humble families. Most of these students do not have the opportunity to study either in their home countries or abroad, due to the significant expenditure of resources that would imply. Students from more than 120 countries have studied in Cuba on Cuban scholarships.

The scholarship program began in 1961. At this time, many African countries were just emerging from colonialism and were struggling to improve their social and economic development. Cuba shared similar goals with these countries and later increased its interaction with them through the Non-Aligned Movement. In the 1960s, scholarships were mainly directed toward the training of students from selected African countries. Young people came to study from grades 7 to 9 of secondary education (middle level), and in medium-level technical schools that trained them to become skilled workers in areas such as agriculture, construction, mechanics, electricity, accounting, and commerce. The majority of these students returned to their home countries with polytechnic training, and a minority went on to higher education at Cuban universities.

During the 1970s and 1980s, Cuba greatly expanded its general and technical secondary schools, and an increasing number of countries in Africa and the Middle East asked Cuba to provide basic secondary schooling up to grade 9 for some of their young people. In order to do this, the Cuban government decided to build special secondary schools on the Isle of Youth for each country involved. As the educational capacity of the countries increased, they needed more assistance in educating their students at higher levels. Some went to senior secondary schools (grades 10, 11, and 12), and from there to university, and others went directly to mid-level technical schools.

In the early 1990s, the collapse of the Socialist bloc of COMECOM countries, combined with the continuation of the US blockade, caused a serious economic situation in Cuba. In spite of the difficult economic conditions of the "special period", the Cuban Government decided to maintain the scholarships of the 20,300 overseas students in Cuba until they could graduate and return to their homelands. By the turn of the new century, there was a different pattern of scholarships. Fewer scholarships were supporting secondary education, while the number of overseas university scholarships increased.

In the academic year 1986–87, there were about 6,000 foreign scholarship students in Cuban universities, and about 12,000 in basic secondary schools. Up to 1987, this total of 18,000 was the largest number of overseas scholarship students in Cuban educational institutions at any one point in time. During the special period, a period of economic restructuring made necessary by the collapse of economic partnership with the Soviet bloc, the number of university scholarships began to decrease, reaching its lowest point of about 3,000 in the 1998-99 academic year. It is remarkable, however, that it was even possible to sustain the program at this lower level, given the severe economic circumstances that the country was going through. When the economy started to recover, the government made the decision to increase scholarships again. In the 1999-2000 academic year, 8,220 university scholarships were awarded to overseas students, the highest figure for this level in the whole history of the program.

By 2008, the number of overseas scholarship holders went up to 31,000. Part of this increase came about because of the creation of the Latin American School of Medical Sciences (ELAM) and the International

School of Sports and Physical Education. As was indicated in chapter 1, the Latin American School of Medical Sciences was established because of the commitment of former president Fidel Castro and the people of Cuba to boost the number of scholarships given to students from very poor backgrounds, particularly after the devastation of severe hurricanes and floods in Central America reinforced the need to dramatically increase medical care in impoverished countries.

By 2005, Cuba was also offering a new and revolutionary program in the teaching of medicine in overseas countries, utilizing new programs of in-service medical training designed by Cuban medical educators. Venezuela is a leading example of a country in which this in-service training is being carried out. This approach utilizes local and Cuban doctors who act as teachers. With the aid of computers and videos, they help students to integrate work and study, carrying out professional practice in community polyclinics from the beginning of their studies.

More than 55,000 foreign scholarship holders from 148 different countries have graduated in Cuba between 1961 and 2008. Of these, over 30,000 are university graduates and over 24,000 are graduates of vocational and technical non-degree programs. University studies for foreign students cost an average of $30,000 in many countries, and medical courses cost $50,000 or more. This gives an indication of the huge financial contribution of the Cuban government to South-South collaboration in education.

Before 1990, the majority of all overseas students who graduated from Cuban universities came from African countries, and the minority came from Latin America and the Caribbean. These proportions changed during the 1990s, so that now the majority of university students are from Latin America and the Caribbean. Students also come, in smaller numbers, from the Middle East, Asia, Europe, and even a few from needy families in the United States. Table 4.2 shows the numbers of students from different regions of the world in the 2005–2006 academic year. In 2010, there were approximately 30,000 overseas students studying in Cuba from more

Table 4.1 Overseas graduates from Cuban universities, by region of origin, 1961–2009

Geographical regions	Total	Percent
Sub-Saharan Africa	11,012	34.9
Latin America and the Caribbean	17,359	55.1
North Africa and Middle East	1799	5.7
Asia	1143	3.6
Europe	53	0.2
North America	162	0.5
General total	31,528	100
In addition, middle-level graduates: 23,660 Total: 55,188		

Source: *Prontuario* (Higher Education Compendium) 2010, p. 12.

Table 4.2 Number of foreign students studying in Cuba on Cuban scholarships, from different countries, 2005–2006

Sub-Saharan Africa	Latin America	The Caribbean	Asia
South Africa 305	Bolivia 4,700	Haiti 960	East Timor 497
Nigeria 213	Venezuela 4,499	Dominican Republic 417	Vietnam 240
Mali 157	Honduras 1,099	Jamaica 319	
Equatorial Guinea 154	Peru 1,070	Guyana 342	
Republic of Guinea 126			
Angola 102			

Source: Figures compiled by the author from his work in the Ministry of Higher Education.

than 123 countries. The vast majority of these (23,535, or 79.3 percent) are studying medicine. Between 1961 and 2009, approximately 10,241 doctors from Latin America and the Caribbean have been trained in Cuba (*Prontuario* 2009–2010).

Organization of the Scholarship Program

The Cuban scholarship program provides completely free education for the students awarded scholarships. The Cuban government meets all costs, including tuition, textbooks, food, boarding, accommodation, and medical attention. There are no differences between Cuban and overseas students. The only cost that the participating governments have to meet is that of the air travel to and from Cuba. The Cuban government gives the scholarship holders a small allowance in national currency of about 100 pesos monthly. Some countries augment this allowance.

The scholarship program is organized through Cuba's Ministry of Foreign Affairs, negotiated by this ministry's diplomatic missions in the participating countries. The main collaboration is with governments, but occasionally social organizations and individuals apply for scholarships. After the arrival of the students, the responsibility of looking after them is assigned to the corresponding institution. For example, the Ministry of Health attends to students with medical scholarships, not the Ministry of Education.

Five government bodies are involved in Cuba's overseas scholarship program. They are: the Ministry of Public Health (MINSAP) that manages and administers courses in the medical universities, leading to medicine, dentistry, and nursing degrees; the Ministry of Education that administers a variety of teaching specializations in the pedagogic sciences; the Ministry of Culture that administers courses in the creative arts; and the Institute of Sports, Physical Education and Recreation that organizes degree programs in physical culture and sports. The Ministry of Higher Education is responsible for policy and regulation related to all Cuban universities. In addition, it is directly responsible for 14 universities that offer 39 types of careers in fields including economics, the humanities, and the technical, agricultural, social, natural, and mathematical sciences. In total, these ministries organize the provision of 57 career programs for foreign students.

The rights and duties of the scholarship holders are the same as that of Cuban students. This includes the right to belong to the Federation of University Students (the FEU). Some overseas students have been elected to posts within this union. A national resolution was written specifically for overseas students, setting out their rights, duties, and functions, relating to the university.

Representatives in the various embassies or diplomatic missions in Cuba are periodically informed about the educational results of students from their countries, as well as of any difficulties relating to their work. Each university has a university council to look after management and administration. The overseas students democratically elect one from their midst to represent them on the university council.

Main Achievements of the Scholarship Program

i) Development of Human Resources

Cuba, arguably, has contributed, proportionately to its size, more than any other country in the world to educating highly qualified workers and professionals for underdeveloped countries. This demonstrates the viability and efficiency of South-South cooperation based on the solidarity approach rather than the traditional market approach.

There are two ways in which the Cuban scholarship program demonstrates efficiency. One is that 88 percent of scholarship students complete their studies and graduate. This however, varies between different countries, with students from some countries encountering more difficulties than others, as will be discussed herein. In the 2004–05 academic year, students from 23 countries had a 100 percent rate of graduation.

The second aspect of efficiency is that most of the students return to their countries to work in the careers for which they have been trained. The curriculum is designed with this aim. It strengthens the overseas students' understanding of their own culture and society, and develops their self-esteem and commitment to their countries. Since Cuba respects the principle of cooperation based on solidarity, and knows the great need of these countries for professionals and technicians, its main aim is to produce graduates to go and practice in their countries, not to keep them in Cuba. Recent research by Sabine Lehr (2008) indicates that some of the students depart from the goal of practicing as professionals in their own countries, and take up jobs in other countries of the global South. A also few pursue further studies at the graduate level in third countries. Nevertheless, the representatives of many countries have expressed their appreciation that the majority of Cuban-trained graduates return to their countries to work.

ii) Professionalism of the Graduates

Another achievement is the satisfaction of the participating countries with the professional level of Cuban-trained graduates. These graduates show a great willingness to do whatever is needed in their field of work, even when this involves facing difficult conditions. This is not surprising to Cubans, since Cuban higher education is internationally recognized for its integration of theory, practice, and social responsibility. Students are trained not only as professionals. They are given an integrated education—not only in academic aspects but with social commitment toward public and community service as well. This is developed through studying with Cubans and students from many other countries, and through their participation in the daily life of Cuban society.

Higher education immerses students in the principles of scientific and applied research. Students learn by study and work placements, and some of the most outstanding ones also learn by working as teaching assistants in their training institutions. To prepare them for this teaching role, the university gives them a certain level of pedagogical training.

iii) Outstanding Performance of Some Graduates in Their Home Countries

A substantial number of Cuban-trained graduates are working in important and responsible posts in their countries. Some of them are diplomatic representatives to Cuba or other countries. To illustrate this, it is noticeable that the former first secretary from Equatorial Guinea is a Cuban-trained graduate, as is the secretary of the Ministry of Education and Culture of Angola, the representative of CARICOM in Cuba, the honorary consul from Dominica, the ambassadors from Bolivia, the Congo, Mali, Namibia, St. Lucía, St. Vicente, and Vietnam in Cuba, and three ministers of public health of three Caribbean countries, among others. As well, parliamentarians, vice-ministers, and directors with national or regional responsibilities are also graduates of Cuban universities.

iv) Rewards for Excellence

The emulation process that has been developed with the foreign scholarship holders encourages them to strive for excellence, and rewards overall effort. When each semester concludes, the best foreign students of each nationality are selected based on their performance in a wide range of activities. For example, some are selected for having the best performance in academic results, sports, culture, and other spheres; others are selected for having the best rooms and being the most outstanding students in the particular university.

These students receive prizes and certificates, and the diplomatic representatives of their country are informed of their success. Organizing this reward system means planning all the events together with the provincial delegations of the Cuban Institute of Friendship with the Peoples (ICAP). At the end of the academic year, prize-giving ceremonies are organized by ICAP, FEU, and the National Office for Overseas Scholarship holders in the Ministry of Higher Education.

At each annual graduation, the participating organizations offer scholarships at undergraduate, masters (MSc), and doctoral (PhD); to the best overseas graduates in the different universities and other institutions of higher education. About 30 of these scholarships are awarded every year. This constitutes an important reward program from which many countries have benefited.

v) Broadening Cultural Horizons

Overseas students participate in sporting and cultural events that take place at the universities. Many of them have obtained prizes and certificates for their achievements in these areas. The main focus of these extracurricular activities is to promote their national pride and cultural identity. The students acquire an awareness of cultural diversity and an international outlook because of the large numbers of international students participating in the programs. This is also a benefit for Cuban students who learn more about other countries and cultures as the universities organize cultural presentations from many countries throughout the year.

vi) Bilingual Competence

Another important result of the scholarship program is the acquisition of Spanish as a second language. Each university has a preparatory language-training faculty that provides foreign students with training in Spanish, including specialized training in the terminology they will need in their particular studies. To prepare students in Spanish, there are preparatory faculties for medical sciences, pedagogical sciences, physical culture and sport, and so on. This introduction to Spanish takes one year, and the students develop the language as their university program continues.

vii) Solidarity

An outstanding impact of the scholarship program is the expression of international solidarity with Cuba from participating countries When Cuban-trained graduates return home, they usually form or strengthen solidarity groups, that is, friendship societies with Cuba. Foreign students have participated voluntarily and actively, through the Congress of the Federation of University Students from Cuba (FEU), in the debate of ideas between different trends of social thought such as between the "solidarity" and "market" approach to international cooperation. In 2005, about 500 overseas students were part of the Cuban multinational delegation to the World Festival of Youth and Students that took place in Algeria and later on in Venezuela.

Challenges Facing the Program

The program of overseas scholarships naturally has some problems, which the Cuban government is working to solve. Among the problems are the following:

i) *Accommodation.* The condition of some of the student residences in some universities is in need of repair. Because of the special period and the economic difficulties that Cuba has faced, lack of maintenance was a serious problem in many affected buildings. This situation impacted upon Cuban students and international students equally. In the year 2000, the Cuban government spent more than $100,000 (US equivalent) to repair a 12-story building in Havana city. Later, similar sums were spent to repair other buildings. Devastation and damage caused by Hurricane Michelle in Cuba forced the country to reconsider the budget assigned for repairs for other uses. Two facilities that had already been repaired were completely destroyed.

ii) *Telephone and Internet communication.* Another difficulty has been that of meeting the great demand for telephone communication that comes particularly from Latin American and Caribbean students. While scholarship holders from Africa, Asia, and the Middle East did not express the same demand for phone services, a new perspective has been given to this problem by the increase of scholarship holders in the Latin American region and their relative proximity to home. The use of email in all the centers of study alleviates this demand, but in general direct phone communication is preferred, and although some long-distance telephone facilities exist in the centers, the infrastructure is insufficient to satisfy the demand. Access to the Internet is limited by the blockade measures dictated by the US government.

iii) *Gaps in the educational levels of students entering the system.* Not all overseas students arrive in Cuba with high educational levels. Some struggle with university-level work, and this, together with inappropriate selection of careers, can cause academic difficulties during the students' first year of preparatory studies. In some cases, this situation results in low levels of academic achievement that affect the efficiency of the system. This problem is being studied by the Cuban authorities, and it is thought that the solution will require two parallel actions. First, there needs to be an improvement in the selection process in each country, which Cuba could help to carry out. Second, Cuba may need to redesign the objectives of the preparatory studies year. In some cases, remedial courses, mainly in mathematics, physics, and chemistry, are offered to help prepare students for the university program.

Quality Assurance of the Cuban Higher Education System

A graduate trained in a foreign country, in order to work as a professional in his or her home country, has to have a degree recognized by that country. The recognition of equivalence of the Cuban degree is done by bilateral negotiations. Most countries have formally recognized this equivalence, but for a few countries, bilateral negotiations are still in process. The Cuban government has received official delegations from some overseas countries that wish to analyze this particular aspect. On the whole, satisfactory results have been obtained.

The high quality of higher education in Cuba has been maintained, as shown by several indicators.

1. Cuba's Ministry of Higher Education has established internal measures for accreditation to ensure the constant development of the university system. Among these measures are self-evaluation and accreditation systems for each university discipline and career path, established in accordance with international trends and control processes. For each career path, Cuba has created national commissions to accredit and assess the respective programs. These commissions include the best specialists in higher education, who upgrade their professional experience and skills on a regular basis.
2. Cuba has sent specialists to train for masters and PhD degrees to several industrialized European countries, and these scholars have obtained good results.
3. Numerous Cuban specialists are requested in many countries for university teaching on masters and PhD programs, and as consultants in curriculum development.
4. Cuban researchers and specialists are members of local and international research networks and centers of excellence such as CEPES at the University of Havana, which has a UNESCO Chair in Higher Education Administration, and the Institute for Tropical Diseases, which is a reference center for UNESCO. Their work contributes significantly to the latest research in their respective fields.
5. Cuba's Ministry of Higher Education has more than 3,000 collaboration agreements with institutions in numerous countries, and these are being satisfactorily fulfilled.
6. UNESCO, UNDP, and other noted international institutions have recognized the role of Cuban professionals in the development of many of their programs.

Impact of the Cuban Scholarship Program

The Cuban scholarship program has a very significant impact on the countries that have participated in it. The program has played a key role in developing cultural, technical, and educational capacity, and human resources, in each country.

Many countries in Africa, the Americas and the Caribbean, and Asia, have negotiated with Cuba to train specialists in careers of particular importance to their economies and societies. Fields of training that are particularly significant include medicine, nursing (especially the training of male nurses), dentistry, health technology, agriculture, education, physical education, and sports. As was previously explained, Cuban-trained graduates are characterized by two main aspects: their high level of professional education and their willingness to work. After returning to their own country, most of them work in the areas for which they have been trained and contribute a great deal to the development of these areas. These university graduates are also an important source of cultural development, particularly because they have learnt to be bilingual in Cuba.

The impact of the Cuban scholarship program also has an important effect on perceptions about Cuba in other countries. Without doubt, this helps to counteract the effect of the United States' communications blockade against Cuba. The overseas graduates establish good relationships with Cuban friends and keep in touch by email and sometimes make return visits to Cuba. The affection and gratitude of these professionals toward Cuba is shown by the establishment of Cuban friendship and solidarity groups in their own countries.

Conclusion

This chapter has outlined the scale and impact of Cuba's cooperation in higher education with a wide range of partner developing countries, and it has discussed some of the challenges to the program. Thousands of young people who have graduated with Cuban degrees have returned to their countries and are making an enormous contribution to essential professions that otherwise would not be adequately staffed. These graduates also make an impact in terms of the development of their cultural horizons including bilingual skills and the maintenance of international friendships that they established in Cuba. The chapter has shown that the solidarity principle has not only to do with good intentions, but promotes good results as well. All parties involved in solidarity interaction gain benefits. Other countries gain training and qualifications. Cuba expands and deepens its knowledge of and interaction and friendship with many countries of the world. People from all over the world develop bonds of affection and solidarity with Cuba.

References

Lehr, S. "The Children of the Isle of Youth: Impact of a Cuban South-South Education Program on Ghanaian Graduates." Unpublished PhD dissertation, University of Victoria, Canada 2008.

Prontuario (Higher Education Compendium) 2010. Cuba: Ministerio de Educación Superior.

5

The Children of the Isle of Youth: How Ghanaian Students Learned to Cope with "Anything in Life"

Sabine Lehr

Introduction

Many developing countries are faced with the severe problem of underdevelopment of their secondary and postsecondary education sectors, stemming from the inadequacy of educational provision during their colonial past. During the postindependence years, this situation was exacerbated by limitations imposed through structural adjustment loans that had the effect of reducing resources allocated to education and other social sectors. In this context, assistance to education becomes particularly important.

In this chapter, I examine the implementation and significance of a program of Cuban educational assistance in the form of secondary and postsecondary scholarships negotiated between the governments of Ghana and Cuba, which was operational between 1983 and 1996.[1] I discuss the experiences of 48 former Ghanaian students of the program who agreed to participate in research that I conducted into the educational, social, and political implications of their years of study in Cuba. Eight senior administrators and teachers were also interviewed in Ghana and in Canada. By analyzing the participants' reports of their experiences with the Cuban scholarship program, their subsequent reintegration into their home country or a third country, and the policy issues that arose, I explore the significance to a developing country of this model of South-South collaboration. The chapter will discuss my research findings concerning the following specific questions:

1. How did the Cuban scholarship program provide access opportunities for Ghanaians from a spread of geographic and socioeconomic backgrounds?
2. How did the study participants perceive the relevance of the Cuban education they received in regard to academic and practical learning?

3. How did the participants view the role of the Ghanaian government regarding the question of work deployment and reintegration when as graduates they returned from Cuba?
4. What challenges did the former students encounter upon return to Ghana, and how did they overcome these challenges?
5. What were the implications of combining secondary and post secondary studies in this scholarship model with regard to access issues?

Background

My interest in this study developed out of my professional practice as a university administrator in Canada dealing with various dimensions of internationalization at my institution. Working in a country that treats international students as existing outside of the government's mandate to provide education as a public good, and therefore does not provide public funds toward the post secondary education of international students, I became acutely aware of the insurmountable access issues faced by students from lower-income backgrounds. International undergraduate students in Canada often pay triple or quadruple tuition fees compared to their Canadian counterparts, and few full scholarships to Canadian universities are available for students from developing countries. During the 12th World Congress of Comparative Education Societies in Havana in 2004, *Education and Social Justice*, I learned about the Cuban approach to educational development assistance through the provision of post secondary scholarships to mostly underprivileged students from lower-income countries.[2] I was particularly interested in the combined secondary and post secondary scholarship program that was in place for a variety of mostly African countries until the mid-1990s, and that provided the potential to benefit academically promising students who might have otherwise dropped out of school before finishing a high-school diploma. The program emerged from Cuba's earlier interventions during the struggle for independence in several African countries. Instead of withdrawing its assistance once military and other logistical assistance came to an end, Cuba decided to continue assisting these newly independent countries in different ways, including economic and educational collaboration.

Cooperation between Cuba and Ghana started shortly after Ghana gained independence in 1957. However, the educational collaboration program between the two countries, which resulted in the construction of a Ghanaian secondary school on Cuba's Isle of Youth, and the training of about 1,200 Ghanaian students at secondary and post secondary levels, was only formalized in the early 1980s. At that point, Ghana found itself in an economic and food crisis that had forced the country to accept loans from the International Monetary Fund (IMF) for structural adjustment programs that reduced the public sector and had a severe impact on the least privileged elements of society.[3] At the same time, the government introduced educational reforms that aimed at providing Ghanaians with

5

The Children of the Isle of Youth: How Ghanaian Students Learned to Cope with "Anything in Life"

Sabine Lehr

Introduction

Many developing countries are faced with the severe problem of underdevelopment of their secondary and postsecondary education sectors, stemming from the inadequacy of educational provision during their colonial past. During the postindependence years, this situation was exacerbated by limitations imposed through structural adjustment loans that had the effect of reducing resources allocated to education and other social sectors. In this context, assistance to education becomes particularly important.

In this chapter, I examine the implementation and significance of a program of Cuban educational assistance in the form of secondary and postsecondary scholarships negotiated between the governments of Ghana and Cuba, which was operational between 1983 and 1996.[1] I discuss the experiences of 48 former Ghanaian students of the program who agreed to participate in research that I conducted into the educational, social, and political implications of their years of study in Cuba. Eight senior administrators and teachers were also interviewed in Ghana and in Canada. By analyzing the participants' reports of their experiences with the Cuban scholarship program, their subsequent reintegration into their home country or a third country, and the policy issues that arose, I explore the significance to a developing country of this model of South-South collaboration. The chapter will discuss my research findings concerning the following specific questions:

1. How did the Cuban scholarship program provide access opportunities for Ghanaians from a spread of geographic and socioeconomic backgrounds?
2. How did the study participants perceive the relevance of the Cuban education they received in regard to academic and practical learning?

3. How did the participants view the role of the Ghanaian government regarding the question of work deployment and reintegration when as graduates they returned from Cuba?
4. What challenges did the former students encounter upon return to Ghana, and how did they overcome these challenges?
5. What were the implications of combining secondary and post secondary studies in this scholarship model with regard to access issues?

Background

My interest in this study developed out of my professional practice as a university administrator in Canada dealing with various dimensions of internationalization at my institution. Working in a country that treats international students as existing outside of the government's mandate to provide education as a public good, and therefore does not provide public funds toward the post secondary education of international students, I became acutely aware of the insurmountable access issues faced by students from lower-income backgrounds. International undergraduate students in Canada often pay triple or quadruple tuition fees compared to their Canadian counterparts, and few full scholarships to Canadian universities are available for students from developing countries. During the 12th World Congress of Comparative Education Societies in Havana in 2004, *Education and Social Justice,* I learned about the Cuban approach to educational development assistance through the provision of post secondary scholarships to mostly underprivileged students from lower-income countries.[2] I was particularly interested in the combined secondary and post secondary scholarship program that was in place for a variety of mostly African countries until the mid-1990s, and that provided the potential to benefit academically promising students who might have otherwise dropped out of school before finishing a high-school diploma. The program emerged from Cuba's earlier interventions during the struggle for independence in several African countries. Instead of withdrawing its assistance once military and other logistical assistance came to an end, Cuba decided to continue assisting these newly independent countries in different ways, including economic and educational collaboration.

Cooperation between Cuba and Ghana started shortly after Ghana gained independence in 1957. However, the educational collaboration program between the two countries, which resulted in the construction of a Ghanaian secondary school on Cuba's Isle of Youth, and the training of about 1,200 Ghanaian students at secondary and post secondary levels, was only formalized in the early 1980s. At that point, Ghana found itself in an economic and food crisis that had forced the country to accept loans from the International Monetary Fund (IMF) for structural adjustment programs that reduced the public sector and had a severe impact on the least privileged elements of society.[3] At the same time, the government introduced educational reforms that aimed at providing Ghanaians with more practical skills, reducing the time students spent in school (up until that point, students entered university after 17 years of formal schooling), and thus increasing the number of students who would access higher education.[4] At the time of the signing of the agreement between Ghana and Cuba for the scholarship program, educational attainment was low, and attrition rates after the first level of education were high. The Ghanaian education system in the early 1980s was not well developed. In a country with a population of about 12 million in 1983, there were only three universities and three polytechnical institutions. In some rural areas, there were neither primary nor secondary schools, and tuition fees, particularly for boarding schools, were prohibitive for the poorer strata of society.

Based on their policy of nonalignment, Ghanaian president Rawlings and his Provisional National Defense Council (PNDC) developed close relationships in the early 1980s not only with the international bilateral and multilateral funding community, but also with a number of socialist regimes including Cuba. When Cuban president Castro extended an offer to Ghana of educational scholarships at the secondary and post secondary levels, Rawlings accepted because such training fitted well with the PNDC's educational restructuring policy whereby purely academic curricula were to be replaced with more vocational and technical training programs.[5] Cuba agreed to provide the Ghanaian students one basic secondary school in an agricultural region on the Isle of Youth, where there were already some schools for young people of other mostly African nations. All schools were numbered, and the Ghanaian school came to be known as Escuela Secundaria Básica en el Campo (ESBEC) #22.

Entering into an educational arrangement with Cuba that had a clear rural component and attempted to link academic studies with the world of work was timely for a number of reasons. In 1983, Ghana was in the middle of a severe countrywide food crisis.[6] Although labor was in relative abundance to carry out the necessary agricultural work, many youth seemed to have lost interest in the agricultural sector due to the discrepancy between rural and urban living conditions.[7] The agricultural reforms introduced by the PNDC focused on capital-intensive farming methods, and thus represented a radical break with more traditional forms of farming.[8] Cuba was particularly well positioned to offer assistance to countries like Ghana due to Cuba's post revolutionary emphasis on the role of education to tackle societal problems through linking practical and theoretical studies, which had led to the development of a technical/vocational education system alongside the academic stream.[9]

The Cuban offer also came at a time when students from Ghana and other African countries found it increasingly difficult to study at universities in the United States, the United Kingdom, or other European countries that had started introducing higher overseas student fees. As part of their neoliberal fiscal policy pursuits, these countries aimed to introduce full-cost-recovery models for international students, and many Ghanaian and other African students had to abandon their studies midway due to the prohibitive tuition fees.[10] Details of the collaboration program were based on the needs of Ghana at the time. As policy makers saw it, the most pressing human resource needs were for middle-level technical staff, vocationally trained, who would assist Ghana's economic and human development. Secondary schooling and post secondary career choices were negotiated accordingly. At the secondary level, curricula in ESBEC #22 were co-taught by Ghanaians and Cubans in order to provide students with the benefits of the perceived excellent Cuban science education, while also keeping them in touch with their home country through teaching them Ghanaian culture, history, geography, as well as English.

The first group of 609 Ghanaian students went to Cuba in 1983. This was the largest single group ever sent as grades 7–9 at the secondary level had to be filled, as well as grades 10–12 at the pre-university level. After that, an average of 120 students was sent during each of the years 1985, 1986, 1987, 1988, and 1989 (no students went in 1984). Because the program was structured around the work and study principle, students either went to school in the morning and worked for a few hours in the grapefruit orchards in the afternoon, or vice versa. The morning and afternoon shifts alternated every few weeks. The total student intake over the life of the program was approximately 1,200 students. Cuba was financially responsible for providing the school infrastructure and the majority of teachers, food, clothes for students, and other necessities of life. Ghana, on the other hand, was responsible for all transportation between the two countries and for providing several Ghanaian teachers for humanities and social science subjects. Ghana also provided a small stipend to the students.

The Isle of Youth's Ghanaian program technically ended with the last student intake in 1989. ESBEC #22 was closed down in 1996 after the last of the students had moved to the post secondary level. A variety of reasons seem to have led to the closing of the program:

1. a program review that was precipitated by the changing political, economic, and social situation in Ghana;
2. changes in the Ghanaian education system, in particular, the opening of more schools that at least in theory resembled the more utilitarian approach common in Cuba, and, as a result, the desire to assign Ghanaian students to targeted post secondary education in Cuba, rather than secondary level education;
3. a desire by Ghana to establish a similar program by building schools in the countryside[11] in Ghana with the assistance of Cuba (an idea that was never put into practice);
4. changes in Cuba brought on by the global changes in the formerly socialist countries that would have made it economically difficult to sustain the large assistance program for international students on the Isle of Youth over time.

The close collaboration between Ghana and Cuba did, however, continue in a broad range of fields, including education, trade, and health. Under a memorandum of understanding for a permanent joint commission cooperation signed in April 2008, Cuba committed to offering a total of

30 tertiary education scholarships to Ghanaian students. These were for the education of 20 medical students, with the remainder of scholarships awarded in the disciplines of engineering, sports, health technology, and mining.[12] The agreement also included the dispatch of 200 Cuban medical specialists to Ghana to assist with the training of Ghanaian medical doctors.

Questions are frequently asked about the potential benefits that Cuba may have derived from offering such generous educational assistance to a large number of countries. As a country that has been isolated internationally because of US policy and the blockade imposed on Cuba, it is extremely important for Cuba to foster relationships with countries that are reluctant to follow the United States' isolationist policy toward the island nation. The Isle of Youth program started during the Cold War years, when both major blocs of countries were trying to win allies on a global basis. The support that Cuba received as a member of COMECON or the Council for Mutual Economic Assistance (CMEA) in those years[13] allowed the small nation to provide generous educational assistance to other low-income countries. However, after the dissolution of COMECON and the disintegration of the Soviet Union, the close collaboration between Ghana and Cuba did continue in the fields of education, trade, and health, as pointed out earlier. The memorandum of understanding of April 2008 is reciprocal in that Ghana has committed to assist Cuba in gaining access to cocoa purchases from the Cocoa Marketing Company, while Cuba in return will train Ghanaians in the manufacture of artesanal chocolate and agroprocessing technologies.[14] This memorandum is the result of a long-standing bilateral cooperation through the Ghana-Cuba Permanent Joint Commission for Cooperation that has met every two years since the early 1980s.

Theoretical Concepts

In discussing the Cuban scholarships to Ghana, I will draw on four major distinct, yet interrelated, concepts: brain drain or brain circulation; South-South development cooperation; links between tertiary education and development; and colonial legacies. Brain drain has been defined as "the phenomenon whereby a country suffers an outflow of its educated elite, on a scale threatening the needs of national development in the long term."[15] Much of the migration typically described as "brain drain" has been shaped by patterns of colonial domination and the subsequent postcolonial relations.[16] The attraction of skilled migrants from lower-income countries is now commonplace in the more industrialized societies. Declining birth rates, aging and less productive populations, coupled with slow economic growth and major global competition, have led these countries to introduce selective and somewhat aggressive immigration policies.[17] There is broad agreement among economists, development theorists, and human capital theorists that substantial levels of migration need to be understood in the context of global wage differentials where residents of the Global South will find it advantageous to move to countries in the Global North. There is also broad agreement that global economic inequalities between individual countries will not disappear in the short term. My study attempted to provide some answers as to whether the Cuban scholarship program and the Cuban educational model created a demand among the graduates who participated in this study to return and stay in their home country, thus outweighing the demand incentives offered by countries of the Global North toward emigration.

The Cuban scholarship program is predicated on the notion that there is a positive link between tertiary education and economic development and growth, a view widely held among scholars and education specialists.[18] Tertiary level enrolment has grown exponentially for the last 50 years for most regions of the world, but growth has been much less pronounced in Sub-Saharan Africa.[19] The link between development and education has in the past frequently been reduced to the application of human capital theory in the context of the Global South. More recently, the focus has shifted from seeing education simply as a mechanism for human capital formation, to acknowledging the value of human development as an end in itself,[20] a concept that Sen[21] distinguished from human capital by labeling it "human capability." The Cuban scholarship program combines the concept of education's intrinsic value of human development, as formulated originally by Che Guevara in the concept of the "new man," with a utilitarian perspective of education that aligns educational programming very closely with the scientific/technical needs of society.

The frequent lack of relevance of educational offerings to job markets causes problems for students from the South studying in the North, and my study thus also explored the links between the participating graduates' tertiary education programs in Cuba and their experiences integrating into the Ghanaian job market.

The origins of South-South cooperation, of which the Cuba-Ghana program is an example, date back to the late 1960s and early 1970s when colonialism was formally coming to an end, and the newly decolonized countries tried to find ways to cooperate among themselves in the context of the new world order dominated by the Cold War and the existence of two powerful blocs of countries in opposing ideological camps.[22] Over the past 30 years, South-South cooperation has been promoted by the UNDP throughout its activities in all regions and most sectors.[23] Paradoxically, an initiative that started as a counterforce to the former colonial powers has been taken over by a normative intergovernmental framework whose proponents are trying to "mainstream" South-South development cooperation into the global operations of organizations located in and controlled by the former colonial master states. Not surprisingly, much of the literature on South-South cooperation focuses on trade or industrial operations, leaving a dearth of literature on the sharing of education models as a form of South-South cooperation. The Cuban collaboration with other countries of the Global South through the provision of educational scholarships operates without any involvement from the "North," and thus models an applied South-South development relationship, which is significant in regard to both scale and scope. The program was formerly supported through subsidies to Cuba by the Soviet Union; however, this source of revenue disappeared after the final disintegration of the Soviet Union in 1991. Although the Cuban collaboration with other countries changed its nature and scope then, it continued in spite of the economic challenges that Cuba faced after 1990.

Postcolonial theory examines the process of colonization and the resistance by former colonies to free themselves from what has been termed the "colonial syndrome."[24] Postcolonial concepts are used to "analyse discursively the continuing legacy of European imperialism and colonialism and to uncover the oppositional discourses of those who have struggled against its lingering effects."[25] The collaboration between Cuba and African countries occurs against this background. Universities in Africa set up toward the end of or after the colonial period were born into the relationship of dependence on European institutions. They frequently continue to be subjected to external domination in their intellectual structure and curricular offerings.[26] In this context, Kallaway pointed to the lack of vocational education in Africa, arguing that the respective development strategies formulated in the early post independence years, which heavily emphasized rural vocational and agricultural education, had not come to full fruition during later years.[27] Many of these early decolonization efforts and successes of the early postcolonial period were nullified by the advent of structural adjustment programming in the late 1970s and early 1980s, thus reestablishing significant elements of dependence for the Global South in the context of globalization.[28] The Cuban educational model is notably different in that it rejects colonial intellectualism and attempts to invalidate the hegemonic conceptions of development and underdevelopment. It does so by working closely with the recipient countries and taking into account their specific needs. In the secondary program on the Isle of Youth, Cuban and Ghanaian teachers and administrators worked collaboratively in designing curricula. At the post secondary level, the Cuban curriculum is responsive to the needs of other countries with similar socioeconomic structures.

Equalization through Recruitment: Enhanced Access

The structural adjustment policies applied in Ghana during the 1980s had a severe negative impact on the state's ability to provide free education, especially at higher education levels. The new policies dictated that education costs were at least partly to be borne by users, which put higher education out of reach for the lower social classes.[29] One of the main features of the Cuba-Ghana program, and in particular of the secondary-level program component on Cuba's Isle of Youth, was its egalitarian aspiration to provide opportunities to students throughout Ghana, including the more impoverished and socioculturally weaker Northern regions. The main mechanism employed by Ghana to work toward equal access was through the early identification of scholarship students just as they entered the secondary educational level. The majority of students, even in remote areas of Ghana and regardless of economic background, were still in school at the end of the first (primary) level. A 1986 UNESCO document indicated that in 1980, enrollment in the first level of education in Ghana was 73.1 percent, unevenly split between 81.7 percent male and 64.5 percent female students.[30] At the secondary level, however, enrolment had fallen dramatically to an overall 35.7 percent, with the same pronounced gender imbalance of 44.0 percent male and 27.4 percent female students.[31] Early recruitment thus held the promise of an enhanced possibility that selection would be based on academic aptitude and would also reach those students with weaker socioeconomic backgrounds. This feature set the Cuba-Ghana program apart from the common practice of identifying scholarship students in the upper school years or after completion of the equivalent of a high-school diploma; a practice that eliminates a large number of students who drop out of school early due to their families' socioeconomic circumstances.

Ghana is divided into 10 administrative regions, and the regions located in the country's north are socioeconomically and infrastructurally weaker than most of the southern regions. The designers of the recruitment program devised a plan whereby a quota of 10 students was allocated to each of the 10 regions. A competitive application process was instituted in the districts (lower-level administrative units) and regions with the help of parents' organizations. Student applicants wrote exams at the district and regional levels that tested for their aptitude in major subjects taught at school. Final selection took place at the national level in Accra. Thus, 120 students were selected every year for the program: 100 from the 10 regions, with 20 places reserved for "protocol cases"—children of those with political or military links. According to several former program administrators, the application/recruitment process was streamlined over the years, and some regions became aware of the program later than others. This situation resulted in uneven numbers of students selected from each region, in particular during the earlier years.[32]

Since no statistical data existed that would have provided any insights regarding the socioeconomic background of the participating students, I used proxy indicators to get an overview of the students' background. In Ghana, access to advanced levels of education was and still is partly related to students' geographic location. Even in 2002, students' residence was still the most decisive factor with respect to determining their chances of university access. During that year, almost 60 percent of students in Ghana's five public universities came from the two more affluent regions of Greater Accra and Ashanti, whereas residents of two of the most deprived areas, Upper East and Upper West Regions, constituted only 5.5 percent of all students.[33]

Table 5.1 shows the region of residence at the time of application to the scholarship program of 40 of the 48 students who participated in my study: the classification of regions from poorer to richer is based on 1992 data and might thus slightly deviate from the situation in the mid- to late 1980s when the students were recruited. The numbers are somewhat skewed toward the richer regions, with 15 graduates residing in regions where more than 50 percent of the population lived in poverty (Upper West to Volta Regions), and 25 graduates residing in the remaining four regions with less than 50 percent of the population living in poverty.

Table 5.1 also contains information on whether the students' parents would have been able to afford the graduate a similar education in Ghana. This information is self-reported and is only available for half of all graduates interviewed who chose to provide information in this regard when asked the question. The majority of those who responded (13 out of 25) indicated that their parents would not have been able to afford them a similar education in Ghana, or that they would only have been able to do so with restrictions or hardship (two respondents).

The information in the table indicates that recruitment likely resulted in the majority of regions being represented, albeit somewhat unevenly. Given the exploratory nature of my study, I cannot draw definitive conclusions

Table 5.1 Geographic and socioeconomic background

Region of residence at time of application to Isle of Youth program	Total number of students from region
Upper West	3
Upper East	2
Brong Ahafo	0
Northern	5
Western	2
Volta	3
Eastern	3
Central	6
Ashanti	1
Greater Accra	15
Total	40
Place of residence at time of application characterized as a....	*Number of students*
City	12
Town	8
Village	5
Total	25
Parents would have been able to afford the graduate a similar education in Ghana	*Number of students*
No	13
Yes	10
Yes, with restrictions/hardship	2
Total	25

regarding the distribution of students across regions. Noticeable, for example, is the absence in my sample of any graduates from the Brong Ahafo Region (one of the poorest regions in 1992), and a single graduate from the Ashanti Region, the second richest region in the early 1990s. Several administrators who spoke with me indicated that the recruitment process was established unevenly across the country and across different regions. The information in the table does provide evidence, though, that the program reached students throughout the country. In conjunction with the students' self-reported perception about their parents' ability to afford them a similar education in Ghana, it becomes clear that the program was reaching historically disadvantaged groups in society whose educational opportunities would have been limited at home. In this regard, it is important to note that access to post secondary education was constrained not just by attrition and socioeconomic factors, but also by the very limited availability of places at post secondary institutions.

Although the group of graduates interviewed for this study constitutes only a small group of all program graduates, and complete data on all Ghanaian graduates' socioeconomic background are not available, it appears that the program contributed to overcoming the colonial legacy of inaccessibility to educational programs outside of the metropolitan centers. The former program administrators reported that the Cubans provided technical advice in the early stages of the program on how to structure the recruitment process in order to achieve this goal of providing equal opportunities to students across the country. Equal access opportunities have been enshrined in the Cuban educational philosophy since the early days of the revolution, and the Cuba-Ghana scholarship program thus provides an excellent example of how a South-South collaborative model can serve to apply such principles in another country's context. The program also provided other opportunities for learning from a country with a more advanced and diversified education system. Due to the relatively short duration of the Cuba-Ghana Isle of Youth program, these opportunities were, however, not fully developed and implemented by the Ghanaians. Apart from the educational assistance—the training of students who might not have been able to receive the same level of training in their home country—the program shows how South-South collaboration can work at the broader level of providing structural assistance, ultimately enabling the receiving country to build up capacity at home, create its own sustainable models, and become less dependent on the provision of programming by the donor country over time. By "structural assistance," I mean, for example, the idea of "schools in the countryside," where urban and rural students study and work together with the objective of creating a collective consciousness and of breaking down barriers between agricultural labor and a liberal/humanistic education. This is of particular importance in countries that are still heavily agriculture-based (most African nations), but where the structural adjustment policies of the past have deemphasized the agricultural sector. In the context of Ghana, government policies during the 1980s were not conducive to development of the agricultural sector. Although that sector constituted about half of the GDP between 1980 and 1991, the budgetary allocation it received fell from 10.4 percent in 1983 to about 4 percent annually from 1986 to 1990.[34]

Although the program's overall impact on access to education was positive, it must be noted that the program was not successful in addressing the gender imbalance that already existed in Ghana at the time with regard to educational access. The program was heavily gender-skewed in favor of male students. It appears that a combination of factors was responsible for this situation: the arrangement of dormitories at the school; Ghanaian families' reluctance to send their female children to a faraway country for a lengthy period of time; and gender roles in Ghanaian society that favored boys' education over girls' education. During the early years of the program, several pregnancies occurred among the Ghanaian female students, which led to a decision not to send any more girls to the Isle of Youth as of 1987, thus skewing the gender distribution even further.

Absence from Home and Reintegration

Early recruitment at the beginning of the secondary school level resulted in a situation where many scholarship students spent up to 13 years away from their home in Ghana as they grew into adolescents and eventually into adults. None of the former students I interviewed returned for a visit back to Ghana during their years in Cuba: only a few students who were selected competitively every year were able to make such a visit. Although a physical separation between children and their parents or next of kin is more common in principle in some African cultures than in North America or Europe, living without any relatives for so many years is clearly also unusual and undesirable from an African perspective. Nevertheless, the continued separation of the students from their families did not have a noticeable influence on student drop-out rates, which remained low throughout the program.

It is not surprising that the graduates encountered challenges when they returned to Ghana, after having spent half their lives in a country with a very different social, cultural, political, and linguistic context. The return and reintegration process can best be understood in regard to four dimensions:

1. Culture and family
2. Accreditation and employment
3. Perceptions of Eastern bloc education
4. Language

Almost every returning graduate faced challenges with respect to reintegration into the cultural and social fabric of Ghanaian society. Many graduates had adapted to the liberal and expressive Cuban way of life that clashed with the more moralistic and rigid Ghanaian society. The dress code in Cuba was more "revealing" in comparison with the chaste Ghanaian way of dressing. Showing affection between couples was commonplace in Cuba, with couples kissing openly in public. This type of behavior was considered unacceptable in Ghana. In Cuba, the graduates had been used to openly discussing issues, asking lots of questions and making their opinion known—all patterns of behavior and communication that were not appreciated to the same extent in Ghana. Graduates and administrators noted that the returnees were not any longer familiar with Ghanaian notions of family relations and patterns of respectful behavior both inside and outside of family relationships. Anarfi et al. described this phenomenon in the context of return migration, arguing that the frustrations encountered by returnees due to their alienation from the home culture could ultimately result in a push to return to the countries where they previously resided.[35] Such a move back to Cuba, however, was not easily possible in the Ghana-Cuba program since it would have counteracted the spirit of the scholarship program, and it was not facilitated by Cuba.

The same culture clash that graduates experienced inside their families also applied to other spheres of life, in particular the world of work. Clashes there occurred along several dimensions—work attitude, hierarchy, and dress code. In many ways, the graduates seem to have found themselves caught between two worlds: they had longed to go home for so many years, but once they got there, their excitement quickly abated when they started to understand the new reality in which they found themselves.

Accreditation issues affected the graduates in two main ways: first, there were a few disciplines that required professional accreditation, and second, those graduates who wished to pursue further studies had to deal with academic accreditation issues. The extent to which individual graduates were affected by accreditation problems depended on their credential and on their location after leaving Cuba. Although most graduating students initially returned to Ghana, a few went to live in the Bahamas, an island group near Cuba, which at that time had immigration policies in place that allowed for relatively easy settlement of those graduates. The first graduates from Cuban polytechnical institutions on returning to Ghana in the late 1980s and early 1990s found themselves caught up in the ongoing debate around polytechnical credentials. Their polytechnic diplomas, a post-school vocational qualification common in Cuba, were not recognized at the higher education level and were frequently seen by potential employers to be little more than a grade 12 qualification. When some of these graduates wanted to upgrade their education at a university, they regularly encountered situations where transfer credit was not provided for their Cuban diploma, and they had to undergo the same training as Ghanaians entering such programs directly from high school.

Ghana had only three polytechnical institutions when the Isle of Youth program started. Polytechnical credentials were not well understood in society until well into the late 1990s. In the context of an educational reform program in mid-1997, the Ghanaian authorities still grappled with accreditation procedures for Ghana's Higher National Diploma (HND) awarded by the country's polytechnics. It was conceded that there were problems placing HND graduates in the civil service and public service sector, yet they were apparently more easily recognized by private-sector organizations.[36]

In regard to professional accreditation, university graduates were better off than graduates from polytechnical institutions once they returned to Ghana. Graduates from human and veterinary medicine programs and university-level accounting programs generally encountered few challenges and received their professional designations more or less promptly after returning to Ghana. The situation was somewhat different for those who went to the Bahamas. I interviewed 10 Ghanaians who had settled in this Caribbean state after obtaining their post secondary credentials in Cuba. Graduates perceived Bahamian regulations around licensing as arbitrary and full of paradoxes: at the same time as Bahamians were sent to Cuba for post secondary (polytechnic/vocational and university) education, professional accreditation was denied to several Ghanaians with Cuban postsecondary credentials.

Regardless of whether there was a formal professional accreditation or certification process added on to the Cuban qualification, finding employment was closely linked to the recognition of Cuban credentials. Study participants reported that graduates who returned to Ghana had to complete one year of national service. Most of the graduates whom I interviewed in Ghana found adequate employment within three years after their return, and several of them found employment almost immediately when they returned. This situation must not be overemphasized or generalized, though: the majority of graduates who agreed to speak with me were university graduates, not those who completed a polytechnic certification. Although I made an attempt to include more graduates of vocational programs in my research, there was a higher reluctance by those with polytechnic credentials to speak with me. Based on circumstantial evidence, I contribute this to a number of factors: (1) lower general confidence; (2) linguistic challenges communicating effectively in English; and (3) a sense of being a "second-class" Cuban graduate with "only" a vocational certification. The majority of graduates interviewed who are now living in Ghana, regardless of whether they had experienced challenges upon their return, are now gainfully employed in positions directly related to their field of study. The overall level of professional satisfaction that I encountered in Ghana was higher than in the Bahamas. The most obvious reason for this enhanced job satisfaction is the higher incidence of graduates in Ghana working in their field of expertise, rather than in a position that is only peripherally related to the graduates' training, as is the case for a number of graduates in the Bahamas. The status of Ghanaians in the Bahamas as immigrants may also contribute to their lower professional satisfaction since they are constantly, overtly or covertly, subjected to the common discriminatory perceptions and/or practices that immigrants frequently experience in their host countries.

The difficult situation of those returning with polytechnical certifications is one of the most paradoxical aspects of the graduates' experiences with the Isle of Youth program since it was exactly the technical/vocational, mid-level professions that were the primary intention of the program. Although the designers of the program had presumably correctly analyzed Ghana's needs and structured the program accordingly, the country's employment sector does not appear to have been ready to absorb the Cuban-trained polytechnical graduates. In addition to doubts about the quality and relevance of the graduates' Cuban education, employers appear to have lacked understanding of certain professional career programs that were available in Cuba, but did not exist in Ghana at that time. Some graduates also mentioned that they had not learned how to market themselves properly in a job interview and later on, in a job. Once some graduates had established themselves in positions, they were able to create their own small networks and help their peers find employment. This is one of the reasons why clusters of graduates can be found in certain work environments.

The graduates' problems finding employment were also related to negative perceptions of their education from a country in the Socialist bloc. According to several former administrators and graduates, since the time of Ghana's independence, education in Eastern Europe had been a contentious issue, and holders of credentials from any country affiliated with the Eastern bloc suffered from the same stigma. The graduates reported having experienced discrimination based on their Cuban credentials, even though the scholarship program had been set up at the highest presidential level. By the time the majority of graduates returned from Cuba, the political climate in Ghana had changed. Governmental support in Ghana for the Isle of Youth program appears to have waned over the latter part of the 1980s and in the 1990s, particularly as far as the returning graduates were concerned. Considerable resources had been put toward the design, preparation, and administration of the program, whereas little to no attention was given to the meaningful reintegration of the graduates. The sociopolitical changes that occurred in Ghana during the 1980s are likely at least partly responsible for this situation. In 1983, Ghana received its first IMF loan for its economic recovery program that came with the condition of adherence to certain criteria formulated in Washington that had not been part of Ghana's own economic recovery measures.[37] While the Isle of Youth program was underway, the Ghanaian government's initial socialist economic orientation changed to a market-based model according to the prescriptions of the IMF's structural adjustment program (SAP). The

SAP limited the government's ability to create jobs, and thus hindered the graduates' integration into the Ghanaian job structure. At the same time, Ghana became the classical example of a postcolonial, neoliberal success story in the West.

Word traveled quickly from Ghana back to those still in Cuba, who felt discouraged by their colleagues' negative reports of the return experience. However, only a minority of graduates appeared to have initially decided not to return to Ghana because the alternatives were limited. Graduates were not permitted to remain in Cuba after the end of their study program. Once some graduates had established themselves in places such as the Bahamas, however, they encouraged others to go there, too.

One of the concerns of the program designers was the possibility that the Ghanaian students would lose their English language abilities while in Cuba. During the years on the Isle of Youth, teaching of the English language by Ghanaian teachers was supposed to prevent this from happening. When the students moved to the post secondary level, the Ghanaian teachers and administrators did not have any further control over the students' English language proficiency. The graduates reported that, upon their return from Cuba, most of them spoke Spanish better than English, which resulted in some initial problems expressing themselves in English; however, catching up with the English language was an automatic process for most returnees. Language challenges were not a major concern in the graduates' work environments. In technical/scientific fields such as engineering and in "universal" disciplines like accounting, graduates found that the technical language did not differ much between English and Spanish. Those living in the Bahamas found their fluency in Spanish useful due to the island nation's proximity to other countries where Spanish is the first language, and where several graduates were able to make use of their Spanish language skills.

On numerous occasions, graduates referred to encountering an attitude of a perceived superiority of European-derived educational programs and degrees, in particular among employers. They saw this type of bias as being directly linked to the ongoing legacy of colonial education systems as educational institutions in Sub-Saharan Africa were designed as carbon copies of metropolitan universities in Europe.[38] Tertiary institutions set up after independence largely followed the same curricula and academic practices prevalent in the former colonizers' countries. In spite of the widespread preference accorded to education systems originating in Western Europe, several African countries have found it worthwhile to collaborate with socialist countries for the strengthening and development of their own educational infrastructure and philosophies. It can be argued that education in socialist countries, precisely because it is somewhat lower-tech, may be more relevant to African countries that find themselves at the lower end of the technology spectrum. This realization seems to have slowly taken hold. During the interviews, one administrator indicated that it was now recognized in Ghana that those educated in Cuba had superior problem-solving skills and were not easily discouraged when they faced difficulties on the job. The conventional notion is that socialist countries place a lot of emphasis on the sciences and technical knowledge in their education system. This was certainly also true for the Ghana-Cuba program. However, the sophistication of technical equipment and machinery at the disposal of students was much lower than is typically the case in industrialized countries. Thus, students were forced to constantly engage in problem-solving thinking to handle technology that was outdated or tended to break down, or to substitute, if the requisite technical equipment was simply not available.

The question of whether the Ghana-Cuba program was less likely to contribute to brain drain than programs in the North, is not easy to answer; however, certain conclusions can be drawn from my research. There is a dearth of exact statistics on how many graduates live in Ghana, and how many live outside the country. A website maintained by a graduate living in the United States provides a useful tool with regard to graduates' locations. By November 9, 2008, a total of 351 graduates, or roughly 30 percent of all Ghanaians who had attended the Ghanaian school on the Isle of Youth, had registered with full name and location as members on the website. Their current location is self reported: A total of 179 members reported living in Ghana, 11 members live in other parts of Africa, 47 members live in the Caribbean region, and 114 members reside in other parts of the world, out of which 108 live in industrialized countries (primarily the United States, the UK, Canada, and Spain), with six graduates living in the Middle East, Asia, or Russia. These figures have to be treated cautiously. It is quite likely that those living in other parts of the world feel more of a need to stay connected via this medium and may thus be overrepresented among those registered through the website in relation to graduates living in Ghana. Also, graduates living and working in remote areas of Ghana frequently have little or no access to the Internet and are thus less likely to register as members.

What is clear, though, is that the Ghana-Cuba program completely lacked the "pull factor" that is currently at the core of immigration policies in many industrialized countries facing steep declines in birth rates and a rapidly aging and less productive population. Canada, for example, has recently introduced a new "Canadian Experience" immigration class that targets persons with a Canadian post secondary education as potential immigrants through a fast-tracking mechanism. Such programs allow graduates to take up permanent residence in their country of study without ever returning home. The Cuban program did not provide such an option, and the majority of graduates returned to Ghana. The program as such was designed in a way to minimize brain drain from the scholarship-receiving country. A graduate's decision to leave Ghana was more likely related to her or his experiences upon reentry into the home country and was thus related to conditions prevailing there, rather than being built into the structure of the scholarship program.

Relevance: Academic and Practical Learning in Tandem

Post revolutionary education in Cuba has been characterized by a close alignment of education with the social economy of a predominantly rural and agricultural society, in particular through a focused effort to break down barriers between academic and manual labor, rural and urban life.[39] Consequently, Cuban education emphasizes the link between academic and practical learning at all levels of the education system. The Ghana-Cuba assistance program was organized according to the same principles. At the secondary level, this link between academic and practical learning manifested in the work and study program on the Isle of Youth. At the post secondary level, all study programs had theoretical in-class components and strong applied components in laboratories or real-world settings. Furthermore, organized volunteer productive labor programs had been instituted in Cuba as part of higher education programs in the 1970s.[40]

The work and study program on the Isle of Youth was undoubtedly a novel experience for the Ghanaian students since such programs did not exist in Ghana. Students from rural areas of the country, however, were used to helping their families with work in the farms after school and on weekends. The more formal work and study program on the Isle of Youth was thus similar to what they were used to at home. For students from larger urban areas, such work was less common or unknown, and there were many complaints and resistance on the part of those students regarding the work component of their scholarship program. Looking back at that program from today's perspective, opinions ranged widely among the graduates about the program's purpose: some saw it as a healthy, fun activity, others as a nuisance that interfered to some extent with the academic part of the program since the work imposed physical demands upon them that compromised their ability to be attentive and to learn in class. A more extreme and rather isolated view was that the work program aimed to make the students indirectly pay for the costs of their education; however, this perspective was clearly not borne out by the economics of the scholarship program. In spite of the different opinions and emotions that the discussion of the work and study program evoked, the majority of graduates agreed that it contributed to their general education by providing them with the tools to cope with challenging life situations. They mentioned that the work component had instilled a sense of discipline, duty, and purpose in them, which carried over into their life as professionals many years later. The setting of the Ghanaian boarding school in Cuba's countryside and the structure of the work and study program taught the students much about the realities of life in a communal setting where work was a collaborative effort.

The work component was not just an add-on to the academic studies that the students conducted on the Isle of Youth: it formed part of the overall evaluation process and contributed to the students' position on the "order of merit," which, in turn, determined the post secondary programs available to individual students. In a modified and less formalized manner, this system has now been partially adopted by universities in the Western world that may take into consideration students' community involvement and other nonacademic factors in addition to students' grade point averages when making decisions about prospective students' admissibility.

At the post secondary level, the integration of academic and practical work occurred primarily within the post secondary curricula themselves. Voluntary work was far less frequent at that level. At certain times of the year, students participated in work organized by the students' organization, the FEU. In particular, in times of crisis, such as natural disasters, but also during the annual harvest, universities might close down, and students were asked to help out with farm work. Many universities closed down for two weeks every year, and students were expected to engage in volunteer work programs. Apart from these compulsory activities, participation in further volunteer work was up to the students' discretion.

Most graduates with whom I spoke reported a perception that their post secondary studies in Cuba had prepared them well for working in a low-tech improvisation context of the type they found upon their return to Ghana. They frequently described their study experience as "do it yourself" and "learning from scratch" to express how the applied components of their academic programs were carried out in an environment with few material resources and little advanced technology, thus constantly challenging their resourcefulness and problem-solving skills. While this was generally seen as a situation that strengthened their resolve and constantly trained them in regard to a wide variety of practical problems encountered, some graduates felt that working with very basic or outdated equipment during their formative years was potentially problematic if they were to later work with organizations or companies that had the opportunity to acquire state-of-the-art technical equipment.

Taking veterinary medicine as an example, it becomes very clear how the students' classroom learning was significantly enhanced through practical applications. Students had extensive training sessions on farms and focused on working with livestock, suitable to an agricultural society, rather than on companion animals, which is frequently the focus of veterinary studies in Western countries. All diagnostics were done manually without any advanced technical equipment. Students who were interested in companion-animal treatment were able to take courses for that purpose; however, the focus was on livestock and animal husbandry for consumption. This example shows the relevance of the Cuban practical training to the students' home-country context, thus providing a further argument for why this kind of South-South collaborative model in education may be more suitable to the development of human capability in lower-income countries than Northern countries extending such assistance. Such enhanced relevance of the training received has the potential to lower the "push factors" out of a graduate's home country, which frequently lead to outmigration if the graduate finds that the education received in the host country is not applicable in the home country's context. As the present example shows, though, relevance of one's training program alone is not sufficient: the specific training undertaken and respective credentials obtained must also be supported by the necessary infrastructure in the home country, which allows for absorption of the returning graduates.

The Cuban educational philosophy combines the concept of education's intrinsic value of human development with a utilitarian perspective that closely aligns education programming with the scientific/technical needs of society. There is a trade-off, though, between such close alignment and the ability of students to freely choose those post secondary programs in which they are most interested. This trade-off also occurred in the Cuba-Ghana scholarship program: although several graduates commented on the advantages of a tightly planned system of aligning education programs with societal needs, they also bemoaned the fact that certain study programs were not available to them since they were not seen as having significance for Ghana's development priorities. The reference here is mostly to programs in the humanities, arts, and social sciences, such as language study programs or subjects like sociology and political science. The fact that Ghanaian program designers placed the emphasis on vocational and scientific-technical fields to further Ghana's technical/industrial development is one explanation, particularly for the absence of access to programs in the humanities. Another possible explanation is the reluctance by Ghana to place students into Cuban university programs with a strong political orientation as Ghana, although sympathetic to the Cuban government, did not have a socialist or communist political and economic system.

Conclusion

In this chapter, I have discussed the experiences of a number of former students and administrators involved in a South-South educational collaboration program between Ghana and Cuba that provided full scholarships for secondary and post secondary studies and trained approximately 1,200 Ghanaians over the course of 20 years. My discussion has focussed on three main topics:

1. Ways in which the program increased access to education to socioeconomically disadvantaged groups, in particular through the combination of secondary and post secondary studies;
2. Reintegration of graduates and questions of work deployment;
3. Relevance of the Cuban educational model of combining academic and practical learning in the context of Ghana.

Although the relatively short duration of the program did not allow for the program-recruitment procedures to be fully optimized, the model used by the program designers resulted in enhanced opportunities for students from different socioeconomic backgrounds. Recruitment at the secondary schooling level was a vital strategy to combat the high attrition rates at early stages of schooling in Ghana. Reintegration into Ghanaian society, as well as integration into Bahamian society as immigrants, proved to be difficult for many graduates. In Ghana, returning graduates had to overcome challenges related to their partial adoption of a Cuban culture that clashed with the fabric of Ghanaian society. They also faced barriers relating to the perception of Western degrees being superior to degrees from Eastern bloc countries and their affiliates. Furthermore, graduates who returned with credentials that were unknown in Ghana at the time, in particular from polytechnical institutions, struggled with accreditation issues. Those graduates living in the Bahamas had to cope with the additional challenges typically experienced by immigrants, and thus had their credentials scrutinized much more closely than returnees to Ghana. The majority of graduates interviewed felt that their education "made in Cuba" had provided them with a mix of academic and practical experiences that were well suited to the careers they were now pursuing. In their own words, the need for adaptability and ingenuity that they had constantly experienced in Cuba had instilled in them a feeling of being able to cope with "anything in life". Outside of the strictly technical skills they had acquired, graduates also appreciated the general work ethic that the Cuban program had instilled in them. They mentioned, however, that they would have wished for more training to develop a general set of skills in areas like leadership and negotiation, which would have helped them with employment issues.

In a world where post secondary education is less and less regarded as a public good and is in many countries provided on a fee-for-service basis, scholarships offer the only opportunity for students from lesser privileged backgrounds to obtain a higher education. Very limited numbers of full scholarships to institutions in the Global North for students from countries of the Global South are available. This research has showed the significance of the Cuban scholarship program not only in terms of its scope, but, more importantly, as regards the horizontal and vertical integration of different levels of education. At the post secondary level, the program provided opportunities for university and polytechnic/vocational education, and in regard to vertical integration, students received scholarships at the secondary and post secondary levels. The research also points to a fundamental shortfall of many scholarship programs that potentially enhances the likelihood of brain drain. Scholarships alone—whether North-South or South-South—to low-income students in the Global South do not ensure that the human capacity thus created at the personal level will be used effectively for the development of the graduates' home countries. Nor do such scholarships ensure that returning graduates will be welcomed by their governments and by potential employers to allow for a smooth transition back into society and the world of work. It may be challenging for governments to implement scholarship policies that include a post scholarship and reintegration component, but such policies would be an immense opportunity for future South-South educational relationships to diminish some of the adverse affects associated with reintegration into one's home country after spending years studying abroad.

Notes

1. S. Lehr, 2008.
2. A. Hickling-Hudson, 2000.
3. J. Herbst, 1993; P. Nugent, 1996.
4. Nugent, 1996.
5. Ghana Country Studies.
6. J. A. Dadson,1983a; J. A. Dadson, 1983b.
7. Dadson, 1983b.
8. Dadson, 1983a.
9. M. Carnoy and J. Samoff, 1990.
10. A. Perry, 1983.
11. The concept of "schools in the countryside" became a significant component of the Cuban education system after 1970. Prior to that, students from the cities went for about seven weeks every year to the countryside to break down the barriers between urban and rural life, a concept known as "schools to the countryside." The "schools in the countryside," on the contrary, were boarding schools for students of grades 7–10,, which combined work and study on a year-round basis (Carnoy and Samoff, 1990).
12. S. Sackey, April 19, 2008.
13. G. E. Curtis, 1992.
14. Sackey, April 19, 2008.
15. B. Jalowiecki and G. J. Gorzelakm 2004.
16. S. Robertson, 2006.
17. J. Buchan and J. Sochalski, 2004; A. Roisin, 2004; D. Teferra, 2005.
18. M. M. Gandhi, 2000; T. Lakshmanasamy, 2000; UNESCO, 1998.
19. E. Schofer and J. W. Meyer, 2005.
20. A. W. Little, 1999.
21. As cited in T. Manuh, S. Gariba, and J. Budu, 2007.
22. A. Abdenur, 2002.
23. United Nations Development Programme, 2004.
24. B. Chilisa, 2005.
25. L. Tikly, 2004.
26. J. Samoff and B. Carrol, 2003.
27. P. Kallaway, 2001.
28. S. Federici and G. Caffentzis, 2004.
29. N'Dri T. Assié-Lumumba, 2000.
30. S. Y., Cisse, 1986.
31. Ibid.
32. Lehr, 2008.
33. Manuh, Gariba, and Budu, 2007.
34. J. Anarfi 2003.
35. J. K. Anarfi, S.O. Kwankye, and C. Ahiadeke, 2005.
36. "Council on Tertiary Education Throws More Light on HND Programme," *Ghanaweb*, 1997.
37. N. K. Bentsi-Enchill, 1984.
38. K. L. Nkulu, 2005.
39. M. Richmond, 1990.
40. R. G. Paulston, 1991.

References

Abdenur, A. "Tilting the North-South Axis: The Legitimization of Southern Development Knowledge and its Implications for Comparative Education Research." *Current Issues in Comparative Education* 4, no.2 (2002): 57–69.

Anarfi, J., Kwankye, S., Ababio, O.-M., and Tiemoko, R. *Migration from and to Ghana: A Background Paper (Working Paper C4)*. Brighton, UK: University of Sussex, Development Research Centre on Migration, Globalisation and Poverty, 2003.

Anarfi, J. K., Kwankye, S. O., and Ahiadeke, C. "Migration, Return and Impact in Ghana: A Comparative Study of Skilled and Unskilled Transnational Migrants." In *At Home in the World? International Migration and Development in Contemporary Ghana and West Africa*. Edited by T. Mnuh, 204–226. Accra, Ghana: Sub-Saharan Publishers, 2005.

Assié-Lumumba, N'Dri T. "Educational and Economic Reforms, Gender Equity, and Access to Schooling in Africa." *Comparative Sociology* 41, no.1 (2000): 89–120.

Bentsi-Enchill, N. K. "A Testing Year for Ghana." *West Africa* 3465 (1984): 107–108.

Buchan, J. and Sochalski, J. "The Migration of Nurses: Trends and Policies." *Bulletin of the World Health Organization* 82, no.8 (2004): 587–594.

Carnoy, M. and Samoff, J. *Education and Social Transition in the Third World*. Princeton, NJ: Princeton University Press, 1990.

Chilisa, B. "Educational Research within Postcolonial Africa: A Critique of HIV/AIDS Research in Botswana." *International Journal of Qualitative Studies in Education* 18, no.6 (2005): 659–684.

Cisse, S. Y. *Education in Africa in Light of the Harare Conference*. Paris, France: UNESCO, 1986.

"Council on Tertiary Education Throws More Light on HND Programme," *Ghanaweb*, July 12, 1997, accessed January 7, 2008, http://www.ghanaweb.com/GhanaHomePage/NewsArchive/artikel.php?ID=1286

Curtis, G. E., ed. *The Council for Mutual Economic Assistance*. Federal Research Division, Library of Congress, 1992. http://www.shsu.edu/~his_ncp/CMEA.html.

Dadson, J. A. "Food and the Nation." *West Africa* 3439 (1983a): 1596–1597.

Dadson, J. A. "Food and the Nation—2." *West Africa* 3440 (1983b): 1659–1660.

Federici, S. and Caffentzis, G. "Globalization and Professionalization in Africa." *Social Text* 22, no.2 (2004): 81–99.

Gandhi, M. M. "Equality and Excellence: Socio-Economic Perspective of Higher Education for Human Development." In *Higher Education for Human Development: Papers Presented at the International Conference on Higher Education for Human Development, held at New Delhi on February 22-24, 2000*. Edited by K. B. Powar, 141–165. New Delhi, India: Association of Indian Universities, 2000

Ghana Country Studies, Other Countries. Country Studies. http://www.country-studies.com/ghana/other-countries.html.

Herbst, J. *The Politics of Reform in Ghana, 1982–1991*. Berkeley: University of California Press, 1993. http://publishing.cdlib.org/ucpressebooks/view?docId=ft2199n7n7&chunk.id=d0e643&toc.depth=1&toc.id=d0e643&brand=ucpress.

Hickling-Hudson, A. "The Cuban University and Educational Outreach: Cuba's Contribution to Post-Colonial Development." In *Local Knowledge and Wisdom in Higher Education*. Edited by G. R. Teasdale and Z. Ma Rhea, 187–207. New York: Pergamon, 2000.

Jalowiecki, B. and Gorzelak, G. J. "Brain Drain, Brain Gain, and Mobility: Theories and Prospective Methods." *Higher Education in Europe* 29, no.3 (2004): 299–308.

Kallaway, P. "The Need for Attention to the Issue of Rural Education." *International Journal of Educational Development* 21, no.1 (2001): 21–32.

Lakshmanasamy, T. "Education and Economic Growth in a Knowledge Based Economy." In *Higher Education for Human Development: Papers Presented at the International Conference on Higher Education for Human Development, held at New Delhi on February 22-24, 2000.* Edited by K. B. Powar, 166–181. New Delhi, India: Association of Indian Universities, 2000.

Lehr, S. "The Children of the Isle of Youth: Impact of a Cuban South-South Education Program on Ghanaian Graduates." PhD diss., University of Victoria, British Columbia, Canada, 2008.

Little, A. W. "Development and Education: Cultural and Economic Analysis." In *Education, Cultures, and Economics: Dilemmas for Development.* Edited by F. E. Leach and A. W. Little, 3–32. New York: Falmer Press, 1999.

Manuh, T., Gariba, S., and Budu, J. *Change and Transformation in Ghana's Publicly Funded Universities.* Accra, Ghana: Woeli, 2007.

Nkulu, K. L. *Serving the Common Good: A Postcolonial African Perspective on Higher Education.* New York: Peter Lang, 2005.

Nugent, P. *Big Men, Small Boys and Politics in Ghana: Power, Ideology and the Burden of History, 1982-1994.* Accra, Ghana: Asempa, 1996.

Paulston, R. G. "Cuba." In *International Higher Education: An Encyclopedia.* Edited by P. Altbach, 931–942. New York: Garland Publishing, 1991.

Perry, A. "The Cost of Foreign Study." *West Africa* 3448 (1983): 2127–2129.

Richmond, M. "The Cuban Educational Model and Its Influence in the Caribbean Region." In *Education in Central America and the Caribbean.* Edited by C. Brock and D. Clarkson, 63–99. London: Routledge, 1990.

Robertson, S. "Brain Drain, Brain Gain and Brain Circulation." *Globalisation, Societies and Education* 4, no.1 (2006): 1–5.

Roisin, A. "The Brain Drain: Challenges and Opportunities for Development." *UN Chronicle,* 4 (2004): 51–52 and 57.

Sackey, S. "Cuba Gives 200 Medical Brigade." *Modern Ghana News.* April 19, 2008. http://www.modernghana.com/print/163124/1/cuba-gives-200-medical-brigade.html (accessed January 10, 2009).

Samoff, J. and Carrol, B. "Continuities and Dependence: External Support to Higher Education in Africa." Paper presented at the Annual Meeting of the Comparative and International Studies Association, New Orleans, LA, March 2003, 1–62.

Schofer, E. and Meyer, J. W. "The Worldwide Expansion of Higher Education in the Twentieth Century." *American Sociological Review* 70, no.6 (2005): 898–920.

Teferra, D. "Brain Circulation: Unparalleled Opportunities, Underlying Challenges, and Outmoded Presumptions." *Journal of Studies in International Education* 9, no.3 (2005): 229–250.

Tikly, L. "Education and the New Imperialism." *Comparative Education* 40, no.2 (2004): 173–198.

United Nations Development Programme. *Forging a Global South: United Nations Day for South-South Cooperation.* New York: Author, 2004. http://ssc.undp.org/unssc_uploads/Other_documents/Forging_a_Global_South.pdf

United Nations Educational, Scientific and Cultural Organization. *World Conference on Higher Education. Higher Education in the Twenty-First Century: Vision and Action.* Paris: Author, 1998.

6

Studying in Cuba, Returning Home to Work: Experiences of Graduates from the English-Speaking Caribbean[1]

Anne Hickling-Hudson

Introduction and Background

Cuba's higher education scholarship program has received little attention in the literature on education and development. In this chapter, I discuss themes that emerge from my interviews with graduates from English-speaking Caribbean countries who studied in Cuba, as well as Cuban educators, on the nature of their academic programs and their subsequent careers. This facilitates exploration of a number of questions, including the following:

1. How, in the perceptions of scholarship students and graduates, have they experienced the philosophy of combining study, practical work, and research in the tertiary education curriculum in Cuban universities?
2. What impact does studying in Cuba appear to have on graduates after they return to their home countries?
3. How does the experience of the graduates throw light on the relationship between tertiary education and national development?

My research on Cuban university education arose from my experience as an educator in Grenada during two years of its 1979–1983 revolution.[2] The People's Revolutionary Government of Grenada accepted an offer of educational assistance from the Cuban government, and negotiated some 350 university and polytechnic scholarships, as well as assistance from Cuban educators to help improve secondary school teaching in mathematics, science, Spanish, and sports. I was on the team that annually renewed negotiations for this assistance, and realized how important this kind of help was in a country that had very little access to higher education. With a small population of just under 100,000, Grenada received only about five scholarships a year to the University of the West Indies, as well as some private financing of overseas university education; therefore, it had few graduates in any field.

As a graduate of British-derived universities in Commonwealth countries (the West Indies, Hong Kong, and Australia), I knew little about the type of education offered in Cuba. I wanted to find out how university education was influenced by a socialist paradigm of educational organization, and to seek to understand the cultural and political implications for the Caribbean of the Cuban style of university and Cuba's scholarship program. On two visits to Cuba, in 1993 and 1996, I interviewed 12 undergraduates from the English-speaking Caribbean who were studying there, as well as seven university professors and officials in charge of higher education. In 1996, traveling on a Rockefeller Fellowship to Guyana, Grenada, St. Lucia, and Jamaica, I interviewed 20 graduates who had been educated at Cuban universities in a wide range of fields. Since then, on several visits to the region during the 2000s, I have interviewed other scholarship students in Cuba and graduates in the Caribbean about the impact of the scholarship program. This chapter sets out some of my findings. The interviews with graduates provide an introductory picture of the nature of education offered in Cuban universities and the use made of it by graduates or returning to their home countries. The small numbers interviewed do not permit broad generalizations to be drawn, but do provide a picture of aspects of the undergraduate experience, and suggest trends and patterns for further research. The chapter concludes by considering the significance for Caribbean countries of continuing higher education links with Cuba in a regional quest for sustainable social and economic development, and by summarizing the importance of qualitative comparative research in higher education.

The Cuban Higher Education Scholarships

Chapters 1 and 4 of this book provide information on the Cuban higher education scholarships that for 50 years have educated some 31,000 young adults from scores of countries as university professionals, and over 23,000 as skilled workers with middle-level technical qualifications. It was noted that in the early 1990s, with Cuba's economic difficulties, the numbers of scholarships were drastically reduced. By the mid-1990s, overseas students were coming to Cuba from 85 countries (mainly in Africa and Latin America) compared to the 114 countries from which students came in the heyday of the scholarships. Yet, in the 1995–96 academic year, there were still some 3000 overseas undergraduates and a further 200 postgraduates, and the numbers of students rose again at the turn of the century. In the latter part of the 1990s, a modest charge of fees for selected programs for about 10 percent of overseas university students accompanied the reduction in scholarships. Some overseas students were now able to enter fee-paying degree programs in the field of health (medicine, dentistry, radiography, etc.), but other degree programs were still paid for by the Cuban government. Fees were being charged for postgraduate scholarships, US$1,000 a year if the overseas student had a Cuban degree, US$3,000 if the degree was from elsewhere (Interview at Ministry of Higher Education, 2000). In the mid-1990s, Cuba was offering English-speaking Caribbean countries about 25 university scholarships a year. Instead of negotiating bilaterally with the government of each country, the Cuban government works through the Caribbean Community (CARICOM), the Caribbean trade and political association.

The Cuban Degree: Study, Work, and Research

Cuban universities have played an important role in helping to reshape worker identity along lines consistent with revolutionary ideals, and to promote a type of cultural nationalism that seeks to end the traditional large disparities between wealth and poverty. The formal and informal curriculum promoted the practice of internationalism and challenges to imperialism. Socialist thought influenced these reworkings. Cuba's universities were developed to counter what revolutionary ideology analyzed as the problems of colonial capitalist education, particularly its elitism, imitativeness, and insufficiently practical orientation. Besides contributing to the expansion of access to tertiary education, an important impact of the Cuban scholarships on the Caribbean region is that they have demonstrated a model of university education different from that inherited from Britain, France, and the Netherlands by previously colonized countries. Based on my current research, and subject to future more detailed comparative research, it appears that the most innovative feature of Cuban higher education is the way in which it integrates study, work placements, and research in university programs that are deliberately oriented to the perceived needs of the society. This section will examine the graduates' experience of the "study, work and research" approach as an induction into a professional field.

As has been described in previous chapters, the three pillars of *Académico, Laboral e Investigación*—academic study, labor, and research—are the foundation of higher education in Cuba. Most degree courses are five-years in length, ending with a research component (medicine takes longer). In the first and second years, students concentrate mainly on the academic aspect of the program. In the third and fourth year they integrate theoretical studies with "labor" (practical work in an industry or profession), and in the fourth and fifth year they write a research thesis that combines all three aspects. Labor of a different sort, that is, non academic manual work, is also expected of students for two weeks each year. Overseas students are told that, for them, this is on a voluntary basis. This usually takes the form of assisting with food production, sometimes for student meals, in the fields or in the university kitchens, and sometimes in the general agricultural harvest.

My interviews with Cuban-educated graduates working in four Caribbean countries gave me an insight into the kind of study and research they had completed for their degrees, and how this prepared them for working as Caribbean professionals. This picture is vividly painted by the graduates themselves in selections from interview transcripts (all graduates are given fictional names to preserve privacy). Their information is categorized to draw attention to two aspects, the first looking at the nature of the degree (subjects and work-study), and the second at the type of research projects embedded in the degree.

The subjects studied in a degree were both broad-ranging and specialist. During the first year, the Spanish language was studied intensively, and foundation studies in the student's chosen discipline were introduced in the language. David, an agronomist and agricultural officer working in Grenada's Ministry of Agriculture, explained that the first year of Spanish and preparatory studies oriented him toward the rest of the degree by introducing the scientific terminology that he would require to study agronomy in Cuba. He said that the first year experience

> made it evident to us that you had to do disciplined study. One of the key strategies was frequent consultation with the teacher and regular evaluation to monitor progress, a strategy that helped me later when I became a teacher in a Grenadian high school.

Subjects were combined with annual work placements that introduced students to every aspect of the job, including the manual work that in many other countries is likely to be regarded as unsuitable for university students. This was particularly noticeable in the information I received from engineers. In the first year of studies, the students were placed in work projects for a month. Each year this time increased, until in the fourth year the work project lasted for three months. These placements, supervised by professionals approved by the university, provided experience in the practical side of production at factories, farms, or some enterprise.

The level of work increased in complexity each year. Christopher, a civil engineer in Grenada, described how

> in the first and second year we worked like labourers for three months, off loading cement trucks, mixing cement on a construction site and so on. In the third and fourth year we worked as engineering technicians, in an office along with other technicians. We attended all the site meetings. In the final year we worked as engineers, strictly on problem solving. In that year we did our research project along with our coursework.

Carlyle, an agricultural engineer from St. Lucia who studied irrigation and drainage, soil and water conservation, hydrology and meteorology, agricultural mechanization, and agronomy, explained:

> In the first year you did general tasks on the farm. In the second year you did a specific task such as working on a mechanical task supervised by an engineer. As you go through those programs you begin to identify problem areas in production which you start thinking about for your final thesis ....In years 3 to 5, the subjects become more applied. We studied the use of machines, the agricultural economy of managing those machines, the design of a farm development plan with respect to mechanization of irrigation systems. These are the areas in which you are expected to participate when you start work. In years 4 and 5 you also did some project management, project cycles etc. Work on your thesis intensifies in year 4, because by the start of the 2nd semester of year 5, you should have finished it.

David, the Grenadian agronomist who studied at ISCAH, the Higher Institute of Agricultural Sciences near Havana, related how his understanding of the relevance of pure science subjects to agriculture developed through his annual work placements on farms. He was puzzled, at first, that in agronomy, which is "...the study of crops and things related to them, like soils, climate, plant diseases and pest control," students were given a thorough grounding in the pure sciences—mathematics; physics; organic, general, and inorganic chemistry; biostatistics, and calculus. It was not that he had a negative attitude to science. In fact, he said, he loved science and mathematics, but

> didn't understand why the subjects we were learning were so vital to agriculture. My understanding of that developed through practical work. We did this on farms and cooperatives, and it became clear why the sciences were so necessary to caring for crops and soils. For example, it was a basis for studying soil chemistry and fertilizers—why too many sulphates make soils acidic. And it helped you to explain things like fertilizers and pest control to people. At the end of the first semester we spent a month doing practical work on a farm. In later semesters we could spend from two to four months on farms. During the term, we also visited farms regularly to study each crop individually, like sugar cane, or some which fell within a group, such as legumes, vegetables, roots and tubers such as dasheen and cassava, and fruit including pineapple, citrus, mango and avocado.

The variety of work and research projects during the degree appeared to give students a wide overview of and insights into their professional field. For example, Cynthia, a Guyanese veterinarian who works in Georgetown as an animal health officer in government-controlled wildlife exports, said that by the third year, after two years of study of the basic sciences, chemistry, mathematics, biochemistry, anatomy, and microbiology,

> we got deeper into the courses that a vet needs such as [the study of] animal disease. We studied pathology, preventative medicine, poultry, cattle, horses,

pigs, sheep, goats, bees, rabbits. We also did pharmacology for treatment, physiology, physiopathology, animal rearing (nutrition, conditions, cases), and surgery. At the end of each year a group of students would be placed on a farm and work there. You would feed animals, milk them, dip for ticks, vaccinate them and so on. Sometimes you would live on the farm ....The university has its own farm, and this would serve for practicals during the year. A research centre was nearby where ISCAH students went to do work. After five years you graduated as a doctor of veterinary medicine. After that you could do postgraduate work. An undergraduate thesis had to be done in a specific area. Mine was on lymphatic diseases, and the case study was mice.

Anna, a Jamaican, studied modern languages (French studies) in Havana and then worked in Jamaica as a teacher, a translator and interpreter, and a businesswoman. As a student she did her work placements in libraries and as a translator at Radio Havana at the news desk. Her final examinations included a lot of oral work. For example, she wrote a chapter in French on the Algerian Revolution and presented it orally. The students were examined in instantaneous translation: "I was put in a booth and was asked to do an instantaneous translation. It was taped, and the tape was submitted for the exam." All her subjects except social science were done entirely in French: "In translating, I went from French to Spanish or Spanish to French. So when I came home, I could think of the phrase in Spanish or French before I got it in English. Now I can switch to anyone of them. I'm trilingual."

Another linguist, James, from Grenada, studied Spanish in a degree course at a pedagogical university. This was organized differently from Anna's French degree in a humanities faculty. All of James's practical work was done in schools, with a placement during each year of the degree. He specialized in methods of teaching Spanish, both to foreigners and to native Spanish speakers, and his teaching practice was assessed in both of these settings. The linguistics strand introduced students to the linguistics that related particularly to Romance languages—French, Portuguese, and Italian—showing their similarities and differences to Spanish. "We studied Latin for one and a half years—there was an emphasis on how it formed the root of Romance languages. We had to be able to translate competently from Latin to Spanish and vice versa." The literature strand gave students an overview of the literatures of several nations including Spain, France, Italy, and China. The course used selected books to illustrate changes in stylistic approaches in the context of the cultural history, the art, architecture, and sculpture that related to geographical areas and historical periods. For his specialization in the literatures of Spain and Latin America, James studied poetry, plays, and novels in their historical settings.

Two of the graduates working in Jamaica in health fields, physical culture, and general medicine, gave some insight into the importance accorded to the study and development of community health. Laurence said that the degree course in physical culture that he did was much broader than the physical education for teachers that people outside of Cuba assumed his training to be. The focus of physical culture was on the health and fitness of different generations in the community, and of women and men. His research project investigated how a certain course of physical education influenced the motor skills of children of different age groups. Peter, a doctor, provided this vivid image of how his internship in a rural community taught him to work with the community not just as a doctor, but as a participating member who thereby got to know the families and their health patterns:

> As medical interns, each of us was sent into an agricultural area in the countryside to be the doctor in charge. You are assigned a nurse and some medicines. The whole population of that community is your responsibility for three months. You treat them, send them to hospital if necessary. You have to integrate yourself into the community. You visit their homes, ask about their health, sometimes even go into the fields and help them reap the harvest. Those are the sorts of initiatives you have to take to win the confidence of the people. At the end of the three months, people in the community plus the nurse and the head of the region, evaluate your medical service, and this evaluation is a part of your final grade.

From the descriptions by graduates of their research fields (all within their first degree except for Matthew's research, which was for a PhD in medicine), it appears that the research projects focused on intellectually challenging problems directly related to a professional field of work important to the improvement of the national economy, or of social welfare. Some of the research was organized as joint projects, with each student or group of students studying a different aspect of a single problem. Research was supervised by one or more professors who specialized in the field. Christopher, the Grenadian civil engineer, said that his research project was to work in a team of students designing composite beams of concrete and steel to build columns used in high-rise buildings. Each student researched a different aspect of the project. Christopher went on to do an engineering masters degree in Canada, and worked there for two years afterward. He said that group research in Cuba into different aspects of one project in his undergraduate degree was an approach similar to what was undertaken in the program for the master of applied science that he did in Canada, at Nova Scotia Technical University.

Edward, an energy engineer, chose his specialization with an eye to what he felt was urgently needed in St. Lucia, his home country. He did projects using water to generate electricity, emphasizing small-scale hydroelectricity. His main research project was on computer applications in power systems. Carlyle, the agricultural engineer from St. Lucia, started work on his thesis during his third year of studies:

> By then I had sufficient theoretical foundation to start developing a literature review and formulating research plans for my thesis. My topic was the

design of harvesting equipment for citrus. The Cubans had three different kinds of equipment for citrus. We compared these and worked on designing the optimum parameters. The general area of harvesting machines was the responsibility of the professor with that specialisation—he had different students working on different projects. In my project, I studied the research done so far on harvesting machines in Cuba, the US, Israel and other countries, saw how these compared, and from that base worked out an optimum design. Production systems are much larger in these countries than here. But my topic was useful in that it helped me to consider appropriate technology for small harvesting here.

Marie, an economics graduate who studied both in Cuba and in Britain and who is now a leader in national planning in St. Lucia, felt that Cuban university education "as opposed to an education elsewhere" had the advantage of giving students a grounding suitable for tackling the problems of a developing country:

I did my degree in economics. In my first year for our work project we went to a sugar factory and did an inventory. In the second year we went to another factory and learnt how to cost products. In the third year we learnt how to break down a five-year plan into one-year plans. In 1983, we went back to Grenada with our professors to help prepare Grenada's first five-year development plan. I worked on tourism, others worked on all the various economic sectors. This was our research project for our degree. Because of this education, I feel that I have a much more thorough understanding of development than UWI economics graduates.

Sometimes the students made use of libraries or centers outside of Cuba to extend research, as did Thomas, an economist working in the finance ministry in Grenada, and Matthew, a Guyanese medical specialist. Taking a degree in economics and policy planning, Thomas also did two subsidiary courses in industrial investment appraisal and in pedagogy. He felt that students' experience of workplace projects and research that contributed to the field increased their desire and will to contribute to national development. His research thesis was on the impact of trade on development in the English-speaking Caribbean:

I carried out the research when I came home each summer to see my wife. I liaised with the Ministry of Finance for my thesis materials. In Havana I did some of the research at the *Centro Estudios de América* (CEA). There was a lot of material there on Grenada and Jamaica. Cuba has a very good library, the José Martí Library, which helped me a lot. I also did some of my research at the University of the West Indies in Mona, liaising with the Consortium Graduate School of Social Sciences.

Matthew, a specialist in ophthalmology, is Guyana's first indigenous Amerindian doctor. He spent ten years studying in Cuba, six years training in medicine, and did a four-year research degree in ophthalmology, traveling back to Guyana for several vacation periods. This enabled him to obtain material in Guyana that not only helped with his research on the frequency and treatment of eye disease in specific social groups, but also to share this with Cuban colleagues:

> My thesis was on fundoscopic alterations in myopic patients. This includes a category of patients where the myopic disorder becomes a disease and could lead to blindness. I looked at the frequency of the disease in groups according to age group and gender, also according to occupation and health, and developed recommendations as to how they could improve eye health. My access to the literature in English was very helpful. I accessed journals when I came back to Guyana, and was able to share this with colleagues in Cuba. A related finding from my research was fundoscopic alterations in AIDS patients. Some cases are treatable (for example, virus infections, diabetic complications), others not (atrophic). Part of my research focus was on the treatment.

The interviews with these graduates illustrated that a characteristic feature of the Cuban degree is that of providing students with experiential knowledge of how their special area of study relates to rural or urban communities, or to a particular industrial, agricultural, or service enterprise. In an interview with lecturers, I was told that the academic system "aims to improve our social and cultural environment and improve interaction between farmers, workers and professionals." Practical work familiarizes students with the kinds of places where they may be asked to work in the future. "Psychologists will work in hospitals, schools and factories, foreign language students in tourism, teaching, interpretation and translation, economics students in banks, tourism, services, accounts, finances—any section of an institution with an economic aspect" (Interview: Universidad Central de las Villas, 1993). Another feature of the degree is the demanding nature of the research project, which springs from the students' work placements and is oriented toward investigating and proposing solutions for problems in the particular industry, enterprise, or community. The systematic integration of study, work, and research in the degree helps to induct students into their professional fields.

Returning Home to Work

The graduates I interviewed were all working in influential professional positions vital to the socioeconomic development of their home countries. Doctors, economists, engineers, agronomists, veterinarians, linguists, teachers, and one businesswoman, all spoke of how they perceived their education and experiences in Cuba as having prepared them for these professions. This suggests answers to the question of how far the qualifications, skills, knowledge, and values acquired by students in studies abroad were likely to contribute to national development, particularly in the aspect of serving the poor majorities in their countries. Having encountered the fears and prejudices of some bureaucrats and employers about the presence of Marxist ideology in their training, some, such as Christopher (a civil engineer in Grenada) and Carlyle (an agricultural engineer in St. Lucia), stressed the role of philosophy and political economy classes in developing their awareness of current affairs and a "grass-roots" orientation. In Carlyle's view:

> A Cuban graduate has been trained in how to deliver professional service within a framework of nationalism and patriotism. Cuba has trained thousands of foreigners and the world isn't turning Marxist because of this. If you are level headed, you can't be brainwashed. Our discussion in political economy classes was an open forum. Like with any other subject, you do what you had to do to pass it.
>
> You don't have to study in Cuba to develop patriotic consciousness, but the Cuban system deliberately trained you to be a patriotic intellectual.... You never see yourself as just a doctor or an engineer, but as a fortunate person whose education was supported by the masses, so you get an orientation to serve. It's a more all-round education: it neutralises the drive that intellectuals have to be the elite, because in Cuban universities they absorb a working-class philosophy, important as a broad guideline.

Donovan, a veterinarian in Grenada, felt that veterinary training in Cuba appropriately emphasized the care of animals for food production rather than the care of small animals as pets. Veterinary students were trained to run production units, on dairy farms, beef farms, and poultry farms, and to practice animal care and preventative medicine "not in a vacuum, but for the goal of increased production." He felt that Grenada should be producing more of its own food animals instead of relying so heavily on imports, including "beef that's four years old from England." Two of the doctors interviewed, Peter and Matthew, showed a particularly strong commitment to community work. Peter, the Jamaican doctor with vivid memories of his internship in rural Cuba, talks of how he was able to transfer the skills he learnt to working in a unique way with Jamaican rural communities, where doctors are notoriously scarce:

> As soon as I came back to Jamaica I transferred the skills I learnt as a medical intern in a rural community. I set up my practice in Linstead's agricultural belt and in Riversdale, and climbed hills and rode donkeys to talk with people about public health. My clientele stretches far and wide—from grandmother to grandpickney.

Matthew, a chief medical officer and the only ophthalmologist in public hospital practice in Guyana, set up a national eye-care program. He spoke of his regular travels into the remote forest-dwelling Amerindian communities to provide eye care that would not otherwise be available, and lectures part-time at the University of Guyana. He estimated that Guyana needed at that time (the late 1990s) at least four more ophthalmologists in public health work. Because of Guyana's low-income base, it would be very difficult for the country to obtain the ten-year training program needed for each of them unless it could rely on the sort of scholarship provided to Matthew by the Cuban government.

On her return to Jamaica, Anna, the Jamaican linguist, worked for some years both in public and private sector educational institutions, teaching, translating, and interpreting. After doing a masters degree in business training in New York, she returned home and set up a collaborative business with a community orientation. James, the Grenadian who took his Cuban degree in Spanish with education, was employed in the Division of Arts and Sciences at the Grenada National College as a lecturer in Spanish studies preparing pre-university students for the British Advanced Level GCE examination in Spanish. James's description of his teaching methods revealed him to be an outstanding teacher, with his students getting excellent results—nearly 100 percent passes and several distinctions in their Cambridge Advanced Level examinations. James was involved in many voluntary professional activities outside of teaching, such as textbook evaluation, interpreting, and in the leadership of professional associations. David, the Grenadian agronomist, spent a few years teaching agriculture to students doing the school-leaving CXC (Caribbean Examinations Council) agriculture course at a high school, his students also gaining unprecedentedly good examination results. He left teaching to work in the Ministry of Agriculture, and used his knowledge of agronomy to develop expertise as a government adviser in horticulture, one of the economic growth areas in the Caribbean.

To summarize, the graduates felt that their Cuban education had deliberately trained them to be a certain kind of professional, one who is oriented toward finding out the needs of people or of industries in a particular field, and gearing his or her career toward meeting these needs. Especially striking was the Jamaican doctor who made it his business to penetrate deep rural areas, sometimes in peasant mode on the back of a donkey or on foot, to talk with people about public health. The closeness of study with work placements geared the graduates toward thinking about what their own countries could do to increase the production of food, non-traditional crops, or goods and services. The two Cuban-trained linguists were striking for the variety of linguistic fields to which they applied their skills, spanning teaching, interpreting, training students to interpret, helping with teacher training, and a community-oriented business consultancy.

"When You Do Things as Differently as the Cubans Do ...."

In 2008, on a visit to Jamaica, my homeland, I interviewed a Jamaican medical student who was in his final year of a medical degree at a university in southern Cuba. Though not yet a graduate, his reflections on his studies and his career aims endorsed the information that had been given to me by my interviewees more than a decade previously. Donovan spoke of the significance of the Cuban public health system, and of his intention to work as a doctor in a rural area of Jamaica where there was desperate need for medical professionals. He described how he valued the political knowledge and global contacts he had gained in Cuba, and his acquisition of Spanish. I include extracts from my interview with him:

> Before going to Cuba, I never used to think about the Latin American countries, even though we live in this region. Now I'm deeply interested in them and my Spanish allows me to follow events there. Cuba is a very political place. You learn a lot about world politics. Foreign students start their program with a first year which teaches them Spanish, prepares them for their specialist university subject, and gives a class in political economy and philosophy which gives you a context for understanding global events. During your university studies, they encourage you to go to events like rallies and celebrations, even though as a foreign student you don't have to. And many classes start with talking about current affairs and what's happening globally.
>
> In the medical degree, you get a lot of practical experience. From the third year they encourage you to work with a specialist to help care for the patients, and that specialist gives you the chance to do a lot of supervised work. The specialist also does a lot of general medicine. They work in a very different way from the system in Jamaica, which is still very influenced by the British and US system of medicine. Jamaican doctors are somewhat dependent on them and our routines are similar to theirs.
>
> Cuba is confident in the unique medical system they have developed. They emphasise community medicine and this is based on a lot of research, for example, risk factor analysis. In every community there's a doctor responsible for every 200 people. The doctors and other health professionals study the health profile of this group, so they know how many are hypertensive, pregnant, or with other health issues. The doctor must see patients with a health condition at least four times a year: twice in the patient's home and twice in the clinic. They can get into trouble if they can't show that they have given this level of health care. Patients are encouraged to come to the doctor and tell them that their blood pressure is up, or whatever. Pregnant women are given special care, and Cuba has one of the lowest rates in the world of infant mortality—5 per thousand live births, compared to 20 per thousand in Jamaica; you can check the exact figures on the WHO web site.
>
> There are lots of group activities through the CDRs (Committees for the Defence of the Revolution), and doctors sometimes use these events to come and talk to people about health, prevention of infectious diseases etc.... When you do things as differently as the Cubans do, you have to be confident about it. They can show the success of their method by their health results.
>
> When I come back to Jamaica as a qualified doctor, I will be required to do my first four months at the Kingston Public Hospital. After that, I would prefer to go to work as a doctor in the Manchester/Clarendon area where I come from. I think there are big health care needs in the rural areas, and my training in Cuba has prepared me to deal with them. Many doctors prefer to work in the

city, and yes, there are urgent needs there too, but I studied in Guantánamo, a rural province, and I want to go back to help in my rural area.

Before I studied in Cuba, the only countries that I used to be interested in were Jamaica, the USA and the UK. They were the world to me. But Cuba opened my eyes to the rest of the world. I met so many students from all over the world there, even some from places which I had no knowledge of, like Mongolia and Bhutan. Studying in Cuba opens your mind and you see the US and UK in context and realize how many other countries you can engage with.

Higher Education and Development

Caribbean countries, like all new nations, must tackle this question: from the point of view of national planning and development strategies, how much should the state invest in providing for education at school, post-school, and tertiary levels? The strategy has usually been to limit state support for higher education so that more resources can be spent on improving the foundations of education—schooling and middle-level technical education. Can nations make the sophisticated response necessary to improve both education and the economy, without a huge increase in the numbers and proportion of people with higher education? The answer is not necessarily evident, since some countries, including Barbados, Trinidad-Tobago, and the Bahamas, have greater per capita incomes than Cuba although their systems of higher education are much less developed. On the other hand, most other Caribbean nations with their underdeveloped higher education systems have lower per capita incomes than Cuba.

The Cuban experience is interesting in that it enables us to reflect on the connection of highly educated professionals with development or the lack of it. Cuba saw the socialist path as its way of challenging and countering the negatives of dependent capitalism. However, the kinds of arguments outlined by Rosset and Benjamin (1994)[3] and Rosset (1996)[4] suggest that aspects of Cuba's development were constrained by the model of dependent socialism. The intrinsic economic limitations of this model, as well as the extrinsic problems caused by the US embargo, mean that many aspects of the economy did not develop in a healthy way. For example, although Cuba achieved

> rapid modernization and a high degree of social equity and welfare, (it) never achieved truly independent development...as much as 57 percent of the total calories consumed by the population were imported prior to 1989. Cuban agriculture was based on large-scale, capital-intensive monoculture...a model showing signs of strain everywhere...as soil erosion and pesticide resistance lead to rising costs, and stagnant and falling yields.[5]

The collapse of Cuba's Eastern bloc support brought out the postcolonial contradictions of Cuba's faith in a model that made it as dependent on external support as is the dependent capitalist Caribbean. The resulting immense economic crisis for Cuba was the sudden loss of 80 percent of its financial aid and trade, and concomitant hardships for the population. Some Cuban agricultural scientists and ministry officials interviewed by Rosset and Benjamin expressed resentment toward Eastern European advisers who were responsible for this model of technology transfer to Cuba: "They criticised themselves for having had a 'colonized mentality' that accepted a model that promoted extreme dependency and external vulnerability."[6]

The "alternative model" that Cuba decided to adopt because of the crisis of the 1990s was one that has been advocated since the early 1980s by the nation's research scientists. It promotes crop diversity rather than monoculture, organic fertilizers instead of chemical ones, and biological pest control instead of synthetic. Animal traction is substituted for tractors, and planting is planned to take advantage of seasonal rainfall patterns in order to reduce reliance on irrigation, and local communities are to be more intimately involved in the production process.

The connection between the alternative model and the universities is extremely important. Cuba has only 2 percent of Latin America's population, but 11 percent of its scientists, and a well-developed research infrastructure. The government was able to call for "knowledge intensive" technological innovation to substitute for imported inputs that became unavailable. University researchers had been advocating the development of the "alternative model," described earlier, since 1982, and many research results, which had previously remained unused, were available for immediate implementation. New research has been modified to emphasize this direction and further develop it. The government supports the implementation of the alternative model with the creation of attractive communities in the countryside offering better housing than in the cities, to try to reverse or at least stem rural–urban migration.[7] In the meantime, city dwellers are encouraged to grow vegetables in small gardens. On walks in Havana during my visits there, I saw some of these gardens in the grounds of public buildings such as ministries and offices, something that would be unimaginable in Jamaica because of the high incidence of crop theft.

Agriculture is not the only sector that is gearing itself toward implementing a new model of self-sufficient, sustainable development. Since the early 1980s, Cuban leaders had become increasingly disillusioned with the model of dependent socialism that limited their production to light industry and raw agricultural commodities for export. During the 1980s, an estimated $12 billion was invested in developing human capital and infrastructure in biotechnology, health sciences, computers, and robotics. The long-term plan was to change Cuba's role in the world economy to that of purveyor of high technology, scientific consulting, and top-quality health services. Having emphasized the development of human resources, Cuba had, by the 1990s, a large pool of scientists and researchers who could come forward with innovative ideas to confront the crisis. The economic potential of these ideas seems to rest on the willingness of the government to move out of a rigidly state-controlled economy, and to experiment with solutions that allow a highly educated workforce to be creative. Current economic restructuring together with the use of this workforce—not just the latter on its own—has enabled Cuba to move into a period of modest economic growth after the difficulties of the "special period" of economic contraction, hardship, and adjustment that followed the collapse of the Soviet bloc.

The globalization of the international economy has presented developing countries, including the English-speaking Caribbean, with a crisis of development. The structure of global production has changed along lines made possible by developments in microelectronics and information technology, fields in which most of these countries are barely at the margins. The previous raw material mainstays of their economies are becoming less relevant and less in demand. Multinational corporations are becoming stronger rather than weaker in their ability to exploit the cheap labor of these countries. Latin American and Caribbean governments have made such inadequate commitment to the development of science and technology that the education system inherited from the colonial era, even if expanded and improved, is unlikely in the short term to produce populations that are highly educated and skilled enough to respond effectively to these global changes. At the same time, the conditions of globalization, the huge foreign debt, the reduction in foreign aid, and the reduction in the opportunity for migration, are combining to worsen the poverty and social plight of the majority.[8]

The enormous gaps in higher education in the capitalist Caribbean are unlikely to be filled without significant external help. These countries need to put in place both an education system that enables them to develop their human resources in a culturally suitable way and in appropriate fields, and a system of national and regional development and planning that could guarantee appropriate utilization of skilled people. Cuba has excess university capacity that could help immensely in the rapid development of regional science and technology skills—arguably to a greater extent than any other country would be willing to. On the other hand, Cuba lacks the economic experience, expertise, and connections needed to seize the opportunities of producing for constantly changing "niche markets" in a globalized economy. The Caribbean region has considerable natural resources (especially Guyana) and pockets of expertise in market-oriented business, tourism, and commerce that could be expanded. If it were possible to put in place a Caribbean project that combined the research capacity of Cuba with the physical and entrepreneurial resources of the rest of the region, immense changes would become feasible.

The keen insights of Marie, the Cuban-trained economist in the St. Lucian Ministry of Planning and the Environment, stressed the connection between educational cooperation and economic cooperation in a broad

Caribbean regional project of development. She commented that, given the excess of trained experts in Cuba, and

> the relevance of their situation to ours, we could absorb them as advisers much more than we do now. After Hurricane Debbie last year, we got many World Bank and other international experts coming in to assist. But we also got a Cuban expert who recommended some excellent strategies for recovery and development, including building micro dams for irrigation. None of the others came up with this. CARICOM should take a policy decision to allow Cuban experts to assist our countries in this way. The governments could easily afford them, since they would not be as expensive as regional experts, let alone those from North America and Europe ....(Caribbean) Governments should contribute more to Cuba to encourage it to offer more scholarships.

Cubans fervently believe that their expansion of access to higher education makes an important contribution to economic growth, development, and the improvement of equity in education. Their provision of overseas scholarships is linked to this assumption. Politically, Cubans see themselves as being willing to share some of the benefits of its achievement in higher education with poorer countries because of their desire to build solidarity in the developing world. The scholarships constituted a way in which the Cuban government could assist countries of the Global South "by offering the kind of help we are able to give," in the words of one professor I interviewed in Havana. He also felt that increasing the numbers of professionals would help these countries to build up stronger educational structures.

Idealistic goals aside, educating thousands of young people from across the globe in a socialist university system must have benefits for Cuba such as spreading knowledge about the revolution and its achievements, building networks, and creating an international reservoir of goodwill about Cuba. This must be important for a country as pressured as Cuba has been by the hostility of the United States government. The drive for solidarity was expressed in this view of the benefits of increasing the political links between Cuba and the Caribbean:

> We belong to the Caribbean. This is our region, and we would like to have a stronger presence in regional organisations—the one that is exclusively for the Caribbean region and the other which includes Latin America. We understand that the economic war nowadays is a war of groups. Integration is necessary to be competitive. The war today, after the end of the Cold War, is more difficult than before. The big countries have no difficulty in having a strong economy. But the small countries need to help each other to develop, otherwise we will continue to be in a very weak position. (Orlando Lancis, Interview, Ministry of Foreign Relations, Havana, 1996).

Yet, there are contradictions surrounding the role of the Cuban scholarships in expanding the access of the Commonwealth Caribbean to tertiary education. The region's need for tertiary education does not necessarily mean that it is willing to turn to Cuba for assistance. For most of the 50 years of independence, the education system of this region has been savagely selective in denying university education to all but between 1 percent and 5 percent of the 20–24 age cohort. In the 1990s, the three major Commonwealth Caribbean universities (the University of the West Indies (UWI), the University of Guyana, and the University of Technology, Jamaica) provided about 25,000 places between them, while non-university tertiary institutions provided about 46,000 places.[9] With the development of "offshore" degree programs provided by overseas universities entering the region, the number of fee-paying university places increased. However, there is still a large unmet demand for tertiary education from people who have completed school. Paul Sutton observes that for the Caribbean, "the numbers in tertiary education at 15 percent in 2000 remain below the Latin American average of 26 percent."[10] Added to this problem of insufficient tertiary places is that of the huge migration of professionals who have been educated in the region. A recent study by Mishra (2006) reports that an average of 70 percent of tertiary-educated people migrated from the Caribbean between 1965 and 2000, this figure rising to 89 percent in the case of Guyana. Remittances sent home by the Caribbean diaspora (more than 3 million in North America alone) are an important source of income, but Mishra argues that the loss of development potential due to skilled migration outweighs remittances and is a serious issue for the region.[11]

Cuba has provided the Anglophone Caribbean with over 900 tertiary education scholarships in the past 30 years. This is an unprecedented gesture of South-South solidarity that no other developing country has yet matched. Yet, because the region has been in the postcolonial vortex of "Cold War" politics, Caribbean students have not taken up as many scholarships as Cuba has offered. Cuban degrees are seen as being associated with Marxist perspectives, and North American degrees and diplomas are viewed as having more status and "saleability." Thousands have sought higher education in the United States and Canada, most without scholarships. In the 1990s, the estimate was that there may have been, in any one year, up to 12,500 Anglophone Caribbean students in US colleges and universities.[12] Many have been able to change their status from student to US or Canadian resident, which has contributed to the loss of highly educated people from the Caribbean region. Some of the Caribbean professionals whom I interviewed felt that Cuban trained graduates were less likely to be part of this "brain drain" of qualified people, because the degree prepared them both technically and attitudinally for contributing to the region's development.

The Cuban scholarships respond primarily to the Caribbean region's urgent need for training scientific personnel, which establishes their vocational relevance to the region, and which also has led to most of the applicants being men, whose high schooling is still much more oriented toward the sciences than is that of women. The largest numbers of scholarships taken up by English-speaking Caribbean students in Cuba have been in the fields of medicine, dentistry, and engineering. A smaller number has been in agronomy and economics, while the smallest number has been in the humanities including education, languages, physical culture, and the fine arts. The two-year polytechnic diploma level has trained people in technical specializations, including a few in film studies. Cuban scholarships cover all educational and living expenses, and Caribbean governments usually finance the airfares to and from Cuba (some provide travel home each summer vacation), as well as "topping up" living-expense stipends. The scholarships have enabled many students from low- to middle-income backgrounds, and a selected few from political groups, to study at universities or vocational polytechnics. The poorest people are not in the picture since some of these do not have the opportunity to complete even primary, let alone secondary, education.

Conclusion

Cuba's educational outreach has been significant in expanding higher education in Africa, Latin America, and the Caribbean. The type of education—its philosophy and practice—appears to have had beneficial results in preparing graduates to tackle the problems of material and social underdevelopment characteristic of many postcolonial countries. Cuban higher education pedagogy insists on the integration of study with practical work and applied research for all students. Academic study is combined each year with work placements related to the degree, and a high level of social responsibility is encouraged in the process. This chapter has described and discussed the significance of this "way of knowing" in the context of higher education policy in developing countries.

The material discussed in this chapter is a contribution to a qualitative and contextualized study of higher education that is rare in the literature on this field.[13] Further research along similar lines applied to other countries could help illuminate important questions. These include questions such as how far university education is organized to relate theoretical and practical work, and to guide students to become creative, research-oriented, and socially responsible graduates. If university structures are found wanting in these areas, then it behoves societies to find more suitable higher education strategies, such as those that could give researchers more responsibility for improving professional fields, and that could enable universities to share skills and resources productively with each other for the social good. Higher education in the twenty-first century in the Caribbean, as elsewhere, is faced with immense changes. In the new learning environments, the Internet removes nearly all constraints on time and space so that learners can potentially create their own education programs selected from across the globe,[14] indigenous and local knowledge have increasing influence on reshaping academic curricula. Developing nations are going to have to ensure that they manipulate and monitor very carefully the quality of higher education to ensure that it brings optimum benefits to their societies.

The Cuban educational model is at the same time an educational system, a set of education principles and practices, and a strategy of educational change shaped in a particular historical context.[15] Unless there is change, current Latin American and Caribbean regimes are unlikely to be able to bring about educational advances comparable to those achieved by Cuba since 1959. While the Cuban higher educational model has several limitations and difficulties, it nevertheless has considerable relevance for the situation facing neighboring states. It may challenge universities in the Global South, based as they often are on models inherited from the colonial period, to examine their own goals, values, structures, and strategies. The Cuban government, through its scholarships, and also through its bilateral agreements offering the technical assistance of skilled technicians and professionals, demonstrates on a practical level "the meaning as well as some of the benefits of the Cuban educational model...above all, it is the failure of other states to satisfy the educational needs of their populations which ensures the relevance of (this) model."[16]

Notes

1. This chapter derives some of its material from a previous publication: A Hickling-Hudson (2000), "The Cuban University and Educational Outreach: Cuba's Contribution to Post-Colonial Development," in *Local Knowledge and Wisdom in Higher Education,* edited by G. R. (Bob) Teasdale and Zane Ma Rhea, New York: IAU Press, Pergamon/Elsevier.
2. Hickling-Hudson, 1989.
3. Rossett and Benjamin, 1994.
4. Rossett, 1996.
5. Rosset, 1996:159–160.
6. Rosset and Benjamin, 1994:28.
7. Rosset and Benjamin, 1994:6–7.
8. Levy, 1996; Levy, 2009; World Bank, 2005; Deere et al., 1990.
9. World Bank, 1993:112.
10. Sutton, 2006.
12. Mishra, 2006.
13. World Bank, 1993.
15. Altbach, 1995.
14. Inayatullah, and Gidley, 1998.
15. Richmond, 1990.
16. Richmond, 1990.

References

Altbach, Philip. "Research on Higher Education: Global Perspectives." *Change* 19, no. 4 (1995): 56–59.

Deere, C., P. Antrobus, L. Bolles, E. Melendez, P. Phillips, M. Rivera, and H. Safa. *In the Shadows of the Sun: Caribbean Development and US Policy.* San Francisco, CA: Westview Press, 1990.

Hickling-Hudson, Anne. "Education in the Grenada Revolution: 1979—83." *Compare* 19, no. 2 (1989): 95–114.
Inayatullah, S. and J. Gidley (eds.) "The University: Alternative Futures." Special Issue. *Futures* 30, no. 7 (1998).
Levy, Horace. *They Cry "Respect!" Urban Violence and Poverty in Jamaica.* Mona, Jamaica: University of the West Indies Press, 1996.
Levy, Horace. *Killing Streets and Community Revival in Urban Jamaica.* Kingston, Jamaica: Arawak Publications.
Mishra, P. "Emigration and Brain Drain: Evidence from the Caribbean." In IMF Working Paper WP/06/25. Washington DC: International Monetary Fund, 2006.
Richmond, M. "Revolution, Reform and Constant Improvement: 30 Years of Educational Change in Cuba." *Compare* 20, no. 2 (1990): 101–114.
Rossett, P. "The Greening of Cuba." *In Green Guerillas: Environmental Conflicts and Initiatives in Latin America and the Caribbean.* Edited by H. Collinson, 158–67. Nottingham: Latin American Bureau, 1996.
Rossett, P. and M. Benjamin. *The Greening of the Revolution: Cuba's Experiment with Organic Agriculture.* Melbourne: Ocean Press, 1994.
Sutton, P. "Caribbean Development: An Overview." *New West Indian Guide / Nieuwe West-Indische Gids* 80, no. 1 & 2 (2006): 45–62.
World Bank. *Caribbean Region: Access, Quality and Efficiency in Education.* Washington, DC: World Bank 1993.
World Bank. *A Time to Choose. Caribbean Development in the 21st Century.* World Bank Report No. 31725–LAC, 2005.

Acknowledgments

The author gratefully acknowledges the kindness of the following people for providing detailed material in interviews: Francisco Martínez (2000), Ministry of Higher Education; Jesús García del Portal (1996), late professor in higher education, CEPES (Center for the Improvement of Higher Education), Havana; Orlando Lancis (1996), Ministry of Foreign Relations, Havana; professors at the Universidad Central de las Villas (UCLV) (1993); and graduates in Grenada, Guyana, Jamaica, and St. Lucia (1993, 1996, and 2008).

7

Cuban Support for Namibian Education and Training

Rosemary Preston

Introduction

Cuba's first African mission set parameters integrating military and human development, in particular training, education, and health, that became typical of Cuban international interventions over the next 25 years. The paragraphs below draw on published histories to synthesize tangled experiences from Algeria in 1962 to the end of the Angolan civil war in 1988 and Namibian independence two years later. Focusing on Cuban support for Namibians in exile, they track Cuba's role in Angola and northern South West Africa, and its support of education in Cuba for Namibian victims of South African attacks and later refuge-seeking groups. They compare Cuba's educational provision for Namibians with that of other countries, before turning to examine what is known of post-return labor-market integration and new Cuban interventions in the independent state.

From Algeria to Angola

Numerous writers stress the importance of previous Cuban missions in Africa to understand Cuba's contribution to the development of Namibia. Here, reference is made first to what became a key model of Cuban internationalism, taking the case of its mission to Algeria, before outlining its involvement in Angola, which quickly became inextricable from its role in Namibia.

The strength of Cuba's commitment to international solidarity and education was tested very shortly after the 1959 revolution.[1] Within a year, Cuba was welcoming small numbers of African students on Cuban scholarships (the first came from Guinea Bissau), simultaneously offering support in Latin America. Staying with Cuba's African mission, Cuba in 1961 sent armaments to the liberation forces in Algeria, receiving in return wounded fighters for treatment and orphaned children to educate. These were to be nurtured in Cuba, until they were able to return as Algerian citizens. A year after Algerian independence in 1962 and the flight of professional cadres to France, it was Fidel Castro who, early in 1963, inspired the first cohort of 50 medical students and related personnel to pioneer Cuba's international solidarity abroad, providing health services for the Algerian people. Later in 1963, Moroccan incursions across the Algerian border and continuing internal unrest saw the rapid formation and dispatch of a Cuban military training force, the Grupo Especial de Instrucción (GEI). A fully equipped artillery battalion, nearly 700 strong, its role was to train the depleted Algerian forces.

To help the members of the mission survive hardship, maintain dignity, and promote Cuba's reputation in North Africa, the GEI was to be guided by Fidel Castro's codes of good personal conduct for Cuban internationalists and his resounding mantra to *fight and train, train and fight*.[2] In the event, the GEI did not fight, but did give military training and general education to the Algerian fighters, while the medical teams were in high demand from the civilian population.[3]

The haste of the 1963 departure of Cuban forces from the Caribbean to Mediterranean Africa was predicated on relations established in the 1950s with Algerian freedom fighters. For Fidel Castro, this required immediate allegiance to Algerian co-revolutionaries as they fought to end the oppressive French regime. Cuban departure for North Africa was so quick that it preceded the signing of bilateral agreements, the establishment of basic mission infrastructure or key financial arrangements. The haste resulted in inadequate provisions, irregular stipends, and frequent hunger. In the end, in spite of its own straitened resources, Cuba bore the major costs of the expedition. Quoting Machado Ventura, Gleijeses notes that it was an unusual gesture for an underdeveloped country (Cuba) to tender free aid to another in even more dire straits, at a time when the donor was already stretched to meet its domestic needs:[4]

> It was like a beggar offering his help, but we knew that the Algerian people needed it even more than we did, and that they deserved it. It was an act of solidarity that brought no tangible benefit and came at real material cost. It was a special moment...because it was when this process of internationalist aid began.[5]

However hastily mobilized, the 1963 mission to Algeria bore hallmark traits of the internationalist strategy that Cuba was to make its own over decades of support to liberation movements, before and after independence, and to other subjugated peoples. These traits included consolidating previously established trust with like-minded activists, providing assistance in Cuba, as well as in the country seeking support. In the first three decades it included a military presence, military training, and technical assistance to civilian populations, wherever needed, notably in medicine and literacy. Scholarship opportunities in Cuba at all levels (from basic schooling and vocational/professional training, to advanced higher learning) became the norm over time. Crucially, the Algerian and other African campaigns, including Angola, often began as Cuban initiatives. Tripartite arrangements kicked in afterward, such as when the USSR agreed to meet costs of military ordnance for the new Algerian government and likewise in Angola, over a decade later. Tripartism remains a feature of Cuban internationalism, initially with third governments and now with multilateral and other organizations, as well. In terms of Algerian reciprocity, it reached a peak when Ben Bella made a much publicized visit to thank Castro in Cuba and when Algeria came to serve as Cuba's headquarters in Africa,[6] albeit for a short period. In Angola, after defeating pro-Portuguese UNITA and US-backed South African Forces (SAFs), reciprocity has been more complicated. It included major involvement in Namibia's independence movement and agreements for large-scale civilian development programs, with delivery in both Angola and Cuba.

Through the 1960s, working primarily with Ben Bella and Nkrumah, president of Ghana, through the Casablanca Group,[7] Cuba was offering similar multimethod contributions elsewhere in Africa (to Zanzibar, Zaire, Congo, Guinea-Bissau, Tanzania, Cameroon), and to other world regions. Resented by the United States, Cuba became known in revolutionary milieus as the champion of internationalism, making no demands and giving unconditional aid.[8] Down the decades, Cuba came to be seen as offering a human development alternative, predicated on reciprocity across sectors and disciplines. More recently, Cuba is working with more than 50 nations in all regions of the world, including sending expertise to a number of richer states, offering multiple forms of education and training.[9]

Cuba, Angola, and Namibia

If the Cuban mission to Algeria set parameters for five decades of international cooperation, its unprecedented support for Angolan liberation through the 1960s and 1970s, before and particularly after independence from Portugal, led to the infrequently acknowledged Cuban involvement in Namibia's emergence as an independent state.[10]

As with Algeria, a supportive relationship had long existed between the different anticolonial movements in Cuba, Angola, and Namibia. The Movimiento Popular de Libertação de Angola (MPLA) had been in solidarity with Cuban revolutionaries since 1956, before and after they came to power in 1959. Formed in 1959,[11] the South-West African People's Organization (SWAPO), the principal Namibian liberation movement, was a close ally. Both MPLA and SWAPO cadres, and from 1967 SWAPO's military arm, the People's Liberation Army of Namibia (PLAN), benefitted from years of Cuban military, political, and other training, through the

1960s until the end of the post independence war in Angola (1988) and the achievement of independence in Namibia (1990).

For Dugdale-Pointon,[12] Cuban training had been instrumental in developing Maoist tactics of shifting between full-scale guerrilla warfare and small-scale terrorism, deployed by freedom fighters in Angola and Namibia, as operations demanded. This was to be a significant factor in the later rout of South African forces, despite "South Africa's excellent counter-insurgency tactics of fortifying villages and striking against rebel bases in safe havens instead of trying to police a huge and desolate border.[13]" As important, it must be remembered that the Angolan and Namibian struggles for independence were in many ways proxy wars, provoked by the Cold War battles of the super powers, seeking to protect South African business interests on the one hand and the socialist development on the other.[14]

Cuba, with Namibian PLAN fighters alongside, played a key role in Angola's 1975 independence from Portugal. This triggered arrangements to be made for young Angolans to be educated in Cuba, from primary and sometimes through to tertiary levels. As Hatzky reports in chapter 8, this was to result in tens of thousands receiving formal schooling and a range of vocational and other professional training. Since then, streams of Cubans have come to Angola offering major cross-sectoral, in-country contributions to Angola's development, not least educational support.

Angolan independence allowed a number changes in support for the Namibian cause. There was a Namibian exodus to safety from Ovamboland, across the Angolan border. Camps were created to receive them and in turn provided primary schooling. SWAPO moved its headquarters. Angola, supported by Cuba, provided PLAN with a protected military base. Multi- and bilateral organizations supporting Namibia were creating operational centers in Luanda, and what was to become a huge international educational program for Namibians was set to take off.

Although the Cuban military was to withdraw within three years of Angolan independence, its mission complete, the fragile MPLA foreseeing further South African incursions, requested it to remain when the coalition government collapsed as civil war loomed. With USSR finance,[15] Cuba remobilized for what was to become its largest and longest military operation in Africa, first in Angola, later in Namibia. They fought the combined SAFs that were seeking to consolidate control north and south of the border to protect commercial access to Namibia's mineral wealth. Between 1976 and 1988, some 250,000 Cuban fighters were to serve in the border area, as many as 40,000 at a time. They stayed on long after the 1976 rout of the SAFs to protect the fledgling Angolan government, and to continue advising Angolan and Namibian forces, as the United States set about refinancing the enemy from the south. A further decade was to pass before an alliance between SWAPO, Cuba, the African National Congress (ANC) of South Africa, and Angola defeated the apartheid military forces in southern Angola and northern Namibia, permitting the implementation of UN resolution 435 relating to Cuban and South African withdrawal and eventual independence in Namibia.

Educating Namibian Exiles

I note[16] that, as frequently the case with anticipatory migratory movements, including exile movements, many of the earliest Namibian exiles had been experienced political activists and comparatively well educated. A number were secondary school students, from families better situated than the majority black population in apartheid South-West Africa. Once in Angola or Zambia, they were hungry to learn, already seeing themselves as the future intelligentsia and leaders of the liberation. For this to happen they needed advanced training. They quickly attracted support from the host country and international sources to complete secondary schooling in Tanzania, Zambia, and elsewhere in SE Africa, while those who had left through Botswana were offered equivalent opportunities in Dukwe and Francistown.

With the exodus after Angolan independence, transit centers were created to sort Namibians entering Angola. As numbers increased, their options were to join PLAN, follow an educational track with a view to leadership in exile and professional roles after repatriation, or move with dependents to long-stay camps further into Angola and there perhaps obtain elementary education.

Preston observes that over the years, international shifts in thinking on the appropriateness of different modes of education for Namibians in exile evolved as demand changed and grew.[17] Throughout the period of the Namibian struggles, sympathetic international commitment was to develop human resources in exile capable of sustaining an independent nation. Educational priorities also reflected changing international thinking over the decades of the conflict, in general and for refuge-seeking groups more specifically. The much more diverse demand that was growing, with larger, less-well-educated populations in exile meant that lower-level provision was needed, catering to large numbers. In the early 1960s, social science had been prioritized at upper secondary and tertiary levels. By the 1970s, more practical professional training was emphasized, with economics, law, and public administration accorded increasing importance. By the 1980s, governments and agencies were in the main providing technical education and vocational training, for greater numbers and for shorter periods in a wide array of countries in most world regions.

In the early 1970s, whatever the military training PLAN fighters were receiving from Cubans in Angola, it was not until 1978 before Namibian children and young people were offered the chance to study in Cuba. This came immediately in the wake of the infamous South African air attack on the Cassinga refugee camp. In the ensuing battle, 150 Cuban soldiers lost their lives, the highest number of any Cuban operation in Angola. Cassinga was destroyed. There were 624 dead, 611 injured. Among the dead were 167 women, and 298 teenagers and children.[18] Located 250 km inside Angola, it was where the women and children accompanying the fighters and other exiles were based.[19] Cuba gave massive military support to counter the attack, the only force from outside Africa to do so. It arranged for some 600 women, children, and adolescents to go to Cuba for medical attention and, later, education, primarily on the Isla de la Juventud, alongside children already there from other war-torn African nations.[20] Many stayed and received the education they were denied back home. Some eventually graduated from Cuban universities. Over the next decade, Cuba went on to furnish several thousand of the Namibians exiled in Angola with educational and training opportunities in Cuba, from primary schooling through to vocational, tertiary, and advanced professional development. It seems that a number with high aspirations and hesitant at staying on the Isla de la Juventud were able to obtain secondary places in Havana.[21]

The World Offers Namibia Education

Several data sets provide insight into the extent of the internationalization of Namibian education in the 1970s and 1980s and what it achieved. They include funding agency lists of those awarded scholarships to study in a range of countries and independent studies of their impact in later years.[22] Post independence research on war-affected Namibians includes two studies on the educational experiences in exile of those who returned: (i) a community-wide survey in three areas of the country and (ii) a large tracer study of people sponsored by different organizations.[23] The Namibian government in exile also kept records. They include data from the 1988 SWAPO Manpower Survey, which reached me as a collection of tabulated files on floppy disks.[24] There is no claim that these data are all of those derived from the survey, nor any information as to what proportion of the potential population of scholars was included in the sample. Indeed, in a number of cases, numbers are small. Certainly, data for students going to the UK represent no more than 15 percent of the 800 Namibians recorded as going to Britain under varying funding arrangements. Nor is there any account of children in Cuba or the GDR at presecondary levels of schooling, of whom there were many hundreds.

With these cautions, the SWAPO Manpower Survey data refer to 2400 people who had received educational support in 38 countries, from 1969 to 1988. Of the 2397 valid cases recuperated, 91 percent had enrolled on a broad array of practical vocational courses oriented to semiprofessional white collar, and skilled and semiskilled manual work in (i) service sector provision (e.g., health, education, law, and administration); (ii) trades and commerce, manufacturing, vehicle repair, physical infrastructure maintenance; and (iii) primary sector skills in agriculture, fishing, and mining. The remaining 9 percent of the sample were in secondary and higher education, and following undergraduate and postgraduate courses.

Table 7.1 SWAPO Manpower Survey (1988): Cuba's provision compared with the overall survey

	N	Qualifications			
		Vocational[1]	Secondary	UG	PG
Whole sample	2397	1791	154[2]	29	35
Cuba	200	169[3]	9		4

[1] The category combines those explicitly described as certificates, cert/voc and vocational qualifications. It omits a number who might also have been included.
[2] About one-third of these are Ordinary Level certificate candidates.
[3] Includes diplomas associated with basic teacher training.

Of the total captured in the SWAPO data set, the majority (36 percent) had been enrolled in southern African institutions. Twenty percent were split between the United Nations Institute for Namibia (UNIN) in Zambia and the UN Vocational Training Centre for Namibia (UNVTCN) in Angola. More than 100 went to Sierra Leone, fewer to a dozen other Sub-Saharan states. Outside the region, most had gone to the then GDR (30 percent) for basic vocational training, with the exception of two lone university students. Cuba received about 200, 8 percent of the total, the UK 113 (5 percent), and the USSR only 2.5 percent.

While most of those going to Cuba were taking vocational certificate courses, 15 percent were enrolled in secondary and higher education. This compares first with the 25 percent of those from the survey who went to the UK (N = 113) to continue academic work, and second the 0.2 percent in the GDR (N = 710) who continued in formal schooling. All four of those listed by SWAPO as having gone to the US were in graduate programs (100 percent), although they had previously held scholarships elsewhere that had served to raise them to such levels.

Back in Namibia

Exiled Namibians returned home in time to vote at independence and witness the creation of the new state. The experience was very different for those with and without good qualifications, even before the elections took place. For those without any qualifications, especially former fighters, life was hard. Many were to travel long distances, often on foot, between towns in search of work, usually ending frustrated.

Of those with qualifications, many had been primed prior to return to fill administrative positions in the new state, with attendant housing incentives, but they had not been prepared to find fully functioning national systems that had continued without them so well for so long.[25] To a degree, many of these returnees were overconfident on the grounds of what often proved to be their superior levels of education. They failed to consider the merits of the years of routine office management experience gained by those who had remained, of which they knew very little. Stayers, in their turn, were fearful of how the well-educated new leaders would treat them, at work and in other areas of their lives.

As in other newly independent African nations, international advice to independent Namibia had been to expand the bureaucracy in the early years, so as to integrate victorious returnees without the wholesale displacement of incumbents, regardless of cuts that may have to be later introduced. A program of training sought to bring incumbents and newcomers together around the new democratic politics of public administration and new ways of working through a legally grounded process of transition. Part of this required the recognition by the public service commission of newcomer qualifications and their implications for eligibility for particular levels of employment. The process was complex and slow as the staff in educational equivalence units worked through thousands of applications from returnees seeking access to the labor market, in the process constructing Namibia's own recognition system, no longer dependent on that of South Africa.[26] Gradually, the proportion of returnees gaining formal sector employment increased, to the point that it overtook the proportion of those who had remained, but there were numerous tensions.[27]

Problems arose associated with the very different educational offerings at different moments of the exile period, in very different parts of the world. These affected employer readiness to accept qualifications, depending on the levels of expertise implied and importantly on the political philosophy of the states that had given them. Those returning with academic qualifications from, for example, western Europe had little difficulty in finding work, once they had been granted recognition. Those with more practical vocational skills fared less well. Occupational certificates from the UK, three quarters from institutes of higher education, were in the main quickly recognized. With vocational qualifications from GDR, it was much more difficult. It was easy for employers to justify their rejection of practical skills by disparaging as solidarity qualifications those acquired in the socialist states of Eastern Europe or Cuba, but this more accurately masked the economic reality in post independence Namibia: formal opportunities for the semiprofessional and more and less skilled manual expertise, obtained by thousands of returnees, were in fact very limited.

In the event, people returning from Cuba could be seen to be faring quite well, as early as 1992. A complex study of post war reconstruction[28] undertook a mix of surveys and qualitative studies on different aspects of labor-market integration.[29] The tracer study of returnee destinations (N = 651) found that of the 75 sampled who had been in Cuba, three-quarters had returned with upper secondary, graduate, and postgraduate qualifications. Of these, half were already in management and other professional employment (Preston, 1993b), a number of them after subsequent training at higher levels than those they had obtained in Cuba. Cases in point would be the present minister of education, Abraham Iyambo, who had completed postgraduate study in the UK, after completing upper secondary in Cuba.

The same is true of Grace Ushoona. A victim of Cassinga, she is currently Namibian ambassador to Cuba, proud of having been a student there as well. Bience Gawanas, with a law degree from the UK, taught Namibians in Angola, Zambia, and Cuba, before returning to one of the most distinguished careers in Namibia and Africa more widely. This in spite of a period as a SWAPO detainee, along with other cadres, who had studied and taught in Cuba.[30] Although the numbers are small, the rate of senior management employment after study in Cuba is better than the rates for either the USSR or the GDR, at 40 and 32 percent, respectively.[31]

Less successful were returnees from Cuba who had spent 12 years on the Isla de la Juventud undertaking production-oriented training in farming. One group, unable to return to their Ovamboland homes because of political differences with their families, had been allocated resettlement land on an abandoned capitalist estate to the southeast of Windhoek.[32] Whatever their initial basic education, their ability to communicate was poor and much better in Spanish than in English or Afrikaans. By 1993, as poor Owambo originating from the north, they were isolated victims of abuse from neighboring Afrikaner communities, with few prospects other than tilling the soil with a hoe, attempting to ward off baboons, on what had once been a highly mechanized agribusiness.[33]

Cuba and Namibia since Independence

There are numerous interpretations of the circumstances of Cuba's withdrawal from Angola in 1988 after the defeat of SAFs at Cuito Cuanavale. In some measure, they mask the limited recognition Cuba received for this victory and for Namibia's subsequent independence, in spite of US acclaim for Cuban achievements.[34] This does not imply a period without communication, far from it. The Cuban delegation to independent Namibia was quickly involved in planning Cuban support in post-conflict reconstruction. Following the recommendations of a Swedish consultancy, Cubans were by 1992 providing urgent training to rehabilitate the most difficult veterans: those not selected for the new peacetime army or reconstructed police force. They found themselves assigned to the development brigades.[35] The Cuban task was daunting, with minimal resources on military bases, vandalized when the SAFs abandoned them. They were working with men and a few women, brutalized after decades of bush warfare and seeing no personal fulfilment or other promised returns for fighting to achieve independence.

Since 1990, there have been regular delegations between Cuba and Namibia, negotiating further social and economic cooperation, much of it educational. In 2000, there were more than 50 Cuban doctors in Namibia.[36] Cuba also assists with Namibian literacy program development and urban planning.[37] In 2007, Cuba was still supporting literacy education in Namibia. In 2010, Cuban health professionals were in Namibia as part of a program to fight HIV/AIDS, malaria, and other diseases that kill thousands every year. Dozens of young Namibians have graduated or are currently studying medicine in Cuba. Of Cuban doctors working in Namibia, a number wish to remain. Cuba also assists Namibia in the fields of education, sports, energy, and mining, among others, reiterating the solidarity that has inspired 50 years of ongoing collaboration between the two.

Notes

1. The opening section draws significantly on the works of Gleijeses. They are the product of detailed historical research, referring to primary documentation and interviews with those who were active in Cuba's engagements first with Algeria, later with Angola.
2. See Castro, R., 1963.
3. Gleijeses, 1996, 182.
4. Gleijeses, 1996, 166.
5. Gleijeses, 1996.
6. Gleijeses, 1996.
7. By 1963, this had become the Organisation of African Unity; see Krook, 1998.
8. Gleijeses, 2002, 199.
9. Cuban Collaboration and the World, n.d.; *CubaNews*, 2003.
10. Hennig, 2011.
11. There is some confusion over this date. Dugdale-Pointon (2002) cites 1959, Bloomfield and Moulton (2000) suggest 1961.
12. Dugdale-Pointon, 2000.
13. Ibid.
14. Gleijeses, 2002, 2006.
15. Bloomfield and Moulton, 2000.
16. Preston (1994) draws on a major post independence study, Preston, R., 1993 ed..
17. Preston, 1994.
18. von Sychowski, 2011.
19. Baines, G. (2008) A recent critique review of continuing debate from South African and Namibian perspectives.
20. McManus (2005) provides a history of the island, including a chapter on the international schools.
21. Preston, 2010. (Abraham Iyambo is currently minister of education in the Namibian government. He completed secondary schooling in Havana 1985, later undertaking advanced studies in the UK.)
22. For example, Preston and Kandando, 1993.
23. Solomon and Kandando, 1993; Tamas and Gleichmann, 1993.
24. Nahas Angula, now prime minister, then minister of education in independent Namibia, provided disks with these data in 1991.
25. Namibians in exile were given considerable amounts of training to manage sectoral administration in government departments. After independence, lack of preparation for the obstacles to innovation in the long-established systems still in place was frequently observed at even the most senior levels of the new government.
26. See Tamas and Gleichmann, 1993, for an explanation of these processes.
27. Solomon and Kandando, 1993; Preston, 1994.
28. Preston, 1993.
29. Solomon and Kandando, 1993; Tamas and Gleichmann, 1993; Preston 1993, 1993a, 1993b.
30. Preston, 1992.

31. Preston, 1994.
32. Preston, 1992b.
33. Preston, 1992b.
34. Bloomfield and Moulton, 2000a.
35. Preston, 1997.
36. Ampupadha, 2000.
37. African Press 2007; *Cuba Standard*, 2008.

References

African Press (2007) Cuba Pledges to Help Namibia Lift Literacy Rates, November 15, http://africanpress.wordpress.com/2007/11/15/cuba-pledges-to-help-namibia-lift-literacy-rates/

Amupadhi, T. (2000) Cuba Acts to Stop Doctors Jumping Ship in Namibia, *The Namibian*. September 8.

Baines, G. (2008) Battle for Cassinga: Conflicting Narratives and Contested Meanings, Accessed June 12, 2011; http://eprints.ru.ac.za/946/1/baines_Cassinga.pdf

Bloomfield, L. P. and Moulton, A. (2000a) Cascon Case ACW: Angola Civil War 1974. http://web.mit.edu/cascon/cases/case_acw.html

Bloomfield, L. P. and Moulton, A. (2000b) Cascon Case NAM: Namibian Independence 1947–90. http://web.mit.edu/cascon/cases/case_nam.html

Castro, R. (1963) Instructions to Majors Bravo and Seguera before Efigenio's Departure, Havana, Ministerio de Fuerzas Armadas, October, 20, p. 1.

Cuba News (2003) *Cuban Literacy Stirs up Kiwis, CubaNews*, November 01, http://www.thefreelibrary.com/Cuban+literacy+program+stirs+up+kiwis.-a0109917546p

Cuba Standard (2008) Cuba assisting Namibia in Town Development, http://www.cubastandard.com/2010/12/08/cuba-assisting-namibia-in-town-development/

Cuban Collaboration and the World (n.d.) http://www.cubanembassy.net/documents/AFC3D06CD1A6A9850A8F4AB1423C8B5AED4915A8.html

Dugdale-Pointon, T. (2002) *Namibia 1966–1990*, September 9, http://www.historyofwar.org/articles/wars_namibia.html

Gleijeses, P. (1996) Cuba's First Venture in Africa: Algeria, 1961–1965, *Journal of Latin American Studies*, 28, 1, pp. 159–195.

Gleijeses, P. (2002) Conflicting Missions: Havana, Washington, and Africa, 1959–1976, Chapel Hill: The University of North Carolina Press, p. 199.

Gleijeses, P. (2006) Moscow's Proxy? Cuba and Africa 1975–1988, *Journal of Cold War Studies*, Spring 8, 2, pp. 3–51 (doi: 10.1162/jcws.2006.8.2.3)

Gleijeses, P. (2007) Cuba and the Independence of Namibia, *Cold War History*, 7, 2, pp. 285–303.

Hennig, R. Chr. (2011) *afrol News*, [No title] February, 11, http://www.afrol.com/articles/17553

Krook, D. (1998) Cuban Internationalism in Angola 1975–1991, New York, Krook Network in Hist 379, http://playagiron.net/ppr/cubang.php

Machado V. and Ramon, J. (1995) Note to Piero Gleijeses, Havana, July 12, p. i.

McManus, J. (2005) La Isla Cubana de Ensueño. Voces de la Isla de Pinos y de la Juventud, Premio Memoria 1996, Ediciones La Memoria, Centro Cultural Pablo de la Torriente Brau, La Habana, 2005, 81–85.

Namibia Reiterates Solidarity with Cuba, last modified November 08, 2010, http://www.escambray.cu/Eng/cuba/namibiasolidarity1011081144

Namibian (2008) Students In Cuba Await Stipends Again, October 24.

Preston, R. (1992a) Detainee Interview Transcripts, Windhoek.

Preston, R. (1992b) Field Notes in Mariental.
Preston, R. ed. (1993) *The Integration of Returned Exiles, Former Combatants and Other War-Affected Namibians*. Namibia Institute for Social and Economic Research: Windhoek, p. 504.
Preston, R. (1993a) Trained in Britain: Namibians on the Labour Market at Home. Report commissioned by the Overseas Development Administration, INCED, University of Warwick, WP 11.
Preston, R. (1993b) The Situation of AET Sponsored Students after Their Return Home. Report to the Africa Educational Trust, NISER, Windhoek, p. 33.
Preston, R. (1994) States, Statelessness and Education: Post-Return Integration of Namibians Trained Abroad. *International Journal of Educational Development*, 14, 3, pp. 299–319.
Preston, R. (1997) Demobilising and Integrating Fighters after War: The Namibian Experience, *Journal of Southern African Studies*, 23, 3, pp. 453–472.
Preston, R. (2010) Notes of a Meeting with Abraham Iyambo, London, Namibian High Commission, January.
Risquet Valdés, J. (2005) The Deep Roots of Cuba's Internationalism, *TRIcontinental*, May 13. http://www.tricontinental.cubaweb.cu/REVISTA/texto22ingl.html.
Solomon, C. and Kandando, D. (1993) Integration at the Community Level: Case Studies of War-Affected Areas, in *The Integration of Returned Exiles, Former Combatants and Other War-Affected Namibians*. Namibia Institute for Social and Economic Research: Windhoek.
Tamas, K. and Gleichmann, C. (1993) Returned Exiles on the Namibian Labour Market, in *The Integration of Returned Exiles, Former Combatants and Other War-Affected Namibians*. Namibia Institute for Social and Economic Research: Windhoek.
von Sychowski (2011) Remembering the Massacre of Cassinga, *People's Voice*, February 15–28, 2011.

Section 3

Cuban Educators: Sharing Skills Internationally

8

Cuba's Educational Mission in Africa: The Example of Angola[1]

Christine Hatzky

Introduction

During the 1970s and 1980s, Cuba maintained several small educational missions in some African countries, for example, in Mozambique, Benin, Guinea-Bissau, Sao Tome and Principe, Tanzania, and Ethiopia. But Cuba's largest educational mission in Africa, and its largest educational mission ever, was in Angola. This example will be explored in this chapter. Altogether about 10,000 Cubans from the field of education carried out their internationalist duties in Angola as teachers, educationalists, and advisers between 1976 and 1991.[2] They were part of an even larger civil mission of about 50,000 Cubans carrying out civilian duties who lived and worked in Angola over this period of time. This civilian cooperation primarily covered the areas of health, education, and civil engineering. It was initiated because of a request by the Angolan government, and it was structured and fixed by various bilateral agreements and contracts over the years. Although much has been written and discussed about Cuba's long-lasting military engagement in the conflicts that occurred after Angola won independence from the Portuguese, Cuba's civilian mission in Angola is less well known and has not yet been thoroughly explored.[3] This was the largest, longest, and most varied civil cooperation in Cuban history and the most broadly based. Furthermore, it is a unique example of South-South cooperation.

This chapter explores some basic questions about the genesis, the specific structures, and the programs of this exceptional cooperation between two developing countries. It provides insight into the methodological work of the Cuban teachers and educationalists in Angola, and shows the significance of their challenging work as well as its limits. The chapter also discusses two outstanding educational experiments that emerged within this cooperation: the sending of brigades of Cuban higher education students to Angola and the establishment of the Angolan schools on Cuba's Isle of Youth.

Background

Following the massive exodus of the Portuguese population after independence on November 11, 1975, the Angolan government felt impelled to request international help, initially to ensure the integrity of Angolan territory by means of military support, but also to maintain essential administrative and social functions. A transitional phase from colonialism to independence did not occur in Angola because of the hasty departure of the Portuguese colonial power. The Portuguese had filled not only all the important positions in the government and the economy, but also secondary ones. Adequate substitutes could not easily be found for these positions because of the enormous lack of qualified staff. As a result, the industrial and agricultural productivity of Angola was run down. Another difficult circumstance was that, about 85 percent of the population of about 4.5 million inhabitants in 1975 was nonliterate.[4] Further, Angola was involved in armed conflicts with South Africa and the rival independence movements FNLA (Frente Nacional para a Libertação de Angola) and UNITA (União Nacional para a Independência Total de Angola) both of which asserted claims to the governmental power held by the MPLA (Movimento Popular de Libertação de Angola).[5] Only Cuba's military support in the post independence conflict on behalf of the MPLA had helped them to come to power. Between 1975 and 1991, almost 380,000 Cuban soldiers fought on the side of the MPLA in order to defend their power against the internal rivals and the external enemies.

It is for this reason that Cuba's involvement was crucial both in the military and in the civilian sector. Cuba, in the first years of its civil presence in Angola, partly took over the responsibilities that would have been carried out by the former colonial power. These responsibilities included support in reconstructing the government by providing advisers for organizational and administrative areas. Industrial structures were sustained by the deployment of qualified staff. Additionally, educational programs for qualified employees for all economic and social fields were initiated. Right from the start, Cuba was involved in the development of the new education system and the campaign for literacy.

Cuba's Civilian Cooperation in Angola: Genesis and Characteristics

Although the military mission and the presence of Cuban soldiers in Angola were closely linked to the civil cooperation with regard to organizational and political matters, civilian work developed an autonomous strength with its own structures and styles. The civil cooperation emerged directly from the military one. After the end of the conflict, named the Second Liberation War, on March 27, 1976, in which the South African army was driven out of Angola with the help of Cuban forces, the Cuban soldiers were meant to return home gradually. Due to an urgent request by Angolan president Agostinho Neto for civil support in the reconstruction of the country, Raúl Castro appealed to the Cuban soldiers, mostly reservists, whom he addressed on his visit in Angola, to remain there for a longer period of time and to aid the reconstruction by using their knowledge of civil professions. One thousand reservists responded to this appeal. Some of them became advisers to Angolan ministries, among them, the Ministry of Education.[6] They helped not only to restructure the ministry but also to establish a whole new national system of education. They also supported the literacy campaign, made suggestions for new teaching materials and syllabuses, and offered courses for training and further education for Angolan teachers.

An educational pilot project had already been started in the economically and politically important enclave of Cabinda two months earlier. A team of 12 Cuban teachers had been sent into the country to investigate the logistics of undertaking a nationwide campaign for literacy on a regional basis and to develop further the education and training of teachers. According to the personal testimonies of some of the members of the first expedition, the basic principles of the civil cooperation between Cuba and Angola were already determined at this early stage.[7] These principles included helping with the reconstruction, to aid and give advice but not to dominate.

Though the focus of the pilot project in Cabinda was education, it is still an example of how the combination between civil and military missions worked. The members of both missions had the duty of strengthening the presence of the MPLA government, and of helping to build up and establish national structures, especially in this region known for its resources of crude oil and that also became the center stage for fierce battles.

Instituting Cuban-Angolan Cooperation

In July 1976, President Neto went on his first state visit to Cuba and publicly thanked the Cubans for their support. During his visit, a convention on further civil cooperation was fixed in a broad skeleton agreement that established the terms of technical and scientific cooperation between Cuba and Angola. This was the first step to institutionalize the support that already existed in the civil area, and to form mechanisms of control and efficiency. On this occasion, President Fidel Castro, for his part, emphasized the tight political cooperation with Angola and the historical, cultural closeness and even blood relationship of the two countries: "Many things link us to Angola: the common goal, shared interests, politics and ideology. But we are also connected by blood, blood in its double meaning: the blood of our ancestors and the blood that we've spilled together on the battle fields."[8] In this speech, Castro prepared the Cuban population for a broad, long-lasting, and massive civil effort in Angola. The Cuban civil mission also envisaged another important issue: the education of Angolans in Cuba. Accordingly, the first 40 Angolan students arrived in August 1976 to study or to finish a specialized education in Cuba.[9]

The fast-growing civil cooperation required further agreements, structures, and organizations on both sides. Government ministries signed more precise agreements based on the skeleton agreement of July 1976. These were supported by the creation in Cuba of the State Committee for Economic Cooperation (Comité Estatal de Colaboración Económica, CECE), in November 1976. Its task was to organize and to shape the international cooperation with foreign countries in an efficient way. Through CECE, the governments of Cuba and Angola settled a special agreement on education. It included the deployment of Cuban professors in Angola to support the building of higher education, the first scholarships for Angolan students to enable them to study at universities in Cuba, and, most important of all, a fundamental analysis of the specific educational needs of Angola by exchanging delegations and experts. The agreement was valid for a year in each case and was renegotiated every year, depending on Angola's needs and Cuba's capabilities to fulfil them.[10] A structure for exchanges and communication was also fixed. A bilateral commission discussed the necessities and problems of the cooperation on a regular basis and prepared the signing of the agreement every year. For its part, the Angolan Ministry of Education (MED) formed a special section (Office for International Cooperation) in 1977 that was exclusively responsible for the maintenance and control of any cooperation agreements with foreign countries. The majority of these were with Cuba. The Cuban organization "Cubatécnica" took responsibility for organizational and logistic implementation of the cooperation. The Angolan counterpart was the "Logitécnica," founded in 1980.

The Angolan Reform of Education

The education policy of the new Angolan state was passed at the first Congress of the MPLA in December 1977. It featured for the first time principles for a radical reform of the whole national education system that had been neglected during colonial times. Following the principles of the constitution of the independent state, education was one of the basic civil rights of all Angolans independent of their sex, skin color, religion, ethnic and cultural affiliation, or social status. Four years of compulsory basic education were to be free of charge and available for every Angolan.[11]

During Portuguese colonial rule, education of the Angolan population with African ethnicity scarcely existed. The educational system was almost entirely directed toward the children of the white settlers. Schools were concentrated in the urban centers of the country such as the capital

Luanda, Huambo, or Benguela, where the majority of the white settlers lived. Schooling was poorly developed in the countryside, where the majority of the black population lived. Colonial education was subject to the economic interests of Portugal. Until the 1960s, 99 percent of the African Angolan population had almost no civil rights. Many of them served as laborers on the agricultural farms that produced cash crops such as cotton, sisal, sugar, and, above all, coffee. Although the colonial educational system was reformed with the outbreak of the anticolonial struggle at the beginning of 1960s and offered some limited educational opportunities to the country's African and mixed-race population, as a whole it went on discriminating against the Africans.[12] Angola had registered half a million primary pupils in 1973, but most of them, as well as those teachers who were trained appropriately, were Portuguese. The majority of them left the country between 1975 and 1976.

After independence, the new educational policy of the MPLA was designed to construct a socialist society and to unify the country in order to build a nation. A fundamental document stated that courses of study and labor should be closely interlinked and become the first principles for the education of future generations. Education was to promote physical and intellectual abilities. It must build the patriotism of the Angolan people, and facilitate the development of a socialist personality—the so-called "New Man." These basic principles reflected the Cuban philosophy of a modern socialist education system and were transferred from Cuba to Angola.

A 12-year school system with three levels was introduced. Basic education spanning eight years was organized in three grades $(4 + 2 + 2)$, followed by high school lasting for four years, with the possibility of leading to specialization in a profession or entry into a university degree course. Due to the critical shortage of specialized staff, the attainment of a three-year university degree was made possible at a special college. Primary school was reduced to six years, the secondary level to two years, and the sixth form to one year in adult education.[13]

Angola's Postcolonial Educational Development: The Cuban Contribution

Both governments agreed with the view that only an educated population could free itself from the aftermath of colonialism and should therefore be enabled to undergo broad economic, social, and cultural modernization through education. They were also in general agreement that Angola should follow the Cuban example and transform itself into a socialist society. One of the greatest challenges for Angola was how to transform education within this context. This involved abolishing the colonial system of education and replacing it by a system of a universal mass education. This section will show how Cuba assisted Angola in this task by helping to reduce the high rate of illiteracy, teaching in schools, colleges, and universities, and providing scholarships to thousands of Angolan students to study at schools, polytechnics, and universities in Cuba.

The Literacy Campaign

Luis Ramírez Villasana, a Cuban reservist who stayed on in Angola for the civil reconstruction, became one of the most important advisers of the national committee for literacy in the following six years.[14] Together with the Angolan educationalists, he and other Cubans helped to lay the foundations for the literacy campaign that was then proclaimed by President Neto on November 22, 1976. Additionally the campaign's aim was to consolidate the national unity of Angola: "Literacy from Cabinda to Cunene," was one of the slogans. Only an educated population could actively participate in the political and economic construction of the nation. The idea that learning is a revolutionary obligation became the leitmotif of the campaign and the reform of education.[15]

This was the first Cuban experience of helping to conduct a literacy campaign in a foreign country. It soon became obvious that implementing adult literacy in Angola was not comparable to the Cuban experience. The country is more than ten times larger than the island. Except for the common colonial experience, Angola had little cultural or linguistic similarity with revolutionary Cuba. Cuba had become independent in 1902, over 70 years earlier than Angola. The educational system that was introduced after independence allowed at least the education of an urban middle class. After the revolution, this educated middle class was able to provide sufficient provisional teachers for the literacy campaign in 1961 whereby 1 million Cubans were taught to read and write within a span of one year. In addition to this, Spanish had always been the main language even in colonial times, and the population was culturally much more homogeneous than in Angola, where the cultural and linguistic situation was much more complex. Over 30 African languages were spoken by an Angolan population with wide variations in habits, traditions, and religions. Despite this, the new educational system prioritized the comprehensive introduction of Portuguese as the official and national language. A multilingual education program teaching literacy in the main African languages spoken in Angola was introduced only in 1997.

According to leading Angolan educators like Pepetela (Artur Pestana), one of the most important contemporary Angolan novelists, deputy minister of education between 1976 and 1981, and one of the initiators of the education reform, they had been in close contact with the Brazilian educator Paulo Freire. Freire's literacy campaign in Guinea-Bissau in 1973, based on his radical interactive method, and his concept of education for liberation, had many followers in Angola.[16] In spite of this, the Angolan educationalists decided finally to utilize only some aspects of Freire's method and not others. Their decision was based on pragmatic and ideological reasons. They used Freire's syllable-based pedagogy for teaching word recognition, but instead of Freire's approach of developing literacy through interacting with the particular interests of the students, they decided to use the Cuban method for literacy based on predesigned primers with highly political expressions aimed at achieving the goal of building a socialist society. The goal was that literacy in one language, using the same symbols, should promote the unity of the new state under the rule of the MPLA.[17]

In contrast to Cuba in 1961, the campaign for literacy in Angola was not accomplished by an intensive nation-wide action, but in stages. Priority in the campaign was given to developing literacy in the members of the political and social mass organizations that were closely linked with the ruling MPLA. These included political groupings, workers' unions, armed forces, and women's organizations. In addition, the Angolan campaign was based on long-term considerations and was not determined by time constraints. One of the greatest challenges of the whole educational reform was to develop the literacy campaign and construct the education system simultaneously. The aim of this simultaneous development was to integrate recently literate people into the formal education system, and thus guarantee the lasting success of the campaign.

Cuban Teachers in Angolan Schools

The biggest Cuban contribution to the construction of the Angolan educational system was the provision of thousands of teachers and students to teach in primary and secondary schools. From 1978 onward, Cuban teachers were employed on a large scale in order to achieve the goal of transforming the school system into one of mass education. The number of teachers needed for this was lacking in Angola. The school year of 1978/79 saw an explosive increase of primary school pupils of over 2 million (compared to 513,000 primary pupils in 1973).[18] The Cuban presence was still low between 1976 and 1978. Mainly specialists were sent in that period, for instance, advisers for the construction of a new educational system and for the design of school books and curricula. The significance of these advisers diminished as more Angolans took on positions of responsibility in the central structures of education.

Between 1980 and 1984, between 800 and 2,000 Cuban teachers per year were sent to Angola, and were employed in nearly all Angolan provinces, staying for an average of two years. The teachers were sent through the "Contingente Pedagógico Frank País" that was established in 1978. Cuban teachers were usually assigned to teach pupils from the sixth school year onward. It was obviously a problem that recently literate Angolan schoolchildren were taught by teachers who had no command of Portuguese. The Cuban teachers were not intended to teach Portuguese as a subject—Portuguese teachers were employed for that. To lessen problems in communication, Cubans were deployed to teach mathematics, physics, chemistry, and biology, as well as geography and history. The Angolan Ministry of Education (MED) annually determined the demands for the teachers for each subject and prepared a list of requirements for the Cuban Ministry of Education (MINED). Angola was always in need of teachers with work experience. This was a request that Cuba could not always fulfil because of shortage of personnel in its own educational system.[19]

The presence of Cuban teachers in Angolan schools had a decisive influence on the curriculum and teaching methods used in lessons. The goal was to liberate the Angolan educational system from its colonial heritage in terms of structure and content, which meant that its concepts had to undergo considerable change. Colonial education was characterized by an authoritarian "chalk and talk" teaching style, didactic teaching, and boring teaching methods. The Cubans brought with them very modern teaching concepts that had been developed and tried out in Cuba since the 1960s. The lessons became more communicative, and pupils were motivated to participate actively. Students were assisted in mastering difficult subject matter until every pupil was able to pass the exams. The best pupils were selected as monitors who were appointed as teaching assistants, whose tasks included responsibility for other pupils with weaker performance. In addition, special interest groups were introduced in which pupils had the opportunity to try out an introductory version of different specializations and professions, and to gain practical experience. Furthermore, the Cuban teachers took care of the extracurricular concerns of their pupils and their social environment. They offered extra assistance in supervising the homework of their pupils and encouraged parents and other family members to be more involved in the education of their children than was done previously. The Cubans took part in the recreational activities of the children and organized sports competitions and other meetings.[20] They also encouraged their Angolan colleagues to engage in systematic reflections on education, for example, in two educational symposia that they organized in the 1980s. These conferences offered educators the opportunity to discuss educational, didactic, and ideological issues and an exchange of experiences on a national level.[21]

Assisting with the Training of Angolan Teachers

Another important aspect of the Cuban cooperation was providing education and training for Angolan teachers. The main intention of the cooperation was to substitute Angolan teachers for the Cuban teachers, because the principle of the Cuban educational mission was assistance for self-emancipation (an ambitious aim that could not be fully achieved, as will be explained at the end of this chapter). A prelude to the teacher-training program was an intensive year-long course in the capital established for participants of all regions in 1977/78, organized and conducted by Cuban teachers. This successful and rapid training program could not be continued in the long run. One problem was that there were insufficient future teachers with the minimum qualifications to participate successfully in the course. Another problem was that those teachers who participated in the courses in the capital left a gap in their schools in the countryside. It was therefore decided that the graduates from these courses should be deployed to promote the establishment of teacher education institutes in the regional capitals.

Cuban Assistance in Higher Education

Cubans began sharing their experience in the area of higher education in 1976. Over 500 professors worked at the University of Angola (after the death of President Neto in 1979 it was named Agostinho-Neto University) in Luanda, Huambo, and Lubango, till the end of the 1980s. This enormous deployment of Cuban lecturers took place mainly in science disciplines, including engineering, medicine, veterinary medicine, and agricultural sciences, but some Cubans also lectured in philosophy, economics, and political science. Other foreign lecturers in higher education in Angola also came from Portugal, the Eastern bloc states (predominantly the GDR, Bulgaria, and Czechoslovakia) and the Soviet Union, a few from South America, and some European countries, but Cuban teaching personnel were by far the majority.

The presence of the Cuban academic staff was an indispensable part of the reconstruction and expansion of the Angolan university system. The University of Angola had especially suffered from the flight of academics after independence. The academic staff had been exclusively composed of Portuguese during the colonial past. The majority of students had also been children of the Portuguese immigrants so that Angola had no academic junior staff of its own.

Cuban Student Teachers: The Destacamento Pedagógico Internacionalista "Che Guevara"

As a result of analyses carried out in the field of education, it became obvious in 1977 that the training of Angolan teachers for the primary and secondary schools would not be sufficient for the near future to make up for the vast deficiencies in the school system. This was the reason why President Neto asked Fidel Castro in 1977 to give extra support by sending some 2,000 teachers. However, in the middle of the 1970s, Cuba itself had immense difficulties satisfying its own demand for secondary school teachers. Thus, in his speech at the beginning of the school year in 1977/78, Fidel Castro announced a unique educational experiment to meet Angola's request, at least in part: he appealed to the best students at colleges of education to complete their work experience by staying and teaching in Angola for one year. This launched the Destacamento Pedagógico Internacionalista "Che Guevara," a deployment of student-teachers that was a totally new feature of the Cuban internationalist mission in the field of education.[22] This initiative was not only to satisfy Angola's request, but also to help build the internationalist experience and commitment of the Cuban volunteers. The students were to experience the character of Cuban internationalism and would learn what was involved in supporting altruistically a politically like-minded state with the utmost effort. The appeal applied to students who had started their studies in the recently founded Pedagogic University (ISP) and who belonged to the Destacamento Pedagógico Manuel Ascunce Domenech. All of them were then participants in a special educational program to relieve the enormous shortage of secondary school teachers in Cuba at the beginning of the 1970s. The students were carrying out the maxim of "work and study" while teaching at schools from the second year of their education.[23]

Castro's suggestion to deploy them in Angola was an international extension of a successful educational experiment that had already taken place for six years in Cuba. These principles—the combination of study and work—have often been considered genuine socialist elements of the Cuban educational system, but they have their roots in the Americas. Cuba's national poet, intellectual, and outstanding visionary of Cuban independence in the nineteenth century, José Martí (1853–1895), can be seen as a pioneer for the development of education to ensure an integral development (of body and spirit) of a human being. Martí's ideas had been taken up again after the revolution and had a great influence on the development of Cuba's revolutionary educational methods.

A huge number of student teachers volunteered for the assignment in Angola. The Cuban Ministry of Education had to develop selection criteria very quickly and design a program to prepare the students for their mission. The majority of students chosen were those studying sciences as these were the specialities requested in Angola. Other crucial criteria were performance of students, their discipline, and the extent to which they had demonstrated positive social engagement. Belonging to a political organization was important but not crucial. The 878 students chosen for the first brigade were given a four-month intensive term in which they continued their studies and, at the same time, were prepared for their stay in Angola. In intensive courses, they were taught the Portuguese language and the politics and history of Angola, and they received basic military training. During the training, their psychological and social suitability for the big experiment was also tested. Finally, 732 students of educational studies, mostly female, went to Angola in March 1978.[24]

In Angola, the student teachers shared housing and everyday life with their Cuban colleagues of the civil mission. They were part of the Cuban civil organization structure that was established in 1977. Additionally, in order to continue their university education in Angola, they were accompanied by Cuban professors. These young Cuban student teachers, just 17–20 years old, were employed in all parts of the country to teach the sciences, history, and geography to pupils from the sixth grade onward. This was a great challenge, although the students were supervised by local tutors and were supported by their professors and by experts, in curriculum and pedagogy, who helped them with preparations of their lessons as well as with all questions they might have on content and method. For most of them, it was the first long absence from home and their first visit to a foreign country with another culture and a language they were learning but had not mastered. On top of that, they had to deal with the precarious way of living that awaited them and the sometimes life-threatening war situation with which they were faced. Although during the second year, students were prepared for their assignment in intensive courses in Cuba, the reality in Angola often proved to be harrowing. They had to teach huge school classes of children of widely varying ages with different levels of education. Another problem was that the children's mother tongue often was not Portuguese, but an African language. In addition, the Portuguese of the Cuban student teachers was also quite problematic—one reason being the linguistic closeness to Spanish. Predictably, communication was often difficult. The students were often in charge of many of these classes and additionally had to teach evening classes for adults. It turned out that the experiment of the student teachers was not as successful as expected, because the students were too young and too inexperienced. When the annual sending of several hundred education students stopped in 1986, a total of 2,026 had taught in Angola.[25] Meritorious participation in the program seems to have been the basis of career opportunities for the Cuban students. Nowadays many participants of the program are important educators, leaders, and managers in the Cuban educational system.

Scholarships for Angolans to Study in Cuba

Another main focus of the cooperation between Cuba and Angola were the scholarships for Angolan pupils and students, enabling them to complete their school education on Cuba's Isle of Youth, or to finish their studies at a polytechnic or university in Cuba. The first allocation of 1,200 Angolan children, among them many orphans or children of civil war refugees, came to the Isle of Youth in August 1977. In June, Cuba had announced the opening of four schools for Angolan children with an overall capacity of about 2,500 primary and secondary level pupils. After completing school, they could go on to a polytechnic or university education, depending on their achievements. This program for scholarships is carried out even to this day. About 7,500 Angolan scholars have graduated from schools, universities, and technical colleges in Cuba, and up to 2001, a further 2,500 Angolans were receiving further education.[26]

The choice of the scholarship holders was made by each country. This often led to a very uneven proportion of boys and girls, normally 70 percent male and 30 percent female students. This can be traced back to the fact that families often sent their male offspring to be educated in foreign countries while their daughters stayed at home.

The Isle of Youth as a center for international education was and still is unique worldwide. The establishment by the Cubans of African, Latin American, and Asian schools on the isle was an integral part of the civil cooperation overseas, and another component of Cuban internationalism.

This was probably one of the most significant projects of Cuban internationalism in the field of education. The challenges for this educational experiment were enormous from the beginning. At times, youngsters from 34 nations of the world lived and studied on the island. The foundational principle of education there was the nurturing of the specific cultural traditions of the students. This was expressed by the annual festival of friendship and culture beginning in 1978, where students from the different nations displayed their expressive culture through music, dance, art, theater, sports, and literature in festivals and friendly competitions. Although the language of instruction was Spanish, students were taught the literature, geography, and history of their home country by teachers from the respective mother country who used their own national language for lessons.

Primary and secondary schools were organized according to nationality in order to strengthen their identification with their country of origin. Students of all nationalities could go on to tertiary education in polytechnic institutions and universities if they met the entry standards, specializing in education, military training, and a variety of other fields. The students and teachers of each country chose representatives who took care of all matters concerning them. For example, these representatives kept contact with embassies and organized holiday activities.

Another central principle of the schools on the Isle of Youth was the close connection between studies and work. Apart from their classes, the students also had to work either in the school gardens or the citrus plantations, from an early age onward. The intention was to teach students to attach great value to practical work within an educational context. Other principles were the development of a culture of science and the education of a spirit of research, as well as the encouragement of physical and mental abilities, the acquisition of cultural capabilities, and the observation of strict discipline.[27]

There has still been little research carried out on the experience of Angolan pupils and students on the Isle of Youth. Many of them lived in the boarding schools for years, far away from their families and familiar surroundings. In interviews they expressed their satisfaction about their education in Cuba, recognizing that most of them would never otherwise have had a chance to achieve a qualifying school or academic education. Nevertheless, they had to face numerous difficulties in adapting. Just as the Cubans had to adapt to Angola quickly, so too the Angolan children and young people had to get quickly used to the new Cuban surroundings, the foreign culture, and the different habits, as well as to accustom themselves to the new language of instruction, different food, another interpretation of discipline, and living together in large, but closely knit groups, observing order and organization as well as the strict ethos of work. Another problem was that rivalries sometimes emerged between the young men of different nationalities leading to violent outbursts that had to be reconciled.

How Cuban Educators Experienced Angola

Statistics of November 1980 from the Angolan Ministry of Education show that 1,168 Cubans were employed in education at that time. To be more precise, 902 Cuban teachers taught in primary schools, 67 in colleges, 79 at institutes for teacher training, 15 in secondary schools, and 25 in higher education. According to these figures, the participants were present in all provinces except for the southern region of Cunene. The majority of Cuban teachers were always located in Luanda, the capital. The statistics also show that the Cuban quota constituted up to 80 percent of all foreign assistance in education between 1980 and 1983. Of the remainder, 10 percent were from Portugal, and the rest were from Bulgaria, the GDR, the USSR, Cape Verde Islands, and elsewhere. This general pattern continued, though with different absolute numbers, until the beginning of 1984. The number of Cuban participants increased steadily until 1983 and reached its climax in that same year with more than 2,000 persons.[28] After that, the Cuban presence in the educational field decreased rapidly. There were different reasons for the large-scale withdrawal of Cuban civilians in all professional fields, but most notably, the security situation in various regions worsened with intense fighting from the opponents of the government (UNITA, among others). Thus, the security of foreign civilians could not be guaranteed anymore. In a bomb explosion carried out in 1984 by UNITA in Huambo, a regional capital, 14 Cuban construction workers were killed in a building in which Cuban civilians lived. Shortly afterwards, a Cuban teacher was killed and five others were seriously wounded in a UNITA attack in the coastal town of Sumbe (province of Kwanza Sul).

Sometimes, it has been assumed that the Cubans who worked in the civil mission had a double function as civilians and as soldiers.[29] The fact is that all adult Cubans had basic military training because of a specific Cuban strategy of defense based on Cuba's situation as a small island just off the US shore and constantly subject to threats. This basic military training, which was refreshed regularly during duties in Angola, was intended to enable Cubans to defend themselves against attacks (like those in Sumbe) and to be able to protect their fellow human beings. These military skills of the Cuban internationalists were considered an additional qualification for working in the difficult circumstances in Angola compared to other participants from foreign countries who had no defense training—for example, the personnel from Eastern bloc states. This was also an important reason why it was possible to send Cuban teachers into conflict zones in remote regions. In the case of an attack, they could defend themselves as well as be protected and defended by any Cuban military present. As mentioned earlier on, the civil mission developed from the military one, and a lot of civilians possessed more than the basic military training. In conflict zones, some even went armed to their lessons. Nevertheless, the civil mission should not be considered as a "disguised" military action. This can be supported by various documents that I inspected at the Angolan Ministry of Education.

These documents were the result of bilateral agreements between the two governments. The job specifications for teachers were not about military qualifications, but about the professional, educational, personal, and political qualification of Cuban teachers. Many of the interviews I conducted with Cuban teachers show that they perceived the regular military training programs in which they had to participate, in Angola, as being bothersome. They also mentioned that the war situation included a permanent latent military threat, which was noticeable in towns as well as provincial areas. This was experienced as extraordinary stress.[30]

Many of the Cuban civilians were traumatized by their experience in Angola. Although in general the teachers and professors had been prepared for their stay in Angola and had been informed about the difficult situation there beforehand, they had no perception of the effects of a war or the meaning of "Africa" or "Angola." Many recollect the cultural shock that they had to overcome in connection with hygiene, food, and the precarious living conditions of the population. In this complex situation, separation from their families added to the overall difficulties, because most of them left their partners and children behind in Cuba. Nevertheless, many civilians also felt that their work in Angola had been a great learning experience and had taught them a great deal in personal, political, and pedagogical aspects.[31]

Conclusion

The close political relationship between Cuba and Angola changed drastically after the summer of 1991. The independence of Namibia was linked to the withdrawal of troops in Angola according to the New York Peace Accords that were signed by Angola, Cuba, and South Africa under surveillance of the US government in December 1988. With the withdrawal of military units the civil cooperation ended as well. Thousands of soldiers and civilians returned to Cuba in 1991. The war in Angola continued, and with the collapse of the Soviet Union, Cuba faced the beginning of the most dramatic crisis in its history. Though the cooperation was continued in some fields, it was scaled down considerably and with a few exceptions, such as—as mentioned earlier—granting of scholarships for Angolan pupils. The swiftness with which the New York Peace Accords were negotiated was a surprise to everyone, so that selective solutions for the crisis in the field of education could not be found. The deployment of Cuban educational specialists to Angola had never been free of charge, but in comparison with the workforce sent from other countries, between 1976 and 1991, the costs for Cuban specialists had been much lower. Until 1991 the Cuban civil mission in Angola was realized within the frame of "internationalist solidarity." After 1991, Cuba's deep economic crisis forced the government to charge appropriate prices for the deployment of their civil specialists, and the cost of Cuban advisers, teachers, and professors rose considerably.

Despite Cuba's enormous efforts, Angola's huge problems in the field of education could not be solved in the 15 years of the Cuban presence. The combination of the specific postcolonial situation and the long-lasting external and internal war prevented the country from dealing adequately with its most important social concerns. Above all, illiteracy could not be effectively brought to an end, because the school system did not work consistently. A UNESCO study in 2005 makes it clear that the situation got worse again after 1991. For instance, just 27.7 percent of 15–19-year-olds were able to read and write at the end of the 1990s. The cohort of 20–35-year-olds showed a 51 percent literacy rate, while the other age groups had a rate of 21 percent.[32] One reason why the gaps in literacy could not be removed was that the country did not manage to build up a steady Angolan teaching staff in 15 years of Cuban presence. A memorandum of the Angolan Ministry of Education dating from August 1990 confirms this fact and draws a disillusioned conclusion. The document shows that the withdrawal of Cuban civilians in the field of education left an immense vacuum behind that was visible as early as 1990. The memorandum critically reflects the fact that after independence the Angolan Ministry of Education quickly became used to relying on the deployment of Cuban teachers in all school types from primary school to university. This fact and simultaneously the inadequate financial and social stimulus for Angolans to strive for teacher training tended to prevent the development of a comprehensive strategy for the education and promotion of Angolan staff.[33] The principle of assistance for self-emancipation could not be realized also because of the magnitude of the country's needs and the problems that occurred during this war-time period.

The modesty, strong will, and high degree of organization that characterized the Cuban internationalists led to their deployment in remote regions. This was seen as an enormous saving for Angola and left a positive impact. Many young Angolans experienced their Cuban teachers or their education at the schools of the Isle of Youth in a positive way given their better pedagogical training in comparison to that of the Angolan teachers. Cubans could take the credit for the education of at least one generation of Angolans, as one of my Angolan interview partners stated.[34] Incidentally, many of today's leading figures in the Angolan economy, culture, and politics have benefited from their Cuban education. Cuban involvement in this cooperation thus helped to lay the foundations for postcolonial educational development in Angola, although its political and ideological principles were changed in different reforms following the Cuban withdrawal.

Notes

1. This article is based on findings from my postdoctoral research project at the Institute of History at the University of Duisburg-Essen, Germany, entitled "Cubans in Angola: South-South Cooperation and Educational Transfers 1976–1991" (in press, 2012, Oldenbourg Verlag, Munich). Thanks to the support of the

Deutsche Forschungsgemeinschaft (German Research Foundation) I was able to carry out my investigation between 2004 and 2006 in archives in Angola, Cuba, Portugal, and the United States among others. I also interviewed 139 contemporary witnesses (Cubans and Angolans) whom I would like to thank for their trust in me. My interviewees were "experts" as well as "normal" eyewitnesses. The experts include educationalists and politicians, many of them involved in the development of the Cuban educational mission in Angola or in the Angolan educational reform project. The "normal" eyewitnesses were generally Cubans who taught in Angola and their former Angolan pupils. Some of the eyewitnesses had worked in other fields and/or in other African countries.
2. The figures are taken from statistics by the Cuban Ministry of Education. Compare Jiménez R. L. *Mujeres Sin Fronteras*. La Habana: Editoria Política, 2008 p. 96f. as well as García Pérez Castañeda, A. "El Internacionalismo de Cuba en la Colaboración Económica y Científico-Técnica. Esbozo histórico de un cuarto de siglo de la Revolución Socialista Cubana 1963–1988.". La Habana: Instituto de Historia de Cuba, n.d. (unpublished) p. 241f.
3. Hitherto, the broadest representation of Cuba's relationships to Africa can be found in Gleijeses, P. *Conflicting Missions. Havana, Washington, and Africa, 1959–1976*. Chapel Hill: University of North Carolina Press, 2002; Gleijeses, P. "Moscow's Proxy? Cuba and Africa 1975–1988." *Journal of Cold War Studies* 8, no. 4 (2006): 98–146; and George, E. *The Cuban Intervention in Angola: From Che Guevara to Cuito Cuanavale*. London: Frank Cass, 2005. However Gleijeses's and George's works focus on the political, diplomatic, and military history. Both mention the civil cooperation only at the margins.
4. In the speech of the Angolan president at the occasion of the start of the literacy campaign on November 22, 1976, he mentioned that 85 percent of the Angolan population was illiterate. *Jornal de Angola*, 23.11.1976, p. 2.
5. Further information on the post colonial armed conflict in Angola and the challenges of independence in Angola can be found, for example, in Birmingham, D. *Frontline Nationalism in Angola and Mozambique*. Trenton: Africa World Press, 1992; Chabal, P. and Vidal, N. eds. *Angola: The Weight of History*. London: Hurst & Company, 2007; Messiant, C. 1961; and *L'Angola Colonial, Histoire Et Société: Les Prémisses Du Mouvement Nationaliste*. Basel: P. Schlettwein Publishing, 2006. Messiant, C. "Angola: The Challenge of Statehood." In *History of Central Africa*, edited by D. Birmingham and P. Martin, 131–65. London: Longman, 1998; Bender, G. *Angola under the Portuguese: The Myth and the Reality*. Berkeley: University of California Press, 1978.
6. Ramírez, V. "Algunas experiencias de la batalla de alfabetización en la República de Angola. Concurso sobre la colaboración internacionalista en la educación": maestros internacionalistas, Género: Testimonio. La Habana, n.d. (unpublished).
7. See the interviews with J. Z. in Luanda on February 01, 2006 and S. L. in La Habana on June 16, 2006. Both participated in the expedition.
8. Castro, F. "Acto conmemorativo del XXIII Aniversario del asalto al cuartel Moncada, 26.07.1976." In: Castro, Fidel (1979). Discursos, Tomo III, 227–43. Havanna: Editorial de Ciencias Sociales, 1979.
9. Cf. Interview with D. D. in Luanda on January 20, 2006. He belonged to these first young Angolans who had finished their studies in Cuba.
10. Cf. "Acordo especial de Colaboração entre o Ministério da Educação da República Popular de Angola e o Ministério da Educação da República de Cuba" and "Acordo especial de Colaboração entre o Ministério da Educação da República Popular de Angola e o Ministério da Educação Superior da República de Cuba," signed in La Habana on December 5, 1976 (Archive MED, Department GII). (Author's

remark: The documents that I quoted are from the archives of the Angolan Ministry of Education [MED]. The archives were not classified or given a call number; therefore, they are cited by giving the title, date, and habitat.)
11. MPLA. *Princípios de base para a reformulação do sistema de educação e ensino na RPA*. Luanda: Edição do Ministério da Educação da República Popular de Angola, 1978.
12. Silva, E. M. "O papel societal do sistema do ensino em Angola colonial (1926–1974)." Revista Internacional de Estudos Africanos, no. 16–17 ((1992–1994)): 103–30; Vela, A. "Transnacionalismo E Políticas Educativas: O Caso Angolano (1975–2005)." Porto: Dissertação apresentada à Universidade Católica Portuguesa para a obtenção do grau de Mestre em Ciências da Educação, 2006.
13. MPLA, *Princípios de base*.
14. Ramírez, V. "Algunas experiencias de la batalla de alfabetización."
15. See *Jornal de Angola*, 23.11.1976, p. 1 and p. 2.
16. See the interview with Pepetela (his real name is Artur Pestana) in Luanda on January 27, 2006, and March 17, 2006.
17. Ministério da Educação e Cultura, *A vitória é certa. Guia do alfabetisador*. Luanda: Edição do Ministério da Educação e Cultura da República Popular de Angola, 1976b; Ministério da Educação e Cultura, *A vitória é certa - a luta continua. Manual de Alfabetização*. Luanda: Edição do Ministério da Educação e Cultura da República Popular de Angola, 1976a.
18. Cf. the project suggestion of the UNICEF for the Ministry of Education (MED) to improve the Angolan education system, dept. INIDE, 15/12/1984 (archive MED, dept. GII).
19. Pepetela referred to this problem in his interview (in Luanda, January 27 and March 17, 2006). I was able to partly retrace this lack of experience in some of the personnel files at the archives of the Angolan Ministry of Education.
20. The information on the Cuban innovations and their influence on Angolan pupils I gathered from my various interviews with Cuban teachers and Angolan pupils.
21. Cf. "Contingente Educacional Cubano en la RPA 2. Jornada Pedagógcica." Programa y Libro Resumen, Mayo 1983 (archive MED, dept. GII).
22. Castro, F. "Discurso Pronunciado En el Acto de inauguración del curso escolar 1977–1978, Efectuada en la escuela vocacional 'José Martí,' Holguín, El 1ro. de Septiembre de 1977." Versiones taquigráficos. Consejo del Estado. www.cuba.cu /gobierno/discursos 1977.
23. Turner, M. L. *Breve Historia De Un Destacamento*. La Habana: Editorial Pueblo y Educación, 1996.
24. Cf. Bohemia 1/02/1978, "La hermosa flor de la solidaridad humana", pp. 32–35, here p. 34.
25. Turner M. L., *Breve Historia*, p. 30.
26. Ortega, V. et al. "Estudiantes Extranjeros En La Isla De La Juventud (1977–1996)." La Habana: MINVEC, 2004 (unpublished document).
27. Most of the information about the international schools on the Isla is taken from an interview with one of the former general school-directors of the Isle of Youth. Cf. Interview with Oscar Elejalde Villalón in La Habana on September 21, 2006.
28. The figures are taken from the files of the Office for International Co-operations (GII) of the Angolan Ministry of Education (MED) that comprehensively registered the numbers and biographical profiles of all the international cooperants from 1980 onward.
29. George, E., *The Cuban Intervention in Angola*, p. 157f.
30. Between 2004 and 2006, I conducted over 80 biographical interviews with Cubans who were in Angola for the civil effort. The majority had been working in the

educational mission. In the Interviews, they expressed their subjective perspective of their experiences in Angola.
31. These conclusions from my interviews can be generalized across many informants, and are significant.
32. Cf. Comissão Nacional para a UNESCO/Direcção Nacional para o Ensino Geral (2005), p. 6.
33. See Gabinete de Intercambio Internacional do MED, "Problemática da Retirada da Cooperação Cubana da RPA," Luanda October 15, 1990 (archive MED, dept. GII).
34. Cf. Interview with O. in Luanda on November 29, 2006.

References

Bender, G. *Angola under the Portuguese. The Myth and the Reality*. Berkeley: University of California Press, 1978.
Birmingham, D. *Frontline Nationalism in Angola and Mozambique*. Trenton: Africa World Press, 1992.
Castro, F. "Acto Conmemorativo Del XXVIII Aniversario Del Asalto Al Cuartel Moncada, 26.07.1976." In *Castro, Fidel (1979). Discursos, Tomo Iii*, 227–43. Havanna: Editorial de Ciencias Sociales, 1979.
———. "Discurso Pronunciado En El Acto De Inauguración Del Curso Escolar 1977–1978, Efectuada En La Escuela Vocacional 'José Martí,' Holguín, El 1ro. De Septiembre De 1977." In *Versiones taquigráficos. Consejo del Estado. In:* www.cuba.cu/gobierno/discursos, 1977.
Chabal, P. and N Vidal, eds. *Angola: The Weight of History*. London: Hurst & Company, 2007.
Comissão, Nacional para a UNESCO/Direcção Nacional para o Ensino Geral. "Analise Da Situação Da Alfabetização E Educação De Adultos Em Angola." Luanda: Ministerio da Educação, 2005.
Cultura, Ministério da Educação e. "A Vitória É Certa." In *Guia do alfabetisador*. Luanda: Edição do Ministério da Educação e Cultura da República Popular de Angola, 1976b.
———. "A Vitória é Certa—a Luta Continua." In *Manual de Alfabetização*. Luanda: Edição do Ministério da Educação e Cultura da República Popular de Angola, 1976a.
García Pérez Castañeda, A. "El Internacionalismo De Cuba En La Colaboración Económica Y Científico-Técnica: Esbozo Histórico De Un Cuarto De Siglo De La Revolución Socialista Cubana 1963–1988." La Habana: Instituto de Historia de Cuba, n.d.
George, E. *The Cuban Intervention in Angola: From Che Guevara to Cuito Cuanavale*. London: Frank Cass, 2005.
Gleijeses, P. *Conflicting Missions. Havana, Washington, and Africa, 1959-1976*. Chapel Hill: University of North Carolina Press, 2002.
———. "Moscow's Proxy? Cuba and Africa 1975–1988." *Journal of Cold War Studies* 8, no. 4 (2006): 98–146.
Hatzky, C. "Kubaner in Angola. Süd-Süd-Kooperation Und Bildungstransfer 1976–1991, Essen." München: Oldenbourg Verlag, 2009.
———. ""Os Bons Colonizadores": Cuba's Educational Mission in Angola, 1976–1991. Safundi." *Journal of South African and American Studies* 9, no. 1 (2008): 53–68.
Jiménez, R. L. *Mujeres Sin Fronteras*. La Habana: Editoria Política, 2008.

Messiant, C. *1961. L'angola Colonial, Histoire Et Société. Les Prémisses Du Mouvement Nationaliste*. Basel: P. Schlettwein Publishing, 2006.

———. "Angola: The Challenge of Statehood." In *History of Central Africa*. Edited by D. Birmingham and P. Martin, 131–65. London: Longman, 1998.

MPLA. "Princípios De Base Para a Reformulação Do Sistema De Educação E Ensino Na RPA" Luanda: Edição do Ministério da Educação da República Popular de Angola, 1978.

Ortega, Vivino et al. "Estudiantes Extranjeros En La Isla De La Juventud (1977–1996)." La Habana: MINVEC, 2004.

Ramírez, V. L. "Algunas Experiencias De La Batalla De Alfabetización En La República De Angola. Concurso Sobre La Colaboración Internacionalista En La Educación." In *Maestros internacionalistas: Género: Testimonio*. La Habana n.d.

Silva, M. "O Papel Societal Do Sistema Do Ensino Em Angola Colonial (1926–1974)." *Revista Internacional de Estudos Africanos*, no. 16–17 ((1992–1994)): 103–30.

Turner, M. L. *Breve Historia De Un Destacamento*. La Habana: Editorial Pueblo y Educación, 1996.

Vela, A. "Transnacionalismo E Políticas Educativas: O Caso Angolano (1975–2005)." Porto: Dissertação apresentada à Universidade Católica Portuguesa para a obtenção do grau de Mestre em Ciências da Educação, 2006.

9

Capacity Building in Latin American Universities: Cuba's Contribution

Boris Tristá Pérez

Introduction

A large and growing number of foreign students are enrolled in postgraduate degree programs in Cuba. During 2002–2003, about 5000 professionals from approximately 30 countries were studying in different postgraduate courses in Cuba. Of these 5000, about 1000 were enrolled in masters and PhD degree programs.[1] A number of Cuban postgraduate courses are offered in Latin American countries. Their universities arrange for Cuban professors to travel and teach the courses requested. In some countries, the Ministry of Education accredits the Cuban degree. Others do not find this necessary. In addition, Cuban professors are invited to take part in teaching postgraduate courses offered by foreign universities. They are also sometimes invited to help with restructuring university policies and programs and with the improvement of management systems.

How is it possible for a country of limited economic resources like Cuba, to assist other countries in developing the management capacity of their university systems? How is this assistance carried out? And how has Cuba become one of the most important countries in Latin America for providing professional upgrading through postgraduate courses? My interest in exploring such questions in this chapter comes out of my more than 40 years of experience in working as a Cuban university academic. My work has included the coordination and management of large university programs, participation at the Ministry of Higher Education in the national planning of university development, and researching and teaching educational management studies at CEPES, the Center for Higher Education research at the University of Havana, as well as at several universities in Bolivia and Mexico.

The contemporary world with its explosion of information in science and technology more than ever requires professionals to widen and continually update their knowledge to tackle the immense global problems of development in an ethical, scientific, and holistic way. Many developing countries, weighed down with the dysfunctional patterns of neocolonialism, have university systems that are too poorly developed to produce adequate numbers of graduates and postgraduates for their needs. International collaboration is essential to help them develop their higher education systems, but traditional forms of assistance from the wealthy countries have not been suitable for achieving this goal.

The argument of the chapter is that Cuba's university strength is a foundation for collaboration in building university capacity overseas. Cuba's strong postgraduate education system and its systematic professional development of university academics provide the foundation that enables it to help other countries develop their postgraduate capacity. This involves the training of their students and supporting them to develop their administrative and curricular systems of higher education. In the following sections, I provide: 1) an overview of how Cuban postgraduate education developed within the university system, and of other factors that demonstrate how the principle of solidarity with other countries underpins Cuba's sharing of its higher education expertise; (2) principles underlying the help with administration and institutional development that Cuba provides to overseas universities; and (3) a case study of a particular experience of Cuban collaboration with a university in Bolivia, South America.

The Strength and Dynamism of the Cuban University System

The starting point of Cuba's ability to share expertise to help postgraduate education and university management in other countries has been the development of a strong postgraduate sector in Cuba's higher education system. This will be outlined next.

The Development of Postgraduate Education in Cuba

In 1959, at the time of the triumph of the Cuban Revolution, postgraduate education was practically nonexistent in Cuba. Only a few professionals, who received funding or worked for foreign companies, were able to study abroad to improve their qualifications.

From 1959 onward, and particularly after the university reform of 1962, postgraduate education started to develop. This was possible mainly because of assistance from different countries, especially in the Socialist bloc. It cannot be said that an internal postgraduate education system existed as part of a national vision until after the promulgation in 1976 of Law No. 1281. Before that, there were only isolated postgraduate programs that were useful but far from adequate to fulfil the needs of the country. This law established the integration of the system of postgraduate studies. It created the Ministry of Higher Education (Ministerio de Educación Superior) to carry out national policy related to higher education, including the organization and management of the whole system of postgraduate education in universities. This was a new stage in the development of postgraduate education.

From this time, two parallel policies were launched. One provided for the award of academic degrees and other professional qualifications. Simultaneously, there was provision for the upgrading of academics, because of the importance of this for the development of the whole of the higher education system. This new system of professional upgrading gave university graduates the possibility of continuously acquiring new knowledge and widening the skills necessary for them to work effectively as professionals with a high level of culture. The three main types of postgraduate provision are long periods of training in higher degree programs leading to a research degree, short courses, and upgrading diploma courses. Other types of professional upgrading that are more responsive to short-term needs include conferences and workshops.

Postgraduate education in Cuba is offered in universities and other institutions, such as research centers. This constitutes the highest level of the national system of education. Currently, postgraduate education is offered in 52 universities and research centers throughout Cuba, and in more than 250 institutions related to teaching and research. These are authorized by the Ministry of Higher Education to offer postgraduate degrees below the PhD level. Only 41 institutions in Cuba are authorized to offer PhD programs. There is a system of 45 national panels of experts to examine doctoral theses in different specializations. When a thesis is submitted, about seven experts from the relevant panel are selected to examine it.

During the 1990s, a new type of economy emerged. Having lost support and trade from the COMECON bloc, Cuba had to find new economic modalities. The state established the opportunity for private sector interests to invest in state enterprises, and new trading arrangements were made with countries that had not been partners before. New skills such as marketing, advertising, and others had to be acquired to work with market conditions, and new skills were also needed for electronic communications technologies. Thus, Cuba's postgraduate education system faced a new economic context that led to unprecedented demands. In response, postgraduate training was redesigned to support a wide range of new skills, to produce new qualifications and labor profiles and even the development of new mentalities and attitudes.

University postgraduate courses, responding to the significant changes during that period, showed a large increase in quantity, both in the number of courses and number of participants. By 2000, the number of courses (short professional courses, training programs, and diploma programs) was 3572, and the number of participants was 95,869. Postgraduate courses were improved and became a basic instrument to support the cultural, economic, social, and scientific and technical strategies of the country. The number of university graduates went up to over 6 percent of the Cuban population. Another significant fact in this period was the high number of professionals who had graduated from study programs conceived in the 1980s under the strategy of training university graduates with a broad labor profile, capable of working in a wide range of posts. Specialization was left mainly to postgraduate training in the particular knowledge needed in specific professional occupations.

Between 2000 and 2004, Cuban universities developed more than 4,100 short professional courses ranging from 20 to 60 hours in length, 693 mentorships (individualized training programs carried out by a mentor or tutor), and 661 diploma programs of 240 hours each in length. About 200,000 professionals participated in these postgraduate activities. At a higher level, more than 1,900 professionals graduated with masters degrees, and 183 with PhDs, according to the official figures of the Ministry for Higher Education.[2]

An important trend of postgraduate courses is to seek technologies to increase the use of distance education. This will facilitate access to postgraduate studies throughout the country especially for people who work in places far away from the main cities. During 2002–2003, five new diploma courses and 121 short courses were developed by distance education.[3]

University Support for Solidarity as National Policy

The Cuban Revolution emphasizes solidarity as a foundational national value. It is understood as being of key significance at both the individual and institutional levels. Therefore, when an individual is asked to support a foreign university in teaching a course, the university has an obligation to support that person by granting him or her leave to carry out this activity. Similarly, when a foreign institution asks a Cuban one for assistance, the Cuban institution will try to select staff members and give them paid leave to travel for this purpose.

This national policy of cooperation can be demonstrated in many ways in addition to teaching. For instance: the Cuban people donated blood for the victims of an earthquake in Peru; and sent 500 medical doctors to assist Pakistan in helping the victims of the 2005 earthquake.

The constant practice of solidarity has reinforced the willingness of Cubans to cooperate at the level of the state, institutions, and individuals. This includes the staff and students in the university sector.

Scientific and Professional Development

It is not enough to be willing to cooperate. This willingness has to be supported by high-quality mechanisms to facilitate cooperation. Cuba's scientific and professional development is what supports its cooperation in postgraduate education.

Scientific development is based on the fact that research and technological innovation are very important in the work of a university department. The participation of professors in research tasks has steadily increased, currently reaching 80 percent of academics. Research activity has also been developed in locations other than university departments, such as centers of advanced studies and research centers in different fields of specialization. An example of one such center of advanced studies is CEPES, which is the Center for the Improvement of Higher Education at the University of Havana. An example of a research center is the Institute of Animal Sciences, which is part of the Agrarian University of Havana. There are 60 centers of advanced study and 20 research centers supervised by the Ministry of Higher Education.[4]

Apart from formal postgraduate degree studies, professional upgrading courses enhance the capacities of academics in both teaching and research. For example, new academics with a recent PhD would be required to take short courses in the pedagogy of higher education in order to enhance their professional skills.

Internal Cooperation within Cuba

Institutional cooperation offered by the Cuban universities is based on a wide experience of cooperation among national institutions.

It must be taken into consideration that from the mid-1970s to the mid-1980s, there was a great expansion of the higher educational system, with the number of general and specialist universities increasing significantly. In the academic year 1976–77 there were 28, by the academic year 1986–87 there were 42, and presently there are 63 university institutions.

This accelerated growth in the number of institutions required a significant effort in cooperation in order to avoid unevenness of quality. When a new institution is established, its academics are guaranteed support and help from older ones. This experience of internal cooperation contributes to the development of the academic's skills in cultural adaptation. For example, when Cubans from Havana work in Camaguey or Santiago de Cuba, they learn to adapt to these local cultures, and this prepares them well for working abroad and interacting in different cross-cultural and educational contexts.

International Cooperation in Undergraduate Education

Cuban higher education has always provided training and qualifications for foreign students. During the period between 1961 and the present, almost 40,000 overseas students have graduated in the country, and 16,500 students out of this group have undertaken university studies. Presently, more than 11,000 overseas students are studying in Cuban universities, the highest number at any one time. Of them, 79 percent comes from Latin America and the Caribbean, 16.2 percent come from Africa, and 3.8 percent from Asia.[5]

Many students who receive their undergraduate degrees in Cuba choose to go on to undertake postgraduate studies there. Another way of organizing this is for Cuban-trained students who have returned to their homelands to request that Cuban professors travel there to provide training and support for a Cuban postgraduate degree. In Brazil and Colombia, the government has to accredit these courses. Other countries, having established parity, do not regard this as necessary. In general, professors stay four to eight weeks to teach or support a subject in a particular program, bringing teaching materials from Cuba with them.

Flexible Delivery and Low Cost of Student-Centered Postgraduate Courses

There is no compromise regarding the quality of Cuban degree and diploma programs. However, there is much flexibility in the ways in which these programs are delivered and the goals are achieved. Adjustments are often made in giving credits that recognize professional experience for entry and in the type of exams that are set for particular groups of students. Some students request that their theses be supervised partially by email correspondence with the Cuban professor. Workplace research is encouraged as part of the assessment. Schedules and timetables are adapted to specific student conditions.

One of the most important elements of Cuban cooperation in postgraduate courses is the approach focused on individualized student-centered attention. This approach is particularly necessary to help the participants integrate what they are studying with their current professional realities. For example, if a Cuban academic is teaching a computer education course in a small Latin American town, he or she will take great care to help the students relate it to their local conditions and possibilities.

Another important feature of Cuban postgraduate cooperation is its very low cost for low-income countries, compared to the cost of studying elsewhere in programs similar in quality and content. Postgraduate courses are usually offered by the Cuban government free of charge, which is particularly significant given the economic situation of low-income countries.

North-South Link

Promoting professional upgrading for Cuban professors and researchers involves utilizing opportunities for them to have a variety of relationships with some of the best universities and institutions in more developed countries. Cuban academics visit these universities for postdoctoral programs, periods of exchange, conferences, seminars, and so on. This is illustrated by the following:

1. More than 15 percent of Cuban professors and researchers travel abroad each year to exchange experiences in foreign universities and institutes.

2. Each year more than 5 percent professors and researchers stay for a significant period of time in excellent universities overseas.
3. One thousand highly qualified foreign specialists come to Cuba each year to work and to exchange scientific points of view with Cuban academics.
4. More than 50 academic and professional conferences are held in Cuba each year. Thousands of delegates from overseas universities take part in these events, which serve to establish relations of collaboration.
5. In 2002–03, Cuban universities financed the participation of 750 of their academics and researchers in international academic conferences abroad.
6. Teachers and researchers from Cuban universities are members of more than 100 international networks.[6]

When exchanges take place between Cuban specialists with universities and other scientific institutions in developed countries, the Cubans are firmly grounded in an understanding of the needs of developing countries. This allows them to gather knowledge and experiences keeping in mind the national context. Their new knowledge is not considered suitable for automatic transfer but becomes the basis of an adaptation process that facilitates the development of appropriate technology. Cuban specialists thus adapt new knowledge and experiences for Cuba's needs and share it with the other developing countries in which they are working. This way, the new knowledge and approaches to contemporary development are introduced within an appropriate vision to specific contexts. This is one of the features that differentiates the type of assistance given by Cuban specialists and the assistance offered by specialists of other countries.

When Cuban academics return from this kind of overseas travel, they are expected to give a report on what they have learnt from the exchange of ideas. They look out for opportunities to develop and apply policies influenced by this exchange, in their own and other institutions. Often they work out with foreign counterparts a draft agreement to be considered when they return home. Sometimes, more than one institution works in a single program that they have jointly negotiated. For example, Cuba is collaborating with one of the Peruvian universities to provide a doctoral program in health management. CEPES in the University of Havana teaches the courses in management, and the Cuban Higher Institute of Medical Sciences teaches the health component.

Cuban Collaboration in Helping Overseas Universities with Administration and Institutional Development

One of the important areas of collaboration is Cuban assistance in helping foreign universities to develop their institutional and administrative capacity. Most of the elements that characterize Cuban postgraduate cooperation—low cost, North-South links—are applied to institutional development cooperation. However, there are some specific elements that should be recognized.

Promoting Endogenous Development

An important principle of cooperation with overseas universities is to encourage the strengthening of the internal capacities of the different institutions in order to develop their independence. Independent institutional capacity is developed when policy making, administration, and teaching are all strengthened. Cuban professors do not just teach their program, return to Cuba, and then go again when invited. The goal is to enable the institution to teach the program, sometimes adding modifications, using its own staff and resources. Following this principle, these institutions select counterparts that systematically work with the Cuban specialists, so that eventually these counterparts may replace the Cuban teachers, and the programs may be implemented without Cuban assistance, or with occasional invited input from Cuba. However, some institutions choose to continue with Cuban programs that are very popular with students. Also, in some cases, students request that their doctoral examination panels include Cuban professors.

A Nondirective, Customized Approach

Cuban specialists consider carefully the knowledge and experiences of the institutions in which they are advisers. They do not go with a suitcase full of answers before they have studied the problem and the context. Therefore, they avoid giving abstract formulas that might not work in a specific context.

Taking that into account, Cuban consultancies are carried out on the basis of a wide comprehension of culture, politics, and institutional development. Consultancies always involve a team of local participants working together with the Cubans. The team works to develop consensus that integrates the views and visions of all participants. They are not necessarily looking for the most up-to-date model, but for the model that will work most appropriately in a given context.

Experience of Systematic Innovation in Cuban Higher Education

Cuban cooperation in administrative and institutional development is based on Cuba's experiences of research and innovation in education. Advice to other countries about ways of developing their higher education institutions is based not only on theory, but on the practical experiences that Cuba has had in educational change. The following are examples of reform in Cuban higher education that have had national and institutional impact on increasing quality and relevance in the university system. These reforms become part of the knowledge on which Cuban advisers can draw when discussing reforms with universities in other countries.

A new administrative approach was developed in Cuba's universities. Every university has a strategic plan that fits into the national interest, and works out administrative strategies based on the objectives set out in the strategic plan. For example, each year, staff in CEPES work out a proposal of academic and administrative objectives that relate to the strategic plan of the University of Havana. The university management evaluates this proposal and agrees on it. At the end of the year, the university checks to see how far the objectives have been carried out. The advantage of this procedure is to integrate the goals and operations of the entire university in a rational manner.

There is a systematic approach in Cuba to evaluate and revise study plans and programs. For each professional area, there are representative national commissions of experts who evaluate the curricula in accordance with the experiences of graduates in the workplace. These workplace experiences may suggest that the curriculum needs to be changed or developed in a particular way. This whole process equips Cuban advisers with the kind of knowledge needed to advise other countries how to conceptualize and carry out systematic curriculum and administrative innovation and updating.

Cuba has developed integration between the workplace, research, and teaching. For example, university students studying engineering can learn part of the course in the workplace relevant to their field of specialization. Their work and their research projects related to the workplace are supervised both by their professor and by experts in the workplace. This combination of university teaching and applied professional experience is a useful model for other developing countries to consider.

Curricular strategies have been developed to provide future professionals with updated information and useful techniques. For example, many careers require a high level of competence in, say, the English language and information technology. Students are taught these two areas and are expected to utilize them systematically in their degree programs, particularly in engineering, economics, natural science, management studies, and studies of the environment.

A great deal of importance has been given in Cuba to working in interdisciplinary groups in the different levels of the university. These groups develop interdisciplinary solutions to national problems. This experience of interdisciplinarity is important to Cuban experts when they are working with other countries.

Cuban academics are skilled in utilizing new information technologies for assisting with the tasks of national development. When they work abroad, this skill is transferred to the particular context.

Drawing from Cuban Research on Improving Higher Education

Another important element that is a basis for collaboration overseas is Cuba's development of research on higher education.

There are research centers and research clusters in Cuba's universities that investigate higher education in all its dimensions. Apart from this, research about specialist fields of higher education takes place in the different university departments. Over the years, many researchers have been trained in higher education, especially through masters and PhD programs. These professionals constitute a group that can carry out further research and innovation in higher education. CEPES, the center for the improvement of higher education at the University of Havana, produces an academic quarterly journal, the *Cuban Higher Education Review*. This journal is a forum for researchers from all over the country to exchange scholarly communication with each other.

The Ministry of Higher Education identifies specific research needs in improving higher education and asks the various research centers to submit projects that could help to meet these needs. It then chooses one or more of these projects to support. This demonstrates a reliance on research to help meets the aims of improving higher education.

Cuba hosts a large international conference in education each year. Every two years the conference (Universidad) is on higher education, and this alternates with a conference (Pedagogía) on general education. Five of these international *Universidad* conferences have been held (1998, 2000, 2002, 2004, and 2006), and seven *Pedagogía* conferences have been held between 1986 and the present. Other events are also held in specific fields of education such as special education, and education to counter HIV/AIDS. Thousands of overseas participants attend each of these conferences. For example, about 2,000 visitors attended the last university conference in 2006. This demonstrates that the research carried out by Cuban professionals in education has great power to attract participants.

Research, Responsibility, and the Modeling of Collegiality as Elements of Collaboration

Further elements that are important in Cuban collaboration with overseas universities include research-based advice, the responsibility shown by consultants, and the modeling of collegiality.

Cuban collaboration is based on scientific and technical research, not on "ideology." Sometimes, for example, a Cuban team might recommend that a university needs to increase its fees. This may not be in keeping with their view that education should mainly be paid for by the state, but if it is seen to be necessary in the particular circumstances, it will be recommended. Cuban collaboration teams show a high degree of professionalism.

Consultancies undertaken by Cuban specialists are characterized by a high level of responsibility and dedication. They will not limit themselves to working for a few hours in the day, but will do what it takes to get the job done on time and to the highest level of quality possible. A Cuban consultancy team not only achieves concrete results, but also demonstrates a particular type of collegial behavior. For example, a collaborative process is followed, and the counterparts are fully involved in helping to solve the problem. This gives them the foundation for learning how to tackle similar problems in the future.

A Case Study of Cuban Cooperation with the J. M. Saracho University (UAJMS) in Tarija, Bolivia

Background to the Project and the Bolivian University Context

In 1998, UNESCO held an international conference on higher education in Paris. UNESCO experts prepared documents identifying the large gap between the current operations of many universities and socioeconomic needs of the countries. The study of these documents by academics and administrators at the J. M. Saracho Autonomous University (Universidad Autónoma J. M. Saracho—UAJMS) in 1997, and the process of institutional self-evaluation that took place, motivated them to prepare the first Five Year Development Plan for the complete transformation of the university.

At the conclusion of the self-evaluation process, IESALC, the Latin American and Caribbean office of UNESCO located in Venezuela, sent a group of international experts to UAJMS to study the report. To help in identifying the main needs of change, IESALC advised that the university needed the following changes:

1. To relate more closely to social needs
2. To modernize its structure and governance
3. To improve teaching, research, and outreach
4. To strengthen human resources, materials, and finances
5. To increase the relations of cooperation with other universities.

The UAJMS team felt that their development plan could serve as a model of change for other universities in similar contexts. IESALC was impressed with the plan, praising its quality and relevance to the process of globalizing knowledge. It agreed to give the plan partial financial support as well as to help the university identify experts in the field who could assist the process. IESALC presented the plan in the 1998 Paris conference. It gained acceptance at the conference, and UAJMS was given the role of being the "pilot university for change and transformation in higher education in Latin America."

UAJMS has about 10,000 students studying in 21 areas of specialization. Of these, 16 are five-year degree programs, and the rest are three-year programs of technical training leading to the middle-level qualification of "Técnico Superior."

The university is in the province of Tarija, in the south of Bolivia. Tarija has a population of about 390,598, of which 135,478 are concentrated in the capital city, also named Tarija. The university is in the capital city, but has campuses in a number of the surrounding areas and municipalities.

UAJMS is an "autonomous" university, which means that it manages its own activities without the control of the government.

Production in the district is mainly based on agriculture, gas, and minerals, which together constitute 48 percent of the economic activity. Other economic activities include commerce, transport, construction, public administration, and services.

The Development Plan: Cuba's Involvement

The first project in the development plan was to computerize the university's administration. When UAJMS asked IESALC/UNESCO for advice on who could help them computerize the administration, CEPES was recommended. Since 1996, there had been interaction between CEPES and UAJMS when CEPES professors had taught a masters of education degree course there, so UAJMS was happy to have a CEPES expert working with them on the computerization project. Following this, the university asked CEPES to continue to send their experts to help in putting the development plan into practice.

When the CEPES experts arrived at UAJMS, they studied the recommendations of the self-evaluation process and identified the priorities for change. On this basis, they, together with the university team, defined the projects that were needed to put these priorities into practice. The projects that had to be carried out may be regarded as being of two types: "soft" projects—those that did not require substantial changes in the institution but would be the basis for other projects (these included the extension of postgraduate programs, and strategic planning); and "hard" projects—those that require significant institutional change (including curricular redesign, new academic structures and governance, new regulations for staff, and new regulations for students). It is important to consider how these projects helped to bring about the transformation of the university.

Postgraduate Training

Four masters programs were developed to relate to regional and institutional development. These were: hydraulic engineering, agricultural development, higher education, and information technology. The university also developed postgraduate diploma courses in the theory and practice of education, the management of higher education, project management, and others. IESALC-UNESCO invited international experts to give lectures and seminars in these areas.

Eight hundred university academics and managers took part in these degree programs, workshops, seminars, and conferences. This process improved the ability of university staff to analyze their work for the purpose of improving it, and developed their research competence. University professionals were upgraded in important fields of regional and institutional development.

Strategic Planning

The university's process of strategic planning facilitated the meeting of academics to achieve consensus about the future of the university and its faculties and departments.

Redesign of Curriculum, Academic Structures, and Governance

University academics became involved in a process of systematic and up-to-date curricular redesign that helped them to increase curriculum relevance and flexibility. Careers in the medical sciences were introduced for the first time in the university.

The old structure employed academics who concentrated on teaching almost exclusively. The new structure introduced was that of academic departments such as those relating to food technology, chemistry, management studies, forestry technology, and so on. This allowed academics to be both teachers and researchers and to cooperate more closely with their colleagues in a similar field of knowledge.

In the new governance structure, the authorities such as deans, rectors, and other administrators were given more executive responsibility, while the university council (of which 50 percent consists of student representatives and 50 percent of academics) had more responsibility for the design of university policy. In the old model, these responsibilities had been less separated, so decisions took a long time to be made.

New Regulations for Academics and Students

In the old model, academics had contracts of up to 14 hours a week, which required them only to teach. In the new model, the contracts were increased to 40 hours a week for full-time staff, and required research, the upgrading of qualifications, and teaching. Performance assessment was carried out annually. The new system integrated academics more closely with the university and allowed them to develop as better professionals.

The new student regulations were linked with curriculum redesign. With the change in study plans came more regular assessment and an increase in expectations for performance.

Institutional Impact of the Development Plan

The practices in the new development plan had a powerful impact on changing the university. Academics gained a wider and deeper understanding of how a university creates and disseminates knowledge. They became more conscious of the links between university and society. They gained a more holistic vision of the institution, whereas before, they were operating mainly within their separate components with little knowledge of the university as a whole. The new system, giving more space for collaboration, allowed better interdepartmental collaboration and facilitated growth. Academics developed more self-confidence and became more proactive in coping with difficulties.

The impact can be defined as the creation of a new culture based on confidence in what the university is, and what it can do.

Conclusion

This chapter has analyzed Cuba's role in contributing to the development of university culture in Latin America. Cuba's contribution includes not only the training of foreign postgraduate students in a wide variety of specializations in Cuban universities, but also assistance given by Cuban university academics in helping Latin American universities to develop their administrative and curricular systems of higher education. The chapter described a case study of how Cuba assisted the improvement of the university in Tarija, Bolivia, but Cubans have undertaken and are continuing with similar projects in many other locations. For example, Cubans carried out this collaboration in higher education development with universities in Nicaragua in the 1980s, and are currently doing so in Ecuador, Mexico, and Peru.

Notes

1. Ministry of Higher Education (2003).
2. Ministry of Higher Education (2001, 2002, 2003, 2004).
3. Ministry of Higher Education (2003).
4. Ministry of Higher Education (2006).
5. Centre of Studies for the Improvement of Higher Education (1993).
6. Ministry of Higher Education (2001, 2002, 2003, 2004).

References

Centre of Studies for the Improvement of Higher Education (1993). *Cuba: Higher Education and the Scope of a Reform*. Havana, Cuba: Cuban University Press.
Centre of Studies for the Improvement of Higher Education (2002). *Cuban Higher Education in the Nineties*. Havana, Cuba: Cuban University Press.
Ministry of Higher Education (2001). Annual Report. Havana, Cuba: Cuban University Press.
Ministry of Higher Education (2002). Annual Report. Havana, Cuba: Cuban University Press.
Ministry of Higher Education (2003). Annual Report. Havana, Cuba: Cuban University Press.
Ministry of Higher Education (2004). Annual Report. Havana, Cuba: Cuban University Press.
Ministry of Higher Education (2005). Annual Report. Havana, Cuba: Cuban University Press.
Ministry of Higher Education (2006). Annual Report. Havana, Cuba: Cuban University Press.
Tristá, B. R. et al. (2002). *Intervention Strategy for University Change: Case Study of Universidad Autónoma "Juan Misael Saracho" de Tarija, Bolivia*. Research Report.

10

"You Help Me Improve My English, I'll Teach You Physics!" Cuban Teachers Overseas[1]

Anne Hickling-Hudson

Introduction

Lending teachers for two-year periods is one of the ways in which Cuba has been able to collaborate with other countries in their efforts to improve educational planning and practice. My field research in 2001 in Jamaica (March and November) and in Namibia (December) enabled me to obtain information about how Cuban teachers are being utilized, and about the educational implications of this project. In Jamaica, I interviewed 15 Cuban teachers in several schools and one in the vocational institute, as well as the Cuban project supervisor in charge of the 51 Cuban teachers. I also talked with officials at the Jamaican Ministry of Education to obtain an idea of the developmental needs in the various subjects that the Cubans had been asked to teach. In Namibia I interviewed personnel in the National Sports Directorate and the Cuban manager in charge of the sports education project. The chapter draws on these interviews to build a picture of how the program of collaboration is organized, and considers its postcolonial significance, in theory and in practice, as an example of South-South collaboration. The chapter contributes to a multilevel style of comparative education analysis based on microlevel qualitative fieldwork within a framework that compares cross-cultural issues and national policies.[2] The discussion of the educational situation of the host countries suggests why Cuban teachers can contribute to meeting curricular needs, particularly in the areas of the sciences, mathematics, Spanish, and sports. The friendly and joking remark of one of the Cuban teachers to school students in Jamaica: "You help me improve my English, I'll teach you Physics!" highlights the reciprocal potential of these cooperation projects, discussed in several chapters of this book.

Decolonization, School Improvement, and the Assistance of Cuban Teachers

Cuba is not wealthy, but its framework of a supportive socialist government has enabled educators to improve vastly the structure and outcomes of the model of education inherited from its colonial period. UNESCO evaluations carried out in 1996 showed that Cuban school students were performing in mathematics, language, and science at a level far exceeding their peers in 16 other Latin American countries.[3] Free-market Jamaica and Namibia also have struggling economies, but in contrast to Cuba, their education systems are floundering. Judging from external examination results, there are pockets of world-class student performance in the best schools, but mediocre to extremely poor performance is common among the majority of students in other schools.[4] In both countries, many teachers are not suitably qualified.[5] In Jamaica the teaching force is also being steadily depleted by teachers leaving the profession for other better-paid jobs at home or overseas. The loss of qualified teachers has been particularly severe in recent years as recruiters from the United States and the UK have stepped up their drive to attract the best-qualified teachers away from Jamaica and into the schools of London and New York.[6]

It is against this background that Cuban professionals are being recruited, as teachers in primary and secondary schools and vocational colleges in Jamaica, and as sports coaches in Namibia. In Jamaica, the Cuban teachers are being asked to help in the existing British-derived system: there is no question of any collaboration to design and develop new structures and approaches to education. Namibia also continues with a British-style education system. However, the Cuban sports coaches have the latitude to help design and develop new systems of sports education. My research investigated how the utilization of Cuban educators was working, while my reflections from a postcolonial perspective focus on how the programs relate to a possible larger picture of long-term educational change.

How the Project Is Organized

Under the collaboration agreements, Cuban teachers and education advisers and planners have worked, and are currently working, in many countries of the Caribbean, Latin America, and Africa. Assistance is offered by Cuba at several levels. Countries can negotiate with the Cuban government to obtain scholarships to send their nationals to Cuba for primary, secondary, and/or tertiary education. They may engage Cuban teachers to teach for a year or two, or they may choose to work with Cuban university advisers on how to improve organizational management and professional courses in universities. Cooperation with other countries is organized according to the particular country's circumstances. Educational assistance, particularly in the form of adult literacy teaching and scholarships to study in Cuba, has been provided free of charge to very poor countries such as Nicaragua and Haiti. However, when countries can contribute to the costs of utilizing Cuban educators, there are cost-sharing agreements of the kind that currently operate between Cuba, Jamaica, and Belize. While the Cuban teachers are working overseas, the Cuban government continues to pay their full salaries at home, so that their families are supported financially. The cost-sharing arrangement means that countries such as Jamaica and Belize pay the Cuban teachers local salaries, which are higher in convertible terms than what they earn in Cuba, and the teachers return a portion of this to the Cuban government.

All Cuban teachers have at least a five-year university degree and receive ongoing in-service professional training. Those chosen to go overseas are often the best in the system. Some of them have additional qualifications such as education up to the masters or PhD level, experience in other developing countries as well as in Cuba, and experience in teacher training, educational administration, and policy development. This is a background that could be of immense value in school systems in other developing countries where many teachers do not have university-level qualifications, where resources are poor, and where pedagogical traditions and organization have proved inadequate to the task of establishing an efficient and effective education system.

In each Cuban province, the education authorities invite applications from teachers who are interested in doing an overseas teaching placement. They draw up a *Bolsa de Colaboración* (collaboration list) of people qualified for overseas teaching and willing to be interviewed. The teachers put themselves forward for countries in which they are most interested. They are interviewed and chosen by selection teams consisting of Cuban educators and visiting education officials from the collaborating country. In the case of Jamaica, the selection team, consisting of Jamaican and Cuban educators, chooses a number of applicants each year to participate in the project, on the basis of their qualifications, experience, and fluency in English. Fluency in English is desirable, but a few are selected in spite of having minimal English. The understanding is that they will work hard to improve their English while they are in Jamaica. One teacher of physics whom I interviewed in Jamaica put it this way:

> English is desirable, although Science has its own language and in teaching you can convey a lot of ideas through signs and symbols. My English is not so good, but they must have felt that it was good enough for teaching Science, and they selected me. When I started to teach in Jamaica, I made a deal with the students—"You help me improve my English, I'll teach you Physics!" and they do help me a lot with my English. (Interview 2, Physics teacher, Jamaica, March 2001)

When teachers are selected by a recruitment team for overseas service, the staff at their schools in Cuba takes a vote as to whether they can be spared to go overseas, since they are responsible for covering for them while they are away. The teachers spend two years in a placement in English-speaking or French-speaking countries, and can apply for a third year, although permission for this is hardly ever granted because of the urgency of getting the teachers back to their posts in Cuba. Teachers going to a Spanish-speaking country are expected to spend only one year overseas. Once selected, the teachers are given a program of orientation to prepare them for their sojourn in the country to which they have been assigned (Interview 1, March 2001).

Different countries have different approaches to utilizing the Cuban teachers. Jamaica is using Cubans who are very highly qualified as teachers and lecturers (some are teacher educators with masters degrees) to fill teacher shortages in the poorer schools that have recently been upgraded. They are usually not placed in the wealthier grammar schools, though a few such placements have been made when a principal has asked for them. When a school requests a teacher for a particular subject and there is no qualified Jamaican applicant, the Ministry of Education may opt to place a Cuban teacher there. Namibia is an example of a country that, in spite of its close relationships with Cuba, has chosen to utilize Cubans as sports teachers in local communities rather than in the schools. These two cases will now be discussed.

Cuban Teachers in Jamaica

In the academic year 2000/2001, 44 Cuban teachers worked in Jamaica, and in 2001/2002, the number requested and sent grew to 51. It appears that the numbers have continued at about this level: in 2011 there were 45 Cuban teachers at the primary, secondary, and tertiary levels, and two Cuban professors teaching at the Caribbean Maritime Institute.[7] In my interviews in 2001, I asked why there were 42 men and only 9 women, and was told that the recruiting team, both Jamaicans and Cubans, had felt that men would be more able to cope with the rough living and school conditions in some areas (Interview 1, March 2001). Some of them were sent to schools in poverty-stricken inner-city areas plagued with violence and other problems. Others were sent to some rural areas that are among the poorest in the country. Nine were at high schools in Kingston, the capital, and a further 11 in Kingston were at technical-vocational institutions that are part of the postschool network of Human Employment and Resource Training (HEART). At HEART, the Cubans were teaching science and technical subjects including electronics, welding, electrical installation, masonry, and carpentry. At the schools they were teaching physics, maths, chemistry, integrated science, biology, Spanish, and music. Most of them are assigned to the middle school (years 7–9) and only a few to classes that are taking school-leaving exams. Twenty-three of the teachers were assigned to teaching Spanish, most at secondary schools, but three in an experimental program of Spanish teaching at rural primary and all-age schools. Only four were teaching mathematics, and 12 were teaching various aspects of the sciences.

Cuba places one of their experienced pedagogical university academics in charge of the Cuban teachers in Jamaica. This support and liaison officer visits each teacher every month, talking with them and looking at their lesson plans, record books, and class assessments, as well as talking with the school principal about them. Monthly talks are held with the minister of education on their progress, and regular written reports are sent to Cuba. The teachers meet every month in three regional groups to exchange pedagogical ideas, problems, and goals with each other (Interview 1, March 2001).

Teachers, including the Cuban visitors, are faced with particularly tough challenges in the newly upgraded Jamaican high schools. "Newly-upgraded" refers to the fact that they have only recently (since the late 1990s) been given additional resources to help them tackle the disadvantage of a history of under-resourcing and neglect.[8] They are the proverbial poor cousins of the secondary system compared to the more privileged "grammar"-style high schools, a status difference reminiscent of that between the secondary modern and grammar schools of the UK. Their relative disadvantage is immediately visible in their crowded, resource-poor environments and in the relative poverty of their students. In spite of the efforts of the Ministry of Education to upgrade them, they are still very visibly schools to which, historically, the poor have been relegated. The distribution of teachers is skewed, with the majority of university graduates teaching in the elite high schools.

More university graduate teachers are desperately needed in the formerly impoverished, now newly upgraded high schools—particularly in subject areas that find it hard to attract graduates—maths, physics, chemistry, and Spanish. These are the areas in which the Cuban teachers are filling crucial gaps. Their task is extremely challenging. Many students in the newly upgraded high schools not only come from poor families which are hard-pressed to support their children adequately at school, but also have had a relatively inadequate primary schooling in under-resourced government schools. Most students lack the sound foundation needed to orient them toward the academic subjects in the regional school-leaving examinations set by the Caribbean Examinations Council (popularly known as the CXC exams). Some, in fact, are only minimally literate and numerate, and others lag far behind the academic levels taken for granted in the wealthier schools. It is a struggle to teach such students the demanding curriculum of the CXC. The science subjects suffer from a shortage of materials, especially in physics and chemistry, which have been newly introduced. Occasionally, far more dramatic problems arise, for example, when two of the Cuban teachers (in schools located in very poor areas) were robbed and knifed by Jamaican teenage boys. They had to be treated at hospitals, and were transferred to other schools.

However, it is not the difficult material conditions in the newly upgraded schools that the Cuban teachers saw as their biggest challenge. Several were of the opinion that the main problem affecting their teaching relates to timetabling. This opinion is summarized in this observation from one of them: "The thirty-five minute sessions are too short. You start teaching, and it's over. There is no time to do anything in depth" (Interview 4 with Mathematics teacher, 2001). Others felt that even when they were given one hour a week for teaching Spanish, it was far from adequate for learning a foreign language. They recalled that when they were studying English at school in Cuba, their timetable assigned them at least one hour a day for classes in the language, and they were expected to supplement this with many hours of homework (Interviews 5 and 6 with Spanish teachers, 2001).

Another significant problem for the teachers was learning to teach in English, a foreign language for all but a few who had grown up in Cuba with Jamaican parents. They were conscious about what they perceived as their own poor mastery of English. But, in the interviews that I conducted, I met only two teachers who felt that their English was so inadequate for what they wanted to say that they asked to speak to me in Spanish and have their responses translated for me. When talking with all of the other teachers, I found their English good enough for communication at the level of sophisticated ideas, although their accent was sometimes difficult to follow. Those who needed to were working systematically and hard, outside of school hours, on improving their English, and their more fluent colleagues were helping them to practise it. All of them appreciated the efforts of some of the school students to help them learn the correct word or phrase in English. Their task of understanding English in the schools was made more difficult by the fact that many of the students constantly switched between Jamaican patois and standard English. Some teachers had bought phrase books of Jamaican patois and were striving to learn phrases from them. One deputy principal regretted that just when the teachers had become more fluent in English in their second year, they had to leave, since it was difficult to get permission for them to stay for a third year (Interview 7 with school deputy principal, Jamaica, March 2001).

One of the two teachers with very little English was a remarkable woman assigned to teach music and dance in one of the newly upgraded high schools. I would not have thought it possible to teach these large classes with so little English; she had only rudimentary skills in the language. But working with a supportive principal who was also passionate about music, she had set up an effective music program in the school, which had never before had a systematic one. I observed a class in which she was teaching students how to recognize and sing notes in music. She also taught students Spanish songs and trained them in putting on dance and music shows. The principal later showed me photographs of the students performing their shows at concerts both at their school and outside of it (Interview 8 with school principal, November 2001). The success of this teacher was due not only to her warm and lively personality and her popularity with the students, but also to her high level of qualifications and experience and excellent pedagogy. With 22 years of experience of school teaching and training teachers in her field at university in Cuba, she has reached the "Categoría Superior," which qualifies her to teach at any level. This fulfilled the request of the Jamaican recruiting team for a teacher of music and dance who could teach at any level (Interview 9 with Cuban project supervisor, November 2001).

In some of the schools, there was a high level of noise and inattention in classes in general. I asked the Cuban teachers how they coped with this. They answered that poor academic discipline—that is, noise, frequent inattention, and casualness about completing assigned tasks—has to do with the oversized classes. In classes of 40 and over, it is inevitable that students interested in learning would be annoyed by the noise and disruption caused by others who were less motivated. Another cause of academic indiscipline seemed to be the fact that many students had a very weak academic background. As one physics teacher put it, "They have not been understanding Science, and so sometimes don't pay attention" (Interview 2 with physics teacher, March 2001). Another teacher said that he wanted to use mathematics to help students understand parts of the CXC chemistry syllabus, but could not because the maths backgrounds of the students was so weak (Interview 10 with chemistry teacher, November 2001). A maths/science teacher said that many students approached mathematics by the use of formulae that they had learnt (Interview 11 with maths teacher, November 2001). He felt that their reliance on formulae and their lack of understanding of the underlying principles was at the heart of their weakness in maths, for if they were faced with new types of problems, they were at a loss. The Cuban teachers were confident that they could utilize their pedagogical skills to improve student interest in learning. In the classes I visited, two Cuban teachers of Spanish were using the method of dividing the students into several small groups and assigning a variety of collaborative written and oral tasks in Spanish according to levels of competence. The teachers of chemistry and physics were using a variety of visual teaching aids as well as practical exercises to help their students develop understanding of science concepts.

Some teachers mentioned their efforts to get to know the students outside of class, talking with them about their problems and counseling them about their studies:

> At first we thought they were badly behaved, but when we found out what their problems were, we say to them, "Your parents have a hard time, they have to pay for your education. Why are you wasting your time?" And they talk to us differently after that. We find that their behaviour has changed for the better." (Interview 12 with group of teachers, November 2001)

From talking to five principals, I gained the impression that the Cuban teachers have a friendly and warm relationship with the community, the staff, and their students, and have coped competently with conditions that are often difficult. Two of the principals said that their schools' needs for maths/science teachers were so great that they would like to obtain the services of many more Cuban teachers than the Ministry of Education could provide. Three said that they would have liked to extend the contracts of the Cuban teachers for a third year and more. They had sent their requests to the Ministry of Education, which passed them on to the Cuban Embassy. But, as the Cuban coordinator pointed out, "They have their jobs in Cuba, and the contract says two years" (Interview 13, November 2001). In order to stay, they would need special authorization from the Cuban Ministry of Education. The view of the Ministry of Education both in Cuba and Jamaica was that contracts should not be extended beyond two years except in very special cases. At that date, none of the Cuban teachers had applied for an extended contract. Most of them had families in Cuba and were happy to go back after the two years.

I was able to visit only one of the 11 Cubans teaching technical subjects at post school vocational colleges. He was teaching integrated science to first- and second-year students in two-year vocational technical courses training them for middle-level practical jobs. Some were to become electricians, mechanics, accountants, textile designers, and garment makers among other fields. It was a challenging pedagogical situation, since the students had different levels of education, some coming from high schools and others not. Most of them had a low level of mathematics education, below the CXC level, and the Cuban visitor was keen to help them improve their maths and increase their interest in science. He was confident that he could do this, as he had been teaching science at a tertiary level for over 20 years. He felt that he was increasing their interest by giving them structured experiments, helping them to establish a close connection between science and their particular subject, and helping them in their choice and study of problems to research and report on at the end of the unit (Interview 14, Science teacher, November 2001).

Cuban Educators and Namibia

My field visit to Namibia was undertaken because of my interest in the close relationship between Cuba and the South West African Peoples' Organization (SWAPO), which won independence in 1990 after over a century of colonial rule, first by Germany and then by the white South African apartheid government. The Cubans were an important component of SWAPO's struggle against South African rule. I wanted to find out how this collaboration was demonstrated in the field of education. I was somewhat surprised to find that there was no project employing Cuban teachers in Namibia's schools or colleges. Yet, there were many Cuban experts in other fields—about 120 doctors, four experts in agriculture, three experts in physical planning, and seven teachers of sports and physical education. Some knowledge of Namibia's recent history is important in understanding the nature of its educational collaboration with Cuba.

Namibia covers a large area, but has a population of only 2 million people, of which over 65 percent live in rural areas, many in very poor circumstances. It has had what one of my Namibian interviewees described as "a rough and difficult history." Namibia won its independence only in 1990. It is emerging from the onerous legacy of German colonialism from 1884 to 1915, followed by the cruel burden of South African rule from 1915 to 1990. South Africa exploited the substantial natural wealth of the annexed country (gold, diamonds, and marine resources), and marginalized black Namibians by virtually excluding them from benefits of the society.[9] They continued the principles of the previous colonial system of German education. Access to schooling was provided for only a minority of the black population, and most of those black Namibians who did get to school were limited to the primary level. Only basic skills of reading, writing, and arithmetic were taught, and less than half the number of primary children was able to move to secondary level.[10] The Germans and South African colonizers intended that education should prepare those Africans who received it for fitting unquestioningly into white political and economic domination.

The educational assistance provided by Cuba between 1978 and 1990 played an important role in educating black Namibians who previously had no chance of receiving a sound education because of the apartheid imposed by South Africa in their own country. Most of the Namibians who studied in Cuba were educated in the internationalist schools (described in chapter 12) on the Isle of Youth. Today, many of those educated in Cuba are professionals and government leaders in independent Namibia. The following quotation is from the transcript of my interview with a young woman who explained how she came to have had her entire schooling in Cuba:

> Hundreds of Namibians have studied in Cuba. The first group that went there to study was over 600. Two secondary schools on the Isle of Youth (in Cuba) were built specially for us. We studied in Cuba from primary to pre-university, and then were given scholarships to do our university studies in East Germany.
>
> When I was growing up, South Africa was in control of our country. My parents didn't want us to study in Bantu schools. They fled the country and went into exile in Angola, as a lot of SWAPO supporters were doing. There was a camp in Angola where women and children stayed. South Africa attacked it in 1977. Many of us children lost our mothers and grandparents and brothers and sisters who were in that camp. We were orphaned. Cuba sympathised very much with us. They spoke with the SWAPO members and offered education in Cuba to the children who had survived, and SWAPO agreed that we could go. With the loss of so many members of our family, we were determined to fight harder, and that's what we did.
>
> In 1978 we went to school in Cuba, on the Isle of Youth. It was a boarding school, and it provided everything for us—food, clothes, books—all. Many teachers lived in the school, and were like parents to us. We learnt to be fluent in Spanish. The interaction of the Cubans with us helped us to become fluent. There are lots of Cubans living on the island. There were lots of other schools near to ours where Cuban children went. We had sporting activities,

tournaments and so on, with our Cuban peers. In most subjects we had the same school programs as the Cuban children, and were treated the same way. The only difference was that teachers came out from Namibia to teach us history, geography and English, because the Cubans wanted us to maintain our culture. But we learnt a lot of Caribbean history too—we were well-informed about the region and the world. We did pre-university schooling, and we decided at that time what fields we wanted to go into for our careers. I was one of those chosen to study medicine in East Germany, which was also helping SWAPO. I started but didn't finish my medical studies because I wanted to come back home when Namibia won independence. I studied here—I did a Diploma in Public Administration. Namibia has no institution for medical studies. (Interview 1 with member of Namibia-Cuba Friendship Society, Namibia, November 2001.)

My interviewee was one of the 1300 Namibians who graduated from schools, universities, and polytechnics in Cuba before 1990. After independence, the new Namibian government decided that most of their students of school-leaving age in Cuba should return to continue their studies in Namibia, which was expanding its tertiary education sector with a new university and more college capacity. As in most decolonizing countries, however, Namibia's education system is still seriously underdeveloped. Although many improvements were made in the decade of independence, this is clearly too short a time to build a new system, particularly given the distorted foundations of the old one.

The Namibian government has established a system that has the goal of providing education for all children to up to year 10. In practice, it does not yet do so. It is still highly selective, and the dropout rates are enormous. The figures in table 10.1 show that in 1999 about 389,000 children started primary school at age six to seven in grade 1 and just over 156,000 finished it with the examination for the Certificate of Primary Education (CPE) in grade 7. By the junior secondary stage (grades 8, 9, and 10), there were only 100,267 students. Only 23,000 stayed to take pre-university schooling in grades 11 and 12. The statistics in table 10.1 clearly demonstrate the sharp selectivity and high dropout rates in the system.

The four teachers' colleges provide training for teachers preparing to teach grades 1–10. In 2005 they were still small, with only 470 places. The University of Namibia is responsible for training the majority of the country's teachers, but most are enrolled at the level of certificates and

Table 10.1 Student numbers in the Namibian school system, 1999

No. of students in all grades	Total primary	Lower primary	Upper primary	Total secondary	Junior secondary	Senior secondary	Other grades
514,196	388,497	232,386	156,111	123,797	100,267	23,530	1,902

Source: Ministry of Basic Education, Sport and Culture, Namibia 2000, p. 100.

diplomas rather than at a degree level. In 2001, the faculty of education had 40 lecturers, 867 full-time students, and 700 distance education students, and it also provided in-service seminars for classroom teachers. One in-service program that has received assistance from the European Union is the Mathematics and Science Teachers' Extension Program (MASTEP), which trains 360 students for the year 12 school-leaving exams in maths and science. The successful ones will become unqualified teachers who can apply for a program of in-service teacher training while they are teaching (Interview 2 with lecturer, University of Namibia, November 2001).

The Namibian government allocates more than 20 percent of the national budget or 7 percent of GDP on education, making Namibia one of the three countries with the highest percentage of GDP spent on education in the world.[11] Since independence, education has improved from a low base, but its development has a long way to go before it even reaches a stage where the majority gets to attend secondary school. I was surprised that in a school system that desperately needed to increase its numbers of qualified teachers, Cuban teachers were not being utilized in the way that they are in the Caribbean. There were divided views on this. Although my Namibian interviewees acknowledged Cuba's valuable educational assistance through scholarships to Cuba before 1990, some felt that Cubans would be inappropriate for teaching in Namibian schools because of the language problem. Their view was that Cubans did not have enough mastery of English to teach Namibian children who were trying to learn English as their second or third language. It was hard enough to learn English, without being taught by teachers whose English was also weak. However, others disagreed, arguing that Cuban teachers could play a useful role, particularly in science and mathematics (Interview 3, group of Namibian educators, November 2001).

As mentioned earlier, the Namibian government utilizes Cuban assistance in the health sector, agriculture, physical planning, and sport. The sports personnel are being used primarily to expand sports training opportunities for Namibians in the rural areas, where the bulk of the population lives. Because of the neglect of the poor under apartheid, little or no attention was paid to developing sports. The present government has set up a sports directorate to organize sports development, with a school sports unit and a community sports unit. It is building sports complexes in several provinces. The sports directorate sponsors regular competitions between regional teams, and the best of these are selected for national and international competitions. Sports associations have started certificate programs to accredit sports performers according to international criteria. The Cuban coaches provided much of the expertise needed to make these developments possible. Meanwhile, four young Namibians have Cuban scholarships to study physical education at the new Higher Institute of Sports and Physical Culture in Cuba.

Under agreements with Cuba, there were six coaches on two-year contracts—three in athletics, one in basketball, one in wrestling, and one in boxing. The policy was to rotate the coaches between Namibia's 13 regions. The coaches worked with adults, but their main emphasis was on after-school training and sports camps for schoolchildren and teenagers. I was fortunate to be able to speak with the director of sports. He had just visited Cuba to try to get more coaches and to extend the contracts of those already there, but said, "It is impossible to get as many as we need and want. I got one more for volleyball and one more for boxing. But they are working in many countries, and have to go home to Cuba" (Interview 4, director of sports, Namibia, November 2001).

The director had a clear appreciation of the role of Cuba in sports development. Namibia gets the Cuban coaches for minimal cost. He explained, "We pay their travel and transport costs and a modest fee for their work, but the Cuban government pays the bulk of their salary." I was told that the Cuban coaches are valuable not only for training athletes and sports performers, but also for capacity building—training the trainers in regular sports clinics. Furthermore, the Cubans work well in difficult conditions and locations. The director said:

> Cuban expertise is ideal for African conditions. They are used to working in rural areas. Recently we had a European coach who said he couldn't train our sprinters without a synthetic track. We do have one in Windhoek, but how can we afford to extend that everywhere? Cubans train world-class experts in their own country, with minimal facilities. That model is useful for us. We have a lot of Cuban doctors in Namibia—they keep track of the health of the sports participants and the athletes. They have the expertise but don't need high tech. (Interview 4, Namibia, November 2001)

The Cuban coordinator of the visiting coaches was based in Swakopmund. He travels to different regions to give courses and clinics for the training of basketball teams and to visit his colleagues in other sports. He trains both schoolteachers and athletics teachers. I asked him about the educational background of visiting Cuban coaches. He explained that all of them were physical education teachers, fully trained and qualified to first degree level, after completing a five-year program of study in Cuba, with an added research component. His own degree had been awarded by the Higher Institute of Physical Education and Culture (ISCF) in Havana. In the degree course they studied a variety of sports, plus pedagogy, physiology, anatomy, health issues, massage, and sports injury treatment. They had had many years of experience in teaching sports and physical education in Cuba. He himself had taught sports in Cuba since 1970. As the head of a sports school in Havana, he coordinated ten teachers on the staff. Included in the team of Cuban sports teachers was a doctor of medicine with a specialization in sports injuries. I was told that this doctor regularly kept up his own physical training, and worked particularly with athletes and boxers. "When there's a boxing competition he moves with the boxers. He checks the boxers for injuries—if they are serious, he stops them fighting" (Interview 5, with Cuban sports coordinator, Namibia, November 2001).

The Cuban coaches were encouraged by the Namibian people's enjoyment of their programs and the demand for them. People that they had trained were already training other teams. The main problem that the coordinator saw was that they could work with the children and teenagers only in the afternoons, as most schools did not have physical education as a subject. He was eager to see Namibia develop facilities such as a physical education institute to enable some of its citizens to specialize in physical education. The director felt that the Cubans had significantly assisted the sports development program, enabling it to expand and enhance local sports training, and that their tuition had caused Namibia's international sporting reputation to be on the rise. Namibian sports performers were competing regularly at the international level. There were Namibian world champions in boxing and athletics, silver medals had been won at the most recent Olympics, and the Namibian football team had qualified for the African Nations Cup (Interview 4, director of sports, Namibia, 2001).

Cuba's Teachers Overseas: Some Policy Implications

There are important policy issues and implications in the Cuban program of sharing its educational expertise in primary and secondary schooling and sports tuition with other countries of the "South." What impact does the program have for the partner countries? How far are the Cuban teachers helping to fill gaps in the teaching capacity of these countries, and how far can their role in schools help to lay foundations for the further educational development of these countries? Equally interesting is the question of the consequences that this program has for Cuba itself.

For a low-income country to offer educational assistance on the scale that Cuba does requires a massive allocation of financial and other resources. Cuba's educational assistance overseas is part of a large program of civilian collaboration with other developing countries of the "South." Cuba has more than 37,000 civilian specialists abroad working in 109 countries of Africa, Asia, Latin America, and the Caribbean, in agriculture, fisheries, sugar refining, mining, transportation, cattle-raising, irrigation, construction, industry, cultural development, and economic and physical planning.[12]

Internationalism in education, therefore, is only one component of Cuban foreign policy. It was only in the 1990s, after the end of the Cold War that increasing numbers of non-socialist governments felt politically able to negotiate the use of Cuban teachers in their own countries. In the 1990s, Cuban teachers went for the first time to Zimbabwe, Botswana, Namibia, and to some Caribbean and Latin American countries. From the perspective of the Cuban government, it must be a sacrifice to "lend" their best teachers and professors for a number of years, but the reciprocity of the program would be likely to include the valuable experience provided for their professionals. Through it, Cuban teachers could improve their foreign language skills, broaden their knowledge of global conditions, in some cases earn foreign currency, and improve their pedagogical skills and professional knowledge by having to teach in difficult and challenging conditions in systems of education different from their own. It might also be regarded as beneficial for the Cuban teachers to appreciate anew their revolution's commitment to education when they compare it with the oppressive educational conditions that they witness overseas. For example, some of the teachers I interviewed in Jamaica were deeply shocked when they encountered the day-to-day problems of poverty of some of their Jamaican students, especially when some students were so poor that they were unable to buy textbooks, and were excluded from school-leaving examinations when they could not pay the expensive entry fees required. A recent improvement is that the Jamaican government now undertakes to pay examination fees for impoverished students, but it is still a challenge for education that so many continue to live in conditions of poverty.

Though the program of sending teachers overseas brings some benefits to Cuba, the fundamental principle of the program is a policy of internationalism that values collaboration between developing countries. When I asked the Cuban supervisor of the teachers in Jamaica why the government encourages teachers to do overseas service, he replied, "International service is our tradition. A lot of people have helped Cuba, and the only way to repay this is to do the same" (Interview 9 with Cuban program supervisor, November 2001). A central belief of Cuba's foreign policy is that countries of the "South" should try to reduce their dependence on the wealthy bloc of countries of the "North," and that this can be achieved if they assist each other. Over the years, some Caribbean governments have assisted Cuba with solidarity and trade within their possibilities, and Cuba has assisted countries of the region with several hundred tertiary education scholarships. This collaboration has simply been extended by the program in which highly qualified Cuban teachers assist other Caribbean countries in selected educational niches within a cost-sharing framework.

The placing of teachers from Cuba in schools in English-speaking countries is on a small scale, yet even this could make a significant impact on educational systems. In 2001 there were only 51 Cuban teachers in Jamaica, and seven Cuban sports educators in Namibia. Two factors suggest that there are potential benefits in utilizing them on a larger scale. One is that Cuban teachers have developed such extraordinary pedagogical skills in mathematics, science, and language that their school students exceed by far the performance of other Latin American students in these subjects.[13] The other factor is the high quality of their work as teachers overseas, appreciated by the educational directors whom I interviewed in the two countries.

Yet, there is ambivalence about the utilization of the Cuban teachers in some of the collaborating countries. From my interviews I learnt that some people, still nervous about the aftermath of the Cold War, are concerned about the possibility that aid from some western countries, particularly the United States, might be jeopardized because of the employment of Cuban educators. Other concerns about the use of Cuban teachers include local suspicions that there might be a danger of them taking away jobs from local teachers. Yet another concern was that the foreign accent or limited English-language skills of some of the Cuban teachers would be a serious impediment in their teaching.

It seems to me, however, that policy makers need to weigh up these fears against the potential value of Cuban educational collaboration. If Cuban teachers and teacher educators were to be used on a much larger scale and more systematically than at present, and if they were to be formally assisted with their study of the local language, they might make very significant contributions to improving the teaching of mathematics, the sciences, and Spanish—subjects at which students need to excel if they are to help their countries improve their economies in the global marketplace. This is not to ignore the fact that there are some very talented and successful local teachers whose students excel. It is simply to recognize that in current conditions, there are not enough of them to meet current needs.

Several modalities are possible to utilize the work of temporary overseas teachers such as the Cubans more effectively. They could be strategically deployed to collaborate in curriculum renewal, traveling around to schools and teacher education institutions to do intensive seminars with students and teachers in selected subject areas. Some could be placed full time in teachers' colleges and university faculties of education for a few years. Exchange programs could be set up between Cuban educators and their colleagues from other countries. They could be used to help develop distance education programs, particularly in subject areas in which host countries are weak. A combination of these and other strategies could be used. It is interesting that the South African government is currently utilizing Cuban teachers of mathematics and science in teacher resource centers in remote rural communities. From this base, they provide in-service seminars for teachers, and visit schools whenever they are requested by principals to help upgrade teaching skills in particular areas. Some of the Cuban teachers in South Africa are the very ones who have already improved their English and their knowledge of a British-derived system by teaching in the English-speaking Caribbean, Zimbabwe, and Botswana. This has all the hallmarks of a promising and productive collaboration, both for South Africa and for Cuba.[14]

Cuba's internationalist goals combined with its significant achievements in improving education have enabled it to develop a unique program of collaboration with other countries in Africa, the Caribbean, and Latin America. Scores of countries have drawn on Cuban assistance in teaching their students at every level of the education system, as well as in educational planning and infrastructural development. It is appropriate to conclude by discussing the theoretical and policy significance of this study of "South-South" collaboration between Cuba and other developing countries that are Cuba's peers, in that they are at a similar economic level and occupy similarly limited levels of power in the international system.

Conclusion: The Significance of Studying "South-South" Collaboration

Small-scale interpretative case studies of policy and practice in education must be carefully justified in order to claim to be useful for the improvement, indeed, the rethinking, of education in the emerging conditions of the twenty-first century. Qualitative comparative studies such as this cross-cultural study of Cuban teachers in Jamaica and Namibia enable us to explore how policy between nation-states plays out at a local level, and the strengths and weaknesses of this policy as it becomes practice. This type of study is important for recording little-known, though important, educational policy exchange between developing countries. The present study examined policies of using Cuban teachers to assist with a range of urgent tasks, from the filling of curriculum gaps in a few key subjects, as in the Jamaican school project, to the collaborative building of a new educational structure, as in the Namibian sports education initiative. Further, studies such as these probe the interaction of cultural context and individual agency in educational settings.

A postcolonial perspective on analyzing "South-South" projects of educational collaboration puts them into the global context of the decolonization of many African, Asian, Caribbean, and Pacific states. Decolonization, as Crossley (2000) points out,[15] is a feature of contemporary geopolitical change that "demands the forging of radically different relations between nation-states, as well as renewed principles and modes of operation for multilateral agencies." However, in practice, many of the old relations of asymmetrical disparities in power have continued in slightly altered guises.[16] The "South-South" projects of collaboration with Cuba demonstrate one approach to the "radically different relations" that are necessary to the decolonization process of building independent capacity and quality in education and other fields.

The work of Cuban teachers in Jamaican schools and Namibian sports programs illustrates many of the issues of capacity and quality that have to be addressed as countries decolonize their education systems. A major problem is that of how to fill serious gaps in staffing, particularly in the poorer schools, and particularly in key science, mathematical, and foreign-language teaching, and the related problem of improving the quality of pedagogy in these subject areas. There is the question of whether placement of most of the Cuban teachers in schools is the best strategy, compared to strategies of utilizing them in teacher support and exchange where the ripple effect might be greater. Some governments, however, have to consider the political dilemmas that may be faced if they were to try to utilize the skills of Cuban educators in a high-profile way. An important issue for Cuba to consider is that of the benefits and costs of utilizing their best educators to do this kind of internationalist work overseas. Do the opportunities for travel, advanced professional experiences, and in some cases extra earnings for Cuban educators outweigh the very great financial costs for Cuba of its project of educational assistance to the "South"?

On a broader scale, another issue is that of the role of the education assistance project in improving political, cultural, and ultimately economic relationships between developing countries. Many promising economic developments could become possible if there were to be increased collaboration between Cuba, which has a large proportion of Latin America's scientists and research capacity, and some of the Latin American and Caribbean countries, which have considerable natural resources and entrepreneurial experience.

Such collaborations could be a springboard for a celebration and development of Caribbean cultures, illustrating, as Tikly (2004) points out in discussing educational change in Africa, the notion of development on political and cultural as well as economic fronts.[17] These are issues that invite deeper exploration as postcolonial educators consider the value of the forging of South-South collaboration, which would be independent of direction and financing with strings from the wealthy countries of the "North."

The study is also important for its ethnographic exploration of the experience of Cuban educators in working in educational systems still weakened by the many negative aspects of the aftermath of colonialism. It is on a small scale, but as Crossley and Vulliamy (1997) show in their volume on educational research on developing countries, qualitative case studies with their richness of contextual and observational analysis can provide important comparative insights into educational issues.[18] Education policy makers in developing countries could draw on studies such as this one to consider how to improve education settings, structures, and pedagogy. They could, for example, consider the potential value of exchanging education personnel for short periods between countries. The Cubans teaching in Jamaica and other Caribbean countries gain cultural knowledge of their island neighbors, which they will certainly use in future teaching in Cuba. They also develop their professional and intellectual skills through grappling with unfamiliar curricula, which they are required to teach in a second language. For my part, my own understanding of policy possibilities and pedagogical concerns for developing countries was enhanced by my fieldwork in this project. I learned much from listening to the Cuban teachers comment on educational issues from the comparative perspective that they had acquired during their experiences in schools overseas, some only in Jamaica, and others in a range of additional countries including Ethiopia, Botswana, and Zimbabwe.

In our free-flowing, minimally structured interviews, Cuban teachers discussed with me the pedagogic significance of the intellectual demands of examination syllabi in the sciences in the English-speaking Caribbean compared with equivalent syllabi in Cuba. We also talked about the social consequences of how different countries organized the education of adolescents in compulsory and post-compulsory education. They analyzed for me some of the problems that their Jamaican students were encountering as they wrestled with traditionally troublesome subjects such as mathematics, chemistry, and physics, their insights challenging my own lack of knowledge of these science subjects. They discussed the kinds of timetabling approaches needed to support serious foreign language study, the effects that they were witnessing of problems of student poverty, and the possibilities for student development when certain policies are put into place. Their conversations reminded me of the importance of peer support among teachers. For example, they spoke of the effectiveness of their systematic efforts to help each other improve their English and of their regular meetings among themselves to discuss their teaching experiences and how they could progress further as professionals. In Namibia I learned about the kind of institutional policy and support that is necessary to stimulate the creation of new educational structures; and in South Africa I learned about additional ways of utilizing the knowledge and skills of Cuban educators in locations other than school-level classrooms.

Colonial histories have taught most decolonizing countries to rely to a large extent on the wealthy countries of the "North" for educational advice, research, ideologies, blueprints, loans, and personnel in order to continue and expand the conventional model of education. Arguably, this model to a large extent fails to engage the minds and hearts of perhaps the majority of students, thus disposing many people to want to discontinue learning after leaving school. An outdated, inefficient, inequitable, and oppressive model of schooling,[19] particularly in developing countries, reduces the ability of individuals and societies to cope with the educational and cultural challenges of the twenty-first century. Cuba's education model is also an imperfect modernist one, but Cuban educators have been supported in developing within it some practices that have successfully tackled some of the deepest problems of the colonial aftermath. The exploration of other insights and models through collaboration between diverse countries of the "South" might at least energize alternative postcolonial thinking, a necessary step in facilitating the building of a high quality of "education for all."

Notes

1. This chapter is based on an earlier article: Anne Hickling-Hudson (2004) South-South Collaboration: Cuban Teachers in Jamaica and Namibia, *Comparative Education*, 40:2, May, pp. 290–311.

2. Broadfoot, 2000; Crossley, 2000.
3. See Unesco, 1998; Gasperini, 1999.
4. In 2008, the performance of Jamaican students in the key subjects of English language, mathematics, and science for the Caribbean Secondary Education Certificate (CSEC), examined by the Caribbean Examinations Council (CXC), had improved compared to previous years, but was still poor. For example, the average pass rate for the sciences was 62.1 percent, while the pass rate in English was 66.8 percent, and in mathematics 40.9 percent. (*Economic and Social Survey, Jamaica*, 2009, Planning Institute of Jamaica, p. 22.12). It is unfortunate that data for the older elite high schools and the newly upgraded high schools have recently been merged, thus making it impossible to see which types of schools are performing at varying levels, or how teachers with different qualifications are distributed among the different school types. Comparative social analysis is thus made difficult or impossible.
5. In 2008, university graduates with additional education training comprised 34 percent of all teachers, compared to 52 percent with a diploma from teachers' colleges. Untrained teachers comprised 6 percent of the teaching force, while university graduates without teacher training comprised 8 percent (*Economic and Social Survey, Jamaica,* 2009, Planning Institute of Jamaica, p.22.13).
6. Jules, 2006.
7. Personal communication, Cuban embassy in Jamaica, January 2011.
8. Evans, 1998.
9. Avoseh, 2000, SACMEQ, 2011.
10. Katzao, 1999, pp. 67–68.
11. USAID, 2008.
12. Keck, C. W., 2007. This article includes a table setting out the total number of Cuban personnel serving overseas in different professional fields. The table shows 37,342 Cubans serving in 111 countries, with 28,664 (76.8 percent) in the health sector in 68 countries, and 578 in education. Most of the latter are in Latin America, with 71 in the Caribbean and about 30 in Africa. Dr. Keck acknowledges the assistance of MEDICC personnel, as well as his 20 or more trips to Cuba, in putting together his data.
13. Carnoy, M., A. Gove, and J. Marshall 2007; A. Hickling-Hudson, 2002: 573–574; UNESCO/ OREALC 1998.
14. See Mbeki, 2001.
15. Crossley, 2000, p. 324.
16. King, 1991; Crossley, 2000; Samoff, 2003.
17. Tikly, 2004, p. 124.
18. Crossley and Vulliamy, 1997.
19. Hickling-Hudson, 2002, p. 571.

Bibliography

Avoseh, M. (2002) Postcolonial Education in Namibia: A Critical Analysis. *Journal of Postcolonial Education*, 1(1), pp. 27–44.

Broadfoot, P. (2000) Comparative Education for the 21st Century: Retrospect and Prospect. *Comparative Education*, 36(3), pp. 357–371.

Crossley, M. (2000) Bridging Cultures and Traditions in the Reconceptualisation of Comparative and International Education, *Comparative Education*, 36(3), pp. 319–332.

Crossley, M. and Vulliamy, G. (1997) *Qualitative Educational Research in Developing Countries: Current Perspectives* (New York: Garland).

Evans, H. (1998) *A Study of Secondary Education in Jamaica: Improving Quality and Access* (Washington: World Bank).

Gasperini, L. (1999) *The Cuban Education System: Lessons and Dilemmas*. Unpublished paper at World Bank seminar entitled "Interchange of Experiences on the Education Systems of Colombia and Cuba."

Hickling-Hudson, A. (1998) When Marxist and Postmodern Theories Won't Do: The Potential of Postcolonial Theory for Educational Analysis. *Discourse: Studies in the Cultural Politics of Education*, 19(3), pp. 327–229.

Hickling-Hudson, A. (2000) The Cuban University and Educational Outreach: Cuba's Contribution to Postcolonial Development. In: *Local Knowledge and Wisdom in Higher Education*. Edited by G. R. Teasdale and Z. M. Rhea (London: Pergamon).

Hickling-Hudson, A. (2002) Re-visioning from the Inside: Getting under the Skin of the World Bank's Education Sector Strategy. *International Journal of Educational Development*, 22(6), pp. 565–577.

Jules, D. (2006) Power and Educational Development: Small States and the Labors of Sisyphus. In: *Current Discourse on Education in Developing Nations: Essays in Honor of B. Robert Tanachnick and Robert Koehl*. Edited by M. O. Afolayan, D. Browne, and D. Jules, 17–29. New York: Nova Science Publishers.

Katazao, J. J. (1999) *Lessons to Learn: A Historical, Sociological and Economic Interpretation of Education Provision in Namibia* (Windhoek: Out of Africa Publishers).

Keck, C. W. (2007) Cuba's Contribution to Global Health Diplomacy. In: Global Health Diplomacy Workshop, March 12, 2007. Retrieved June 14, 2011 from http://igcc.ucsd.edu/research/globalhealth/presentations/keck.pdf.

King, K. (1991) *Aid and Education in the Developing World: The Role of Donor Agencies in Educational Analysis* (Harlow, UK: Longman).

Leiner, M. (1989) Cuba's Schools: 25 Years Later. In: *The Cuba Reader: The Making of a Revolutionary Society*. Edited by P. Brenner, W. LeoGrande, D. Rich, and D. Siegel, 445–456 (New York: Grove Press).

Lutjens, S. (1996) *The State, Bureaucracy and the Cuban Schools: Power and Participation* (Boulder CO: Westview Press).

Lutjens, S. (2000) Política educativa en Cuba socialista: lecciones de 40 años de reformas [The politics of education in socialist Cuba: lessons of 40 years of reforms] In: *Cuba: construyendo futuro* [Cuba: Building the Future] Edited by M. M. Pérez, M. Riera, and J. Valdés Paz, 287–330 (Barcelona: Fundación de Investigaciones Marxistas/Viejo Topo).

Mayo, P., Borg, C., and Dei, G. (2002) Editorial Introduction: Postcolonialism, Education and an International Forum for Debate. *Journal of Postcolonial Education*, 1(1), pp. 3–8.

Mbeki, T. (2001) Cuba's Selfless Contribution to African Liberation Driven by a Genuine and Passionate Humanism. Letter to ANC Congress, March 30, 2001. *ANC Today*—Online Voice of the African National Congress, Volume 1, No 10:March 30–April 05, 2001. http://afrocubaweb.com/southafrica.htm Accessed June 12, 2011.

Ministry of Basic Education, Sport and Culture, Namibia (2000) *Annual Report* (Windhoek: Ministry of Basic Education, Sport and Culture).

Ministry of Education and Culture (1999) Education: The Way Upward. A Green Paper for the Year 2000. Unpublished paper. Jamaica: National Council on Education.

Richmond, M. (1990) Revolution, Reform and Constant Improvement: 30 Years of Educational Change in Cuba. *Compare*, 20(2), pp. 101–114.

SACMEQ (Southern and Eastern Africa Consortium For Monitoring Educational Quality) (2011) Education in Namibia. http://www.sacmeq.org/education-namibia.htm. Accessed December 7, 2011.

Samoff, J. (2003) Institutionalising International Influence. In: *Comparative Education: The Dialectic of the Global and the Local*. Edited by R. Arnove and C. Torres, 52–91 (Lanham, MD: Rowman & Littlefield).

Tikly, L. (2001) Post-colonialism and Comparative Education Research. In: *Doing Comparative Education Research: Issues and Problems*. Edited by K. Watson, 245–264 (Oxford: Symposium Books).

Tikly, L. (2004) Globalisation and Education in Sub-Saharan Africa. In: *Disrupting Preconceptions: Postcolonialism and Education.* . Edited by A Hickling-Hudson, J. Matthews, and A. Woods, 109–126 (Flaxton, Brisbane: Post Pressed).

UNESCO/OREALC (1998) *Laboratorio Latinoamericano de Evaluacion de la Calidad de la Educación: Primer estudio internacional comparativo sobre lenguaje, matemática y factores asociados en tercero y cuarto grado* [Latin American Laboratory for the Evaluation of Quality in Education: An initial study of language, mathematics and relevant factors in the third and fourth grades]. (Santiago, Chile: UNESCO).

USAID (United States Agency for International Development) (2008) Quality Primary Education. USAID, Namibia. http://www.usaid.gov/na/so2.htm. Accessed December 6, 2011.

Appendix

Interviews in Jamaica

Interview 1—Cuban program supervisor, March 2001.
Interview 2—Physics teacher, March 2001.
Interview 3—Education officer in Spanish, Ministry of Education, Jamaica, March 2001.
Interview 4—Mathematics teacher, March 2001.
Interviews 5 and 6—Spanish teachers, March 2001.
Interview 7—School deputy principal, March, 2001.
Interview 8—School principal, November 2001.
Interview 9—Cuban program supervisor, November 2001.
Interview 10—Chemistry teacher, November 2001.
Interview 11—Mathematics teacher, November 2001.
Interview 12—Group of Cuban teachers in Jamaica, November 2001.
Interview 13—Cuban program supervisor, November 2001.
Interview 14—Science teacher, November 2001.

Interviews in Namibia

Interview 1—Member, Namibia-Cuba Friendship Association. November 2001.
Interview 2—Lecturer, School of Education, University of Namibia, November 2001.
Interview 3—Group of Namibian educators, November 2001.
Interview 4—Director of sports, Government of Namibia, November 2001.
Interview 5—Cuban ports coordinator, November 2001.

11

Cuba's Contribution to Adult Literacy, Popular Education, and Peace Building in Timor-Leste

Bob Boughton

Introduction

In Timor-Leste, a national adult literacy campaign supported by a small team of Cuban advisers was launched in 2007. By 2010, three years later, over 70,000 people completed a 13-week basic literacy course, and the campaign looks set to have a major impact on the country's 50 percent illiteracy rate. This chapter, drawing on findings from in-country fieldwork funded by the Australian Research Council, outlines the achievements of the literacy campaign, and assesses the contribution that Cuba's adult literacy work is making to post-conflict peace building and the achievement of postcolonial independence. This unusual and innovative experiment in mass popular adult education, undertaken with high levels of local involvement and minimal donor support, stands in sharp contrast with the more dominant neoliberal models of education and training for state building, favored by international agencies such as the World Bank.

Background and Context

August 30, 2009, marked the tenth anniversary of the historic UN-supervised referendum in Timor-Leste (population 1 million), in which 97 percent of the adults voted, and an overwhelming majority (78.5 percent) rejected the offer of becoming an autonomous province within the Republic of Indonesia. In line with an international agreement reached a few months earlier, this required Indonesia to end its 24-year military occupation of this tiny island nation. In the weeks that followed, the Indonesian army withdrew, but not before they had organized and supported a punitive scorched earth process of killings and the destruction of thousands of homes and public buildings. In a report commissioned by the UN High Commission for Refugees, Geoffrey Robinson wrote:

> The worst of the violence followed the announcement of that vote on September 4. Over the next few weeks, Indonesian soldiers and police joined armed pro-Indonesian militiamen in a campaign of violence so sustained and so brutal that it shocked even those who had predicted a backlash. Before a UN-sanctioned military force arrived to restore order in late September, hundreds of people had been killed and an estimated 400,000 people—more than half the population—had been forced to flee their homes.[1]

On October 25, 1999, the UN became the official interim governing authority, a role it played until independence was formally granted in May 2002. The UN Transitional Authority (UNTAET) inaugurated a massive program of international aid and development to assist the processes of post-conflict reconstruction, with an initial budget of over US$500 million pledged by donor countries[2] (UNSC 2000).

In 2009, an Australian feature film called *Balibo* was released internationally, telling the story of the first days of the Indonesian invasion in 1975. The film is named after a tiny town in the westernmost district of Bobonaro, perched high on the plateau above the northern coast of the island of Timor, a few kilometers from the border with Indonesia. For over three decades, Balibo has been the focus of debate and recrimination, arising from the murder there in October 1975 of five young Australian, British, and New Zealand journalists, by forces led by the Indonesian army, illegally invading what was then the sovereign territory of Portuguese Timor.[3] In October 2008, while leading an Australian Research Council study of Timor-Leste's new adult education system, I visited Balibo to meet with a group of adult literacy workers and their Cuban adviser, Barbara Massilanq, about the government's national literacy campaign. The campaign had been launched in the capital Dili in March 2007, and classes began in July of that year in Balibo and the five sucos (towns/administrative areas) surrounding it—Cova, Leohitu, Batugede, Leolima, and Sanirin. Small as it is, Balibo is the sub-district "capital," part of the larger district of Bobonaro. Speaking through interpreters, my colleague and I communicated in Portuguese with the Cuban adviser, and in Portuguese and Tetum with the local Timorese staff, which included all the monitors, five men and one woman; as well as the campaign coordinator for the Balibo sub-district, and the sub-district administrator, the senior civil servant in the area. Each village-based monitor, we were told, was teaching two classes of 12 students. Classes ran for 13 weeks, and already they were up to their third intake.

We met in the council building, across the road from the "Australian" house, where the journalists had originally sheltered in October 1975, recently restored as a museum and community learning center. On the hill above the town square sits the old Portuguese fort where the fighters of FALANTIL,[4] the army of the East Timorese independence movement

FRETILIN,[5] had resisted the Indonesian invasion before retreating into the forest. The fort provides a view to the coast below, from where Indonesian frigates, moored just offshore, shelled the town on that morning 33 years earlier. The historical resonances were palpable. In the face of this illegal invasion, FRETILIN had, on November 28, 1975, declared the independence of their country, and called for international support. Within days, Cuba had given them that recognition, something the Western world, including Australia, refused to do for another 25 years. Three decades later, we were witnessing Cuban solidarity in its new form. In the new independent Timor-Leste, Cuba is now providing doctors and literacy advisers in every sub-district to help deal with the massive health and education problems that were the direct legacy of colonialism and war. This chapter is about this extraordinary story of international solidarity and struggle, and how the ties that formed between the people of these two fiercely independent island states from opposite sides of the globe have produced one of the most compelling examples of international education in the twenty-first century.

Origins of the Adult Literacy Campaign

During the period of direct UN rule, after the Indonesians withdrew and before the granting of formal independence in May 2002, countrywide consultations were undertaken to inform the production of the National Development Plan (NDP). In those consultations, which reached over 35,000 people, "70 percent of the population prioritised education as one of the three most important sectors to be developed for the country's future."[6] In response, the NDP Vision 2020, which had the support of all sectors and political groupings, included this statement:

> For the next generation, in the year 2020, people will be literate, knowledgeable and skilled. They will be healthy and live a long productive life. They will actively participate in economic, social and political development, promoting social equality and national unity.[7]

The NDP went on to nominate three priority areas of education: basic school education, vocational education, and adult literacy. Noting the 50 percent adult illiteracy rate and the high proportion of adults who had never attended school, the NDP called for "the design and implementation of literacy manuals and the implementation of campaigns to address the low literacy level within the population."[8]

Already, in 2000, well before the NDP consultations had begun, young Timorese activists from the Student Solidarity Council (SSC), which had formed the last years of Indonesian occupation, had begun to tackle the problem. A group of SSC women went into the districts in March 2000 to organize literacy classes, at the same time as others among their colleagues were reopening schools.⁹ With support from some international NGOs, most notably Oxfam Great Britain, these young women and their colleagues in other ex-Resistance organizations agitated for the government to undertake a national adult literacy campaign. They drew their inspiration from the work of the first generation of FRETILIN independence activists, who had initiated a mass literacy campaign based on the methods of Paulo Freire in January 1975, prior to the Indonesian invasion.¹⁰

Around the same time, in 2000, the UN–controlled Ministry of Education also began work on literacy, with support from donor countries, especially Brazil. The ministry included many officials whose experience of educational administration had been gained in Indonesian times, and their view of literacy was very different from that of the young student activists and the veterans of the 1975 campaign who had inspired them. The ministry officials were also strongly influenced by the international institutions advising them, in particular UNICEF and the World Bank, and the powerful donor countries of the West who were funding the international assistance program. Their education goals were in tune with the depoliticized, technical discourse of human capital theory and poverty reduction, which is the preferred "genre" of the World Bank and the international donor community.¹¹ In contrast, the earlier FRETILIN manual entitled *Timor Is Our Country,* was characterized by anticolonial images and text.¹²

These differences surfaced in 2003, in two national education conferences, the first a civil society conference, and the second a government one. What was at stake were two fundamentally different approaches to the role of adult education in national development. On the one hand, the students advocated a popular education model, one in which education would be a key element in the ongoing struggle for national liberation that had begun in the 1970s. "We have freed the land," they said. "Now we must free the people," adapting an oft-quoted slogan from the resistance. On the other hand, the international donor community and most of the senior officials of the ministry saw education in terms of human capital development, part of the process of overcoming poverty through the gradual incorporation of Timor-Leste into the global economic system.

Connecting with Cuban Assistance

The first constitutional government, which took office in May 2002, was led by Prime Minister Mari Alkatiri, one of the 1970s independence activists who had founded FRETILIN. In the first two years of the new government, the focus was on basic school education and the rebuilding of school infrastructure. This was in accord with the advice of international donor agencies that were at that stage vital to the country's reconstruction. By 2004, adult literacy was on the agenda, and the ministry, with support from local and international NGOs, agreed to hold the first National Adult Literacy Conference.¹³

Opening the Conference, Prime Minister Mari Alkatiri set the tone:

> Learning to read and write is to liberate...Literacy is a national priority, because Timor-Leste needs all the population to understand the process of development, to consolidate democracy and to have the capacity to intervene in their own life. (Field notes, September 15, 2004)

The final resolutions from the conference called for a government-led national literacy campaign based on the examples of Kerala[14] and Cuba, and on the experiences of the 1975 FRETILIN campaign. However, this idea of a national mass literacy campaign led and coordinated by government was not put into practice. Instead, the Ministry of Education developed its existing literacy program, supported by funding from UNICEF and UNDP. At the same time, UNESCO support focused solely on community learning centers, not on a literacy campaign.

Meanwhile, Cuba had already initiated a comprehensive medical aid program.[15] Under this program, Cuban doctors were being deployed into every administrative unit in the country (called sucos), while at the same time Cuba also provided scholarships for young Timorese to study medicine in Cuba. Toward the end of 2005, Prime Minister Alkatiri visited Cuba, to discuss an expansion of this program. While there, he raised the illiteracy issue, and was immediately offered further assistance, in the form of a team of advisers trained in the Cuban adult literacy method known as Yo Sí Puedo! (This method is described in more detail later.)

Alkatiri seized this opportunity, and in January 2006, the first group of 11 Cuban literacy advisers arrived in the capital Dili.[16] The Cubans were welcomed warmly by the young activists of the popular education network and the FRETILIN political leaders, but their reception among some officials within the Ministry of Education and among the international adviser community was considerably cooler. They also quickly became the targets of anticommunist propaganda emanating from the socially conservative Catholic Church, already at loggerheads with Alkatiri over his government's refusal to continue the Indonesian practice of making religious instruction a compulsory examinable subject in schools. Nevertheless, they were based within the ministry's nonformal education directorate, and in February they began trialling the materials they had brought with them, at sites in Dili and in the nearby districts of Baucau and Liquca.[17]

The Impact of the 2006 Crisis on the Campaign

Within a month of the Cubans beginning their work, the country was engulfed in a major political crisis, brought on by a mutiny within the army and sections of the national police force, which grew into a violent movement to overthrow the elected FRETILIN government. When differences between the president, ex-FALINTIL commander-in-chief Xanana Gusmão, and the prime minister, Mari Alkatiri, could not be resolved, a new government was formed under the leadership of Gusmão's preferred candidate, the ex-foreign minister, José Ramos Horta. The new education minister and her two vice ministers were FRETILIN leaders, and Vice Minister Ildha de Concecão, who took charge of the literacy campaign, had herself been a member of the student brigades that had taught literacy in the rural areas in 1975, before going on to join the guerrillas in the mountains.[18] The new leadership in the ministry was convinced that mass illiteracy, especially among the youth, had made it easier for their opposition to mobilize the mass demonstrations and violence. Therefore they made the national literacy campaign a priority, in the lead up to the presidential elections, scheduled for February 2007, and the parliamentary elections that would follow.[19]

Following the advice of the Cuban team, the government in January 2007 set up a national commission chaired by the education minister to lead the literacy campaign, and a campaign secretariat. The secretariat was independent of the ministry bureaucracy, reporting directly to the minister and the national commission. It included two leaders from the popular education network, namely the coordinator of the Institute for Popular Education, a local NGO; and the coordinator of the Centre for Community Development and Peace at the National University (UNTL). The government allocated substantial funding from its own annual budget, over $700,000, to fund the campaign. Over the next six months, literacy "monitors" were recruited in every suco, and given a basic two- to three-day training program by the Cuban advisers, assisted by staff from the ministry's nonformal education directorate and a group of university students recruited to help in the campaign secretariat. The massive logistical exercise of purchasing and distributing the materials and equipment was also undertaken. The process had a sense of urgency, in that the preparations for the elections were also underway, and there was no guarantee that a new government would agree to continue the literacy campaign if it failed to start before the June 30 deadline.

By the time the elections were held, classes had opened in two-thirds of the country's sucos, and the campaign was underway. FRETILIN, however, although it won more votes in the election than any of the other parties, lost government. The new prime minister was the ex-president, Xanana Gusmão, who was able to form a government based on an alliance with a number of smaller parties, while FRETILIN went into opposition. Meanwhile, it proved impossible to stop the campaign's momentum, although it had slowed in the months following the elections.[20] Eventually, the Cubans were successful in negotiating a new agreement with the new minister of education, João Cãncio.

Bobonaro District and the National Campaign

I returned to Timor-Leste during the second half of 2007, and again in 2008, 2009, and 2010, to conduct fieldwork and complete my evaluation of the campaign. The trip to Balibo in October 2008 was part of this ongoing evaluation work. On this same trip, we also met with campaign workers and observed classes in Maliana, the capital of the district of Bobonaro; in Manatuto and Venilale on the eastern side of the island; and in Dili itself.

The Timorese campaign workers in Balibo with whom we spoke told us that so far, the classes were enrolling more women than men, because the men had to work in the fields. They said people enrolled because they wanted to be able to write their names, and also to learn about health issues (Cuban doctors visit the classes regularly). Sometimes people missed classes, but they attended more than they missed. Classes were held in homes, and sometimes out in the open. The main difficulties were not having fuel for the generators that provided the power to run the TV and DVD on which the audiovisual lessons were shown. When the generators broke down, they had to be sent to Dili to be serviced, leaving the class without essential equipment for several weeks. Every fortnight, the local staff all met with the Cuban adviser for training. The oldest of the monitors, nearly 62 years old, had been a young man at the time of the invasion. The youngest was a young woman in her twenties. They told us that 135 students had graduated in a local ceremony presided over by the *Chefe do Suco* (the equivalent of a mayor) and the district campaign coordinator. According to the Cuban mission coordinator's records, over 1500 previously illiterate people in the district of Bobonaro had graduated from the classes by September 2008. Another 900 adults were currently enrolled, at various stages of the 13-week course. Of the 50 sucos in this district, classes had not yet started in five, because they had not yet received their materials and equipment, due to lack of available transport.

A few hours drive away on rugged mountain roads, in the village of Kulunu, in the "suburb" of Raifun on the rural fringe of the district capital Maliana, we observed a literacy class in progress. The monitor was Victor Sánches, a 30-year-old man who also worked part-time for the local community radio station. He was assisted by the sub-district coordinator, Francisco ("Chico") Pereira and the Cuban adviser, Isnoel Fernandes. In Victor's 3 PM class that day, there were 14 "official" students, two more than the "quota" of 12. There were six men, and eight women. There were also another five or six school-age children with exercise books and pens who were writing everything down and joining in the lesson. The classroom was in a shaded area with a dirt floor, built onto the house of a friend of Victor's. Perhaps because of the international visitors, the class was watched by a large "audience," mainly children, who stood around the edge of the teaching area, behind the plastic chairs on which the adults sat. Old people, young people, men and women, the class worked away for over an hour, variously concentrating on the TV screen, discussing and answering questions, and working laboriously to form letters and words in their preprinted books. While Victor and Francisco did most of the teaching, occasionally Isnoel moved in to the front to help them make a point.

This class that we observed was only one small part of a bigger picture. Bobonaro, the district in which Balibo and Maliana are located, is one of 13 districts in Timor-Leste. Balibo and the suco of Raifun in Maliana are two of the 400 "towns" in which classes have been running as part of the national literacy campaign. Every three months, another group of 20 or more people "graduate" in each suco where classes are held. Graduates pass a test in which they must write their own name and a simple sentence about their life in Tetum (usually) or Portuguese, the two official languages of the country. Here, as elsewhere, the campaign moves through three phases. First, there is the "socialization" phase, during which the Cuban advisers work with their Ministry of Education counterparts to mobilize the local leadership to support the campaign, and to choose the local monitors who are provided with three days initial training. Ideally, a local sub-commission is established, including local officials, elected leaders, representatives of women, youth, NGOs, the church, and the local police. This local group then supervises the recruitment of the first group of students and helps the campaign workers and their Cuban adviser deal with any problems that arise as the campaign proceeds. The second phase begins when the class is officially launched with a local ceremony. Students then attend five classes per week, of one- to two hours duration, over 13 weeks. At each class, the participants sit on plastic chairs around a large TV screen, usually in the monitor's house or the local school or community center, watching a DVD "episode" that shows a class like themselves learning from a literacy teacher. Both Tetum and Portuguese versions of the DVD are available, the latter having been made for a similar campaign in Brazil. The local monitor stops and starts the DVD at prearranged points, to allow the class to practice the same oral and written exercises being viewed by the class on the DVD. Each student has a workbook that contains the exercises. The monitor checks and corrects this work, sometimes with the assistance of the Cuban adviser or the local campaign coordinator, each of whom visit every class in the sub-district on a regular schedule to observe and record progress. At the end of the 13 weeks, students are tested, and those who pass the test take part in a graduation ceremony, attended by local leaders and notaries, at which they are given certificates, and the next group of participants is welcomed into the class. The third phase of the campaign, which was part of the original plan but has so far not eventuated, is for the graduates of the class to join other post literacy activities to consolidate and extend their learning.

Prior to the visit to the districts, I met with the Cuban ambassador, Ramon Vásquez, and the literacy coordinator, José García. The data they presented showed that already 9,800 people had graduated from the campaign, and they expected this figure to rise to 12,000 by the end of December 2008. As a result of this success, discussions had begun with the president, the prime minister, and the minister of education to accelerate the campaign in selected districts, by opening classes in every "aldeia."[21] The ambassador spoke about the need to see the campaign in "humanitarian" terms, to keep it "out of politics," because there were interests in the country, both local and international, who wanted to politicize Cuba's involvement, and it was important for Cuba not to get involved in these internal political disputes. "We have no strategic interests in this country," he said, "only humanitarian interests."[22]

The International Significance of Cuba's Educational Aid in Timor-Leste

Timor-Leste's national literacy campaign, carried out with the cooperation of Cuba, is of international significance as one of very few successful examples of a "South-South" international aid program in the region. Cuba's assistance to Timor-Leste is particularly noteworthy, because it allows for some comparisons to be made between the Cuban aid model and the development assistance provided by wealthy donor countries and international agencies, such as UNICEF and the World Bank. Its unique features include the international solidarity character of the aid, the generosity of its scale, its low cost, the associated "grass-roots" style and approach of the Cuban advisers, and the special features of the Cuban literacy teaching method.

Cuban aid programs in the areas of health and education are by no means a new phenomenon, but they have attracted little academic attention. Hickling-Hudson provides an examination of Cuba's educational aid to Jamaica and Namibia, which also briefly summarizes the history of Cuba's educational aid work, including its scholarships for overseas students to study in Cuba, and its export of many thousands of professionals including school teachers to work in overseas countries. As she points out, Cuba's ability to do this is due in part to its own excellent education system, which produces many more qualified teachers than it needs itself. However, it is also an important part of Cuba's socialist internationalism, and part of its current foreign policy:

> A central belief of Cuba's foreign policy is that countries of the "South" should try to reduce their dependence on the wealthy bloc of countries of the "North," and that this can be achieved if they assist each other.[23]

Of particular relevance to Timor-Leste, which was a Portuguese colony before the Indonesian invasion, is that a major focus of Cuba's assistance programs in Africa has been the ex-Portuguese colonies of Angola, Guinea Bissau, and Cape Verde. In fact, the historical roots of the solidarity links between Cuba and Timor-Leste lie in the relationships that the original independence leaders in Timor-Leste developed and still maintain with their counterparts in the anticolonial movements of these African countries, which, along with Cuba, were its most consistent supporters internationally between 1975 and 1999. The evaluation by Lind et al. for UNESCO of Cuba's adult literacy aid and the Yo Sí Puedo method noted that although the program was running (at that time) in over a dozen countries, theirs was the first independent study of this work. Like Hickling-Hudson, the authors of this report also identified international solidarity as part of the explicit motivation behind the development of the program.[24]

One of the most striking things is the scale of this assistance. For example, the health assistance program includes 305 Cuban health workers in Timor-Leste, including 230 doctors, 25 nurses, and 50 health technicians; while 600 Timorese medical and allied health students are being trained in Cuba on full scholarships, with the first due to return in 2010, and a further 105 are being trained through a new medical program established by the Cubans at the national university, UNTL.[25] While the literacy collaboration is not on the same scale, the initial group of 11 advisers was expanded in 2008 to 35, enough to place one adviser in every two sub-districts.

The third point to note is the low cost and "grass-roots" style of Cuba's aid. Like the doctors, the literacy advisers live on a relatively frugal allowance. In Timor-Leste, most internationals working for UN agencies, international NGOs, or as international advisers in government ministries earn between US$5,000 and US$15,000 per month, in salaries and living allowances. Internationals often also enjoy generous paid leave arrangements, spending time out of country every few months. The vast majority also live and work in the capital, Dili. Each Cuban, by contrast, receives a basic living allowance, paid by the government of Timor-Leste from its education budget. Initially, it was US$170 per month, subsequently raised to US$250 per month when some of Timor's oil revenue began to flow into its state budget. Three advisers are based in Dili, while the rest are posted to the rural towns and districts, where infrastructure is almost always limited and conditions are harsh. Their accommodation is usually a house or part of a house rented to them by a local. They receive a rental subsidy, up to US$250 per month per house (sometimes shared with another adviser or a Cuban doctor); assistance with furnishing their houses; and a small subsidy to buy gas, electricity, and mobile phone cards. Only the coordinator has access to a car, a second-hand 4WD vehicle owned by the Ministry of Education. The others travel around their districts and back and forth to Dili on local public buses and microlets, or on the back of the motorcycles that have been issued by the government to each of the district and sub-district literacy campaign coordinators. The Cubans thus have a lifestyle much closer to the locals than most international advisers, a fact recognized and commented on favorably by many Timorese we interviewed. In total, each of the team costs approximately US$750–US$1,000 per month, or US$12,000 per year, less than many international advisers earn in one month. The Timor-Leste government also pays their return tickets from Cuba, at US$6,000 per adviser per two years. The net cost to the Ministry of Education budget in a full year is therefore only a little over US$400,000, most of which is immediately recycled back into the local economy.

The Cuban advisers demonstrated that they had deep experience and training in education and internationalist adult literacy cooperation. José

Manuel "Llera" García, the leader of the first team, was himself a veteran of Cuba's own literacy campaign in 1961, when, as a 12-year-old schoolboy, he went to the countryside with many other high school students, to help the Cuban peasants learn to read. He also fought in Angola in the 1970s with the Cubans sent there to reinforce the independence army of the MPLA (Movimento Popular de Libertação de Angola), who were fighting to eject their Portuguese rulers. Now 60 years old and a senior administrator in a regional education department in Cuba, he took two years leave from his job to work in Timor-Leste, and extended his stay for a further year to help orient the next team. His assistant coordinator during the first two years, Rafael Ferrer Ortega, somewhat younger, had also been in Angola during the 1980s and 1990s, working on a literacy campaign there that was run via radio. Together with nine others, all of whom were school or university teachers in Cuba, they formed the first technical adviser team. In February 2009, all but Llera finished their tour of duty and returned to Cuba, to be replaced by a new larger team of 35, who arrived in April 2008. In March 2009, just before Llera left, there were 36 advisers, 24 men and 12 women. The oldest (Llera) was 60, the youngest 37; and their average age was 51, making them an experienced team of educators. Just as importantly, all but the youngest were "children of the revolution," people who were born before 1959, or soon after, and who grew up in the first decades of Fidel Castro's rule.

Fifth, the Yo Sí Puedo method, a unique Cuban invention, contributed greatly to the success of the literacy campaign. Its roots lie in Cuba's own 1961 literacy crusade that holds a special place in the pantheon of national literacy campaigns. In that year, Castro's new revolutionary government sent thousands of young high school students to the countryside, to teach the peasants to read and write (Leiner 1986). Cuba's experience with this campaign, which reduced illiteracy from 24 percent to 4 percent, as well as its long tradition of supporting pre- and post independence adult education in developing countries aroused significant interest around the world (Hickling-Hudson et al. 2006). Responding to this interest, especially from other Latin American countries, the Cuban government established an agency in September 2000 to support the dissemination of its work, a research department for youth and adult literacy and education within the Pedagogical Institute for Latin America and the Caribbean (IPLAC) in Havana.[26] Building on experience in a radio-based literacy campaign in Haiti in 1999, the IPLAC researchers developed Yo Sí Puedo, which is a unique method of teaching literacy via audiovisual lessons. The method itself is in some ways fairly traditional, according to current international adult literacy thinking, in that it is based on learning the letters of the alphabet, followed by words, followed by sentences. However, the Cubans have introduced their own innovation, which they call alphanumeric. This involves the learners in first associating each letter of the alphabet with a specific numeral. The rationale for this is that many nonliterate people do in fact have basic numeracy, and will thus learn their letters more easily by this associative method. By December 2005, when Prime Minister Alkatiri visited Cuba, the IPLAC program had been adopted in 15 countries: Argentina, Bolivia, Dominican Republic, Ecuador, El Salvador, Guinéa Bissau, Haïti, Honduras, Mexico, Mozambique, New Zealand, Nicaragua, Paraguay, Peru, and Venezuela.[27] The number of countries employing the method has now almost doubled, to 28.

Adult Literacy and Peace Building

In the specific circumstances of Timor-Leste, a highly volatile post-conflict society, Cuba's adult literacy work is making a direct contribution to the international peace building and reconstruction effort, one that is, however, hardly ever mentioned in the extensive peace-building literature.[28] One of the most confronting aspects of the recent history of Timor-Leste is the way in which it illustrates how much damage is done to a preexisting society by a violent colonial military occupation. Until 1999, the people of Timor-Leste had lived for more than 200 years under not one, but three fascist colonial regimes, those of Portugal, Japan, and Indonesia. None of these regimes had shown any respect for their basic human rights and had responded to any local attempts to challenge their rule with extreme and arbitrary violence. To achieve decolonization the people have been asked to transform themselves and their communities, in the space of just ten years, into active participants in a process of building an independent nation based on the principles of democracy and the rule of law. The miracle is that they have achieved as much as they have, but one should not be surprised that the process is full of problems yet to be overcome. The three biggest challenges today remain the establishment of national unity, overcoming the divisions inherited from the colonial period; the creation of social and political institutions and practices that sustain democracy and the rule of law; and the creation of an independent and sustainable economic base, capable of feeding the population and moving it out of extreme poverty. Each of the three challenges, interrelated in practice, is part of the process that the United Nations calls peace building.[29]

However, while peace building as a term in international development practice and theory is relatively new, the processes it describes are not. During the twentieth century, many societies emerged out of long periods of brutal colonial rule, often only after protracted wars of national liberation to expel their occupiers. Others, which had enjoyed formal independence but which had been ruled by local elites still beholden to their excolonial masters, likewise fought wars of national liberation before achieving genuine independence. In fact, it was the inspiration of such movements in the Portuguese colonies of Africa that first inspired the young students who formed FRETILIN in 1974, and their anticolonial ideas and organizing techniques owed much to the literature of those movements. They also drew heavily on the much longer tradition of socialist thinking and revolutionary practice that had developed from the popular democratic struggles in Europe in the mid-nineteenth century, and inspired anticapitalist revolutions in Russia, China, and large areas of eastern Europe in the first half of the twentieth century.[30] As documented by Arnove and Graff, national literacy campaigns have a long history that connects strongly to these socialist and anticolonialist traditions.[31] However, it is only recently that writers in the field of education have begun to make the link between adult literacy and the practices of post-conflict peace building.[32]

The situation the Timorese people faced following the August 1999 ballot and the violence that preceded and followed it is hard to convey to people who did not witness it.[33] On my first visit in May 2000, Dili looked as if it had been bombed into rubble, but the destruction was in fact more targeted and systematic than a simple bombardment. Every public building, including every government office, school, and health clinic had been deroofed, and its internal plumbing and wiring removed. Most had then been burned as well. Whole suburbs of houses had been reduced to shells, underground water pips and stormwater drains destroyed, and even the wires removed from every power pole. However, this physical destruction was not nearly as serious as the human destruction. Every family had lost someone during the 24-year war, with over a third of the original population having died violently or as a result of famine. Almost every person had been relocated from their home district, and Dili itself was home to thousands of displaced people. There was almost no functioning government, since most of the senior positions in the public service, including in education, had been occupied by Indonesian "transmigrasi" who had fled with the Indonesian army.

To rebuild a country that has suffered like this would be difficult even if the population was already well educated, and had an ample supply of skilled tradespeople, professionals, and public servants to undertake the work. In Timor-Leste, the situation was the opposite. At least 50 percent of the population was illiterate, and over 80 percent eked out an existence in subsistence agriculture and fishing in the rural areas, suffering from chronic food insecurity. The health situation was likewise appalling, with almost no public health infrastructure, extremely high rates of maternal and infant mortality, with many thousands of people suffering physical and mental injuries from the treatment they had received at the hands of the occupiers and their local allies. Moreover, there were no democratic institutions, since the country had been under Indonesian military rule for the last 24 years; and prior to that under a Portuguese civilian dictatorship for several centuries, in which few local people had any civil or political rights.

It is against this background that the campaign to reduce and hopefully eradicate adult illiteracy can be seen for its true value. It is impossible to imagine how else a country of only 1 million people, despite its significant oil wealth, can build a functioning democracy and an independent economy when such a large proportion of its people remain illiterate. The literacy campaign has the potential to mobilize many thousands of people as agents of their own development, not just in an economic sense, but also in a political and a cultural sense. Moreover, by bringing people into this process across the country, in every single district, sub-district, and suco, it creates a form of national unity, a common experience from which everyone can begin to see themselves as "an imagined community." For those who have more education and take part in the campaign, it also connects them directly with the experience of the majority, hopefully ensuring that, as with the first literacy campaign, this will help form a new generation of nationalist leaders committed to improving the conditions of the majority of people.

Already, the campaign has proved its ability to mobilize women, who form the majority joining the classes. This is a key factor in the ability of a society to move beyond conflict and its aftermath, which almost always makes women the prime targets of violence.[34] In becoming literate, Timorese women will be more able to participate in the political life of their community and the nation, and carry through on the implementation of the rights that they have won in the new independence constitution. We know also from follow-up studies on the Nicaraguan literacy crusade that women who participate in these classes are much more likely to have healthier children and lower rates of infant mortality.[35] It is also known, and women participants in the campaign are already reporting this, that they will feel more able to assist their children in school. This suggests that the acquisition of literacy by parents in Timor-Leste will help overcome the intergenerational transmission of educational inequality, as it has in other countries.[36]

In summary, then, the national adult literacy campaign that Cuba has helped Timor-Leste to undertake is an essential component in the strategy to rebuild peace, for at least five reasons:

1. Education is a basic human right, and literacy is the first step in every educational pathway. As a basic human right, it is part of what must be achieved to overcome inequality. It is also the means to achieving other rights;
2. As they acquire literacy, it becomes easier for the mass of the population to participate in the development debate on a more equal basis;
3. The campaign model is a campaign for national unity as it brings the whole population together over a shared goal, connects people across regional and political divides, and involves the state, the government, the president, and the parliament in playing a part;
4. It creates bonds between the less and more educated, encouraging the better educated to share their skills with the least educated in their villages;
5. It directly addresses the status of women, especially in the rural districts.

Conclusion

Cuba is well aware of the contribution that both its literacy mission and its health mission are making to the restoration of peace and stability. Cuba's ambassador in Timor-Leste indirectly reinforced this point to me, when the literacy campaign was experiencing financial difficulties in early 2008. He asked me whether Australia, which was at that time providing over a thousand peace-keeping troops, might not be able to assist with funding for the campaign. "This country needs teachers, not soldiers," he said.[37]

In September 2010, on my most recent visit, the national literacy campaign in Timor-Leste had classes running in 558 sites, and 73,600 people had successfully completed the initial 65-lesson course. Such an achievement in the space of two-and-a-half years is remarkable. It remains to be seen whether the necessary follow-up post literacy programs will be established, and whether this momentum can be maintained. If so, this campaign will form a solid foundation on which to build a genuine movement for lifelong education, a learning society, a society in which "education for all" is not an empty slogan, but an achievable goal. On the other hand, a successful national literacy campaign, as the international evidence shows, is a complex and costly task, one requiring above all a very high level of political commitment, and a capacity for managing and coordinating united action across all sectors of government, and in society as a whole. It can only work with such united action, and if it is not sustained, then results will fall short of expectations, and those who succeed initially will revert back to illiteracy in a short time.

With the Timor-Leste national literacy campaign, Cuba has succeeded in facilitating the first national adult literacy campaign to be undertaken in the Pacific region. Moreover, it has done this largely outside the normal international aid and development structures, as an expression of South-South cooperation and solidarity. This experiment is destined to provide a new benchmark against which the aid efforts of other countries in the region will be assessed by recipient countries. The campaign is also providing a test of the value of the innovative adult literacy method invented by Cuba, known as Yo Sí Puedo, against a background of extreme poverty and devastation, and the effects of three decades of war and violence. It also therefore provides the international community with an object lesson in the contribution of literacy to post-conflict reconstruction and peace building. If it succeeds, and the problem of illiteracy in Timor-Leste is overcome, the Cuban mission will have provided an essential foundation for the development in the longer term of a sustainable national system of adult education to support the country's national development goals.

Notes

1. G. Robinson, 2003.
2. United Nations Security Council (UNSC), 2000.
3. J. Jolliffe, 2009.
4. FALINTIL is an acronym for Forças Armadas de Libertação Nacional de Timor-Leste.
5. FRETILIN stands for Frente Revolucionária do Timor-Leste Independente.
6. East Timor Planning Commission, 2002.

7. Ibid., p. xvii.
8. Ibid., p. 144.
9. S. Nicolai, 2004, 77
10. D. Durnan, 2005, 101-111; A. B. Da Silva, 2008.
11. B. Boughton, 2009, 74–87.
12. Anon, 1975.
13. J. Gutteres, 2004.
14. The state of Kerala in India mounted a successful mass literacy campaign in 1989–90, which resulted in Kerala achieving the highest rate of adult literacy in the country (Tonquist 2000).
15. T. Anderson, 2010, 77-86.
16. Interview, Mari Alkatiri, Dili January 2010.
17. Interviews, Cuban literacy coordinator, Dili, September 21 and 25, 2006.
18. Interview Ildha Da Concecão, October 3, 2006.
19. In late 2006, the education minister, Rosaria Corte-Real, invited me to come to Timor-Leste to work full-time on assisting the development of a strategic plan for the national adult education system, and with the preparatory work of the national literacy campaign. Since this coincided with the Australian Research Council adult education research project, on which the ministry was a partner, I was able to comply, and between November 2006 and July 2007, I spent most of my time in-country, working in the nonformal education directorate (Boughton 2008).
20. Boughton, 2008.
21. A pilot program to test whether this is feasible has since begun in the district of Oecusse, and in the subdistrict of Atauro, a small island off the coast of the capital Dili. If the plan goes ahead nationally, it will require a massive increase in resourcing, as there are over 2500 aldeias (villages) in which classes would need to be opened. It appears the current government wishes to complete the campaign in time for the next elections in 2012.
22. Interview with Cuban ambassador, October 25, 2008.
23. A. Hickling-Hudson, 2004, 289–311.
24. A. Lind, N. Askoornool, and N. Heinsohn, 2006.
25. M. Leach, 2008/09, 8–9.
26. IPLAC's website is at www.iplac.rimed.cu. See also a website (in Spanish) established by international supporters of Yo! Sí Puedo, following the 2005 World Conference on Literacy in Havana, at www.frenteinternacional.yosipuedo.com.ar
27. R. M. Torres, 2009; Lind et al. 2006.
28. World Bank, 2007; James Scambary, 2009.
29. D. Durnan, 2005.
30. H. Hill, 2002; A. B. Da Silva, 2009.
31. R. F. Arnove and H. J. Graff, 1987.
32. J. McCaffery, 2005: 443–462.
33. I. Kristalis, 2002.
34. S. Mojab and Stephan Dobson, 2008, 119–127.
35. P. Sandiford, J. Cassel, M. Montenegro, and G. Sanchez, 1995, 5–17.
36. A. Lind, 2008.
37. Discussion with Cuban ambassador, May 2, 2008.

References

Alkatiri, M. (2005). Keynote Address. Cooperating with Timor-Leste Conference. Iwaki Auditorium, Melbourne, June 16, 2005. *Development Bulletin* (No. 68), pp. 6–10.

Anderson, T. (2006). Timor-Leste: An Independent Economic Path under Pressure. *Lusotope*.
Anis, K. (2007). *Assessment of the Effectiveness of Literacy and Numeracy Programs in Timor-Leste*. (Commissioned Report, USAID Timor-Leste Small Grants Program, November 2007).
Anon. (1975). *Rai Timor. Rai Ita Niang (Timor Is Our Country)* (Photocopied reproduction of original, in Jill Jolliffe Collection). Canberra: National Library of Australia.
Arnove, R. F. and Graff, H. J. (Eds.). (1987). *National Literacy Campaigns. Historical and Comparative Perspectives*. New York and London: Plenum Press.
Australian Broadcasting Corporation. (2006). *FOUR CORNERS. Program Transcript. Reporter: Liz Jackson. Date: 19/06/2006* (Downloaded from www.abc.net.au June 2006).
Boon, D. (2006). *Timor-Leste Adult/Adolescent Literacy Project 2005–2008* (Unpublished Project Report 18 December 2006. Copy provided by the author). Dili: RDTL Ministry of Education and Culture.
Boughton, B. (2008). *East Timor's National Literacy Campaign and the Struggle for a Post-Conflict Democracy*. Paper presented at the Australasian Asian Studies Association Conference, Melbourne July 1–3, 2008. Electronic proceedings, at www.arts.monash.edu.au/mai/asaa/bobboughton.pdf.
Boughton, B. (2009). Challenging Donor Agendas in Adult and Workplace Education in Timor-Leste. In *Learning/Work. Critical Perspectives on Lifelong Learning and Work*. Edited by L. Cooper and S. Walters. Capetown, South Africa: HSRC Press.
Cristalis, I. (2002). *Bitter Dawn: East-Timor—A People's Story*. London: Zed Books.
Da Silva, A. B. (2008). Understanding FRETILIN-FALINTIL Popular Education in 1973–1978 and Its Relevance within the Present Political Conjuncture (Unpublished draft PhD Thesis outline. Copy provided by the author).
Da Silva, A. B. (2009). *Amilcar Cabral and the Pedagogy of Liberation Struggle*. Paper presented at the Timor-Leste Studies Association Conference July 2–3, 2009, Dili, Timor-Leste.
Durnan, D. (2005). Popular Education and Peacebuilding in Timor-Leste. *Development Bulletin* (No. 68), pp. 108–111.
East Timor Planning Commission. (2002). *East Timor National Development Plan*. Dili: Republic of East Timor.
Guterres, J. (Ed.). (2004). *Proceedings of the First National Literacy Conference in Timor Leste*. Dili: RDTL Ministry of Education and Oxfam.
Hickling-Hudson, A. (2004). South–South Collaboration: Cuban Teachers in Jamaica and Namibia. *Comparative Education* 40 (No. 2, May).
Hickling-Hudson, A., González, J. C., and Sabina, E. M. (2006). Education in Newly Independent Countries: Problematic Models and the Significance of the Cuban Alternative. *Austrian Journal of Development Studies* 22 (No. 4), pp. 97–126.
Hill, H. (2002). *Stirrings of Nationalism in East Timor: Fretilin 1974–1978: The Origins, Ideologies and Strategies of a Nationalist Movement*. Otford (Sydney): Otford Press.
Jolliffe, J. (2009). *Balibo*. Carlton North: Scribe.
Kristalis, I. *Bitter Dawn: East-Timor: A People's Story*. London: Zed Books, 2002.
Leach, M. "The Neglected State-Builder: Cuban Medical Programs in the Pacific." *Arena Magazine* No. 98, December-January (2008/09): 8–9.
Lind, A. (1997). *Adult Literacy in the Third World: A Review of Trends a Decade Later*. Stockholm: SIDA.
Lind, A. (2008). *Literacy for All: Making a Difference*. Paris: UNESCO.

Lind, A., Askoornool, N., and Heinsohn, N. (2006). *Cuba's Global Literacy Approach "Yo, Sí Puedo"* (Unpublished draft report to UNESCO, May 2006. Copy provided to author).

Lind, A. and Johnston, B. (1990). *Adult Literacy in the Third World: A Review of Objectives and Strategies.* SIDA.

McCaffery, J. (2005). Using Transformative Models of Adult Literacy in Conflict Resolution and Peacebuilding Processes at Community Level: Examples from Guinea, Sierra Leone and Sudan. *Compare: A Journal of Comparative and International Education* 35 (No. 4), 443–462.

Mentjes, S., Pillay, A., and Turshen, M. (Eds.). (2001). *The Aftermath: Women in Post-Conflict Transformation.* London: Zed Books.

Mojab, S. and Dobson, S. (2008). Women, War, and Learning. *International Journal of Lifelong Education* 27 (No. 2), 119–127.

Morrow, R. A. and Torres, C. A. (2001). Gramsci and Popular Education in Latin America: From Revolution to Democratic Transition. *International Journal of Educational Development* 21, 331–343.

Nicolai, S. (2004). Learning Independence: Education in Emergency and Transition in Timor-Leste since 1999. Paris: UNESCO International Institute for Educational Planning.

Robinson, G. (2003). *East Timor 1999. Crimes against Humanity* (A Report Commissioned by the United Nations Office of the High Commissioner for Human Rights, July 2003).

Sandiford, P., Cassel, J., Montenegro, M., and Sanchez, G. (1995). The Impact of Women's Literacy on Child Health and Its Interaction with Access to Health Services. *Population Studies* 49, 5–17.

Scambary, J. (2009). Anatomy of a Conflict: The 2006–2007 Communal Violence in East Timor. *Conflict, Security and Development* 9 (No. 2, June).

Tornquist, O. (2000). The New Popular Politics of Development: Kerala's Experience. In *Kerala: The Development Experience: Reflections on Sustainablility and Replicability* Edited by G. Parayil pp. 116–138. London and New York: Zed Books.

Torres, R. M. From Literacy to Lifelong Learning: Trends, Issues and Challenges in Youth and Adult Education in Latin America and the Caribbean. Regional Synthesis Report. Hamburg: UNESCO Institute for Lifelong Learning (2009).

United Nations Security Council. (UNSC) (2000). *Report of the Secretary-General on the United Nations Transitional Administration in East Timor (UNTAET) 26 January 2000.* New York: UNSC.

World Bank. (2007). *Timor-Leste's Youth in Crisis: Situational Analysis and Policy Options* (Report prepared September 2007 by Markus Kostner and Samuel Clark with contributions from Edith Bowles and Steffi Stallmeister; based on a visit to Timor-Leste in May 2007).

Section 4

The Global Reach of Cuban Education: Participant Narratives

12

Cubans Sharing Education: The Isle of Youth

Oscar Elejalde Villalón

*Interviewed by Anne Hickling-Hudson and
Jorge Corona González
July 14, 2008*

Introduction

The Isle of Youth, an island off Cuba´s southwestern coast, became a significant center of education for young foreigners studying in Cuba. Between 1980 and 1996, thousands of children, adolescents, and young adults from many countries studied in this island. Most were secondary school students and higher education students, but some were also in primary schools.

The Cuban population of the Isle of Youth is about 50,000. Their main economic activities are agriculture, specializing in citrus production of lemons, oranges, and grapefruits, kaolin mining (used in ceramics), and a small amount of tourism based on its beautiful beaches and landscape.

I spent ten years as an educator in the Isle of Youth. I was rector at the Pedagogical College, and then became head of the educational division of the local government, a post that included directing education for foreign students. In these posts, I developed expert knowledge of the educational system on the Isle of Youth. This chapter gives an insight into the type of education programs that Cuba provided for overseas students and reflects on the challenges that I had to meet within the various educational roles that I played.

Schooling and Higher Education on the Isle of Youth

The first wave of overseas students came to study in the Isle of Youth in 1977. Students worked in the work-study modality. Those who studied in the morning worked in the countryside in the afternoon, and vice versa.

The countries that sent these students, all former colonies, suffered from severe underdevelopment of their education systems. They lacked sufficient schools, sufficient trained teachers, and sufficient teacher education facilities. They wanted to rapidly prepare qualified workers for their economic and social development. Cuba gave them the opportunity to do this.

Some of the students who came to the Isle of Youth were survivors of war and conflict in their home countries. This was the case, for example, with many of the students from Namibia, who suffered in the massacre of Cassinga perpetrated by South African troops during the regime of apartheid. South African soldiers bombed a whole camp of Namibian refugees who had fled from South African rule in Namibia. They killed children, women, and men. Afterward they dug a big hole and bulldozed the bodies into it for burial. Many children were orphaned. The liberation movement, SWAPO, organized the children and asked Cuba for help in educating them. The Cuban government agreed to do this, and took them to schools on the Isle of Youth.

When I went to the Isle of Youth, the school for Namibian students was already established and working. The school catered to all ages. Many of the children had a very low level of schooling or were non-literate, and had to be taught from scratch. It was a complex educational challenge, as so many had been orphaned in the war and required substitute parenting and psychological attention for trauma.

In 1986 at the request of the governments of Zimbabwe and Angola, a number of students from these countries were sent to Cuba to study to become teachers at the secondary school level. Several hundred of them had senior high school qualifications, and they were able to specialize in physics, chemistry, biology, mathematics, and geography. We hope that today, many of them are teaching these subjects in their own countries.

There was already a branch of the Carlos Manuel de Céspedes Pedagogic University on the Isle of Youth, to train and upgrade teachers working there. So it was available for enrolling the student teachers from Zimbabwe and Angola from 1986. The Namibian government asked us later to train a small group of their students as primary teachers.

In the island, there was the possibility of developing more citrus and other agricultural plantations. The necessary requisites to develop work/study programs were there. In the program, all students were required to work half a day in school studies, and the other half in agriculture. We had on the island a small population, plantations with land, some boarding schools, and a location in which we could take better care of large numbers of students. Had we scattered them all over the mainland, we could not have had an integrated program for them, bringing in their teachers to look after their cultural development. We did not have the necessary capacity to place extra numbers of students on the mainland, where schools were already overcrowded. The expansion of middle-level schooling took place from the mid-1970s. Schools had been built to take in 500 students, and sometimes we had to send 600 to them.

The number of foreign students studying in Cuba increased annually up to approximately 22,000 in 1995, in different educational levels, including pedagogical studies. They came from 38 countries in Africa, Latin America, the Caribbean, and Asia.

Initially, we placed students of specific countries in schools of their national group. For example, we had schools for children from Angola, the Saharan Arab Republic (Spanish Sahara), the Congo, Nicaragua, North Korea, and the Arab countries. More than 1,600 young people from Zimbabwe were trained as teachers, especially in maths, the natural sciences, and geography. They studied at the Pedagogical University for foreign students that I mentioned, a branch of the Carlos Manuel de Céspedes Pedagogical University. The polytechnical schools, which are Cuba's speciality, were multinational. At these, it was not possible to organize students by ethnic groups. The students came from many countries and had a variety of cultures and customs. Discipline and living together was more complex and difficult than in the junior high schools, where the students were organized according to their nationalities.

It was a mass project. Planeloads of students came to the Isle of Youth.

Seven Pillars of Cuban Education

Cuban educators developed a program of comprehensive education for foreign students based on the principles of education for all Cuban students, but with additional elements. We followed this program on the Isle of Youth.

The program of comprehensive education consisted of seven pillars or foundational principles. These can be separated into three principles of study incorporating practical work, academic work, and research, and four principles of extracurricular experiences.

Three Principles of Learning: Work, Study, and Research

Academic work is the key pillar of Cuban education. This includes education in all the subjects of the curriculum, plus extra education in political ideas to orient students toward helping with the socioeconomic development of their countries. This education in values helps students to build solidarity, commitment, self-determination, collaboration, and so on.

Productive work trains students in a culture of combining work with study. Students learnt to produce some of their own food, for example. Here, educators stressed the development of productivity, responsibility, and discipline.

Research helped to educate students in a scientific culture, stressing the scientific method and its application in solving practical needs. To graduate, students had to prepare a research paper each academic year, and they presented these papers at student forums designed for age and year level. At universities and polytechnics, they had to produce a thesis in the final school year, to show their mastery of theory and practice.

Four Principles of Extracurricular Experience

Sports and Physical Education
Every student had to take these classes. They could select a number of different sports. There were many competitions between different teams, and this gave birth to the Organisation of Sports and Games for Foreign Students, which organized friendly competition between different nationalities. The main sports were soccer, volleyball, basketball, athletics, chess, table tennis, and others. Some foreign students who were outstanding at sports were invited to participate in Cuban teams in some international games. They returned to their countries as well-trained and developed athletes.

Culture and the Arts
Students practised the artistic culture of their countries in dance, music, singing, painting, sculpture, handicraft, woodwork, and other things. We invited teachers from the homelands to work with us to lead the teaching of this cultural program.

Recreation
We took students on school excursions to cultural and historic places including museums. They also went to the beach. Some of them had never seen the sea. It was something wonderful for them, and they loved it. This recreation was important as it contributed to psychological contentment.

Health
When the students came to Cuba they were given a full health check-up and vaccinations. They had full access to health care and were treated for health problems if necessary, the same as the Cubans.

Tasks and Challenges as Program Director

My main task as director was to manage the whole plan of educating and training foreign students on the Isle of Youth. I had special responsibility for middle-level secondary schools and for teacher education at university level as I was director of the Pedagogical University branch. I was head of the educational division of the municipality and was also appointed as vice president of the municipal government, which gave me the necessary authority to secure the facilities required for the development of the overseas student program. I brought years of experience and expertise to these posts, since I had a PhD in pedagogical sciences, and was dean of the education faculty and later, deputy rector at the Pedagogical University of Camaguey. I had also been dean of education and deputy rector at the Pedagogical University in Havana. So I had the experience necessary to combine the direction of secondary and higher education.

On the Isle of Youth, I reported to the Ministry of Education as well as the local government. With authority over the whole educational budget for primary, secondary, and higher education on the Isle of Youth, I could ask my staff to ensure that money was allocated to this or that task.

In my ten years as director, many presidents and ambassadors of African countries came to visit their students on the Isle of Youth. They would talk with all of the educators responsible for their students—the teachers from their homelands, with the Cuban school teachers and administrators, and with me as director, to update them about the sociopolitical conditions in their home countries, and to see if there were any problems for the students and how they could be solved. Many came to attend graduation ceremonies. Some embassies appointed special people with responsibilities for the Isle of Youth. These visits and appointments further strengthened the links of the students with their home countries.

There were students from 38 different nationalities on the Isle of Youth, and it was complex to organize programs that balanced all their needs. In general, the students were disciplined and organized, and showed respect to the Cuban authorities. Most of them were also very good students. However, it was a challenge to deal with the tensions that would sometimes arise between them. For example, some African groups had interethnic rivalries, and these showed in their behavior at the schools. Another problem was that some students complained violently when their governments did not send them money on time. We had to explain to them that this problem was not our fault, and that their behavior was harming the solidarity program.

It was a tough assignment. We brought in Cuban teachers from all over the country. They left their families in the main island and worked on the isle as if they were in a foreign country, living in modest accommodation for two or three years. The director also had to work with the teaching force.

The foreign students in Cuba today are mainly in higher education, not secondary schools. Because of the economic difficulties of the special period, we had to stop bringing new students to the Isle of Youth, although we helped the existing ones to stay and finish their courses.

Life of the Students on the Isle of Youth

The main features of our education of overseas students on the Isle of Youth were that

1. we took good care of the students that were sent to us
2. we helped them to preserve and articulate their national identity in many ways
3. at the same time they learnt a lot about Cuba and our curriculum
4. they all went home.

Sometimes it was not easy to gather some of the students to go home, because they got used to Cuba, liked it here, and wanted to stay. They spoke fluent Spanish and moved freely through the country. Sometimes we had to go looking for them and enlist the help of the embassies to send them home after their study program had come to an end.

We put on cultural festivals each year, and these gained a lot of popularity—especially the performance of national songs, dances, and poetry. There was enormous diversity in the cultural arts—sculpture and art exhibits, and even exhibits of hair styles and fashion. In many of the schools and colleges, the students organized food competitions.

We tried to meet their food preferences within the possibilities we had. The local government gave a high priority to feeding these students a balanced diet, trying at the same time to cater to their food customs and traditions. Fish, chicken, and pork were the main proteins. In each school, the students had a small farm to help meet their food needs. They raised pigs, chickens, and goats. They grew potatoes and malanga, vegetables, herbs, and spices. We tried to develop the idea in them as in all students that people should do productive work as well as study. The food they produced didn't cover all their needs, but did cover some. In their national festivities they always prepared national dishes, and the government would help them as much as possible.

We were not only training them as students at different levels, but as human beings with a creative and productive approach to work and life. We wanted them to realize that food and other goods don't come from the sky. Our aim is to educate students with an approach to society in which they sees themselves as producers, not just consumers, with a humanistic and self-reliant personality, a humane and rational view of their society, a commitment to their home country, and the skills and will to work for its development. This approach constitutes an integrated and holistic education.

The African countries whose governments sent their young people to the Isle of Youth knew that we were offering this educational approach, and wanted their young people to have it. They would ask for particular professional training for different groups of students—for example, in agriculture and economics. The three pillars of the curriculum—the academic, productive, and research principles, applied to all levels—primary, secondary, pre-university, polytechnic, and university. Young people being educated in Cuba all follow this principle. They study and do productive work. For senior students, in their last semester they are assigned to further full-time work and related research. Some university professors go to those workplaces to help students with their research.

Last but not least, all these students maintained links with the communities on the Isle of Youth. They went to parties, had boyfriends and girlfriends, and sometimes this caused problems. They left some seeds in Cuba, and today there are quite a number of Cuban citizens with one African parent.

From the 1990s, the numbers of school students decreased. The schools are now being used for different educational purposes. For example, some of them are being refurbished as university branches.

Conclusion

There is no doubt that the academic preparation given to foreign students on the Isle of Youth had a very beneficial impact both on them as individuals and on their countries. The foreign students who graduated in higher education and as technical specialists went on, in their own countries, to fill positions of great responsibility in government ministries, educational institutions, business enterprises, and various national and international organizations. We feel very proud and pleased to have contributed systematically and without self-interest to the preparation of specialists of high pedagogical and scientific level, who have a well-developed sense of moral and human values, and who are ready to face the challenges of the twenty-first century.

13

The Long Road to Neurosurgery: Reflections from Ghana on 18 Years of Studies in Cuba

Samuel Kaba Akoriyea, with Sabine Lehr

Introduction: My Childhood in Africa

I am Samuel Kaba Akoriyea, born in 1972 in Chiana, a village in the Upper East Region of Ghana. This village is approximately 36 miles away from the regional capital Bolgatanga and at the time only enjoyed the presence of a small health post, miles away from my family house, compelling my mother to deliver at home with the help of a traditional birth attendant and my very experienced great grandmother Tutu who died at 112 years.

At the age of two years, I was taken to my father's house in Navrongo where I had my kindergarten and primary education in a catholic school, Monsignor Abatey Memorial School. I attended Zamse Secondary Technical School at Bolgatanga for a year and continued form two in Navrongo Secondary School.

On August 20, 1986, at age 14, I was among 119 scholarship students to travel to Cuba. We arrived at José Martí airport, Havana, after 16 hours of flight with transit in Dakar, Senegal, to refill the aircraft, a DC 10 of Ghana Airways. From the airport we were sent to a small town called Batabano from where we boarded a ship for a 12-hour journey to the Isle of Youth, my future home for the next seven years. We were conveyed in buses to Kwame Nkrumah Junior High School where we joined many other Ghanaian students who pioneered the journey in 1983 and 1985.

ESBEC 22: My Junior High School in Cuba

We arrived at the Kwame Nkrumah Junior High School (Escuela Secundaria Basica en el Campo, "ESBEC 22"), at 9 PM local time on August 22, 1986. At the entrance was a huge statue of Dr. Kwame Nkrumah and José Martí

(Cuban national hero). We were happily received by the students in the school. Some practically jumped into the buses to see if there was anyone from their home towns to get first-hand information about their families and friends.

The Isle of Youth program was work and study, which meant that academic activities in school were supplemented with work in the surrounding grapefruit orchards. The idea behind this approach was the holistic Cuban philosophy of learning that regarded physical and community-oriented work as being equally important as intellectual development. My program started from the sixth grade, with the first year dedicated to learning the Spanish language. We started our school activities on the 1st of September 1986. We were divided into four groups: two groups attended morning classes and conducted afternoon farm work, while the other two would carry out farm work in the morning and attend classes in the afternoon. This was a well-structured system as the schedule rotated on a regular basis such that all groups were able to experience morning classes and afternoon farm work, and vice versa.

The first six months were focused on learning the basics of the Spanish language. We also participated in farm activities. In our school, farm activities were basically in the "toronja" (grapefruit) plantations, contrary to the false perception in Ghana that we were sent to work on sugar cane plantations. Sometimes we harvested the grapefruits, often a difficult job that entails climbing the "toronja" trees and dealing with the presence of small red ants. Other times we weeded the grass under the trees. I performed both duties during my first three years on the Isle and settled as the bookstore keeper in my final year, distributing exercise and textbooks.

Although farm work was laborious, we learned to produce and enjoy the fruit of our own labor from childhood. Today, when I travel across Ghana as I do every year, I see vast stretches of land being wasted while people beg in the streets and most food products are imported. I frequently ask myself the question: would such an educational system as we experienced in Cuba benefit Ghana if introduced?

Academic Activities

Subjects taught on the Isle of Youth included Spanish language, mathematics, biology, chemistry, technical drawing, labor education, social and political science, physics, and physical education. These subjects were taught by Cuban teachers whereas English language, geography, and history were taught by Ghanaian teachers. I liked chemistry but was also good in biology and mathematics. Among the Ghanaian-taught subjects, I enjoyed history, especially when we studied the history of our national hero Dr. Kwame Nkrumah, the challenges in his life, the sacrifices he had to endure through the struggle for independence, and how he organized the country with a vision, but unfortunately was overthrown by a coup d'état.

The Ghanaian teachers were brought from Ghana to Cuba for a two-year term and were also responsible to guide us and inculcate Ghanaian culture in our upbringing. I personally think this was necessary as we had left Ghana at a very young age. Although there were some instances in which—from my perspective—they overstepped their mandate, they were able to restore discipline and control as they were more empowered than their Cuban counterparts to punish any wrongdoing or even recommend repatriation of any student for extremely bad behavior. Equally important were the subjects these Ghanaian teachers taught, especially history and English language. Most ESBECANs including myself will confess the language tribulations we face in working in English-speaking environments when all our training from childhood has been in Spanish.

Social and Cultural Activities on the Isle of Youth

Schools on the Isle of Youth at the junior high school level exclusively housed students from one particular country, however, this situation changed at the pre-university level when students from different countries attended the same school. Among the countries that operated junior high schools were Namibia, South Africa, Sahara, North Korea, Nicaragua, Zimbabwe, Yemen, Sudan, Mozambique, Angola, Guinea Conakry, Guinea Bissau, Ethiopia, DR Congo, and Cape Verde, just to mention a few. We had annual interschool sports competitions in various games. I was a basket and handball player, winning bronze medals on two occasions. Ghana was usually good in volleyball, football, and athletics. On average, we were not tall enough to match the teams of Sudan, Angola, and the local Cuban team in basketball and handball.

Cultural activities were organized for all countries to exhibit their traditional dances. Likewise, annual academic competitions were organized in the various subjects. The competitions usually took place in the various schools at all grades, and those students who were placed first in the various subjects at their respective school would then compete with students from other schools on the island. The competition finally moved to the national level. In my final year, the ninth grade, I was placed first on the isle in social and political science or "Fundamentos de los Conocimientos Políticos" (FCP).

Pre-University/ Senior High School

In the summer of 1990, together with 43 other students, the first 44 in order of merit out of the original group of 119, I moved into senior high school (Instituto Pre-Universitario en el Campo IPUEC # 28, Andrei Greichkov), in a different part of the Isle of Youth. This constituted a fundamental change of environment for the subsequent three years. The school consisted of students from Mozambique, Ethiopia, Cape Verde, Mongolia, Sudan,

Namibia, Burkina Faso, South Africa, and Ghana. Although we were all under the same roof, the students of each country formed their own academic groups, and we did not mix in the classroom for lectures.

This was a period to socialize, listen, and learn from other nationalities. It was a time to learn about the situation in Mozambique, Namibia, South Africa, the Darfur crisis, and to share experiences as to how we all got to Cuba. Contrary to the selective procedure that took place in Ghana, many students from the Sudan, Mozambique, and Angola explained how they had to flee their country as refugees. Whereas we received letters from our parents, they never saw their parents before leaving their home lands. I then recognized the reasons for their generally poor academic performance as many had not actually been in schools, but had lived in refugee camps before coming to Cuba. I also appreciated the importance of the educational program in which I found myself. It helped save many from suffering and provided an opportunity for thousands of children from Africa and other low-income countries that would have never had the opportunity to progress academically in their countries.

I then understood the links between their history and their academic challenges.

During my senior high school years, we were taught most of the same subjects as in ESBEC, albeit at a higher complexity. Political science and technical drawing were not any longer taught in senior high school. We still had Ghanaian teachers to teach English, geography, and history. The annual competitions continued, and in my final year, the twelfth grade, I was placed first in chemistry and second in biology at the school level. Cultural activities also continued, and it was refreshing to see performances from the Mozambican group as they were very stylish and danced like Michael Jackson.

My "farm duties" were transformed into work in the school garden where we produced vegetables. I learnt a lot from doing this type of gardening. Today most people who visit my house flatter me by saying that I probably have the best garden in Ghana with different types of flowers attracting varieties of butterflies all year round.

My University Years in Cuba

Another 360 degrees turn in my life occurred after completing my preuniversity education. I left the Isle of Youth in the summer of 1993 to start at medical school in the University of Medical Sciences in Santa Clara City, Villa Clara. At this stage, there were no further farm activities. Once a year, students were expected to participate in voluntary farm work for two weeks. This was more like a vacation in the countryside than work and was very exciting. We were mixed in classrooms with Cubans and people from all parts of the world.

After my third year in medical school in Santa Clara, I became the vice president of the Ghanaian Students' Union in Cuba (GHASUC) and was transferred to Calixto García Teaching Hospital in Havana to be closer to the Ghanaian Embassy, as the student representative is required to have frequent interactions with the embassy. A year later, I was voted as the GHASUC President and was reelected for three consecutive years. I was also selected as the representative of foreign students in Calixto García Teaching Hospital for two years. This meant active involvement in political activities, organizing students, defending their interests, and representing them before authorities, in summary, assuming a leadership role. This role increased my experience in leadership skills and team work. I now feel well prepared for any responsibility in society. I graduated from medical school in 1999 and was awarded a scholarship to specialize in neurosurgery.

Neurosurgery

Every year, the Cuban government awarded scholarships to the best graduates to specialize in different fields. I was among the best foreign graduates in Havana and was awarded a scholarship to specialize in neurosurgery. At that time, Ghana with its 18 million citizens had only two neurosurgeons, and I was very glad and grateful for such an opportunity. I immediately started my residency training in the National Institute of Neurology and Neurosurgery in Havana in 1999.

In November 2003, I graduated in neurosurgery with honors. I had also been the chief resident for two consecutive years. In my second year of residency I was selected among the best foreign students to attend the world youth and students festival in Algeria.

I returned to Ghana immediately to work. Despite all the difficulties encountered as a young foreign-trained neurosurgeon, I succeeded in establishing a neurosurgery unit in Ridge Hospital, the regional hospital of the capital, Accra.

I became the only Ghanaian student who stayed in the Cuban scholarship program for 18 consecutive years. Not only did I acquire a profession in Cuba, but I also met my wife, Dr. Yanet Pina, a Cuban. She also works in the Ridge Hospital as specialist in intensive and emergency medicine. We have two beautiful children, Brittany and Glenford. In 2005, I was awarded a scholarship for a PhD program in public health in Spain, sponsored by the Spanish government. I enrolled in the University of Santiago de Compostela in January 2006 and graduated with honors of summa cum laude in November 2009.

I work in Ghana as a neurosurgeon and head of the department of neurosurgery in Ridge Hospital, vice president of the Ghana Academy of Neurosurgeons, and clinical auditor of the Ghana National Ambulance Service. In regard to the latter, my main function is to conduct clinical audits of various ambulance stations in the entire country, setting of standards and training of emergency medical technicians. I am also a lecturer at the Peri-operative and Critical Care Nursing School in Korle-Bu Hospital and the School for Nurse Anesthetists in Ridge Hospital. I have many more goals for developing my professional knowledge and expertise, and the sky is the limit.

Conclusion

The Cuban scholarship program was very beneficial to the students involved. We received an education that many could not have afforded in their own countries. It also benefited the collaborating countries in terms of increasing the number of skilled personnel. However, Ghana could have contributed more to the success of the program. The Ghanaian government failed to organize vacation trips for students to visit their parents in Ghana. Students were neither funded to afford such trips nor did the government attempt to help in any way. I see this as one of the foremost problems of the program. Many students lost touch with their families and friends. Many were afraid to even return home upon completion of their careers due to the fear of the unknown.

Today, many ESBECANs are operating in numerous aspects of the Ghanaian economic and political arena. It is my hope as we continue to develop the ESBECAN association composed of former Ghanaian students from the isle program, others who studied in Cuba, and sympathizers, that we will be able to stay united and together champion countless programs to benefit our homeland, Ghana.

14

The International Film and Television School in Cuba: For a Stronger Media Culture in the Global South

Anne Hickling-Hudson and Melanie Springer

Introduction

A little-known facet of Cuban internationalism is that Cuba shares in the education of young people who want to help build a stronger media culture that represents voices from the global South. Cuba was instrumental in the establishment and operation of the International Film and Television School at San Antonio de los Baños. The Cuban government provided the location and buildings for the school, and among the range of international media professionals who teach the students are selected Cuban professors from the Institute of the Arts, based in Havana. The International Film and Television School is supported by funding from Spain and other countries, and by the willingness of international media professionals to teach short courses for little more than an honorarium. Cuba used to provide full scholarships for students from the South to study a two-year course in film or television, but now charges fees for its three-year diploma course.

In 1996, I (Anne) visited the International Film and TV School, wanting to find out how the school worked for Caribbean students on scholarship there. I interviewed two Caribbean students who had scholarships from the Cuban government, Melanie Springer (Barbados) and Suzette Zayden (Belize). Melanie's description of her experiences of studying at the Film and TV School, and her understanding of how this might influence her future careers, is set out in this chapter in her own words.

I caught up with Melanie again in 2011, and found that in the 15 years since studying at the Film and TV School, both she and Suzette had gone on to further studies and excelled in media/communication careers valuable to their countries and the Caribbean region. Melanie Springer is director of a Barbados-based media production company that provides multimedia products and services in the Caribbean. She manages the production of videos for clients, the design of websites and advertising copy, and the development of both community and entrepreneurial projects. Suzette Zayden manages her own production company and is festival director of Belize's International Film Festival. Among many achievements, she has directed media productions including documentaries and commercials showcasing Belize, and provides local TV stations with advice on programming, accessing markets, and training for employees.

The focus of the chapter is on Melanie, since I was able to have a long conversation with her via Skype in 2011. I set out extracts from this conversation, and follow these with extracts from my interview with her in 1996 while she was a student at the International Film and TV School at San Antonio de los Baños. These interviews illustrate how Cuba provides educational infrastructure, teachers, and a particular cultural environment, all of which help to develop the skills and the 'conscientization' of future media professionals of the Global South.

Melanie Springer—Conversation with Anne Hickling-Hudson, February 21, 2011

Anne
Please bring me up to date with your career since I interviewed you at the International School of Film and Television in Cuba in 1996.

Melanie
After graduating from the School in Cuba, my first jobs were in advertising through media in Barbados. I learnt mostly as a production assistant—but it was very stressful. After a few months I went to Italy, staying with an Italian friend who had been at the Film School. I learnt some more about film production in Italy, but mainly concentrated on writing my novel.

Then I went to Belize to help Suzette set up her business. Suzette was very keen to contribute to her country, but her country was not receptive to her. In a sense they were just not ready. There's not the level of development that we have even in Barbados. It seemed to me that the Mayan groups in Belize are not too interested in a work-orientation, even when they are earning a salary. Work is not the most important thing. And I'm not faulting them—that may be a good way of life. Barbados, by contrast, is a post-slavery environment. We work, and then ask questions after. In Belize I helped Suzette organize a film festival and discovered that I don't like that sort of administrative work. I left after a year. I came back home to Barbados and set up my own media production company, "The Brownest Eye."

Anne

You have now arrived at a work situation where you have many irons in the fire, it seems, with many different facets of media production including advertising.

Melanie

We do film and video production. My clients pay their bills, and hopefully there's enough left over to support me to do my creative writing and other arts projects. Some of the clients ask for things to do with branding their product or service. I don't really like advertising because I don't think it adds a lot of social value. But it pays the bills.

My preference is for social branding. I don't want clients who expect me to be at their beck and call all year round. I like doing a specific project. For example, the coastal conservation department, part of the Ministry of Agriculture, asked me to do a half hour film on coastal conservation.

Anne

What role did your education at the Film School in Cuba play in your work at present?

Melanie

I certainly wouldn't be doing any of this if it were not for studying in Cuba at the Film School. I would probably have been a museum curator, or have dedicated my life to being a creative artist. But through film, I have a forum for telling stories, and there's not enough of that in film in the Caribbean. Cuba brought me to a crossroads, and I took the road of filmmaking. I enjoy the journey. I don't see myself as a businesswoman—that's probably why my business doesn't make a profit but just breaks even. I consider myself primarily an artist. My decision was to lay the foundation of my career in Barbados, and even if I want to travel, that will still be my base.

Anne

Do you want to produce Caribbean feature films?

Melanie

Not necessarily—there are people in the region doing that already—like Asha Lovelace, a Trinidadian woman who runs a company called "Caribbean Tales Worldwide." She studied at the film school in Cuba, and she has made two or three films already. I don't want to use film to explore social issues like abortion or abuse—other people are doing that—I just want to tell stories with a happy ending. In Barbados, we have a Film and Video Association—I'm not trying to blaze a trail alone. My perspectives are unique, though, and I can use that to my advantage.

I went to the Cuban Film School at a time when people went there on full scholarships—that is something I have over many others who went later when the school became fee-paying. It now charges about $10,000 a year, and it's a three year diploma. When I was studying there, the film school was like a family. Like your family, you know you can rely on them, even if you fall out sometimes. I am still in touch with friends and networks I made while I was at the school. It's celebrating its twenty-fifth anniversary this year.

Melanie's Studies at the International Film and Television School, San Antonio de los Baños, Cuba 1996

Extracts from a conversation recorded on February 2, 1996, while Melanie showed me (Anne) around the various classrooms, studios, and departments of the Film and TV School.

Melanie
This Escuela de Cine y Televisión is called the "School of the Three Worlds." Latin America and the Caribbean, Africa, and Asia represent the three worlds which are the focus of this school. In the first year, we use a polyvalent method of studying. Every student has to do direction, production, sound, photography, scriptwriting, editing. We work together to experience each aspect of film production. The aim is to build up a cadre of Latin American and Caribbean film makers who can counter the dominance of US film.

The facilities of the school are very good. In the Equipment Department, you can borrow any type of equipment for making film. There's an excellent Library—but the ethos is "anti scholastic" meaning that you learn mainly by trial and error, not by exams. Only the Sound Department has exams for those specializing in sound engineering, as it is a very technical field. The idea is that you learn from the teachers who come from all over the world to run three or four week courses. I'm specializing in sound, Suzette in production. The head of the Sound Department is Jerónimo Labrada, one of the best in Latin America. He's written a book called *Registro Sonora* or Sound Register. The head of the Music Department is José Rosado. He is a bassoonist, and is a professor both here and at the Instituto Superior des Arte (ISA). Students from the ISA have been brought over to teach us the basic skills of playing the guitar. The idea is to have film students understand the language of music so that they can incorporate it into their work. At the moment of mixing they need to be able to make certain technical decisions. They should also know enough about composers to be able to select suitable ones for a particular type of film. They need to understand musical structure—the difference between a sonata, a rondo, a symphony, and so on. You have to know the different speeds, like allegro, andante, presto, and the origins and types of music, from the Greeks onwards, what kind of story you can tell with music, what mood you create with a violin or an orchestra. Ideally, film professionals who are sound specialists should be advanced enough to able to read a music score. So that's why sound students have exams. We have to incorporate music directing and many other skills....

The polyvalence process that we participate in means that each one of us learns the basics and how to respect the professions of the other people who will form a part of the team. Part of this polyvalence, and part of the reason for the scholarships in general, is so that we will create a stronger cinema in Latin America, Africa, and Asia, to represent us, so that we can have our own film industry. The problem with the United States market is that they manipulate the other smaller markets, so that you either buy what they want to sell, or you don't make money. And the idea is that cinema should not only be about making money, but getting a message across to people, or just sharing ideas and sharing cultures. Europe tends to struggle to maintain that, and we can't expect to rely on them to do it—we have to start doing it ourselves. And that's why there are these scholarships, to bring all these people together, to understand us on a cultural level, to understand us on a professional level. That's why we live together, two years—it's not always easy. But it's a very worthwhile experience, and we realize it again each time we have a visitor come—it slaps us back into reality, and makes us realize that even if we are complaining we are very lucky.

The school is actually the brainchild of the Foundation for New Latin American Cinema, whose base is all of the cinematographers or directors in Latin America - not so much the Caribbean, 'cause in the Caribbean, who can talk about cinema right now is Jamaica, nowhere else. Or Martinique, which can't really be considered part of the Caribbean, 'cause anything they have falls under France. So these people got together. They donate money, they donate equipment, they pool their cinema friends from all over the world together, they try and help get moral support. What Cuba did was say: okay, you have everything, but do you have a place to put it? I will give you this piece of land. This is a school that was already here that was remodeled, and they basically made it into the cinema school that it is now.

For the past few years, every two years we change directors, we get people within the Foundation of New Latin American Cinema. The man that you met downstairs—he is a Colombian, and he's been with us as director for the last two years. But before that, it was a Brazilian. We use Latin American and European specialists, but more European than Latin American ones....

Anne

How does the School get enough money to pay these experts?

Melanie

Well, that's where the Foundation comes in. They sponsor the school with money. Spain offers lots of money, and a lot of the countries support their particular students....There tends to be two students from each country in general—two to three. Colombia and Venezuela and Spain seem to be the countries with the tightest agreements, and they each have three students. The ones from Spain are special, because Spain does not constitute a part of the Three Worlds. Spain gives so much assistance, that in addition to their three students there is usually an exchange student from the

Basque country, which is a department of Spain with its own language and customs. Now there are two of them over here. They stay for about three months, for the first phase of our education, which is how to do cinema fiction—they stay for that. And some, if they're really interested, the school lets them stay on a little longer, but they will not be considered as a group of those who get a diploma. When we leave here we get a diploma.

Melanie takes Anne to meet José Rosado (the music professor)

Anne
Please could we ask him to explain more about his role as a professor of music in both the Film School and the Institute of the Arts (ISA) in Havana?

Melanie (Translating José's reply)

José teaches at the ISA Thursdays and Fridays all day, and at the Film School Monday, Tuesday, and Wednesday. He has two groups at the ISA, those studying conducting an orchestra and those studying choral music—choir and lyrics. He teaches composition also. In order to do the two jobs he works from early in the morning to late at nights, and often on Saturdays with the ISA students.... He teaches the origins and types of music in a multicultural way—music from Asia and Europe and other parts of the world. He tries to give students an understanding of what constitutes different musical "schools," for example, the Italian school, the German and French schools. He teaches the origin of each of these styles, how they came about ....The Japanese have a completely different tonality. So there's all of that variety.

Anne
How much music is it possible to teach students in only two years?

Melanie
Unfortunately, music is only done in the second year. He is fighting hard to see if they will start the music in the first year, to be able to get students further. Students are given a general musical panorama, so that they can identify the most important structures of music, and types—symphony, jazz, Brazilian music, Cuban music, and so on, but we need more time to be able to treat the musical score in a more in-depth way ....It's difficult to read a score...it needs two years. It's an advantage when the student comes in actually knowing a little about music, so you can build on that.

Melanie is continuing to show me (Anne) around the film school to tell me about her experiences

Melanie
One of the opportunities that the school gives us, upon graduating, is to transfer, do a student exchange with Canada, the United States, Europe, or Latin America, to study for up to a year, or sometimes two years—as long as you want—in one of these schools, or to be able to participate in a movie

that's being made, or in general, to make contacts. Being able to participate in the Film Festival—we get to show our ten-minute documentaries, or thesis. Any work we've done, we can present in the Film Festival, where people from all over the world, including Latin America, come to see films that have just recently come out. Prizes can be won, and mention can be made. And the contacts that you make alone, in the Film Festival, are worthwhile. We've met the person who did *Dangerous Liaisons*, we've met some new rising film makers who've done *Shallow Grave*—they're English. And there are lots of people that you meet who offer you, with an open heart and an open mind, possible jobs, and you meet really nice people who are really friendly, and you make friends for life.

Anne

So this is an opportunity to extend your professional contacts, and perhaps to find a job that will start you off in the film industry? And the contacts that this school has allows you to take the opportunity of doing that?

Melanie

Exactly, and present our work. That's what the Film Festival does.

Melanie takes me to see her bedroom, which is very attractive. There is a view across the fields of vegetables and sugar cane, to a factory beyond. She has painted the white walls with excellent artistic decorations, she has her photographs everywhere, she's arranged her bed and sofa and guitar on one side, and then there are her cooking implements.

Anne

You look very comfortable, Melanie!

Melanie

Yes, but I had to work hard at it!

Anne

Melanie, how did you come to be here?

Melanie

I love to watch movies. I love to become involved in a movie, and I love reading and I love imagining. So I like making up stories in my head and I spend hours just thinking about the story, or even years developing a character, even though I never get to put it down on paper because I'm too lazy to write. I like art, and while I was studying Art Education at the Community College in Barbados, I had to do a project on cultural institutions in Barbados. There were about 15 of us in the class, and each one had to present the project in a particular way. We were in groups, and my group was to do cultural institutions, and I chose to do my project in documentary form. And I just had so much fun editing, and filming with the video camera, that I decided, okay, I'm going to do cinema.

I started to think: well where do I want to study cinema? Should I study it in America? And I thought, no...if I'm going to do cinema, I don't need to influence people with more of the same stuff .... And I thought, well, French movies are lovely. And so Mummy said, well okay. And I decided, well let's see if I can be an au pair and learn French in France. But when it was near time to get ready for leaving, Mummy said, no, no, no, France is really far away; maybe you should go to Martinique or Guadeloupe first and see if you like French people, and then decide .... So I went to Martinique, and I should have been there for ten months, and after six months, I learnt French, but I hated being there, and so I left .... And I thought, where am I going to study cinema, then, if I don't want to do French, and I don't want to do American, well, maybe Canada. And I was talking to the son of this lady, Kathleen Drayton, I don't know if you know her, she's at the University (of the West Indies). And I was complaining about people and countries and things I didn't like, and he said, why don't you go to Cuba? And I said—Cuba! Ye-e-ah! There's really great cinema there!

I started getting in touch with people who spoke Spanish, getting in touch with anyone who knew someone who was Cuban. Fortunately enough, Cuba was trying to create a new embassy in Barbados. And I got in contact with this representative of the Cuban government, who is now the Cuban ambassador here, and every time he traveled home he would send papers for me. I talked to Grace (Pilgrim), and Grace had to figure out the exam. Then later on came Damon (Mills) and his mother, and they helped me to communicate with Cuba via fax, because for some reason the faxes couldn't get through to Cuba from Barbados. All this went on for a whole year. Like two weeks before I figured I'd better get a job, I got a letter saying that I was accepted.

I came over to Cuba, and it wasn't anything like what I thought it would be. I thought that you could do cinema, like, you could just make a movie, and I never actually realized that you had to choose a profession out of the 50 different hundred-and-thousand professions in cinema: decoration, make up, sound, editing, production, executive producer, you could be the distributor, you could be this and that—I didn't realize there could be so many! I wanted to do animation. The school said...well, they never said to me they didn't have animation. They said, oh well don't worry, when you finish here you can transfer to some place in Spain, because most of the people who want to do animation go on to Spain.

We've been pretty lucky, Suzette and I—we've had lots of offers of work. There's a guy who came to teach scriptwriting, and he's done scripts for *LA Law*, *Hill Street Blues*, things like that. He said, oh I know so and so who works at 20th Century Fox, he has his own animation company. If you're still interested in animation you can come over there. And we met another man, a Welshman, who says—I've got a friend who's doing animation; maybe I can see if I can get you a job. And even if none of these things come through, it all gives you a feeling that people are willing to help you, that a job is possible.

Anne

So it has opened up a lot of possibilities for you—it's the beginning of a process, really.

Melanie

Yes, a lot of possibilities. Basically, my reason for wanting to do cinema is, I think that Barbadian culture, West Indian culture is a really rich culture. And there are very few people who represent it. My mother, she does Caribbean literature. And I, being the daughter of a teacher, know very well how it is not to appreciate parents and not to listen to half the things they say. I don't know half the Caribbean literature that is within my own walls, for even though I like to read, that wasn't necessarily what I wanted to read. If they put it on television, I'm gonna watch it first. The problem is, they don't put Caribbean literature on television. And that's something I could help to do.

Anne

I've always thought this, Melanie! I've always thought we should do this in the Caribbean! We have such a rich history and literature and culture.

Melanie

The problem is that you have to leave home, for you can't do it in Barbados. You leave home, and then you keep on going.... My vision doesn't go as far as to see myself actually working in cinema, but I can definitely see myself working with Suzette, for example in relation to the CBU—the Caribbean Broadcasting Union. They try to connect the Caribbean countries. The head office is in Barbados, and they do some tremendous documentaries, basically, educating those who have not traveled throughout the Caribbean on how the Caribbean is. And they are trying really hard to extend themselves. Suzette is working on a documentary right now, with this Jamaican-Canadian man who is trying to show the relationship between North American Indian, native American culture, and African culture. If that works out, that's a documentary that will be out there opening people's eyes. You never know. You just take each step at a time. The basic idea is that we can work together to promote our culture. The possibilities of Caribbean cinema aren't going to be that great. The possibilities of TV are stronger, and documentaries are important in that.

15

Air Raids, Bride Price, and Cuban Internationalism in Africa: A Cuban Teacher in the Angolan Civil War

Marta Fernández Cabrera

Interviewed by Anne Hickling-Hudson

My Internationalist Placement at the University of Angola

I was one of the group of Cubans who went to teach in Angola during their war of independence in the 1980s. I was there for two years, from August 1983 to July 1985.

I was chosen by my university in Cuba to join the Pedagogical Detachment "Frank País" as an internationalist worker, and I was asked to work at the University of Angola in the Pedagogical Institute of Educational Sciences, Department of Foreign Languages. This was in the province of Huila, in the capital Lubango. I was supposed to teach methodology for teaching English, but actually I taught other subjects including integrated English practice, and British and North American literature.

When I arrived at the university I was surprised at how few students there were. As a result of colonialism, very few people were able to get as far as the university level. I taught in a four-year degree course, and had less than 20 students studying English across the four years. Each year had a group of only four to six students. They were being prepared as bilingual teachers. Some were studying English and Portuguese, and some, French and Portuguese. The group studying English was less than 20. From the point of view of language teaching, it was good to work with small classes, as we had a chance to get to know and interact with the students. Only a few of the students were Angolans. Others came from different parts of the continent, for example, from Mali and Zaire, I think on scholarship from the Angolan government.

Living in the Middle of a War

During that time, Angola was at war—civil war between the government and UNITA, a party supported by the South African apartheid regime. When I arrived, the battle of Kangamba was taking place. In this battle, a group of Cuban and Angolan soldiers were victims of an ambush from UNITA soldiers and South African troops. Our side managed to win the victory, but this was not an easy task. The male professors joined in military duty on the bridges. They spent a few months there to reinforce the defense, and then afterward they went to teach. We also had to be trained to defend ourselves—to use AKMs to defend our buildings in case of attack.

The south was very dangerous because of all the fighting. The Pedagogical Institute was in the south and that's where I started teaching. But when I arrived, we were kept for about a month in Luanda in the north, the capital of Angola—beautiful, with a wide bay with islands and luxurious hotels that we could see at a distance—we were in a military camp. Cubans were constantly arriving, and there was no capacity in boarding places to put any more. That's why I was at the camp. That's where we were trained to be ready for war. The southern part of the country was "hot" because of the Battle of Kangamba, and we were newcomers and had no experience of war, so it would have been risky to send us immediately to the southern provinces. So we stayed a month in Luanda.

Looking back, for me it was a wonderful experience to work in Angola. I really appreciated the meaning of living in Cuba and what the revolution had achieved in improving conditions in our country. I appreciated what it meant to live in peaceful and quiet conditions, because in Angola I learnt what it was like to live in the middle of a war. At night you could hear the noise of guns and war planes. The planes (23 migs) flew above our building, making the glass of the windows tremble.

It was sad to be a witness to all the suffering—poverty, diseases, misery, infant mortality. I lived near the cemetery and witnessed a stream of people with little white coffins burying their children all day long. Some Africans lived in "kimbos"—very poor slum areas with huts made of poor materials. "Mumuilas" was the name of the tribe that lived in these areas—related to the Bantu people in the southwest of Angola. They were nomadic. Every night you could hear the women crying and wailing because of the death of their loved ones. Some women were expressing their grief not only by crying: they would also injure themselves.

In our spare time we were on duty protecting our buildings—the ones where we lived—to reinforce the duties of the FPLA. Cuban soldiers would visit friends in the building, bringing loaves of bread. They would give us, but the hunger in Angola was so severe that there would be hungry children looking at us. We would give them some bread, and they would take it home for their families without even eating it first, or sometimes they would share it with others on the streets. It was very sad to see those children who were hungry all the time. They called us Cuban cousins—*primo, primo!*

We would constantly have to practise military strategies as the building could be at any time attacked in an air raid by UNITA. So we had to consider ourselves soldiers as well as teachers because of the war. It was at every corner. We were not allowed to walk alone on the streets in the evenings—we had to stay in the building.

There weren't enough Angolan troops. Cubans had to defend the buildings in which they were living. Women defended the building by day, men at night. We knew the necessity of this, because in 1984 in another part of Angola, Huambo province, a bomb had been placed in a car parked outside a building housing Cuban teachers and other workers. Many Cubans died—those who were playing basketball and dominoes, those who were queuing for dinner, even some who were sleeping. One who was playing dominoes was annoyed when a colleague called him to help with typing. He had to go upstairs to do it. As he typed, the bomb went off. His friends were killed.

Markets, Bride Price and Sharing Food

What was strange and interesting to me in Luanda were the "candongas," great fairs or markets in the open, where you could buy anything you needed, but not exactly at low prices. I visited them sometimes. An African man was watching me, and said to me, "You are very pretty," and said to the Cuban men who were walking with me that he was willing to exchange two oxen for me. My friends said "No deal! We won't be exchanging her for two oxen!" And my friends jokingly said to me after that, "Two oxen! Marta, you must be very pretty indeed!"

Angolan women had few rights. I rarely saw a man working—women carried everything. Even when they were looking after lots of small children they still had to carry all the loads. When our Angolan colleagues of Portuguese descent invited us to lunch too, women did all the work—as soon as we finished our lunch, they had to go and wash the dishes. They realized that Cuban women were different. They said, "We are friends. Don't make a revolution in our home, please!"

The women were specialists in preparing food, especially pastries. Bolo was a pastry with chocolate, coconut, or vanilla—delicious! Pork was a customary dish for us Cubans and also for our Angolan colleagues of Portuguese descent. The colonials ate the meat of the pig, but taught their African subjects only to cook and eat the intestines—the Africans would wait for the intestines and cook them up, preferring them to the meat.

Children were always knocking at the door, asking us for milk. There was extreme shortage of food. UNITA placed land mines all over the territory, on land and even in the trees. So trucks or cars were in great danger of being bombed. When Angolans wanted to travel, they would ask to join the military convoy so that they could be protected. They would stop and test for land mines throughout the journey. Most of the food came by air, and this was also dangerous because of the "Mirages"—the war planes of the enemy. Because of a government agreement, food for Cubans was secure, so we did not have to go looking for it. So we were willing to share our food with others who needed it, including some of the Vietnamese professors at the Pedagogical Institute.

We could not go walking freely, and had to spend a lot of time at home. I was very pale as we were indoors so much.

Friends and Assassinations

My English is American in style. The Angolans were used to being taught by the British, although it was very uncertain—there was no planning and a lack of professors. Most professors had left the country, so they depended on overseas ones. There were professors from Mali, from Eastern Europe, from Vietnam, and from South Africa. I had the privilege of being friends with Jeannette and Marius Schoon, from South Africa, members of the ANC. They were persecuted for embracing the ANC—Marius was imprisoned for 12 years in South Africa. On his release he joined the underground resistance and met Jeannette and married her. They moved from one country in Africa to another as political refugees. Marius was an ANC leader and the South African apartheid regime planned to assassinate him, so he had to keep moving. They had two beautiful children, a girl of six and a boy of two. Even the children were trained for a dangerous life. When the girl, Kathryn, opened the door she would only open a crack and if I asked "Is your mother at home?" she would close it and go and check the situation, then return to let me in.

There was a very tragic experience in which this family was involved. A South African member of the ANC, a friend of theirs, was sick, and Jeannette asked me if I could arrange for the Cuban doctors to look after him. I offered to be the translator and went to the hospital with him. Jeannette asked us to come back to have tea with her after the hospital visit.

We heard an explosion. Someone ran to tell us that the building in which the Schoons lived was the target of this. We ran to the apartment block. What had happened was that Jeannette had gone to the post office and collected a parcel. She took it home and she was smoking when she opened the parcel, and it was a parcel bomb. It was destined for her husband, and it went off killing her and her seven-year-old daughter immediately.

A Vietnamese neighbor witnessed this as he was going to join the tea party. He stood at the door and saw what happened—Jeannette's head was blown off, her daughter lost her face, and her intestines spilled out. They were killed instantly. The Vietnamese man suffered cuts all over his face and arms from the shards of glass from the windows and glass-topped table.

This happened on a Thursday in June 1984, around the 27th. I was asked to translate during the investigation and had to pass around the photos of the corpses, but I could not bear to look at them.

Jeannette's husband was away in Luanda at a meeting. At the funeral on Sunday the internationalist Vietnamese teachers prepared beautiful displays of flowers.... The little son, only two, was constantly asking where were his mother and sister. I offered to look after the child if Marius had to travel, and told him of the possibility of the child growing up in Cuba. He said "Thanks a lot, Marta, but he is all I have in the world. If we die, we die together."

In the 1990s I learnt that Marius Schoon had become a part of the cabinet of Nelson Mandela and that Fritzie is a young man now.

Jeannette was interviewed once, and asked if she was not afraid of being killed by a parcel bomb. She said she would take that risk, but was determined to retain her commitment to the struggle.

Antipersonnel bombs can be in the form of a letter with ordinary-looking paper which is actually a bomb. Cuban specialists are trained to look for this. I had temporary trauma for several months after—thinking that every letter I opened would be a letter bomb. I could have easily been killed if I had gone to the tea party as Jeannette invited me.

I was warned by my Cuban colleagues never to be alone, as I was a close friend of the Schoons and UNITA was watching me. Once an Angolan man brought me a letter and I was reluctant to open it. He said it was from Marius Schoon.

The situation was always dangerous. There were actually Cuban counterrevolutionaries on the UNITA side. On one occasion a military jeep arrived with these Cubans, and they offered a lift to other Cubans, who were deceived into accepting the lift. They were kidnapped and taken away. That's why we were forbidden to take lifts.

In February 1985, nearing my departure in July from Angola, I was brushing my teeth, when the cry came round our building—air raid, air raid! Go to the basement! I was a bit annoyed thinking it was yet another rehearsal—but it was real. We dashed to the basement and there was a blackout. Mirage jets were seen on the radar coming towards the city—but they were not able to reach it. So eventually it was a false alarm, but we were so tense that as soon as it was over we all rushed to the bathroom. The Mirage jets reached Leva instead, a mountain located outside of the city of Lubango in the province of Huila. The landscape is so beautiful there that Fidel said once that to know Angola it would be necessary to visit Leva.

Teaching, Translating, and the Legacies of Colonialism

While teaching I was always aware that many of my students were hungry, really hungry. I constantly looked for a pretext to arrange snacks for them. Some of my students were married and had lost one or more of their children to diseases. When I commiserated with them, they would say, it is the will of God.

The signs of colonialism were everywhere. Once I wanted to buy a newspaper and there was a crowd around trying to buy the papers. I stood on the margins of the crowd trying to get in. A white Angolan man of Portuguese descent was watching and rolled up a paper like a baton, and started to beat them back so that I could get through. I was horrified to see this and said, "What are you doing? Stop!" And he said, "You have to treat them like this—they are animals." I said "No! they are human beings and want to get a paper just like I do. Leave them alone!"

My students wanted to do a term paper on the phonetics of English—the sounds that were difficult for them as they did not appear in their African languages. They did a comparative study comparing these sounds with the sounds in their languages. I encouraged them and assisted them to do this, and they enjoyed it.

In the literature course I taught them short stories. Textbooks were sent from Cuba in order to facilitate my teaching. They were anthologies, published as a compilation of stories from British and American writers. I taught the historical background as well as the text—the life and work of these authors, and the literary movements that characterized their life and times. So I taught them history as well as literature. When the Schoons arrived, they both preferred to teach linguistics and integrated English practice, and the Vietnamese were teaching the methodology of the English language and would not allow me to teach it. The director told me that they needed someone to teach literature, so I specialized in that.

The students graduated from the Pedagogical Institute with a four-year degree. I think that the ones who were foreigners returned to their home countries to teach. Many of the Angolan graduates taught a pre-university level. There were other Cuban teachers at the different levels of the Angolan system, from primary to secondary to adult education. Adult classes took place in the evening, and a group of male Cuban teachers would stand outside of the building with their AKs to protect the school from being attacked by UNITA. But of course we would never take guns into any classroom.

Sometimes Angolan soldiers on the UNITA side would invade schools and humiliate the teachers. There was a dance called the "capetula," and the soldiers would force the teachers at gunpoint to dance the capetula naked in front of the students. When we Cubans heard about this we all decided to learn to dance the capetula. But there was no need to demonstrate our capacities as dancers. Nobody dared to force us to dance in such a way.

December 22 in Cuba is Teachers Day, when teachers are celebrated. We wanted to celebrate it for Angolan teachers too and started saving money for it. But unfortunately at that time two Cuban officers were captured by UNITA, tortured, and killed in our province, so we decided not to have the celebration. Instead, we attended their funerals.

I participated as a wartime translator when a CIA agent, a white American, was caught in our province. He said that he was an agricultural specialist in soils, an agronomist, and he really was, but at the same time he was a CIA agent spying on the facilities of the Cuban troops. At first he answered all the questions in a very robotic way. He was well programmed. He looked very innocent, and spoke English only. I had to translate this into Spanish, very slowly in order to be understood by the Angolans. He said that he could not speak Portuguese, though we felt that that was a lie. After a lot of questioning, we eventually found what he was up to. He was taking photographs, with very sophisticated cameras, of what he thought were military installations. After this he was sent to trial, and it was up to the Angolan government what happened to him.

My Portuguese was not good at first and people had to translate for me. I learnt some, but it never developed very much as I usually had translators, and I always gave my lessons in English. It was when I returned to Cuba that I took formal language classes in Portuguese.

Conclusion

Angola represented a challenge for me, both personally and professionally. The internationalist mission gave me the opportunity to prove myself in a variety of fields: as a professional, as a revolutionary, as a human being living under stressful conditions, and as a humanist. After having completed the mission in Angola, I understood perfectly what our national hero José Martí meant when he stated *"patria es humanidad."*

16

Teaching in Rural Jamaica: Experiences of a Cuban Teacher

Emelina P. Pérez Herrera

Interviewed by Anne Hickling-Hudson
Havana, July 2006

Introduction

When I came to "Far Mountain" School in Jamaica (500 students), I was shocked to find that some of the young people in my classes were either functionally illiterate or completely illiterate. At the beginning this was a dissonance for me, as I had been teaching university students for more than 25 years. At the Jamaican school, I taught Spanish to classes from grade 5 (age ten) to grade 9 (age 15). After leaving, I gave a paper at the Literacy Conference in Cuba, on teaching Spanish to students in grade 9. The paper was entitled "An Experience in the Teaching of Spanish to Functionally Illiterate Young People at a School in Rural Jamaica."[1] My aim in teaching Spanish was to contribute to the healthy and rounded personality of young people and adults. But when I saw that some of the teenage students were not literate in their own language, I had to rethink my aims and strategies with these classes. I first found out that they were non-literate when I saw the principal teaching them to read and write. I offered to help her.

The Setting—A Rural Mountain Community

It was a poor rural area—although people hated to hear me say that, because some of them had fancy houses and cars. But some kids were hungry, for their parents were very poor. A "Food for the Poor" Program from the United States donated rice, oil, beans, powdered milk, and flour. It was distributed through the school. The person responsible for the distribution of the food was the guidance counselor—she had a list of the poorest children and would give it to them. I would sometimes eat with the children, though many teachers did not like to eat with them. There was a lot of shame about taking the food, on the part of both teachers and students. Yes, some teachers needed that food too, but they did not want to show they were poor. I don't know if they went and asked for it, but they got some of the food. I got some of it too, and was not ashamed to show it. I said to them, "There is no need to be ashamed, it's just local conditions."

At first, I offered soup to some children who needed it but I had to stop because too many of them wanted to come to my home to have soup, and I did not have enough for all. Another of the memories from my work in Jamaica was that I had the custom of hugging the children and being affectionate to them. At first they laughed at me but it was good for me as a teacher. A way to share with the members of the community and with the neighbors in general and with the people I lived with was going to church on a Saturday, and people treated me like family. I loved Jamaica and that community.

Teaching Spanish at the School

The motto of the school was "Pray and Work," and I taught them to say it in Spanish "Rezar y Trabajar." Most of the children were friendly and well behaved, but I was amazed by the group who behaved and acted in an unruly way. Some were really rude, even to the principal. If they were asked to bring their parents to the school, for instance, they would curse or swear.

I was faced with difficulty when I realized that many could not read and write, and they used patois most of the time. Many students never used Standard English. I decided first to teach them to write the letters of the alphabet in English, and then I taught them to read simple words in English—using phonics.

I hung up a picture of a taxi to encourage the students to talk about that form of transport—as I had seen the vice principal use that same method. Taxis and minibuses were almost the only form of transport in the area. A few kids could afford to come to school by taxi, but others who lived far in the mountains had to wake up and walk miles and miles to school. Some got there by 6:30, an hour before school started, and still found the energy to play energetically before 7:30 assembly, especially the boys.

I had to show these kids how to sound out each of the words in English, then to join the letters and sounds. I would use word games, like getting them to take letters out of a box and put them together to form a word. It was very hard because at that age, 13 and 14, many of them didn't want to be in school—they wanted to be taxi drivers or soldiers to earn good money. When they could read a sentence in English, I would teach them the same in

Spanish. When they learnt parts of the body in biology, I would teach them the names in Spanish. It took me two years to teach these kids to read with comprehension. I used many sources, like *the Children's Own* newspaper and the books *Old Iron Blue* and *King Mirodas* by Elkanah Rhule. I took them on trips to Spanish Town (the former capital city of Jamaica), to the museum and the Arawak museum. On some occasions I worked with other teachers: history, science, religion and art, and they helped me to set up trips, hire a taxi and so on. I used patois poems by Louise Bennett. I could not pronounce patois, but another teacher taught me how to say one of the patois poems. I asked the children to read the poems, or just some short pieces of them, and would get them to translate these poems into English, then to Spanish.

At some moments I felt frustrated, mainly when they laughed at me, but it was different when they showed they could repeat, say or read a word or a phrase in Spanish. I was aware of my objective. I had to make them learn by all means, no matter how.

One day, I was teaching the communicative function *me gusta* and *no me gusta*: I like—I do not like. The examples I used were very funny for them. I said in Spanish *Me gusta la frutabomba*—"I like papaya," and *No me gusta el quimbombo*—"I do not like okra." Every time I pronounced the words *frutabomba* and *quimbombo* there was a burst of laughing. Then, I changed the words. When I had finished my lesson I went directly to see the principal, who was walking around my classroom because of the noise. She kindly explained that the sounds in the words I used at the beginning have a vulgar connotation in patois. I apologized as it was not my intention, but understood this could happen in any foreign language class. I am proud to tell you they learned to say, read, and identify as well as write *Me gusta* and *No me gusta* in Spanish sentences. The objective was fulfilled.

I decided to start a Spanish club as I saw there was a French club with ten students, mainly girls. I put a notice in the school inviting membership of the Spanish club to those who wanted to learn to sing in Spanish and do Spanish dance. I started with only fifth and sixth graders, but then younger children wanted to join, and then eighth and ninth graders did too. So, I ran the club for different age groups at different hours. I started it before school and I attracted some of the early arrivals to come into the school and do club activities. In the club, I taught poems and drama mainly. What really helped was the support of some of the parents. They would help me to buy the cloth for costumes in the Spanish Drama Festival competition, and they would help me make the costumes and take the kids to Kingston on the buses.

The festival offered competitions in poetry, drama, dance, and singing. My primary students in fifth and sixth grades won a gold medal for their recital in Spanish of a long poem by Nicholas Guillén, Cuba's national poet. I had the poem in Spanish and a translation in English, some kids did a verse in Spanish, others in English, then they would alternate. We also won gold for dance. This was amazing as I don't know how to dance well, but I taught them the main steps and gave them the music. The little girls won gold and the older ones, silver. Not many boys took part as they were more into sport, but there were a few boys in drama. They enjoyed dancing but were embarrassed to dance with girls in a competition. It's very different from the situation in Cuba.

Professor Martha from the Jamaican Ministry of Education organized a Spanish camp every year at Easter for kids taking CXC Spanish.[2] I was the only Cuban teacher who went to the three camps she organized, one each year. I woke up before everyone, and I went to the dorms and asked the students to get up in Spanish. I told them everything in Spanish; put them through morning exercises in Spanish and spoke Spanish to them all day long. They were from different schools and went to the campsites with their own teachers. Even the teachers practised their Spanish with me, as it was a chance to practice with a Spanish speaker. At breakfast I walked around and asked them to say the names of all the foods they were eating, for example, *plátano, leche, arroz, pan,* and so on.

I would like to emphasize that I did not teach CXC Spanish at school. However, I prepared kids for the GSAT (Grade Six Achievement Test) and the grade 9 test. After that, they had to leave school. I was happy with my achievement of teaching Spanish to so many students, including some who were non literate.

Parents and Children

Jamaica still has issues with gender. In public, in the daytime, boys and girls are not supposed to be seen together, and they stay apart. When it was International Women's Day, they celebrated it in the afternoon, as we do in Cuba, I said to the schoolboys, "Come on, you must give the girls a kiss for their Special Day!" The vice principal was shocked, and said, "No, no, no Emelina, we don't do that!"

Most of the children's parents were small farmers, but some had small businesses in Spanish Town. Some of these business families lived in really fancy houses. Many women were vendors, others were dressmakers, and some were teachers, but other people didn't have jobs. The majority of them had relatives living in America and England, and they sent money and barrels of goods. Some got enough money to build a big house even though their jobs could not enable them to do this. Others lived in much poorer houses and I know that a lot of the kids I taught came from poor families.

An unusual incident happened with a sixth-grade girl who was supposed to be struck by duppies—she started attacking her father and other people. People started to shun her and so did her schoolmates. I talked with her and hugged her. I worked with her on her lessons and the children said, "Mrs. Pérez aren't you afraid of duppies?" I said, "of course not." And she passed her exams, and they started to share with her again and sit beside her... at least in my class they did.

Reflections

I consider my experience with the Jamaican students great and unique. It was a way to come back to life, to fight, to feel full of energy after having lost my younger daughter. Her name was Dasha. She was suffering from asthma, and at the age of 22 she passed away. It was September 18, 1998.

I especially enjoyed working with the students in the Spanish club. Through it, I felt I was contributing to enrich their values, their knowledge, their understanding of what a student is like, her or his duties and their love for Jamaica. It was really rewarding to listen to the kids reciting or dancing or playing a drama.

I could never forget my years as a school teacher in Jamaica because I realized the success was not only mine, it was the contribution of the school board, teachers, parents, neighbors, and the whole community which made my work meaningful and lively.

Notes

1. This was a paper presented at the International Seminar on *Literacy and Post Literacy. Policies and Programs.* Havana International Conference Centre, Cuba. June 5–9, 2006.
2. CXC is a popular acronym for "Caribbean Examinations Council," the group of educators who set and mark school-leaving examinations for the Commonwealth Caribbean (formerly British colonies). These examinations, of equivalent standard to the British "O" Level school-leaving exams, are usually taken at high schools in grade 10, when students are about 16. The CXC exams are not available to all students in the age group. Some schools, formerly called "All Age" schools, end at grade 9, like the one described in this chapter. If pupils pass the grade 9 test, they can enter a high school, but many do not pass.

17

Cuban Cooperation in Literacy and Adult Education Programs Overseas

Jaime Canfux Gutiérrez
Interviewed by Jorge Corona González
and Anne Hickling-Hudson
Havana, September 2006

Cuban Involvement in Literacy and Post Literacy Campaigns: An Overview

Cuban collaboration with other countries of the world in literacy campaigns is extensive. Countries in which Cubans have collaborated and worked as literacy educators include Angola, Mozambique, Sao Tome, Cape Verde, Grenada, and Nicaragua, from the 1970s to the 1990s, and Nigeria, Haiti, and Venezuela after the 1990s. Cuban literacy educators have exchanged experiences and ideas in Guatemala, Peru, Ecuador, Brazil, Mexico, Colombia, and Argentina.

It is not just a question of implementing adult literacy. A country must incorporate adult literacy in a systematic plan for a full process of education. There must be post literacy education, and studies designed for adults up to the sixth grade, then up to the ninth grade. Adults must then be given the opportunity for senior schooling and must be offered access to tertiary education. It took the Cuban revolution 50 years to achieve this process of full universal education. However, with new technologies, the process can be done faster, and for less cost. If countries want to develop, they must proceed along this path.

Improved adult literacy and education should take place as part of a socioeconomic development program, which improves production, energy use, health, and education for all of the population.

Cuba's Development of Literacy Programs Overseas

Cuban literacy educators working overseas during the 1970s and 1980s followed a systematic method. First they researched the countries and their contexts in order to learn about the socioeconomic conditions, the language(s), and other characteristics of the places in order to work there. Then they helped educators in these countries to develop suitable materials and produce them in booklets. Using these materials, they together with nationals taught students in classrooms.

Low-income countries continued to ask Cuba for help with literacy education. President Fidel Castro realized that it was very difficult to fulfill the needs of these countries by face-to-face teaching. In Cuba, in 1959, we had a million non-literate people, and a quarter of a million teachers were used to carry out the literacy campaign. But when a country has a much larger percentage of non-literates in the population, that proportion of teachers to students is not possible.

The president of Niger, formerly a colony of France, asked for Cuba's help in adult literacy, and President Castro discussed with him the idea of teaching literacy through radio broadcast in order to reach the maximum number of students and reduce costs. So in the 1990s, we worked with national experts of Niger to design and prepare this program, and we carried out a pilot project. Due to political instability within the country, the program did not get further than the pilot. However, this design changed the approach to literacy teaching from that time on.

In Haiti, the experiment with literacy education through radio broadcasts started in 1997. The objective was to reach more people with fewer resources. The result was that 129,000 Haitian people learnt to read and write by radio. Another 130,000 Haitians learnt literacy through face-to-face teaching carried out by Cuban and Haitian educators. The campaign was halted because of political instability. When Préval became president of Haiti, he asked for Cuba's help in teaching literacy by TV as well.

In Venezuela in 2004, Cuban literacy educators assisted with an adult literacy program that was carried out mainly by TV. Within two years, 1.5 million Venezuelans learnt to read and write in this program. In the last 5 years (2001–2006), literacy campaigns by TV and radio have been carried out by Cuban literacy advisers in cooperation with national educators in Argentina, Ecuador, Nicaragua, Peru, Bolivia, Paraguay, and several states of Mexico.

For post literacy education, Cuban educators have conceptualized a continuous program that gives adults approximations of schooling suitable for their maturity, from primary grade one to grade six. For the first level, we have prepared a book with readings to help students develop reading comprehension, writing, oral skills, etc. The post literacy program is implemented through video classes—20 months on TV (divided into two ten-month periods). The most important subjects in the post literacy course are language and mathematics.

How Cuban Educators Organize Literacy Education through TV and Video Classes

Cuban literacy education professors are highly trained university academics. They are responsible for preparing the radio or TV program in the collaborating countries. The literacy classes that they organize and prepare for each program are of a very high quality. Of course, in designing culturally authentic lessons, they consult and work with educators and cultural experts from the particular country. These experts become the video presenters of the programs.

Each video lesson, with its component workbooks, is implemented by a facilitator in a classroom with students. The facilitators are people from the participating country. They do not prepare the lesson, but control the process of implementing it. They watch the program with the learners. The video lesson has points that guide the facilitator to help the students to do their workbook exercises, and they are trained to help the students and assess their work.

The evaluative aspect is partly based on observation of the students—their behavior in the class, their attendance, and the self-evaluation of the student. The process of evaluation, 70 per cent of classwork and 30 percent through a final test, is systematically implemented by the facilitator. The objective is for the students to succeed. If adults experience failure, most of them won't return to the lesson. That's why the facilitators pay individual attention to the needs of the students.

This kind of literacy program features minimum cost, maximum participation. Facilitators would have required three years training or more, plus experience, to design video classes, so it is more efficient to use highly trained professors to do this. The state has to pay for the room, TV time, and the training of facilitators as implementers of the literacy program throughout the country, but the training of facilitators in the old way would have cost far more money.

A Glimpse of Literacy Education in Different Countries

The Caribbean and Latin America

During the Sandinista period in Nicaragua (1979–1985), Cuba collaborated with the Sandinista government for the development of literacy. Five thousand young Cubans went to Nicaragua as literacy educators and primary school teachers.

In Haiti, the students are first taught in Creole. The intention was to teach these adult learners at the second stage in French as a second language. Not many speak French, and Creole reinforces their national identity. This is very sensitive for the people there, and we follow the policies that the people want. During the political crisis in Haiti, it was impossible to carry out the second stage of the program. However, at present, the Haitian government has decided to restart the program with the help of Cuban advisers. The new program will partly be carried out by radio and television.

The method applied in Haiti was our first experience in using radio. In Venezuela, this method was improved and expanded using radio and TV. This method has now been adapted in various sociocultural contexts and using different languages, including English, French, Portuguese, Guinea-Bissau Creole, Quechua, and Aymara (indigenous languages of Peru, Bolivia, and Ecuador), and Guaraní (the indigenous language of central South America spoken in southern Bolivia, Paraguay, southern Brazil and northern Argentina and Paraguay). Even in these languages there are local differences, such as the variations in Quechua in different locations. In Mexico our program has been carried out in Spanish, apart from one in an indigenous language in Michuocán. In Oaxaca, there are monolingual indigenous groups who only speak their own language. The program is adapted for them when possible. Sometimes there are no specialists in these languages, especially when they have no written forms. However, in Mexico, a large proportion of the population speaks Spanish.

In Venezuela, 50 Cuban professors worked as adult literacy advisors. Throughout the country, there were 70,000 locations for the video literacy lessons that these professors designed, and about 75,000 Venezuelan facilitators. Cuba supplied advisers, TV sets, and booklets, but the rest of the cost was paid for by the Venezuelan government. The cultural component of the program is based on input from Venezuelans, and they present the TV programs. The literacy lessons on video are sent to the facilitators. The class watches the video lesson, and the facilitator helps them to carry out the exercises. Facilitators carry out the evaluation tasks. This has proved to be a very economical strategy, as the training of the facilitators is less complex than if they were in complete charge of the lessons. The campaign was so successful that more than 1.5 million adults were taught how to read and write in approximately one and a half years (between 2003 and 2004). Post literacy education in Venezuela currently involves more than 1 million students. About half of them had just completed the first stage of the literacy program (*Yo Sí Puedo—Yes I Can*), and the follow-up program takes them to the sixth grade of general education (*Yo Sí Puedo Seguir—Yes, I Can Follow Up*). Some who enrolled in the post literacy program already had some primary schooling but participated in order to upgrade their education. By 2006, 50–60 percent of these students had completed the post literacy program by TV.

Africa

The methods currently being used are the same as in Venezuela, but they are oriented to the sociocultural context, the language or languages of the country, and existing projects.

Nigeria is an example of a country with a very complex sociocultural context. With a population of about 124 million, some 50 million are non-literate. In 2004, Nigeria asked Cuba for help in adult literacy education, which they wanted to be available to seven linguistic groups that they selected (Hausa, Igbo, Yoruba, Eski, Kamuri, Nupe, and Colocuma). Cuba sent to Nigeria literacy specialists who spoke English. They advised the Nigerian government how to implement a multilingual literacy program. In the Cuban method, the first step is to train native experts who work together with the Cuban professors in program development. This begins with diagnosing the language, then experiment in teaching classes of students. On this basis they develop the program, and together they prepare the booklets. The Nigerian program is being planned for 10,000 adult students for each of the seven languages—70,000 in all.

In the1980s, thousands of Cuban teachers went to teach at the adult literacy and primary education levels in Angola. Mozambique has a 53.6 percent illiteracy rate. In 2004 the government asked Cubans to help them with a literacy campaign. Today there are four Cuban advisers in Mozambique, and they have trained more than 300 national instructors and 3,000 facilitators. There are 80,000 students in radio-based literacy education programs. In both countries, the government selected Portuguese as the language to be used.

The government of the Cape Verde Islands also chose Portuguese, even though the majority of Cape Verde people speak their own native Creole. Fifty percent of the Cape Verde population migrates to Europe in search of work, so they need Portuguese to make a living, facilitating their transition to other European countries. Their economy is based on this overseas work. All of these factors influence the decision about what language is used in literacy education. I spent three years as a literacy educator in Cape Verde, an archipelago of 11 islands off the west coast of Africa. Travel was by plane or sea. My responsibility was to articulate the whole subsystem of adult education, which was nonexistent at that point. They did have a literacy campaign, but not a whole system. The Cuban team upgraded the literacy program and the whole system of adult education.

We had to train the teachers in a face-to-face method of literacy teaching. This was a three-year training program in adult education, which gave them the possibility of getting a diploma by which they could increase their salaries by about $150 per year. The training program gave the teachers a solid base. Now they are requesting help again, with taking those adults into secondary education and beyond.

There are some countries that want literacy carried out in their own languages and relating to their own culture including music. So we assist those places in the way that they request. Programs must be different every time, which is very interesting work. You develop a lot of cultural background and knowledge about those countries.

New Zealand

New Zealand is another different context. It's a developed country, but some groups among their indigenous population expressed a need for literacy teaching. They want literacy in both English and Maori. They put out a tender internationally for a literacy team to teach the program they wanted, and out of several countries which applied, including the United States and the UK, Cuba won the tender. The Cuban team worked with Maori educators, using the Cuban method being used in other countries. This collaboration produced an adult education program called "Greenlight." The program is in English, but in "Kiwi English." We use Maori words to identify the words being studied in English, and Maori cultural symbols are part of the program. Many people in New Zealand, even highly educated ones, have been taking the course, because it has been interesting for them.

The "Greenlight" program teaches literacy from preschool to primary level, through text and media. It is divided into four stages of literacy and numeracy education. Each stage is represented in a workbook with several lessons including text and exercises. A DVD goes with each workbook. Each lesson is presented through a television teacher, who helps the learner to work through the text and exercises.

The Cuban Strategy of Literacy Education: A Non Elitist Approach

My PhD thesis is on Cuba's literacy campaign, its policy and methodology. It is a theoretical synthesis of the adult literacy experience in the early 60s in the midst of the radical changes that were taking place in Cuba. Adult literacy was the core of the stage that we describe as the first Cuban educational revolution. We learnt how to design and implement mass processes of education, beginning with literacy, and going on to sixth grade, ninth grade, senior schooling, and university. This experience is the basis for our ability to carry out literacy programs in other countries.

We had to put aside the elitist advice of experts. In my experience, sometimes native people are sent to study adult education in Europe. Many of them return full of elitist conceptions about literacy, and seeing the problem from the European point of view. We don't say we are the wisest ones, but we are developing methods based on our long experience and study. For us, it is a matter of sharing between equals, and recognizing the intelligence and diversity of others.

Teaching literacy is not as problematic as many experts claim. It has been argued that a great deal of funding is required for the numbers of students involved. However, we take into consideration the voluntary participation of people in the community in the literacy process. We are able to keep the costs down through mass participation on a voluntary basis. We do not agree that a large cost is involved in hiring highly qualified experts to carry out the campaign. We do use experts, and we don't underestimate the necessity of excellent technical design. However, we design and organize mass campaigns with wide community participation, and for this, political will is required. We take many policies into consideration, and respect national identity. We are flexible, and have a deep respect for the national cultural and socioeconomic environment.

I worked for three months on the evaluation and impact of the program in New Zealand. Then I went to a very different context in the Mexican states of Oaxaca and Michuocán. Cuba has the privilege of working in different contexts, and this enriches our theoretical and practical approach to literacy teaching. That's why we have proposed that we could eradicate illiteracy in the world in ten years at a cost of US$1.5 billion.

Now I'm working on a book about the Cuban approach to literacy education—trends, learning processes, and comparisons of what was done in 1961 and now. It will discuss the principles on which Cuba has based literacy programs, here and abroad. These include political will, conception of method, elaboration of program, and how to train experts here and in other countries about structures of management, administration, and control. Other principles are the different flexible approaches that should characterize the collaborative process, and the evaluation of the social impact of literacy programs. The latter is being done in Venezuela, Mexico, and New Zealand.

UNESCO awards have recognized the theoretical value of our method, and the evaluation model, and also the post literacy programs. We have won the "Rey Seijong" award, plus two honorary mentions celebrating the impact of our evaluation methods. The panel consisted of seven international experts, including people from the United States.

18

The Role of the APC (Association of Cuban Educators) in Advancing Cuban Internationalism in Education

Lidia Turner Martí

Interviewed by Anne Hickling-Hudson and Alejandro Torres Saavedra

As an educator, I have been deeply involved with two associations very important to the promotion and exchange of research in Cuba and overseas. They are the Asociación de Pedagogos de Cuba (APC, Association of Cuban Educators) and the Asociación de Educadores de Latinoamérica y el Caribe (AELAC, Association of Educators of Latin American and the Caribbean).

The APC was formed in 1989 as a nongovernment scientific organization quite separate from the teachers' union. The APC has a branch in each of Cuba's 14 provinces, and each branch has its president and deputies on the local executive. It started with 100 members, and by 2009 there were about 39,000 members. The association has research sections related to levels of education—primary, secondary, higher, and adult teaching, and the themes and challenges characteristic of these levels. There are also groups interested in education through community work, comparative education, and in curriculum areas.

AELAC, the Association of Latin American and Caribbean Educators, was created in 1990 as a result of negotiations, led by the APC, between teachers of 18 different countries, during the *Pedagogía 1990* International Congress. The objectives of AELAC were firstly, for teachers in Cuba and the region to work cooperatively and secondly, to create conditions in which they could exchange with each other. AELAC provides a forum for exchanges of ideas between teachers in the whole region. Cuba has provided a place for AELAC's headquarters and financial help to pay for a secretary general. The president changes from one country to another, every four years. The presidency has been held by scholars from Venezuela, Argentina, and the Dominican Republic.

Many countries joined AELAC, and the APC became its Cuban chapter. This provided the APC with an effective organizational framework to interrelate with other countries. I will talk about how the APC divides its international cooperative action in two sections: the section cooperating with Latin America and the Caribbean and the section cooperating with North America. I will also explain how the cooperation with North American educators facilitated the APC's hosting of the 12th Congress of the World Council of Comparative Education Societies in Havana in 2004. I will also talk about Cuban international cooperation in the field of education.

Cooperation with Latin America and the Caribbean

Many Cuban educators travel to Latin America and the Caribbean to assist voluntarily in education. This educational cooperation is organized by associations such as AELAC. It is quite separate from the government-to-government activities that have been described elsewhere in this book.

Through the APC and AELAC, Cuban educators have had a tremendous impact on the life and work of thousands of educators from all over the world, but especially from Latin America, through conferences, meetings, seminars, and exchange visits, all of which promote educational research.

In each of Cuba's 14 provinces, there is a branch of the APC that regularly brings Cuban teachers together and organizes educational events. Each province has "sister" relations with Latin American countries. Some examples are: Pinar del Río with Argentina (a book on the teaching of the Spanish language came out of this), Santiago de Cuba with Mexico, Guantánamo Bay with the Dominican Republic, and Havana City with Venezuela.

Teachers from a province or region in Cuba exchange with another province or region overseas. Cubans are not paid for their work in this exchange, but their travel, accommodation costs, and living expenses are covered. For example, when educators in Havana city exchange with educators in Venezuela, Venezuela pays for tickets and lodgings. Using this procedure, Cubans have worked at different levels of the education system in more than 10 states of Venezuela. They have worked in projects from kindergarten to university, including even developing a postdoctoral course for professors who are already PhDs.

APC professors do not charge fees for the course they teach in these collaborative agreements. Because of this, some low-income teachers can afford to attend their courses. They earn low salaries and sometimes teach at two or three schools, and could not otherwise afford to attend such courses.

In Argentina, when I taught a 15-day course, the organizers charged teachers only a small fee for registration. This covered the cost of my ticket. Although it was a low fee, some teachers could not afford it. There was a teacher who brought her small child and sat outside of the seminar trying to listen to what was going on, because she could not afford the registration fee. But the teachers who do come to the seminar are grateful to the APC professors for giving their expertise and time for just the cost of their travel.

Sometimes, universities in Latin America invite Cuban professors to give lectures, and pay them university rates. Another arrangement is when a university hires a Cuban professor for one or two months in each year, to help with master of education (MEd) programs, especially research methods. Sometimes professors from the APC doing this university work take the opportunity to do extra, voluntary professional development work with classroom teachers in low-income schools. All of this is based on our vision of solidarity and internationalism.

When Cuban professors leave their posts in Cuba to do this collaborative work overseas, there is a cost to the Cuban government. It continues to pay our salary while we are away. Our colleagues in Cuba cover our work while we are teaching overseas. Some visits to teach overseas are not for more than a month, while others are for longer periods, like the two-year collaboration agreements in which Cuban teachers go to Jamaica and other Caribbean countries. Whether short or long, the same principle operates—the Cuban government continues to pay our salary and our colleagues cover our work for us.

Since 1993 the APC and AELAC have organized several seminars in Cuba for educators from Latin America. Their attendance is facilitated by low registration fees, as well as low fees to stay in accommodation owned by the Cuban Ministry of Education. The following are examples of themes around which workshops have been conducted for many years running:

1. Teachers and the challenges of the century
2. Games and children
3. Teachers and community work
4. The teaching of language and literature
5. Education and environmental problems

We were doing this for solidarity, but we did not realize the international impact that this work has had on helping to upgrade the skills of teachers. In the last few years, we have had the opportunity to work with thousands of teachers from overseas. We have them here in our universities, and we work with them in their own countries.

Cuba was expelled from the OAS (Organization of American States), (OEA in Spanish, *Organización de Estados Americanos*) so our relationships with Latin America were for a time more difficult than those with Europe. For years the only Latin American country that I visited was Mexico. Now there is much more opportunity for us to work in various countries of Latin America.

José Martí's ideals are important in guiding us. I have written a book on an aspect of my work overseas—on how children in countries where I have worked react to themes pointed out by Martí. The book is entitled *The Pedagogy of Tenderness*.[1] Martí pointed out how tender relationships create a better human being, and I used examples from seven countries. We asked teachers to keep a journal of the problems they face in the classroom, and this will be the second volume of the *Pedagogy of Tenderness*. For me it is unforgettable, every time I receive letters from those teachers. I ask them when they write to send me pictures of the children, so that they can be in the second book.

For more than 20 years, I have been studying Martí's philosophical ideas on education. His work is in 27 books and is scattered across many types of publication—letters, newspapers. etc. He died at 46. Howard Gardner's "multiple intelligences" idea was talked about by José Martí long ago. From 1887, he was pointing out that children know more than they appear to know. He said that in Cuba we have greater numbers of intelligent people than we have trees, and that genius will disappear when we are able to cultivate everyone's intelligence.

A great achievement of the Association of Cuban Educators has been the production of books in conjunction with authors from other countries of Latin America. An example is the series on preschool education, entitled *Great Latin American Educators* that was produced with authors from Chile and Brazil, among others.

The APC and Cooperation with the USA

After the revolution in 1959, few relations could develop between Cuban and North American teachers, because of the US blockade. In 1981 a conference to analyze Cuban education was held in Boston in the United States, organized by the Cuban Studies Centre in New York. After this, a few scholars from the United States attended some educational conferences in Cuba, and they had to struggle with all the territorial laws implemented by the blockade. Their presence in Cuba was always due to their personal efforts. In the early 1990s, the CIES (Comparative and International Education Society) invited Cuban professors to their conferences in the United States to present papers on Cuban education, but the US government would not give them visas. So the idea was developed to hold a seminar about North American and Cuban education, in Cuba, with the participation of educators from the United States and Cuba.

The *seminario* succeeded in establishing regular relationships between Cuban and North American educators where there had been little interaction before. As the APC president, I worked with Dr. Sheryl Lutjens of Northern Arizona University to organize the first *seminario* in 1994 in the city of Havana. After that we organized it annually in different provinces, including Pinar del Río, Matanzas, Granma, Cienfuegos, Santiago de Cuba, and Havana province.

The general goal of the *seminario* was to exchange ideas and research on the quality of education. Topics included: education policy, comparative education, teacher training and upgrading, methods and learning strategies, values formation, education and society, and the role of new technologies in education. The tenth *seminario* in October 2004 was held in Havana at the same time as the 12th World Congress of Comparative Education Societies, hosted by the APC. The topic was the role of the *seminario* in professional and academic exchange, and the prospects for future collaboration given the difficult conditions. The US government under President Bush was making it more and more difficult for US educators to visit Cuba, so at this meeting the participants discussed other possible ways of continuing the interaction.

The ten-year experience of the annual US/Cuba seminar had important results. Because of this seminar, the informational blockade about education between the two countries was broken. Cuban educators did not know much about North American education, and vice versa, and the *seminarios* provided the opportunity for exchange. North American educators brought with them educational journals, books, and magazines, and Cuban educators were happy to receive these and to introduce the North Americans to Cuban publications. Some of the US participants carried out joint research projects with Cuban educators, mainly about the teaching of foreign languages and the strategies for teacher training. Some books were published jointly by Cuban and North American authors[2]. North Americans established relations with Cuban associations and organizations to which they had no access before. They developed collegiality with professors of education in several universities, and established links with the research center on women's affairs, the center for psychological and sociological research, and the anthropology research center, among others. Some North American educators gave courses in Cuba on methods of participatory action research. Some of them also participated in the *Pedagogía* conferences which they got to know about.

In the first ten years of the *seminario*, 359 American scholars and educators attended the events and presented 340 papers, together with 393 Cubans who presented 360 papers. (see Appendix 2).

The 12th *seminario* was held within the activities of the 12th Congress of the World Council of Comparative Education Societies, held in Havana City[3] in 2004. Since 2004, new forms of educational cooperation have been established between Cuban and US scholars and educators under the title of "Research on Cuban Educational Practices." These new forms of exchange have been held in the provinces of Holguín, Sancti Spíritus, and Villa Clara.

The APC Joins the World Council of Comparative Education Societies (WCCES)

An important result of the cooperation between the APC and North American educators was the inclusion of the APC in the World Council of

Comparative Education Societies (WCCES). The North American educators who were members of the CIES helped Cuba to establish a comparative education section of the APC, and assisted the Cuban educators in preparing a bid to host the biennial congress of the WCCES in 2004. The bid was successful, and the APC organized the hosting in 2004 in Havana City of the 12th World Congress of Comparative Education with the theme "Education and Social Justice." Their work in organizing this congress benefited from the support and advice not only of the WCCES executive, but also of the North American educators through their membership of the WCCES. The congress was held in the Convention Centre in Havana, and was attended by 1022 delegates from 69 countries. The largest delegation was that of the United States with 209 participants.

The organization and development of the 12th World Congress had great significance for Cuban educators and especially for the ones who belong to the Association of Cuban Educators, because it provided the opportunity for valuable exchanges with educators who had never previously visited Cuba. These exchanges allowed increased mutual understanding of different approaches and experiences, and established ongoing professional links of great mutual benefit.

In preparation for the World Congress in Cuba, the Association of Cuban Educators organized conferences in each province, and the best of the papers delivered were selected for presentation at the World Congress. These provincial conferences allowed us to strengthen the existing research groups on comparative education and stimulated further research in Cuba.

After the Congress, the links with other countries and societies were widened. As an example, Cuba attended the 13th World Congress in Sarajevo, Bosnia-Herzegovina, and participated on the international panel that awarded the Pedro Rosello Award for the best research on comparative education in Spain in 2006.

Members of the Association of Cuban Educators, in response to invitations from the host countries, presented courses on comparative education in Turkey and Spain. Other links that should be mentioned are with the South African and Argentinian associations of comparative education, and the publication of the article "Comparative Education as a University Discipline in Cuba" *(La Educación Comparada como Disciplina Universitaria en Cuba),* in the Blue Book published in Sophia, Bulgaria, 2008.

The APC and Conferences on Education

The Cuban Pedagogical Congress, named Pedagogía, meets every other year. It is large-scale event attracting about 5,000 to 6,000 people. Of these participants, some 4,000 are from overseas, mainly from Spanish-speaking countries, but a few also come from English-speaking countries. The congress has met in 1986, 1990, 1993, 1995, 1997, 2001, 2003, 2005, 2007, and 2009. Within the congress there are special mini-conferences for representatives from UNESCO and other international associations.

The APC does important work in organizing Pedagogía. This is an important conference, bringing together thousands of teachers and educational managers from many countries. The conference stimulates educational research and writing, with presentations of high quality and wide variety, addressing themes of great importance to education. Preparing for the conference helps to develop teachers, since preconference seminars and courses are offered throughout Cuba on different topics. Participants enroll in them, and this upgrades their knowledge and skills.

About 2,000 of the participants in Pedagogía present research papers on every aspect of education including planning, administration, supervision, curriculum, special education, and teacher education. The congress is significant in encouraging research on education and important papers from Latin America and Cuba are presented. The best papers from local and provincial education conferences in Cuba are selected by a board for presentation at the Pedagogical Congress. This encourages research among Cuban educators.

The APC has also participated in the biennial higher education conferences entitled *Universidad* where thousands of professors from different universities from different countries have shared their experiences with the Cuban colleagues, including those from the APC.

The APC has also organized many educational events bilaterally with other countries including Venezuela, Colombia, Argentina, Mexico, the Dominican Republic, and the United States (in the annual *seminario*, discussed earlier). Members of the APC play a role in the region through AELAC, as they are often invited to give papers and keynote addresses in different Latin American countries that are members of AELAC.

Appendix 2

Table 18.1 Cuba-US seminars, dates, participants, and provinces

Seminario	Date	Cuban participants	US participants	Province hosting seminar
1	1994	12	10	Havana City
2	1995	36	18	Pinar del Río
3	1996	42	30	Matanzas
4	1997	47	32	Granma
5	1998	42	45	Cienfuegos
6	1999	48	46	Pinar del Río
7	2000	55	52	Santiago de Cuba
8	2002	34	44	Havana City
9	2003	46	64	Matanzas
10	2004	31	28	Havana City
No. of papers presented		393	360	753

Notes

1. Lidia Turner Martí and Balbina Pita (2002) *Pedagogía de la Ternura*. Editorial Pueblo y Educación, Cuba. This book, *Pedagogy of Tenderness*, has been published several times in Venezuela, Chile, and recently in Spain.
2. Examples of scholarly publications on themes related to Cuban education that had their genesis in the *seminarios* include:
    McDonald, J. A. (2000) "Forty Years after the Revolution: A Look at Education Reform in Cuba," *International Journal of Educational Reform* 9:1 (January): 44–49.
    Mickelson, R.A. ed. (2000) *Children on the Streets of the Americas: Globalization, Homelessness, and Education in the United States, Brazil, and Cuba* (London: Routledge).
    Lutjens, S. L. (2000) "Restructuring Childhood in Cuba: The State as Family," in *Children on the Streets of the Americas: Globalization, Homelessness, and Education in the United States, Brazil, and Cuba*, ed. Roslyn A. Mickelson (London: Routledge), pp. 55–64.
    Lutjens, S. L. (2000) "Schooling and Clean Streets in Cuba: Children and the Special Period," in *Children on the Streets of the Americas: Globalization, Homelessness, and Education in the United States, Brazil, and Cuba*, ed. Roslyn A. Mickelson (London: Routledge), pp. 149–59.
    Hanson, D. M. and Tochen, F. V., eds. (2003) *The Deep Approach: Second Languages for Community Building* (Madison, WI: Atwood Publishing).
    Hickling Hudson A., Corona González, J., and Preston, R., eds. (2012) *The Capacity to Share: A Study of Cuba's International Cooperation in Education Development* (New York: Palgrave Macmillan).
3. The 12th World Congress of Comparative Education in the WCCES is discussed in the chapter by Anne Hickling-Hudson (2007) "Improving Transnational Networking for Social Justice: 2001–2004," in *Common Interests, Uncommon Goals: Histories of the World Council of Comparative Education Societies and Its Members*. Edited by Mark Bray, Vandra Masemann, and Maria Manzon, Hong Kong: Comparative Education Research Centre, University of Hong Kong.

Section 5

Endnote

19

Achievements, Celebrations, and Learning

Rosemary Preston

Nation Building

Educationally, Cuba has much to celebrate. From the early 1960s, with an obligation for all to learn, its unprecedented investment in literacy and schools was extended into an ever-increasing multilevel system, reaching into the remotest corners of the nation. Over time, this has taken Cuba to the top of world rankings in several areas of human development, no matter that its economic statistics were not always deemed sufficiently robust to include it among the indicators.

From the outset, Cuba's education mission has been integral to its fight for liberation from the capitalist system. It enabled the mass transmission and internalization of revolutionary values to children, youth, and adults, simultaneously imparting basic and later more advanced technical skills of learning and knowledge. In a country where the majority was poor or destitute, the promise of what education would give was potent. With the departure of much of the professional workforce in 1959, with positions inseparable from their education, such a promise was believed by the less advantaged who remained in Cuba. Educating the masses would in due course replace the expertise of those departed, with solidarity and egalitarianism to sustain the momentum.

So it was that Cuba's educational approach became part of an unsurpassed nation-building strategy, inculcating the idea of a Cuban identity acceptable to all.[1] It committed people to work for the collective revolutionary good, wherever and whenever required. Inspired by the democratic and egalitarian principles for Cuban independence espoused by José Martí in the nineteenth century, it had historical coherence, as well as being grounded in contemporary socialist thinking.

Cuba's education and training mission embraced military and civilians alike. Within months of coming to power, US threats of destabilization and the invasion at the Bay of Pigs had confirmed the need for effective fighters. The long-held revolutionary vision of an international socialism, shared with liberation movements around the world, saw Cuban military sent on countless missions to fight, train, and serve others less well prepared than themselves. For some, Cuba's military excursions up to 1988 were a means of consolidating its revolutionary identity at home, as well as its international repute in like-minded states, often left in wonderment at Cuban generosity.[2] Reports of military prowess were confirmed in Cuba by the tales of wounded fighters and orphaned children from other countries arriving in Havana to receive humanitarian care and education from the Cuban people. On return to their countries of origin, they would talk well of the attention received, admiring the principles of solidarity on which it was grounded (see, for example, chapters 13 and 14). The later arrival of massed cohorts of children from countries at war was to have similar effects, for protracted periods of time. In peacetime, the mechanism remained in place, with scholarships for study in Cuba still awarded to aspiring professional cadres, unlikely to obtain such training at home, and Cuban experts providing multiple forms of training elsewhere, primarily in low-income states.

Changing Economic Direction

Down the decades and after the end of the Angolan campaign, commentators have followed the ways in which the revolutionary government has retained the support of the people, in the face of inescapable and debilitating crises at home and major political and economic changes in the wider world. The plunging sugar market and the loss of USSR support led to Cuba's exceptionally challenging "special period." To survive, Cuba increased trade with friendly states in the Caribbean, in South America, and in Western Europe, exchanging services for urgently needed commodities and encouraging remittances from Cubans resident abroad.[3] At the same time, Cuba remained committed to its ideals of solidarity, not least to mitigate the divisive effects of emerging entrepreneurialism. As in the formative years of the revolution and as the special period waned, the late 1990s saw renewed commitment to education to maintain loyalty to the cause and restore the levels of learning and professional development.[4] The language of reform and empowerment was linked again to images of Martí and Guevara, recapturing the popular imagination and uniting Cubans to overcome hardship through solidarity with each other.

Today, Cubans continue to provide professional services in mainstream public and incipient private sectors, including those which generate overseas income, for example, tourism and fees for certain health and educational services. Abroad and on short-term contracts, tens of thousands of Cuban government employees with advanced expertise assume roles as international advisers, particularly in education, training, and health. They are committed to sharing their understanding of achievable change and development, in solidarity with poorer states and poorer communities in those more affluent. Individually, their financial incentive is a small income supplement, but in terms of self-esteem, they hold their heads high across the world, themselves a model of what the revolution has achieved. For Cuba, they gain experience and their contribution provides material and more important symbolic returns to its long investment in human development. Recently, with the relaxation of migration and foreign-exchange regulations, this revenue is supplemented by private remittances from increasing numbers of Cuban residents abroad.[5] In 2009 they transferred 1.4 billion dollars to the Cuban economy, from as far away as Spain, Kuwait, and Pakistan.[6] For most, it was their education in Cuba that facilitated their income and their willingness to send money home, simultaneously contributing to family well-being, treasury funds, and GNP.

Internationalism, Solidarity, and Aid

It is not certain the extent to which the early years of Cuban internationalism were framed to challenge the then modalities of international technical assistance, but as the number of missions increased, the claim is accepted. The remuneration of Cuban government experts has never been comparable to the charges of international consultants and development agents not committed to the frugality of solidarity and its attendant principles. Indeed, the morality of the Cuban stance reflects the narrowly differentiated structures of pay in Cuba, with maximal salaries no more than four times the minimum. More than modest increments for government employees who do such international work would not accord with the founding principles of Cuban internationalism, although current moves to more market-oriented socialism may see this change.

For the present, with Cuban missions across the world and the weakening of official development aid for human development, Cuban solidarity is a significant alternative. The capacity to share through egalitarian development is a powerful way of improving the lives of ordinary people, above all the poor, oppressed, and marginalized, wherever they may be.

Notes

1. Kapcia, 2005.
2. Gleijeses, 1996, 166.
3. Barberia 2002, 1.
4. León, 2000, 20.

5. Orozco, 2002, 2.
6. Millman, 2009.

References

Barberia, L. (2002) "Remittances to Cuba: An Evaluation of Cuban and US Government Policy Measures," Harvard University, David Rockefeller Center for Latin American Studies at Harvard University, Working Paper # 15, p. 46.

Gleijeses, P. "Cuba's First Venture in Africa: Algeria, 1961–1965," *Journal of Latin American Studies* 28, no. 1 (1996): 159–195.

Kapcia, A. "Educational Revolution and Revolutionary Morality in Cuba: The 'New Man,' Youth and the New 'Battle of Ideas,'" *Journal of Moral Education* 34, no. 5 (2005): 399–412.

León, F. (2000) "Cuba: Human Resources Development and Employment: What to Do after the 'Período Especial?'" Chile, Santiago [CubaSource.org, Canadian Foundation for the Americas (FOCAL) http://ckmportal.eclacpos.org/caribbean-digital-library/labour-and-employment/xfer-966]

Millman, J. "Cuba Receives More Cash from Workers Abroad," *The Wall Street Journal*, March 5, 2009.

Orozco, M. "The Cuban Condition: Migration, Remittances and Its Diaspora," *Inter-American Dialogue*, March 5, 2009, p. 21.

Biographical Notes

Samuel Kaba Akoriyea

Samuel Kaba Akoriyea is a consultant neurosurgeon and head of department of neurosurgery in the Ridge Regional Hospital, Accra, under the Ghana Health Service. He is also a lecturer in the School of Peri-Operative and Critical Care Nursing in Korle Bu and the School of Nurse Anaesthetists, Ridge Hospital, and a facilitator in the training of emergency medical technicians and paramedics in the Ghana National Ambulance Service. He the vice president of the Ghana Academy of Neurosurgeons and deputy director of the Ghana National Ambulance Service under the Ministry of Health of Ghana. He attained his degree as a medical doctor from the Higher Institute of Medical Sciences, Havana, Cuba, in 1999, and graduated in 2003 as a specialist neurosurgeon from the National Institute of Neurology and Neurosurgery, Havana, Cuba. Following his return to Ghana, he helped establish the neurosurgery unit of the Ridge Regional Hospital in Accra in 2004. He obtained a PhD in Public Health from the University of Santiago de Compostela, Spain in 2009. His areas of interest include quality care in medical practice, and developing standards in clinical services, research, medical emergency services, diseases of the spine, endoscopy neurosurgery, functional epileptic surgery, neurovascular surgery, and skull base surgery.

Bob Boughton

Bob Boughton is an associate professor of adult education at the University of New England in Australia. He has been undertaking research in Timor-Leste since 2004, on the role of adult education in post-conflict development. His studies of the Timor-Leste national literacy campaign and the role of the Cuban education mission in that country were undertaken as part of a wider three-year project supported by the Ministry of Education in Timor-Leste and a grant from the Australian Research Council. His other main research interests are Aboriginal adult education, and theories and traditions of popular education. Prior to his appointment at UNE, Bob worked for over two decades as an adult educator and development worker with Australian Aboriginal organizations and communities.

Jaime Canfux Gutiérrez

Jaime Canfux, born in Havana, Cuba, was awarded a PhD in pedagogical sciences from the Enrique José Varona University of Pedagogical Sciences, where he specialized in history. Professor Canfux has worked for 50 years in the field of youth and adult literacy education and was the director of the literacy studies group at the Pedagogical Institute for Latin America and the Caribbean (IPLAC).

Jorge Corona González

Born and educated in Cuba, Jorge Corona González holds a master of science in economics and for many years taught political economy at the University of Havana.His fields of interest include educational planning, educational policies for development, and the impact of globalization on education. A former president of the Pedagogical Institute for Latin America and the Caribbean (IPLAC), he is currently special advisor on international collaboration in Cuba's Ministry of Education, and a member of the UNESCO Chair in Educational Sciences.

Angel Oscar Elejalde Villalón

Angel Oscar Elejalde, born in Guantánamo, Cuba, has a PhD in pedagogical sciences and 38 years of experience as an educator at all levels of education. From 1986 to 1995 he was Rector of the multinational university in pedagogical sciences, Universidad de Ciencias Pedagogías "Carlos Manuel de Céspedes," on the Isle of Youth. He was also the international general secretary of AELAC (Association of Latin-American and Caribbean Educators) from 2003 to 2006. He is a full and consultant professor of the University of Pedagogical Sciences "Enrique José Varona." and was given the "Frank País García" award, the highest award granted by the Council of the State of Cuba in the field of education.

Marta Fernández Cabrera

Marta Fernández is an associate professor at the School of Foreign Languages, at the Enrique José Varona University of Pedagogical Sciences in Havana. She has worked in education at the tertiary level for more than 35 years, and is a member of the Association of Linguists in Cuba. Marta has published several articles on sociocultural studies related to the Anglophone world. She participated in a Cuban internationalist mission to Angola in the 1980s, where she worked primarily as a teacher, and where occasionally, she was also called upon to assist the armed forces as a translator. For more than ten years, Marta has been head of the specialist "History of the Culture of the English Speaking Peoples" group at her university.

Christine Hatzky

Christine Hatzky is professor of Latin American and Caribbean history in the history department at Leibniz University in Hanover, Germany.

Her areas of study include the history of Mexico and Central America, Cuba, and the Caribbean, as well as the history of Africa, especially of the Portuguese-speaking countries Angola and Mozambique. She holds a Leibniz PhD in history (2003) and was assistant professor at the department of extra-European history at the University of Duisburg-Essen, Germany from 2002 to 2010. Her PhD thesis, published in German (2004) and in Spanish (2008), is the biography of Julio A. Mella, the famous Cuban student leader and cofounder of the Cuban Communist Party. The subject of her postdoctoral thesis, completed in 2009, is that of Cuba's civil cooperation in education in Angola between 1976 and 1991.

Anne Hickling-Hudson

Anne Hickling-Hudson is an associate professor at Australia's Queensland University of Technology (QUT), specializing in cross-cultural and international education. Born and raised in Jamaica, Anne was educated at the universities of the West Indies and of Hong Kong. Her PhD, from the University of Queensland in Australia, won dissertation-of-the-year awards both in the United States and in Australia. A Rockefeller fellow, she is widely published, and is a pioneer in applying postcolonial theory to the comparative analysis of educational policy and practice in global contexts. She is recognized for her international leadership in academic associations. As president of the World Council of Comparative and International Education Societies (WCCES) from 2001–2004, she coordinated the 12th Congress held in Havana, Cuba, and was made a member of honor in the Association of Educators of Cuba (APC). She has also been president of the British Association of International and Comparative Education (BAICE), 2009–2010; of the Australian Association for Caribbean Studies (AACS), 2009–2011, and of the Australia and New Zealand Comparative and International Education Society (ANZCIES), in 1998 and 1999.

Sabine Lehr

Sabine Lehr is an adjunct professor with the School of Public Administration at the University of Victoria (UVic), Canada. She was assistant director of the Office of International Affairs at UVic until December 2008 when she took up a one-year volunteer position as an adviser/researcher for organizations of persons with disability in Rwanda. She has an MBA in international management from the University of London (2002) and a PhD in educational studies from the University of Victoria (2008). She now teaches in the area of community development and advises UVic's Office of International Affairs on internationalization of the curriculum. Her fields of interest include making learning environments more relevant to international contexts, the internationalization of higher education globally, and the impact of study/work abroad experiences on students and host environments in North-South and South-South contexts.

Elvira Martín Sabina

Elvira Martín, born and educated in Cuba, is professor of economics and director of CEPES, the Centre for the Improvement of Higher Education at the University of Havana. With a specialization in the political economy of education, she is a leading researcher in organizational change and system development in higher education in Cuba and other countries. She holds a UNESCO Chair in University Organization and Leadership at the University of Havana and is on the university's management council. As director of CEPES, she is also on the management council of Cuba's Ministry of Higher Education, and is a special adviser to the Minister.

Francisco Martínez Pérez

Francisco Martínez holds degrees in engineering, and was a professor and dean of the Faculty of Mechanics at CUJAE, the specialist university of engineering sciences in Cuba. He went on to become head of the department of training for engineers in Cuba's Ministry of Higher Education, and then was in charge of organizing liaison services between overseas students holding Cuban scholarships and the universities and colleges in Cuba which they were attending. He has also worked in the Bahamas to coordinate the program of Cuban teachers in Bahamian schools.

Emelina P. Pérez Herrera

Emelina Pérez is a professor of English and a consultant in the School of Foreign Languages, University of Pedagogical Sciences Enrique José Varona, where she has worked for more than 35 years. Awarded her master's degree in English and Spanish in 1971, she has been part of the National Commission of Experts in the English Language in Cuba and is a member of the Association of Linguists of Cuba. She has taught Spanish at the University of Guyana and in Jamaica, and has written several books on the teaching of English as a foreign language.

Rosemary Preston

Rosemary Preston was director of the International Centre for Education in Development, at the University of Warwick (1993–2005), specializing in aid, organizational relations, lifelong learning, and community development in low-income states. Her interdisciplinary research has prioritized minorities, notably in Andean America, the South Pacific, and southern Africa. Her research in policy and practice for international organizations includes directing multi method studies of: labor and war-related migration; post war reconstruction; technical assistance, consultancy, and partnership. Cross-cutting themes include HRD, training and education; gender, ethnicity, and civil society. Rosemary Preston has published widely, is past editor of *Gender and Education* and *Compare*, and has 25 years experience of I/NGO governance. She has been chair of the British Association of Comparative and International Education, the UK Forum for International Education and Training and the Council for Education in the

Commonwealth, and Deputy Chair of INTRAC. In 2004, she coordinated international links with Cuban organizers of the 2004 World Congress of Comparative Education Societies, held in Havana. A linguist, she is fluent in French and Spanish, with skill in other languages.

Melanie Springer

Melanie Springer is founder and director of "The Brownest Eye," a Barbados-based media production company that provides multimedia products and services in the Caribbean. She leads the production of videos for clients, the design of websites and advertising copy, and the development of both community and entrepreneurial projects. Having obtained her professional education in art education at the Barbados Community College and in cinema and sound engineering at the Escuela Internacional de Cine y Televisión in Cuba, she worked in a wide range of film and television projects in Italy and Belize before setting up her company in Barbados. She has written a novel entitled *Pearl: A Caribbean Story*.

Alejandro R. Torres Saavedra

Born in Holguín, Cuba, Alejandro Torres received his doctorate in pedagogical sciences in 2001. He is vice dean of the School of Foreign Languages of Enrique José Varona University of Pedagogical Sciences, chairs the Group of Caribbean Studies there, and is an honorary member of the Caribbean Association of Cuba. He is a member of the National Curricular Commission in Foreign Languages and Secretary of the National Sub-Commission of Syllabi and Design of Textbooks in Foreign Languages in Cuba. As a member of the Cuban Association of Linguists, he is on the executive of GELI (Association of English Language Teaching Specialists) within the Cuban Academy of Sciences. He is Cuba's representative for international affairs in the World Council of Comparative Education Societies (WCCES).

Boris R. Tristá Pérez

Boris R. Tristá Pérez is professor and senior researcher at the Centre of Studies for the Improvement of Higher Education, Havana University, Cuba. His PhD in Economic Sciences from the University of Havana, Cuba (1984), examines the performance improvement of department heads in higher education. His postdoctoral thesis, completed in 2008, develops a systemic approach to university management. He has worked as an adviser to university administrations in Bolivia, Ecuador, and Mexico, as well as at several universities in Cuba. His fields of interest, research, and teaching focus on higher education as a field of study, change in higher education and higher education management, especially the issues of leadership, institutional culture, and organizational behavior.

Lidia Turner Martí

Lidia Turner was born in Santiago de Cuba. She graduated from the School of Philosophy and Humanities, University of Havana (1956), and holds the degree of Doctor in Pedagogical Sciences (1977). Dr. Turner is a former director of the Central Institute of Pedagogical Sciences of Cuba, an emeritus professor of the Enrique José Varona University of Pedagogical Sciences (the leading pedagogical university in Cuba), and an emeritus member of the Academy of Sciences in Cuba. She is also the director of the Pedagogical Sciences Section of the National Commission of Scientific Degrees. Widely published, she is honorary president of the Association of Educators of Cuba (APC) and of the Cuban chapter of the Association of Educators of Latin America and the Caribbean (AELAC).

Index

12th Congress of the World Council of Comparative Education Societies in Havana, 264

academic qualifications, 134
academic work, 55, 133, 219
Accra Agenda for Action, 36, 90–91, 229, 277
accreditation, 60, 66, 81, 93–95, 102
achievable change and development, 275
activists, 3, 128, 131, 199–201
adult education system, 198, 212
adult literacy, 4, 7–8, 13, 15, 20–21, 43, 146, 176, 197–201, 205–212, 255–256, 258–260, 278
Africa, 2, 4, 6, 8–9, 17–18, 20, 24, 30–31, 36–37, 39–41, 47–48, 56, 67, 74–76, 80–81, 88–89, 97–98, 108, 124, 127–132, 134–136, 141–142, 154, 156, 165, 176, 183, 187, 189, 191–193, 205, 208, 219, 225, 227–228, 234–235, 241, 244, 259, 279, 280
African languages, 146, 246
African National Congress (ANC), 130
Agostinho Neto University, 149
agricultural engineer, 111, 113, 116
agriculture, 2, 21, 26, 42, 45, 59, 64, 74, 81, 92, 110–111, 117, 119–120, 132, 172, 182, 185, 187, 209, 217–218, 222, 233
aid architecture, 36–37
air raid, 241, 245
Algeria, 6, 22, 79, 127–129, 229
alternative model, 39, 120

Angola, 6–8, 18, 20, 76, 78, 127, 129–132, 135–136, 141–158, 183, 205, 207, 218–219, 227–228, 241–243, 245, 247, 255, 259, 278–279
Angolan Ministry of Education, 144, 147, 153, 155, 157
annual academic competitions, 227
annual GDP income, 13
annual graduation, 79
annual US/Cuba seminar, 267
antipersonnel bombs, 245
applied research, 56, 78, 124
appropriate technology, 114, 167
Ashanti Region, 92
Asia, 36, 41, 67, 75–76, 80–81, 98, 165, 187, 219, 234–236
assistance for self-emancipation, 148, 155
assistance from Cuban educators, 107
Association of Cuban Educators (APC), 8, 263–269, 279, 282
Association of Educators of Latin America and the Caribbean (AELAC), 8, 263–265, 269, 278, 282
Australian Research Council, 197–198, 212, 277

Bahamas, 20, 94–97, 102, 119, 280
Balibo, 198, 203–204
basic secondary schooling, 74
Batista, Fulgencio, 14
Battle of Kangamba, 242
Bay of Pigs, 14, 274
Beijing Forum for China-Africa Co-operation (FOCAC), 41
Belize, 21, 177, 231–232, 281

Bennett, Louise, 251
bilateral agreements, 42, 125, 128, 141, 154
blocs, 40, 87–88
Bobonaro, 198, 202–205
Bolgatanga, 225
Bolivarian Alternative for the Americas (ALBA), 2, 41, 43–44, 48
Bolivia, 7, 41, 55, 76, 78, 162, 171, 174, 208, 256, 258, 281
Boughton, Bob., 7, 21, 197, 212, 277
brain circulation, 87
brain drain, 87, 98, 102, 123
brigade, 22–23, 150
British-style education system, 176

campaign coordinator, 198, 203–204
Canada, 29, 35, 56, 83–84, 98, 113, 123, 236, 238, 279
Canfux Gutiérrez, Jaime, 8–9, 257, 278
capacity building, 46, 161, 186
Cape Verde Islands, 153, 259
capitalism, 2, 119
capitalist, 3, 15, 40, 44–45, 109, 120–121, 135, 273
Caribbean, 1–2, 6, 8, 13, 17–18, 20, 27, 23, 25–26, 39–41, 41–43, 55, 59, 67–68, 75–76, 78, 80–81, 95, 98, 107–110, 114, 117, 119–125, 128, 165, 171, 176, 178–179, 184–185, 187–193, 207, 219, 231–235, 239, 253, 257, 263–265, 274, 278–279
Caribbean Association of Cuba, 281
Caribbean Broadcasting Union (CBU), 239
Caribbean cinema, 239
Caribbean diaspora, 123
Caribbean Examinations Council (CXC), 117, 179, 181–182, 193, 252, 253
Caribbean regional project, 121–122
Caribbean School of Medicine in Santiago de Cuba, 25
Caribbean Tales Worldwide, 233
CARICOM, 40–41, 44, 78, 109, 122
Carnoy, Martin, 15, 29–30, 55, 68, 103, 193
Cassinga, 131, 135

Castro, Fidel, 14–15, 47, 75, 85, 128–129, 137, 143–144, 149–150, 156–157, 207, 256
China, 2, 28, 40–41, 112, 209
civil mission, 6, 141, 144, 150, 153–154
civil rights, 144–145
civilian cooperation, 142
clusters of graduates, 96
Cocoa Marketing Company, 87
Cold War, 2, 15, 17, 41, 87–88, 122–123, 130, 156, 187, 189
collaboration agreements, 44, 81, 176, 265
collaboration list, 177
Colombia, 21, 41, 55, 61, 166, 235, 255, 269
colonial education, 18, 97, 145, 148
colonial legacies, 35, 87
colonial period, 89, 125, 176, 208
colonialism, 3, 9, 14, 28, 35, 39, 41, 57, 73, 88–89, 142, 145, 183, 191, 199, 241, 245–246
colonies, 9, 20, 89, 205, 208, 218, 253
combining work with study, 219
COMECON, 87, 163
Commonwealth Caribbean, 122–123, 253
communist, 17, 40, 68, 101, 279
Communist Youth organization, 63
communities, 24–25, 41, 54, 56, 63–65, 115–116, 120, 135, 178, 189, 208, 222, 275, 277
Committees for the Defence of the Revolution (CDR), 118
community health, 22, 112
community medicine, 22, 118
community political power, 16
community-oriented work, 226
Comparative and International Education Society (CIES), 266, 268
conditionalities, 5, 19, 37–38, 42, 46
conference in Havana, 1
Congress of the MPLA, 144
cooperation projects, 175
Corona González, Jorge, 1, 5, 13, 35, 53, 68, 221, 257, 272, 278
cost-sharing agreements, 177
Council for Mutual Economic Assistance (CMEA), 87, 103

Index   285

counterinsurgency tactics, 130
credentials, 94–96, 101–102
Creole, 258–259
crisis of development, 121
Cuba-Ghana program, 88–90
Cuban Academy of Sciences, 281
Cuban advisers, 7, 20–21, 154, 168–169, 197, 202, 204–206, 258–259
Cuban aid model, 205
Cuban educational model, 88–89, 101, 125
Cuban educational philosophy, 92, 101
Cuban educators, 1, 6, 8, 19–21, 43, 107, 139, 153, 176–177, 182, 189, 191–192, 219, 256–257, 263–264, 266–269
Cuban Higher Education Review, 170
Cuban Institute of Friendship with the Peoples (ICAP), 79
Cuban internationalists, 46, 128, 153, 155
Cuban literacy educators, 8, 255–256
Cuban professors, 13–14, 19, 144, 150, 161, 166, 168, 178, 231, 258–259, 265–266
Cuban revolution, 2, 5, 13–14, 53–54, 58, 65, 162, 164, 255
Cuban scholarship program, 5, 73, 76–77, 81–83, 88, 102, 229–230
Cuban soldiers, 131, 142–143, 242
Cuban sports coaches, 176
Cuban student teachers, 149–151
Cuban students, 25, 77, 79–80, 151, 219
Cuban Studies Centre in New York, 266
Cuban teachers, 4–5, 7, 18–20, 53, 141, 143, 147–148, 153–155, 157, 168, 175–182, 185, 187–192, 195, 221, 226, 243, 246, 259, 264–265, 280
Cuban teaching personnel, 149
Cuban universities, 1, 4, 7–8, 24, 28, 74–76, 78, 107–109, 116, 132, 164–165, 167, 174
Cuban university academic, 161
Cuban university system, 6, 162
Cubans sharing education, 11, 217
cultural arts, 222
culture and family, 93

culture clash, 94
curricular strategies, 169
curriculum and program development, 13
CXC exams, 179, 253

Dakar, 36, 225
decolonization, 89, 176, 190, 208
decolonizing countries, 7, 39, 45, 184, 192
dentistry, 24, 76, 81, 109, 124
dependent socialism, 119–120
deployment in remote regions, 155
developing countries, 2, 5–6, 18–19, 28–29, 38, 40, 42, 53, 57–58, 60, 73, 82–84, 121, 124, 141, 162, 167, 169, 177, 187–188, 190–192, 207
development, 1–2, 4–5, 8–10, 13–19, 21, 22–23, 28–30, 35–37, 39–47, 53–54, 56–60, 62, 66–67, 73–74, 77, 81–82, 84–89, 93, 97, 100–103, 107–108, 111–112, 114–115, 119–124, 129–130, 132, 135, 142, 145, 147, 150, 152, 155–156, 161–165, 167–169, 172–174, 177, 185–187, 190–192, 198–202, 205–206, 208, 210–212, 218–220, 222, 226, 232, 255–257, 259, 265, 268, 270–275, 277–281
development assistance, 29, 37, 39, 42, 45–46, 84, 205
development brigades, 135
development of human resources, 77, 120
development paradigms, 39
Dili, 198, 201, 203, 206, 209, 212–212
diploma, 8, 84, 90, 94–95, 124, 163–164, 166, 172, 184, 193, 231, 234, 236, 259
disability, 13, 21, 22, 279
distance education, 164, 185, 189
doctor, 60, 112–114, 116–118, 186, 206, 277, 282
doctoral examination panels, 168
donor countries, 36–37, 198, 200, 205

early childhood, 13, 21, 60–61, 63
Early Childhood education, 60–61
East Germany, 58, 183–184

Eastern bloc, 18, 21, 93, 96, 102, 119, 149, 153
Eastern Europe, 4, 96, 134, 209, 244
Eastern European advisers, 120
economic and market reforms, 17
economic contraction, 121
economic growth, 15, 36–37, 45, 87, 117, 121–122
economic hardship, 17
economic recovery program, 96
economic restructuring, 15, 17, 64, 74, 121
economic weaknesses, 45
economics, 59, 61, 67, 77, 99, 114–115, 124, 131, 149, 169, 222, 278, 280
education for all (EFA), 36, 38, 54, 56, 184, 192, 211, 219, 255
education in Eastern Europe, 96
education of adolescents, 192
education reforms, 63
educational attainment, 85
educational change, 38, 54, 58, 125–126, 168, 176, 191, 279
educational missions, 141
educational policy and practice in Cuba, 60
educational reform, 60, 62, 95, 147, 156, 270
educational research, 59–60, 191, 264, 269
egalitarian, 1, 90, 273, 275
ELAM, see Latin American School of Medicine
Elejalde Villalón, Oscar, 7, 9, 30, 55, 68, 159, 221, 278
elite high schools, 179, 193
embargo imposed by the United States, 16–17
emergency relief initiative, 26
emigration, 15, 88
employment, 3, 15, 29, 37, 64, 93, 95–96, 102, 134–135, 178, 189
emulation process, 78
energy engineer, 113
engineering masters degree, 113
engineers, 5, 18, 45, 53, 65, 110, 115, 280
English, 1, 6, 8–9, 30–31, 41, 86, 95, 97, 107–109, 112, 114–115, 121, 124, 135, 169, 175, 177–178, 180, 184–185, 188–189, 192–193, 226–228, 237, 241, 244, 246–247, 250–251, 258–260, 278, 280–281
English language abilities, 97
equal access, 90, 92
equalization, 89
equitable and high-quality education, 67
equity, 5, 37, 53–54, 119, 122
ESBECAN, 227, 230
Escuela Secundaria Básica en el Campo (ESBEC), 85–86, 225–226, 227
Europe, 4, 9, 27, 35, 75, 93, 96–97, 122, 134, 209, 235–236, 244, 259–260, 265, 274
examinations, 112, 117, 179, 188, 193, 253
excess university capacity, 121
expansion of the university, 64
experiential knowledge, 115
ex-Portuguese colonies, 205
external examination results, 176
extracurricular, 8, 79, 148, 219–220

FALANTIL, 198
family and cooperative enterprises, 64
farm activities, 226, 228
Federation of University Students (FEU), 77, 79
fee-paying degree programs, 109
fee-paying university places, 123
Fernández Cabrera, Marta, 8-9, 243, 245, 278, 280.
film studies, 124
five-year university degree, 66, 177
fluency in Spanish, 97
foreign scholarship holders, 75, 78
Foundation for New Latin American Cinema, 235
free aid, 128
Free Trade Agreement for the Americas (ALCA), 43–44
freedom fighters, 128, 130
Freire, Paulo, 146–147, 200
French, 27, 112, 128, 178, 236, 238, 241, 251, 258, 281
Frente Nacional para a Libertação de Angola (FNLA), 142
FRETILIN, 199–202, 208, 211, 213

friendship societies with Cuba, 79
full-cost-recovery models, 85

gender imbalance, 90, 93
German colonialism, 183
Ghana, 5–6, 20, 83–103, 129, 225–230, 277
Ghana Academy of Neurosurgeons, 229, 277
Ghana National Ambulance Service, 229, 277
Ghana-Cuba Permanent Joint Commission for Cooperation, 87
Ghanaian culture, 86, 227
Ghanaian job market, 88
Ghanaian President, 85
Ghanaian students, 83–87, 97, 99, 225, 228, 230
global economic inequalities, 88
global educational crisis, 5, 36, 39, 46
global financial crisis, 2–3, 60, 62
Global North, 9
global solidarity programs, 14
Global South, 6, 9, 13, 40, 54, 67, 77, 102, 122, 125, 231
globalization, 3, 9, 19, 66, 89, 121, 270, 278
graduates in the Caribbean, 108
graduation ceremonies, 221
grammar schools, 178–179
Grenada, 17, 107–108, 110, 112, 114, 116–117, 255
Group of 77 (G-77), 40, 47, 48
growth in GDP, 2
Guevara, Che, 58, 88, 149, 156
Guinea Bissau, 127, 205, 227
Gusmão, Xanana, 201–202
Gutiérrez, Canfux, 8–9, 255, 278
Guyana, 17, 76, 108, 114–117, 121, 123, 280

Haiti, 19, 21, 27, 25–28, 31, 76, 177, 207, 255–256, 258
Hatzky, Christine, 6, 130, 141, 278–279
Havana, 1, 8–9, 19, 23–24, 30, 40, 48, 60, 80–81, 84, 111–112, 114, 120, 122, 126, 132, 136, 156, 162, 165, 167, 169, 174, 186, 207, 212, 221, 225, 229, 231, 236, 249, 253, 255, 264, 266–268, 269, 274, 277–281

health, 2, 4–6, 11, 13–16, 18–19, 22–30, 36–37, 39, 42–44, 56, 58, 60, 65, 67, 76, 78, 81, 86–87, 109, 111–113, 115–118, 120, 127–128, 132, 135, 141, 167, 185–186, 193, 199, 203, 205–206, 209–210, 220, 225, 229, 255, 275, 277
Helms-Burton Act, 17
Hickling-Hudson, Anne, 1, 5–8, 13, 30, 32–33, 35, 47, 53, 103, 107, 125, 175, 192–193, 205, 207, 212, 217, 231–232, 241, 249, 255, 263, 270, 279
higher education and development, 119
higher education sector, 59, 73
historically disadvantaged groups, 92
holistic education, 222
Huambo, 145, 149, 153, 243
Huila, 241, 245
human and veterinary medicine, 95
human capital, 16, 45, 87–88, 120, 200, 275
Human Employment and Resource Training (HEART), 178
humanitarian, 204–205, 274
humanities, arts, and social sciences, 101
hungry children, 242

ideological camps, 88
IESALC, 171–172
IMF loan, 96
immigration policies, 87, 94, 98
in-service professional training, 177
independence, 6–7, 14, 27, 40, 84, 96–97, 123, 127–131, 133, 135–136, 141–142, 145–146, 149–150, 154–156, 168, 182–185, 198–200, 205, 207–208, 210, 226, 241, 273
indigenous and local knowledge, 124
Indonesia, 197–198, 208
Indonesian army, 197–198, 209
innovation in education, 168
Institute of the Arts, 231, 236
institutional development, 162, 167–168, 172
integrated education, 78

Integrated Health Program, 22
integration of study, work, and research, 58, 115
interdepartmental collaboration, 173
interim governing authority, 198
internal cooperation, 165
international agencies, 7, 16, 26, 66, 197, 205
international aid and development, 198, 211
international collaboration, 3, 44, 162, 278
international education, 5, 9, 18, 151, 199, 266, 279, 281
International Film and Television School in Cuba, 231
international health collaboration, 23
International Monetary Fund, 84
international service, 188
international students, 4, 19–20, 29, 73, 79–81, 84–86
internationalist, 6–7, 16–18, 20, 26, 28, 30, 39, 42, 53, 55, 128, 141, 149, 154, 183, 189, 191, 206, 241, 245, 247, 278
internationalization, 4, 14, 84, 132, 280
internet, 80, 98, 124
IPLAC, 59, 207–208, 212
ISA, 234, 236
Isla de la Juventud, see Isle of Youth
Isle of Youth, 7–8, 19–20, 55, 74, 83–87, 89–93, 95–99, 132, 135, 142, 151–152, 155, 183, 217–223, 225–228, 278
Iyambo, Abraham, 134, 136

Jamaica, 2, 7–8, 13, 17, 21, 40, 76, 108, 112, 114, 116–120, 123, 175–180, 182, 188, 190–193, 205, 235, 249–253, 265, 279–280
Jamaican patois, 180
joint ventures, 3, 45, 64

Kaba Akoriyea, Sam, 8–9, 229, 277
Kingston, 118, 178, 251
Kwame Nkrumah Junior High School, 225

language, 8, 37–38, 55, 79, 93, 97, 101, 110, 115, 146–147, 150–152, 169, 176–177, 180, 185, 188–193, 226–227, 234, 236, 241, 246–247, 249, 251, 256–259, 264–265, 274, 280–281
Latin America, 8, 16–17, 19–20, 24, 41, 75–76, 108, 112, 120, 122, 124, 128, 161, 165, 171, 174, 176, 187, 189, 191, 193, 207, 219, 234–235, 236–237, 257, 264–266, 269, 278, 282
Latin American countries, 2, 41–42, 118, 161, 187, 207, 264, 269
Latin American School of Medicine, 20, 24, 26, 74
Latin American Universities, 7, 161, 174
Lehr, Sabine, 5, 9, 13, 35, 47, 77, 83, 103, 225, 279–280
liberal/humanistic education, 92
liberation movements, 3, 43, 128, 274
lifelong learning, 54, 65, 280
linguistics, 112, 246
links between tertiary education and development, 87
literacy, 4, 7–8, 13, 15, 20–21, 26, 36, 43, 47, 54, 56–58, 65, 129, 135, 142–143, 146–147, 155–156, 176, 197–212, 249, 253, 255–261, 273, 277–278
literacy advisers, 199, 201, 206, 256
literacy campaign, 7, 15, 56–57, 143, 146–147, 156, 197–202, 204–207, 209–212, 256, 259–260, 277
literacy education in Namibia, 135
literacy teaching method, 205
Lovelace, Asha, 233
low-income countries, 4, 13, 17, 23, 87, 166, 228, 256, 274, 280
Luanda, 130, 145, 149, 153, 156–158, 242–243, 245
Lubango, 149, 241, 245

Majoli Viani, Marina, 13, 30
Maori educators, 260
Martí, José, 43, 114, 150, 225, 247, 266, 270, 281–282
Martín Sabina, Elvira, 5, 30, 53, 68–69, 280
Martínez Pérez, Francisco, 5, 73, 280

Marxist ideology, 116
Marxist perspectives, 123
mass organizations, 55, 59, 147
master of education (MEd) programs, 265
masters and PhD degrees, 81
masters degree programs, 65
masters degrees, 164, 178
mechanisms to facilitate cooperation, 164
medical assistance, 22, 24–26, 45
medical brigades, 22–23
medical collaboration, 22–23
Medical Education Cooperation with Cuba (MEDICC), 28, 31, 193
medicine, 4, 8, 19–20, 22–26, 75–76, 81, 95, 100, 109, 111–114, 116, 118, 124, 129, 136, 149, 184, 186, 201, 229
Mediterranean Africa, 128
mentorships, 164
Mexico, 16, 21, 28, 40–41, 162, 174, 208, 255–256, 258, 261, 264–265, 269, 279, 281
Middle East, 74–75, 80, 98
middle-level secondary schools, 220
middle-level technical institutions, 63
middle-level technical qualifications, 108
migration, 38, 87–88, 94, 120–121, 123, 275, 280
migration of professionals, 123
military occupation, 197, 208
military strategies, 243
military training, 128–129, 131, 150, 152–154
Milliennium Development Goals (MDGs), 37
minimum cost, maximum participation, 257
Ministry of Education, 59, 67, 68, 76, 78, 142–144, 147–148, 150, 153, 155–157, 161, 175, 178–179, 182, 200–201, 204, 206, 213, 221, 252, 265, 277–278
Ministry of Higher Education, 59–60, 69, 76, 79, 81, 109, 126, 161, 163, 170, 174, 280
Ministry of Public Health (MINSAP), 67, 76

mission infrastructure, 128
mission to Algeria, 127–129
model of university education, 109
modern languages, 112
mountain community, 8, 249
Movimiento Popular de Libertação de Angola (MPLA), 129–130, 142–145, 147, 157, 207
Mozambique, 20, 141, 156, 208, 227–228, 255, 259, 279
municipal government, 220
municipal university branch, 63
Municipal University Centres (SUMs), 27, 37, 64–65, 80
museum and community learning center, 198
music and dance, 180–181

Namibia, 6–7, 20, 28, 78, 127, 129–137, 154, 175–176, 178, 182–188, 190, 192, 205, 218, 227–228
National Adult Literacy Conference, 200
National Commission of Experts in the English Language in Cuba, 280
National Commission of Scientific Degrees, 282
national commissions of experts, 169
national committee for literacy, 146
National Curricular Commission in Foreign Languages, 281
national development, 35, 87, 107, 114–115, 169, 199–200, 211, 279
National Development Plan, 199
national goals of equity and quality, 54
National Institute of Neurology and Neurosurgery in Havana, 229
National Sports Directorate, 175
national system of adult education, 211
nationalization, 14
Navrongo, 225
neocolonialism, 162
neoliberal fiscal policy, 85
neoliberalism, 2, 9, 66
Neto, President, 143, 146, 149
neurosurgery, 8, 225, 229, 277
new development compact in education, 37
new economic context, 163

new man, 88, 145
new paradigm of North-South educational aid, 37
newly decolonized countries, 88
newly upgraded high schools, 179–180, 193
NGOs, 200, 204, 206
Nicaragua, 17, 21, 23–24, 40, 174, 177, 208, 219, 227, 255–258
Nicaraguan literacy crusade, 210
Nigeria, 76, 255, 259
Nigerian government, 259
Nkrumah, Kwame, 218–226
Non-Aligned Movement, 4, 17, 36, 40, 74
nonalignment, 85
nonformal education, 201–202, 212
non-literate, 22, 218, 249, 256, 259
non-socialist governments, 187
North, 1, 5, 9–10, 14, 28–29, 35–37, 39–42, 44, 46–47, 66, 75, 88–90, 93, 98, 102, 104, 122–123, 128, 130, 135, 156, 166–167, 188, 191–192, 205, 219, 227, 239, 241–242, 264, 266–268, 279
North America, 75, 93, 122–123, 264
North American educators, 264, 266–268
North-South aid, 29, 46–47

occupational certificates from the UK, 134
Operation Miracle, 26, 45
ophthalmology, 114
oppositional discourses, 89
Organisation of African Unity, 40, 136
Organization of American States (OAS), 265
orphaned, 128, 183, 218, 274
outmigration, 101
overseas scholarship holders, 74, 79
overseas students, 5, 19, 55, 73–77, 79–80, 108–110, 165, 205, 217, 221, 280

paid leave, 164, 206
Paris Declaration on Aid Effectiveness, 36
partner countries, 3–4, 7–8, 13, 28, 37, 44–45, 187

partnerships, 2, 37, 46
patois, 180, 250–251
patria es humanidad, 247
peace building, 7, 197, 208–210, 211
Pedagogical University (ISP), 150
pedagogical university academics, 179
pedagogy, 21, 58, 60, 114, 124, 146, 150, 165, 181, 186, 190–191, 266
People's Liberation Army of Namibia (PLAN), 65, 90, 111, 114, 120, 129–131, 168–169, 171–173, 199, 204, 211, 212, 220, 255
perceptions about Cuba, 82
Pérez Herrera, Emelina, 8 , 9 , 251 , 280
Pérez, Tristá, Boris 7, 19, 161, 280
PhD, 79, 81–82, 113, 161, 163, 165, 170, 177, 220, 229
physical culture, 76, 79, 112–113, 124, 185
physical separation between children and their parents, 93
policy of internationalism, 4, 188
political cooperation with Angola, 143
polytechnic vocational training, 18
polytechnical credentials, 94–95
polytechnical institutions, 85, 94–95, 102, 219
polyvalent method of studying, 234
Popular Education, 200–202, 277
Portuguese, 20, 112, 129, 141–142, 144–147, 149–151, 156, 198, 204–205, 207–209, 241, 243, 246–247, 258–259, 279
Portuguese colonial power, 142
postcolonial, 7, 14, 17, 29, 35, 87, 89, 97, 104, 119, 123–124, 145, 155, 175–176, 190–193, 197, 279
postcolonial societies, 35
post-conflict reconstruction, 198, 211
post-conflict society, 208
postdoctoral programs, 166
postgraduate capacity, 7, 162
postgraduate courses, 132, 161, 163–164, 166
postgraduate education, 7, 162–163, 165
postgraduates, 108, 162
post independence, 83, 89, 130, 132, 134, 136, 207
post literacy, 57–58, 204, 211, 255–258, 261

post school, 119, 178, 182
post-Soviet economic difficulties, 45
post war reconstruction, 280
practical productive work, 55
practical vocational skills, 134
practical work, 55, 100, 107, 109, 111–112, 115, 124, 152, 219
pregnancies, 93
preparatory language-training faculty, 79
Preston, Rosemary, 1, 6, 9, 127, 131, 134, 136–137, 270–273, 280–281
pre-university, 86, 117, 184, 222, 227–228, 246
primary and secondary education, 61, 66
pro-Indonesian militiamen, 198
process of transition, 134
productivity, responsibility, and discipline, 219
professional accreditation, 94–95
professional courses, 164, 176
professional satisfaction, 95–96
professional upgrading, 161, 163, 165–166
professionalism, 78, 170
programs for overseas students, 5
Prontuario, 68–69, 76–76, 82
protocol cases, 90
provincial conferences, 268
psychological attention for trauma, 218
public health, 67, 76, 78, 116–118, 209, 229, 277
public health infrastructure, 209

qualifications, 65–66, 82, 108, 115, 133–134, 148, 154, 162–163, 165, 173, 177, 181, 193, 218
qualifying teachers, 54
qualitative case studies, 191
qualitative comparative research, 108
quality in education, 5, 53, 58, 190
Queensland University of Technology, 279

radio-based literacy education programs, 259
Rawlings, President, 85
recognition of Cuban credentials, 95

reconstruction, 26, 134–135, 143, 146, 149, 198, 200, 208, 211, 280
recreation, 22, 67, 76, 220
recruitment, 29, 39, 89–93, 101–102, 177, 204
recruitment program, 90
rector, 7, 217, 220–221, 278
reduction of class sizes, 62
referendum in Timor-Leste, 197
reflections on education, 148
refugee camps, 20, 228
refugees, 4, 6, 20, 151, 198, 218, 228, 244
regional science and technology skills, 121
Registro Sonora, 234
reintegration, 6, 83–84, 93, 96, 101–103
remittances, 123, 274–276
research, 1, 5–8, 13, 17, 22–23, 41–42, 48, 55–57, 59–61, 65, 77–78, 81, 83, 95, 98, 102, 107–115, 118, 120–121, 124–125, 132, 136, 152, 155–156, 162–163, 165–166, 168–176, 182, 186, 191–194, 197–198, 207, 212, 219, 222, 263–265, 267–270, 277, 280–281
research centers, 163, 165, 169–170
research infrastructure, 120
research on Cuban educational practices, 267
research thesis, 109, 114
researchers, 23, 81, 120, 124, 166–167, 169, 173, 207
reservists, 143
restructuring of the economy, 16
restructuring university policies and programs, 161
returnees, 94, 97, 102, 133–135
revolution, 2, 4–5, 10, 13–18, 27, 53–54, 57–58, 64–65, 92, 107, 112, 118, 122, 146, 150, 162, 164, 188, 207, 242–243, 255, 260, 266, 270, 274–275
reward program, 79
reward system, 78
Ridge Hospital, 229, 277
rural communities, 116, 189
rural Jamaica, 8, 249

scholarships, 1, 5–7, 13, 19, 24–26, 45, 53, 58, 73–76, 79–80, 83–85, 87, 89, 101–102, 107–109, 122–125, 127, 132–133, 144, 146, 151, 154, 176, 183, 185, 188, 201, 205–207, 229, 231, 233–235, 274, 280
school garden, 228
School of the Three Worlds, 234
school teacher in Jamaica, 253
schools in the countryside, 62, 86, 92, 103, 149
schools of London and New York, 39
Schoon, Jeannette and Marius, 246
scientific culture, 219
scorched earth process, 197
Second Liberation War, 143
secondary education, 37, 57, 61, 65–66, 74, 193–194, 259
secondary teacher, 61–62
selection criteria, 150
selection process, 80
seminario, 266–267, 269–270
senior high school, 63, 66, 218, 227–228
skilled migrants from lower-income countries, 87
skilled workers, 37, 46, 74, 108
small businesses, 3, 17, 252
small farmers, 15, 252
social commitment, 22, 55, 78
social conditions, 17, 25
social stratification, 53
social workers, 63
socialist, 2–3, 15–17, 36, 43–44, 46, 55, 58–59, 66, 74, 85–86, 96–98, 101, 108–109, 119, 122, 130, 134, 145, 147, 150, 162, 176, 187, 205, 208–209, 274
socialist bloc, 58, 66, 74, 96, 162
socialist economic principles, 44
socialist personality, 145
socialist planning system, 44
socially responsible graduates, 124
socioeconomic factors, 92
sociopolitical conditions, 221
solidarity groups, 79, 82
solidarity in the developing world, 122
solidarity principle, 18, 20, 28, 82

South, 1, 3–9, 13–14, 17, 20, 29, 35–37, 39–48, 54, 56, 67, 75–77, 87–89, 92, 100, 122, 125, 127, 129–131, 134, 136, 141–143, 149, 154–155, 162, 166–167, 171, 175, 182–183, 187–192, 205, 211, 218, 227–228, 231, 242, 244, 268, 274, 279
South Africa, 8, 17, 20, 39, 41, 56, 76, 130, 134, 142, 154, 183, 189, 192, 227–228, 244
South African apartheid regime, 242, 244
South African colonizers, 183
South African Forces, 129
South African rule, 182–183, 218
South-South aid, 47
South-South collaboration, 1, 3–5, 7, 10, 29, 35–36, 39–42, 46–47, 75, 77, 83, 88–89, 94, 100, 141, 155, 175, 191–192, 211, 213
South-South development cooperation, 39–42, 87–88
sovereignty, 3, 5, 27, 42–43
Soviet bloc, 2, 15, 74, 121
Soviet bloc trade and aid, 2
Soviet Union, 2, 14–17, 58, 87, 89, 149, 154
Spain, 3, 98, 112, 229, 231, 235–236, 238, 268, 270, 275, 277
Spanish, 3, 8–9, 13–14, 21, 22, 79, 97, 107, 110, 112, 117–118, 135, 146, 151–152, 175, 178–181, 183, 189, 195, 212, 219, 222, 226–227, 229, 238, 247, 249–253, 258, 264–265, 268, 279–281
Spanish as a second language, 79
Spanish colonialism, 3, 14
Spanish Drama Festival, 251
Spanish language, 8, 97, 110, 226, 264
Spanish Town, 251–252
Special education, 21, 59, 62, 170, 269
special period, 2, 16–17, 66, 74, 80, 121, 221, 269, 274
sports and physical education, 13, 21, 75, 182, 186, 220
sports development, 185–187
sports school, 186
sports teachers, 178, 186
Springer, Melaine, 8–9, 231–232, 281
St. Lucia, 108, 111, 113–114, 116, 126

Index   293

standard English, 180, 250
state sector, 6
state-controlled economy, 121
strategic interests, 38, 205
structural adjustment, 3, 39, 83–84, 89, 92, 96
structural assistance, 92
student drop-out rates, 93
Student Solidarity Council (SSC), 199
study and work placements, 78
study as a full-time job, 63
sub-district administrator, 198
Sub-Saharan Africa, 36, 76, 88, 97
subjugated peoples, 128
substitute parenting, 218
SUM, see Municipal University Centre
Sumbe, 153
sustainable development, 16, 66, 120
sustainable economic growth, 37
sustainable models, 92
SWAPO, 129–130, 132–133, 135, 182–184, 218
SWAPO Manpower Survey, 132
Tarija, 7, 171, 174

teacher education, 35, 61–63, 149, 189, 220, 220, 269
teacher shortages, 178
teachers, 4–7, 18–20, 26, 38–39, 45, 54, 56–63, 65, 67, 75, 83, 86, 89, 97, 113, 115, 141, 143, 145–155, 167–168, 173, 175–193, 195, 205, 207, 211, 218–221, 226–228, 234, 241, 243, 245–246, 250–253, 256, 258–259, 263–266, 269, 280
teaching assistants, 78, 148
teaching capacity, 7, 187
teaching Spanish, 8, 112, 178, 180, 249–250, 252
technical assistance to civilian populations, 129
technical education and vocational training, 131
technical schools, 63–64, 66, 74
technical specialists, 223
technical subjects, 178, 182
telephone facilities, 80
tertiary education, 5, 19, 87–88, 107, 109, 123, 152, 176, 184, 188, 255
Third World, 40, 73
timetabling, 180, 192

Timor, 7, 21, 76, 197–202, 204–212, 277
Timor-Leste, 7, 197–200, 202, 204–212, 277
Timorese women, 210
transfer credit, 94
transforming the content of education, 54
Tristá Pérez, Boris, 7, 19, 163, 280
Torres Saavedra, Alejandro, 9, 265, 281
Turner Martí, Lidia, 8, 9
tuition fees, 84–86

UN, 16, 56, 130, 133, 197–200, 206
UN High Commission for Refugees, 198
UN Transitional Authority (UNTAET), 198
UN Vocational Training Centre for Namibia (UNVTCN), 133
underdeveloped, 1, 9, 22, 36–37, 43–44, 66–67, 77, 119, 128, 184
underdevelopment, 6, 9, 14, 28, 35, 57, 83, 89, 124, 218
undergraduate experience, 108
undergraduates, 6, 108
UNESCO, 30, 38, 43, 47, 55, 66, 68, 81, 90, 103, 155, 158, 171–172, 176, 193, 201, 205, 262, 269, 278, 280
UNESCO Chair in University Organization and Leadership at the University of Havana, 280
UNICEF, 43, 56, 61, 66, 157, 200–201, 205
UNITA, 129, 142, 153, 242–243, 245–246
United Kingdom (UK), 29, 98, 119, 132–136, 176, 179, 260
United Nations Development Program (UNDP), 10, 43, 47–48, 81, 88, 201
United Nations Institute for Namibia (UNIN), 133
United States (USA), 2–3, 8, 14–17, 27, 29, 35, 43–44, 47, 75, 82, 85, 87, 98, 119, 122–123, 129–130, 156, 176, 189, 235, 236, 249, 260–261, 266, 268–269, 279
universal mass education, 145
universalization of literacy and primary education, 65
universalizing literacy, 54
Universidad, 115, 170–171, 269, 278

universities, 1, 4, 7–8, 13–14, 18, 20, 24, 28–29, 57, 59–60, 63–65, 67–68, 74–76, 78–80, 84–85, 89–90, 97, 100, 107–11 1, 116, 120, 123–125, 132, 144, 146, 151–152, 161–171, 174, 176, 184, 220, 265, 267, 269, 279–280, 281
universities and colleges in Cuba, 18, 280
universities in Africa, 89
university access, 90
university graduates, 57, 75, 82, 95, 163–164, 179, 193
University of Angola, 149, 241
University of Havana, 19, 30, 60, 81, 162, 165, 167, 169, 278, 280–281
University of Medical Sciences in Santa Clara City, 228
University of New England in Australia, 277
University of Santiago de Compostela, 229, 277
University of the West Indies, 108, 114, 123
University of Victoria (UVic), 279
university outreach center, 63
university professionals, 108, 172
university reform of 1962, 162
university scholarships, 74, 109
university system, 6, 18, 64, 81, 122, 149, 162, 168
unmet demand for tertiary education, 123
UN-sanctioned military force, 198
Up the Down Escalator, by Michael Manley,40
upgrading of academics, 163
urban planning, 135
US blockade, 18, 66, 74, 266
US embargo, 4, 17, 29, 119
US film, 234
utilitarian perspective, 88, 101
utilitarian perspective of education, 88
utilization of skilled people, 121

values, 15, 22, 55–56, 58–59, 62, 67, 115, 125, 188, 219, 223, 253, 267
Venezuela, 3, 5, 17, 21, 24–26, 28, 40, 43–45, 55, 61, 75–76, 79, 171, 208, 235, 255–256, 258–259, 261, 264, 269

veterinarians, 115
veterinary studies, 100
video literacy lessons, 258
violence, 178, 198, 202, 208–211
vision of an international socialism, 274
vocational and agricultural education, 89
vocational and technical nondegree programs, 75
vocational and technical training programs, 85
vocational education, 3, 37, 56, 58, 89, 102, 199
vocational qualification, 94
vocational qualifications from GDR, 134
vocational technical courses, 182
voluntary farm work, 228
voluntary work, 100

weakening of official development aid, 275
West Indian culture, 239
withdrawal of Cuban civilians, 153, 155
Work, Study, and Research, 55, 219–220
work and study, 75, 86, 99, 103, 150, 226
work and study program, 99
work placements, 63, 78, 109–112, 115, 117, 124
work projects, 45, 110
work-study modality, 217
worker identity, 109
workplace research, 166
World Bank, 7, 38, 122, 125, 197, 200, 205, 212
World Congress of Comparative Education Societies, 84, 267, 281
World Council of Comparative Education Societies (WCCES), 267–268, 270, 279, 281
world youth and students festival, 229

Zayden, Suzette, 231–232
Zimbabwe, 19, 187, 189, 192, 218–219, 227

GPSR Compliance

The European Union's (EU) General Product Safety Regulation (GPSR) is a set of rules that requires consumer products to be safe and our obligations to ensure this.

If you have any concerns about our products, you can contact us on

ProductSafety@springernature.com

In case Publisher is established outside the EU, the EU authorized representative is:

Springer Nature Customer Service Center GmbH
Europaplatz 3
69115 Heidelberg, Germany

www.ingramcontent.com/pod-product-compliance
Lightning Source LLC
LaVergne TN
LVHW021947060526
838200LV00043B/1942